The Tudor Wolfpack
and the Roots of Irish America

Jack Bray (signature)

The Tudor Wolfpack
and
the Roots of Irish America

Jack Bray

NEW ACADEMIA
PUBLISHING

Washington, DC

Library of Congress Control Number: 2016933528
ISBN 978-0-9966484-7-9 hardcover (alk. paper)

NEW ACADEMIA
PUBLISHING

4401-A Connecticut Ave., NW #236, Washington DC 20008
info@newacademia.com

More titles by New Academia at www.newacademia.com

To Joan

Contents

Illustrations

Acknowledgments

The typical brief expressions of gratitude allowed to authors often do not convey the kind of gratitude owed to the individuals who have helped with this project. Nor is it easy to identify who has helped the most, but profound thanks are due to Ambassador Robert Shafer for so many years of sharing a deep interest in Ireland and its history, for his exceptional knowledge of all eras and for his extraordinary memory of the people and events; to Dr. Carole Sargent of Georgetown University whose superb counsel and assistance have been of immense value in every aspect of this work; to Meghan Finlay for sharing her deep knowledge of Irish history honed at Kings College, London, and for her guidance in the presentation of the text; to my son, John, for all the help he provided in research, securing permissions, locating elusive source material and providing wise advice; to authors James Conaway and Finlay Lewis for their generosity in sharing their shining talents with language, and for many years of guidance on the challenges of nonfiction writing; to Dr. Charles Cashdollar of Indiana University of Pennsylvania for perceptive advice from his distinguished career in history; to Robert Muse for his keen knowledge of modern Ireland and his dedication to Human Rights causes in Ireland, Britain and America; to my longtime secretary, Margaret O'Brien, for many years of devoted help with the early days of this project, and to my secretary, Deborah Yates Carney, for her fine work in bringing the final manuscript to life.

Foreword

Winston Groom

The Irish people have suffered mercilessly at the hands of conquerors over the past thousand or so years of history. Peoples from at least a dozen European nations had invaded Ireland, including Vikings, Celts, Gaels, Spaniards, and the evangelical St. Patrick himself, sent in the Fifth Century by his Bishop and the Pope to convert the heathen Irish.

The Normans tried with only limited success to conquer the Irish in 1167, a hundred years after their takeover of England. The Normans at first seemed easily to overcome the clans and tried to rule like feudal lords. In time they intermarried with the Gaelic Irish and assimilated into their culture with a mind towards putting as much distance between themselves and England as possible. That remained the situation for some four hundred years until the mid 16th Century when Irish resistance to British rule provoked King Henry VIII to invade once more and re-establish his authority.

This touched off a lengthy war between the clans of the Irish chieftains and the English soldiers during which little quarter was asked and less was given. Irishmen were tortured, after which they were hanged by the thousands and their heads often impaled along roadsides.

At one point the Spanish sent a small army to assist the Irish but in the end the British prevailed. They confiscated the lands once more and instituted such harsh and outrageous controls (among other indignities, they ordered the Irish to give up their Catholicism) that it ultimately resulted in the great Irish emigration to the United States.

Jack Bray tells this thrilling story from an immense wealth of knowledge and such a writer's eye for detail that no one even remotely interested in the period will want to miss it.

Many of Winston Groom's 20 books are histories, including his latest, *The Generals*, about WWII generals MacArthur, Marshall and Patton. His Civil War histories include *Vicksburg, 1863 and Shiloh, 1862*, and his fiction includes *Forrest Gump*. His book *Conversations With the Enemy* was nominated for the Pulitzer Prize.

Preface

The seed of England was planted in Ireland by the Plantagenet dynasty with the 12th century Norman invasion, and it spread its deepest roots during the 16th century as courtiers of the Tudor dynasty confiscated large tracts of the most valuable lands owned by the Irish. As profound as the Tudor impact was on Ireland, none of the Tudor Kings and Queens ever laid eyes on it. Instead, for more than 100 years of Tudor lordship and Tudor monarchy, a succession of Deputies was sent to rule the Irish from Dublin. These Deputies delivered hands-on governance with the fists of a brawler and the nimble fingers of a pickpocket as they jockeyed for assignments, hoping to take from the Irish the kind of spoils that eluded them at home. Most of them governed so brutally that their Queen likened them to wolves.

They confiscated prized estates by violence and fraud, which alienated the Irish and provoked resistance that turned into rebellions. At the conclusion of those unsuccessful rebellions, even more of the best land of the Irish was confiscated. After the 17th century English Civil War and the Wars of the Three Kingdoms, England banished a large part of the Irish population from their homes in the fertile areas of Munster, Leinster and Ulster to the barren areas west of the River Shannon. Huge numbers of impoverished Irish wound up farming tiny plots, trapped in an extremely fragile life at the mercy of English landlords, and highly vulnerable to the slightest downturn in their health, in the weather, or in the economy.

The Irish were treated as a separate race conquered by the Tudor army, ostracized by Penal Laws in the early 18th century which denied them most fundamental rights of property, voting, and education. England officially discriminated against the Irish and the Scots Irish on the basis of their Catholic and Presbyterian religions. The Irish had become serfs, and many were little but slaves.

By the dawn of the 18th century much of the gentry of the Irish and Anglo Irish had fled. These so called "Wild Geese" went largely to the Continent to escape an intolerable life in Ireland, but a few began to go as far as America. Scots Presbyterians in Ulster, feeling increasingly disenfranchised and abused by the Penal Laws, left Ireland in significant numbers between 1707 and 1775, and many of them emigrated to America.

For those still in Ireland during the 19th century, the Tudor and Stuart and Cromwell land confiscations had created a poor tenants' nightmare. When a fungus spread through the farms of Europe in 1845 killing potato crops, it had some fatal impact in the Low Countries, but in Ireland the poorest Irish were almost entirely dependent on potatoes; they were devastated by several years of failed potato crops, and they died of starvation and famine diseases in huge numbers while their British overlords and landlords governed them and evicted them as though they could have cared less. More than a million desperate Irish fled to America and elsewhere during and after The Great Famine, and they and their robust progeny produced an outsized impact on the cultures and the institutions of America, Canada, Australia, New Zealand and other nations. The flight to America offered a special allure for the penniless Famine immigrant who saw America as "the refuge of his race, the home of his kindred, the heritage of his children and their children."[1]

The roots of this plight were the land confiscations by the Tudor monarchs and Deputies. The banishments of the Irish from their lands were shrouded by the benign-sounding names "plantations" and "settlements," but they began the ruination of the relationship of England and Ireland, and lead to a catastrophic famine. The failure of centuries of intelligent governments to heed the numerous warnings of their own staffs and commissions that such a crisis would occur should make clear the deep complexity of the problem.

Huge personalities dominated the period—they were men and women as captivating as the most interesting 21st century leaders. Many of the chieftains who resisted the Tudor conquest earned colorful sobriquets — "Shane the Proud," "Silken Thomas," "The Great O'Neill," "Grace of the Gamesters," and "The Grand Disturber." The central figures were seldom angels, neither the Irish chieftains nor the Tudor Deputies, the Privy Council nobles, or the Tudor royalty. Some whose achievements were the most significant were flawed leaders; and some who performed shamefully received great accolades from their contemporaries. Their achievements should not be diminished by their personal shortcomings, nor exaggerated by imaginary virtues.

Elizabeth I, one of England's strongest, most accomplished rulers, whose 1588 "heart and stomach of a king" speech to her troops at Tilbury is one of history's best, used that same gifted voice to urge slaughter and exclaim her joy at reports of gruesome torture. The Great O'Neill, who transformed the Irish military and led the greatest clan war against England, was a difficult, ambitious, dissembling leader, and a philandering husband. The powerful Rebel Earl of Desmond, Gerald Fitzgerald, was headstrong, foolish, self-destructive, arrogant in the presence of the Queen, and so erratic he was called the "Mad-brained Earl," but he was courageous, loved by his wives and a talented poet. Sir Anthony St. Leger and his protégé, Sir Thomas Cusack, were competent, restrained and respected officials, but their tenure was clouded by allegations of corruption. Sir Henry Sidney fathered a revered poet, served effectively as Deputy, but facilitated the misuse of government power to help confiscate estates from the Irish and the Anglo Irish. The worst of the Tudor Deputies had impressive credentials and no shortage of pedigrees. Sir John Tiptoft was a humanities scholar, but he impaled victims and killed so readily he was given the sobriquet, "The Butcher of England," well before he was sent to govern Ireland. Lord Grey de Wilton, whose tenure in Ireland has been called a "rule of extermination," had enough of a heart that he wept as he ordered his men to torture officers who had surrendered and then to hack to death their 600 followers. Sir Richard Bingham presided over many arbitrary executions and the wholesale slaughter of 1,000 Scots men, women and children, but he helped fashion a system of modern taxation in Connaught. Walter Devereaux, the First Earl of Essex, who ordered the massacre of several hundred Scots men, women and children, was a Knight of the Garter, Earl Marshal of England and the head of a distinguished family.[2]

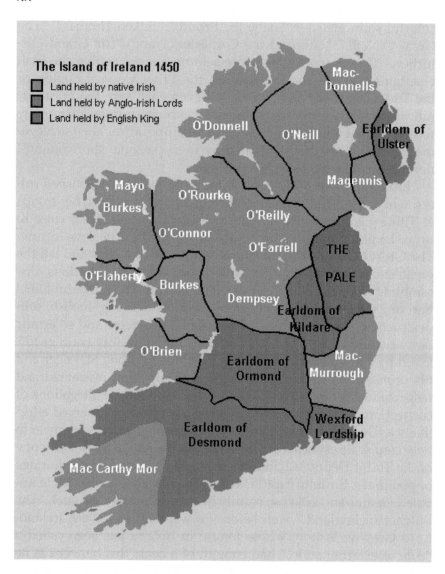

Map of Ireland in 1450

1

Autumn Turns to Winter

I find that I sent wolves not shepherds to govern Ireland, for they have left me nothing but ashes and carcasses to reign over.[3]
— Elizabeth I

The O'Neill awaited news from Spain, and this time he was hopeful. The autumn of 1601 was beginning to show its colors in the trees of Ulster as if to decorate the scene for the arrival of welcome news. Things had gone wrong two years ago when Spain tried to send him troops to support his rebellion. Storms drove the Spaniards away; but now the sea was cooperating. He was hoping for a message that reinforcements had landed. O'Neill knew the message would be brought by some young clansman scampering up the hill to the O'Neill Castle at Dungannon, breathless, to bring exciting news to Hugh O'Neill, (*Aodh Mór O'Neill*), former Earl of Tyrone, now Ireland's rebel chieftain.

The Spanish army tossing about at sea in 33 ships on their way to Ireland was a small force of about 4,000, but enough reinforcements to make the Irish chieftains confident of victory. For O'Neill, this could mean the difference between life or death. The Spaniards' arrival could save him from the grisly fate of a rebel — a death that might start with his arms and legs being broken, then dragged out for many days. England had decided upon "the extirpation of the native and so-called Old English population, and the resettlement of the cleared countryside and towns by British immigrants."[4] By O'Neill's day in the sun it was abundantly clear to the Irish chieftains that Her Majesty Queen Elizabeth I had come to view the native Irish as savage and disloyal and had despaired of

Hugh O'Neill, Earl of Tyrone

peaceful Anglicization. Exasperated, she was now bent on ridding Ireland of the disloyal Irish.[5] "[T]he sword of extirpation hangeth"[6] over the Irish, O'Neill wrote as he tried to encourage other potential rebels.[7] He was now confident the English sword would hang above them no longer if Spanish troops landed in Ireland. The native Irish could begin to renew their society which Tudor England had been busily erasing from history.

The most recent Spanish emissary, Ensign Pedro de Sandoval, had come to Sligo in late Summer 1601 and met with The O'Donnell, the chieftain Red Hugh O'Donnell (*Aodh Ruadh O'Domhnaill*), to coordinate the plans for the arrival of the Spaniards. He told O'Donnell that troops were ready in Spain and would soon sail for Ireland. They were fewer than the chieftains hoped for, but still a strong force to bolster the clans' forces. The chieftains, however, alerted Sandoval that Queen Elizabeth had sent a very large English army into Ireland under her new Deputy, Charles Blount, Lord Mountjoy, and much of his army was currently massed in the south. They warned Sandoval that such a small Spanish force should avoid the south at all cost. Sandoval agreed and hurried back to Spain to warn that the armada must sail farther north to avoid the English troop concentration and instead land where it would be welcomed by northern Irish clans, and then together prepare to fight the English in Ulster.

That was now many weeks ago. Sandoval arrived back in Spain on October 1 where he was met with disheartening news — the Spanish troop ships had already sailed, and they had selected Kinsale on the south coast as their landing site. They had been at sea for several weeks and there was no chance to reach them.

The Spanish troops did land at Kinsale the very next day, October 2. And when the breathless clansman brought that news to O'Neill, his elation was gone in an instant. The Spaniards were already trapped by English troops. Mountjoy's army had set up siege camps on the four hills outside the walls of Kinsale while the rattled Spaniards huddled inside. The Spanish had turned themselves from welcome reinforcements into a demanding distraction.

O'Neill hoped that the Spanish might escape Kinsale by sea and sail north, but the Spanish leader smuggled a message out to O'Donnell that their ships had all left and they had no way to escape. The Spaniards urged the northern chieftains to march to Kinsale and rescue them. The clans would have no choice but to leave the safety of their lair in Ulster, march in mid-winter the length of Ireland, and they would likely have to fight the decisive battle that would decide the fate of the Irish on open ground against English troops well trained for cavalry charges and lines of musket fire, free from the confines of the Ulster woods favored by the clans.

2

Collapse of the British Lordship

Hibernia Hibernescit (Ireland makes all things Irish)[8]
— An ancient observation

By this time, the Ulster clans had been at war against the Crown for 9 long years. How had the centuries-old relationship of England and Ireland come to this? Long ago the Irish had become used to the English lordship. They had accepted the English monarch as the overlord of Ireland back in 1175 when the Plantagenet, Henry II, accepted the submission of many of the Irish kings. The lordship had been reaffirmed in the mid-16th century and had not even then seemed a threat to the Irish people. Henry VIII had obtained the agreement of most of Ireland to surrender their lands, but he immediately regranted those lands to the chieftains and they accepted him as their distant overlord. In 1541, Henry VIII had also proclaimed himself their King, and the Irish accepted that as well. What had happened between 1541 and 1601 that had so badly derailed this time-honored relationship? There had been only scant rebellion[9] in the previous 400 years[10] since the English first arrived. Most disturbances had consisted of raids by chieftains on the Old English, the descendants of the Normans, who had settled in the Pale. Those raids were more like cattle rustling than rebellion.[11] Most Irish had given little thought to rebellion against their English overlord. Yet in the middle of the 16th century rebellion had begun, and by 1601 some in Europe had begun to wonder whether England would prevail.

Most puzzling to Europeans as well as many London courtiers was that the rebellion was led by a lifelong ally of the English, the Earl of Tyrone, Hugh O'Neill. He and the other Ulster chieftains were well aware that previous stories of a swashbuckling rebel challenging a powerful king or queen that began as rousing tales often ended with the rebel's head on a pike. They knew also that one man's rebellion is another's treason. Why did O'Neill risk death for himself, his family, and attainder for his clan? Why had he turned against a Queen he had praised for her kindness to him, the Queen for whom he had such affection that, later, at her death, he burst into tears.

Something new and very unsettling had found its way into England's Irish policy during the 16th century. England was no longer merely punishing the Irish countryside with coercion measures used to pacify unruly clans; that was certainly nothing new. English officials had been using coercion to pacify the "Wild Irish" for centuries. Efforts to Anglicize some of them had also been around a long time and, in areas of the south, the east and the west those efforts had achieved considerable success. The extensive Ormond earldom in Kilkenny had become loyal to the Crown; it had "gone English." The earl of Clanrickard in the far west in Galway had gone so English he was called "The Sassanach" (Englishman). The Pale in the east, and Dublin, had long been loyal. So were other walled cities. While other areas outside The Pale and the cities remained Irish, their political temperature rarely rose to the raging fever of rebellion even through the early 16th century.

Earlier rebellions had erupted over distinct localized provocations in regional lordships — in Kildare in Leinster under the Earl of Kildare in 1487 and under the Earl of Offaly in 1534, in Tyrone under Shane O'Neill in Ulster in 1567, in Desmond Munster under James FitzMaurice in 1569 and under the Earl of Desmond in 1579, in Leinster under Lord Baltinglass in 1580, and in Connaught under the Burkes in 1572, 1576 and 1586. Those rebellions had not spread throughout Ireland; they had been regional — disorganized, even chaotic, and all had been crushed. This was different.

Map 1 LORDSHIPS, *c.* 1534, by K. W. Nicholls

Map of 16th Century Irish Lordships, circa 1534.

The 16th century Irish chieftains had not simply grown weary of foreign rule and rebelled to achieve independence. They had tolerated rule by a foreign monarch, and they were used to foreign settlers — the Danes who invaded in the 9th century and the Normans who invaded in the 12th century. By the Tudor era the Normans or Old English were a wealthy Irish peerage. Some of that nobility had bonded very well with the native Irish and all had become comfortable with the fact that their overlord was the English monarch. And they were used to accepting the notion that the King could choose his subjects' religion.[141] This was the reality of 16th century Ireland.

Central to that reality was that, to the 16th century Irish, there was no Ireland.[12] Centuries earlier there had been a High King, but the concept of a modern Irish nation had not yet been born. As Professor Edmund Curtis described 16th century Connaught: "There was indeed as yet no Irish nation and the aims and local pride of the Connaught lords were a whole world removed from those of burgesses and landlords in the Pale."

Outside of Dublin and a few walled towns, the Irish were provincial small villagers. Many of them were allies only of those in their small settlements. Few, if any, felt loyalty to some incomprehensible all-island nation or to distant peninsulas or towns with which they were totally unconnected. Most Irish had experienced only vicious clashes with other villages, and those clashes had made them enemies, not friendly neighbors.

Tudor Courtiers Discovered the Riches of Office in Ireland

What had changed in the 16th century was that Tudor courtiers had awakened to the fact that local governance by the Irish kept the riches of Ireland out of the hands of the Crown and out of their own pockets. England under Henry VIII at times had severe financial worries. Few of the Tudor era courtiers had any wealth and many were in debt. None had much hope of being rewarded with rich lands in England. Ireland was very tempting to Lord Chancellor Cardinal Thomas Wolsey, to Thomas Cromwell, and other Tudor officials.

A new era of political corruption came about in England and Ireland and it became possible for English courtiers to grow rich off the Irish, but the sources of wealth, land and cattle, were already owned by native Irish and Anglo Irish and, therefore, had to be confiscated from them.[13] The weapons the courtiers needed to confiscate Ireland's lands were a strong royal army, control of the Dublin Council and parliament and the tribunals that would decide disputes. Such control enabled the Tudor courtiers to confiscate vast Irish lands, to take some by murder, some by fraudulent claims, and some by escheatment.[14] Martial law executions allowed them to take specially targeted lands; by securing the attainder of a wealthy Irish lord, they could confiscate his entire lordship. And if an earl could be toppled, his entire earldom, a significant fraction of Ireland, could be confiscated in one fell swoop.[15]

The Tudor courtiers of the 16th century set out to use all of these ploys. Fines were levied arbitrarily. False title claims to valuable Irish estates were presented to compliant and complicit Tudor officials. Tudor martial law soldiers they named seneschals were permitted to execute arbitrarily any Irish they deemed guilty of treason, and to confiscate their property. The local death rate in an Irish lordship rose dramatically when the seneschal and his goon squad came calling.

The Tudor courtiers who came to 16th century Ireland lined up for the appointments and the chance to dip into the lucrative honeypot of Ireland.[16] They would lobby for appointment as an under treasurer or provincial official, hoping ultimately to rise to the post of Deputy. Many of the courtiers were related, yet they competed intensely with each other for the best posts in Ireland. They would backstab each other, becoming bitter enemies in the process. It was said they agreed only on one thing — they all hated the Irish. Chief among the Irish in their way was the House of Kildare.

Early in the Tudor monarchy, the Earl of Kildare and his noble family controlled the government, and stood directly in the way of English courtiers' pursuit of Irish spoils. The 8th Earl of Kildare had achieved a new level of authority using his great political and military skills. He controlled the political apparatus in Dublin. He had changed the Grand Council; it became in substance a Kildare Council, not a Tudor Council, and by his exceptional fighting skill he achieved dominance over a wide area. He formed alliances with the House of Desmond and the great northern clans of the O'Neills of Tyrone and the O'Donnells of Tyrconnell. Governing as no Irishman had before him since the English first came, Kildare seemed to have effective control of Ireland by the dawn of the 16th century.[17] But just a few decades into that century, Henry VIII's chief minister, Cardinal Thomas Wolsey, and his protégé, Thomas Cromwell, saw that as well. England, by then, was strapped financially, and hungry for the land and cattle of Ireland. If they could end the power of the House of Kildare, Ireland would be without the protection and support of the alliances the Earl had forged, and would be ripe for piecemeal confiscation. The Tudor solution to the Irish problem eventually became ridding the most valuable Irish lands of the Irish.[18]

3

What Alarmed Tudor England

He that would Old England win, must first with Ireland begin.[19]
— 16th century European belief

Something different had also caused England to pursue a new aggressive goal with a new urgency to achieve it. The Tudor Court was not only tempted by wealth, but also driven by fear that grew to a state of high anxiety as threats from European powers escalated in the 16th century. Ireland was the perfect platform in enemy hands from which a Continental power might invade England. From Spain, it was a long sea voyage to reach England. Some English wondered why Spain had not seized upon the tactic of taking Ireland earlier as a base from which to conquer England. Many doubted Spain would wait much longer. In the mid-16th century, Spain had political, financial and religious reasons to invade England. Spain's King had received a virtual papal order to take down an English Queen seen by Spain as a heretic who was leading her followers to spiritual doom. The Spanish Armada tried to invade from Spain in 1588, but the long sea voyage crippled the effort. Ireland, however, was very close, and there was abundant evidence that the rebellious Catholic Irish were natural conspirators for King Philip II.

Control of Ireland had come to be seen as essential to England's own security. "If England was to become a great power, the annexation of Ireland was essential to her, if only to prevent the presence there of an enemy; but she had everything to lose by treating her as a conquered province, seizing her lands, and governing her by force."[20] Queen Elizabeth decided she would, nevertheless, conquer and transform Ireland entirely and make it another England. It eventually became clear to Irish lords and chieftains that there was no place for the Irish in this scheme.

The European Crises

England's angst and the Irish rebellions occurred within an intriguing, stormy European political landscape. The conditions that led to the Tyrone rebellion occurred primarily in England and Ireland – Henry VIII's split with Rome, the murders of the York princes, and the Wars of the Roses — but the events in England and Ireland were heavily influenced by events across Europe — the Dutch Revolt, the assassination of Prince William of Orange, the French Catholics' slaughter of Protestants on St. Bartholomew's Day, the Spanish Inquisition, the execution of Mary Queen of Scots, and the Invasion by the Spanish Armada. They all had an impact on England's Irish policy, and they all ricocheted off the Irish.

In the Netherlands, the Dutch revolt that began in 1568 heightened the Elizabethans' fears that the Catholic Spanish might decide to bond with Irish Catholic rebels, use Ireland as a launchpad, and invade England simultaneously from Ireland and the Netherlands. Protestant Prince William of Orange was assassinated in 1584 in the Netherlands by a deranged Catholic, while England was fighting an Irish rebellion in Munster. The Tudor Court feared that Catholics in Europe were banding together. Elizabeth's fear of the Irish Catholics escalated, and her goal in Ireland became more ominous than the goals of any Tudor before her.

England also had to contend with the threats from the "auld alliance" of Scotland and France. The powerful House of Guise, French Catholics, was determined that Mary Queen of Scots should depose Elizabeth. The great spymaster of the Tudor era, Sir Francis Walsingham, regularly received intelligence warning of one plot or another to bring Mary Stuart to power.

These fears, in turn, stimulated several Tudor schemes to create an alliance with Spain. One such alliance — the marriage of Queen Mary I of England, a Catholic, to the Catholic King Philip II of Spain – was a form of insurance against invasion, but it carried a price — the creation of legitimized claimants to the English Throne

Spanish King Philip II and Queen Mary I of England

among the Catholic Spanish. It lasted only a few years, however; Mary died young and King Philip II had no success wooing his late wife's very Protestant sister, Queen Elizabeth.

Instead, Tudor counselors turned to France. They stimulated near-farcical courtships with French royalty. These serial overtures to wed Elizabeth to someone who would create stability and reduce the religious tensions in Europe placed Ireland and England on a political seesaw. As romance with a French royal heated up, threats from France cooled down. As the Netherlands revolt against Spain drained Spain's treasury and dominated its plans, the risk that Spain would undertake the cost of aiding the Irish in fighting England subsided. Either Spain or France could, however, at any time, try to take Ireland for themselves, then turn their sights on England.

It had taken the Tudor monarchs virtually the entire 16th century to Anglicize and control the south of Ireland, and by 1592 only Ulster eluded their grasp.[21] When England's Sir Richard Bingham, President of Connaught, began strikes[22] that threatened Ulster,[23] a great rebellion began.[24]

By 1598 the chieftains had piled up victories in surprise attacks and the English forces had at times fallen into disarray.[25] The chieftains of the north who fought each other for centuries[26] had at last joined together against the Crown of England. The Maguire of Fermanagh and The O'Donnell of Tyrconnell had begun the rebellion in Ulster. O'Neill, who led the largest clan and greatest fighting force in Ulster, had vacillated, but finally he had joined the rebellion.[27] O'Neill used his long experience as a cavalry commander for the English, and a good share of his wealth, to improve substantially the clans' military power.[28] Victories at Clontibret, The Yellow Ford and elsewhere had an "astonishing effect on the country." People had begun speaking of The O'Neill as "King of Ireland."[29] On the Continent, royal Courts had a new-found respect for The O'Neill. Messengers sent to them by O'Neill were treated with the deference they would show ambassadors.

But now, in the Autumn of 1601, the Spanish were trapped at Kinsale. As soon as the disappointed Irish chieftains regained their equilibrium, they saw what they needed to do, and they fashioned a new strategy. Together the Irish and Spaniards might be able to surround the English exposed on the wintry hills above Kinsale, set a siege of their own, then let Winter take its toll and end the English rule of Ireland that began more than 400 years earlier.

4

Why the English Came to Ireland

Some Irish were "gentle and cultured," but others were "wild men of the woods."[30]
— Polydore Vergil

The taking of Irish land by adventurers, courtiers and governors from England began long ago. It began like a creak on the stairs. The Irish did not see the English coming. For centuries Ireland hovered across the Irish Sea almost unseen, separated from England and the Continent, spared the onslaught of Huns and Romans so dreaded by the tribes of Europe.[31]

The Normans had come to Ireland in 1167, then again in 1169 and 1170. Ironically, the Normans had been invited into Ireland. A 12th century regional Irish king, Leinster King Dermot MacMurrough (*Diarmaid MacMúrchada*), had fled Ireland under heavy attack from other Irish Kings, and he traveled to England, to Aquitaine and to Wales to seek help from King Henry II and Welsh Norman lords. MacMurrough lead the Normans to think that the conquest would be quick, that the ill equipped Irish would easily be overcome by Norman archers' superior tactics.

A Norman Beginning

The Normans came quietly to the Irish shore.[32] In 1169 two small ships drew the attention of Irish on the far southeast coast. The foreigners came ashore at Bannow Bay near Baginbun. Some sounded French, others Welsh. This would not have been the first time peaceful fisherman or voyagers had wandered off course, but these visitors began building breastworks and they had weapons. News of the arrival of the strangers was sent all the way to the High King, Rory O'Connor (*Ruadri Ua Conchobhair*), in far western Connaught, but it raised only the modest concern of local plunder. Far more, however, was about to happen. This modest force of French and Welsh – speaking Normans would turn out to be the beginning of the English in Ireland.

The Normans disturbed Ireland's ancient civilization far more than the Vikings had,[33] but they did not fundamentally alter it. For several decades there was sporadic Norman expansion, but the Norman effort to take all of Ireland finally ended[34] with a number of Irish kings entering into a treaty and accepting the lordship of Henry II, but no genuine Norman conquest of Ireland ever came to pass.[35] The efforts to expand the Anglo Norman frontiers were hampered by tenacious clan resistance[36] and other difficulties,[37] by England's poor finances, by trouble from the Scots, by preoccupations with other parts of Europe, and by the Black Death. All this combined to prevent the Norman parts of Ireland from becoming or behaving as English.[38] Earldoms were awarded to loyal Normans, in part to infuse Ireland with an Anglo Norman nobility, but two of the earldoms, Kildare and Desmond, became more Irish than English. The English oversight remained distant and ineffective;[39] even by the 14th century, the English King ruled in the manner of a distant lord and the Irish remained steadfastly Gaelic. The native clans not only survived Norman assaults, they began to absorb Anglo Norman influences. The Normans in the far south intermarried freely with the Irish and many Normans became indistinguishable from native Irish.

The Norman descendants in Ireland became known as the Old English or Anglo Irish. To the New English who came in the next two centuries and huddled together in Dublin and the surrounding Pale, the rest of Ireland was an alien, hostile wilderness. The area of the Pale close by Dublin was called the maghery. Nearer the frontier the areas were called the Pale marches. The frontier itself was still dangerous to the English of the Pale by the 15th century. The clan territories beyond it where the "Wild Irish" lived were utterly terrifying.

THE NORMAN INVASION OF IRELAND

Ireland's High Kingship was often contested. The most bitter of these struggles brought about the Norman invasion of Ireland a century after the far different 1066 invasion of England by William the Conqueror. Henry II, the first Plantagenet King of England, as early as 1155, had considered invading Ireland, but he could not gain papal approval. In 1166 the perfect invitation fell into Henry's lap.

King Dermot MacMurrough of Leinster. The events that created the opportunity were instigated by a provocative and ambitious regional king, Dermot MacMurrough, the King of Ui Cennselaigh (Wexford and South Wicklow). MacMurrough had killed or blinded *Donal MacFaelain,* lord of north Leinster, and thereafter reigned as King of Leinster.

In the north of Ireland, *Murchertach MacLochlann*, the powerful King of Ailech (northern Ulster) had seized the high kingship from the rightful successor Rory O'Connor with Dermot MacMurrough's assistance. Years earlier, in 1152, MacMurrough, had abducted another king's wife. The fabled "rape of Dervorgilla," the wife of Tiernan O'Rourke (*Tiernan O'Ruairc*), the King of Breifne, was actually an abduction at her invitation, but the enraged O'Ruairc had invaded Leinster and secured her return from Dermot MacMurrough. But the old score was unsettled.[40]

Rory O'Connor and the king of Oriel, *Donnchad O'Cerbhal*, attacked and slew the usurper High King, MacLochlann, and reclaimed the high kingship. MacMurrough was suddenly on his own and exceedingly vulnerable, and under renewed attack from *Tiernan O'Ruairc*, still bitter over Dervorgilla.

(continued)

(The Norman Invasion of Ireland, continued)

O'Connor and O'Ruairc decided to join forces against MacMurrough and finally defeat or kill him. The Danes of Dublin and many other Irish also turned against MacMurrough.

In 1166 O'Ruairc led the attack on MacMurrough and on August 1, 1166, MacMurrough was forced to flee to England and Aquitaine where he secured an audience with Henry II and requested help. Henry approved MacMurrough's request to enlist Norman knights and barons in Bristol and south Wales to help Dermot reclaim his lost provincial kingdom of Leinster.

Henry, however, saw this as his own opportunity to claim Ireland. Constantine the Great, so it was believed, had granted all islands to the papacy and this grant was the authority on which Pope Adrian IV gave Henry a Papal Bull titled Laudabiliter ("laudably and happily," it began), which authorized his taking Ireland.[41]

Strongbow. The mixed group of Normans who invaded Ireland came from Bristol, France and westernmost Wales. These Normans were largely Anglo Welsh and Flemish. They spoke French as did many in England. Despite the Norman conquest of England, by 1166 Welsh Normans were hard pressed for land. Rhys ap Gruffydd, the King of the Welsh area of Deheubarth, was hostile to their expansions, and thus these barons and knights proved receptive to Dermot's promises of vast Irish lands as a reward for their help to reclaim his kingdom of Leinster.

One of the Norman knights in Wales, Richard FitzGilbert de Clare, Earl of Pembroke and lord of Strigoil, known as

(continued)

(The Norman Invasion of Ireland, continued)

Strongbow, was the overlord of many of the knights who came to Ireland. Strongbow was the great leader who could deliver victory. Dermot laid great inducements at the feet of Strongbow, including his beautiful daughter Aoife (Eva) in marriage and succession to the kingdom of Leinster. Almost as important as Strongbow was a Norman lord from Wales, Maurice FitzGerald, the son of Gerald of Windsor. Dermot enlisted Maurice and Maurice's half-brother, Robert Fitz Stephen, for his invasion.

The Norman Landings. Dermot MacMurrough returned to Ireland with a small Norman force in August 1167 together with Richard FitzGodebert de la Roche of Rhos, and a very small advance force of mercenaries from Pembrokeshire. On May 1 and 2, 1169, the Norman Invasion of Ireland began with the landing at Bannow Bay in Wexford of two ships carrying Robert FitzStephen, Maurice de Prendergast, Robert de Barry, Meiler Fitz Henry, Miles Fitz David and a number of archers. They built earthworks at Baginbun, and soon they had taken Wexford. Strongbow arrived with his men in 1170. Strongbow joined with the Normans at Baginbun and together they overwhelmed Waterford. They marched north and led an attack on Dublin, then a city of Danes living alongside some native Irish. After a long siege, the Normans captured the city and executed Haskulf the Dane, ruler of Dublin.

Henry II himself then came to Ireland in 1171 with an army filling 400 ships.[42] He received submission of many of the lords of Leinster and Munster. As the Normans [43] went about attempting to subdue native Irish chieftains, kings and clans, Norman walled cities, castles and strongholds[44] were

(continued)

(The Norman Invasion of Ireland, continued)

established. Norman Irish Earldoms were created to reward the Norman leaders and begin efforts to pacify Ireland. In 1175 Henry II signed The Treaty of Windsor recognizing High King Rory O'Connor as leader of the native Irish under Henry's lordship. But over the next 200 years the Normans found themselves unable to entirely dominate the country, and Gaelic life continued to thrive in many places. For this pivotal episode that infused an entirely new people, the Normans, into Ireland, MacMurrough became known as Diarmaid na nGall (Dermot of the Foreigners).[45]

The Clans the Normans Encountered

Like a primeval thicket created to nurture and protect native tribes, the lush island spread from Dublin through the rough and rustic terrain of hillsides run by the O'Tooles in Wicklow and the O'Mores in the east midlands, and other septs in the many crannogh, glens and in the rugged mountains peopled by woodsmen.[46] The north, Ulster, was virtually sealed off. Access was difficult, rarely attempted, and always dangerous. Drumlins, hills, forests and bogs were broken only by a few passes controlled by the Irish chieftains of the north — the O'Neills of Tyrone, the O'Donnells of Tyrconnell and the Maguires of Enniskillen.[47] These three great clans were supported by smaller northern clans, all of whom lived by the ancient customs of Gaelic Ireland.[48]

A clan's chieftain, and his chosen successor (*Tánaiste*), together with a group of clan leaders (*cenel*) led by a governing leader (*Taoiseach*) commanded subservient lords (*uirrithe*), and their urraghs, kerne, vassals and churls.[49] The greatest chieftains were not far different from the Irish kings. Though each regional king had been independent, they had bonded somewhat loosely prior to the Norman invasion under a High King (*Ard Ri*).

The strongest clans had by the late 15th century been battling among themselves[50] for centuries. Internecine warfare had helped prevent the cohesion[51] Ireland would need, if any were possible, to launch a successful war against England. Moreover, the Irish could field comparatively few foot soldiers, most of whom were unskilled in the discipline and the weaponry needed in a typical 16th century English battle. Other countries were reluctant to join or aid the Irish.[52]

The tribal subjects of Gaelic chieftains had greatly different appearance and habits from the English. They spoke only Irish. Their hair was long and matted. On many Irish their hair hung down in their faces and was cut high in the croppy style above the ears.[53] The Irish still celebrated ancient festivals of *Lughnasa, Imbolg, Bealtaine* and *Samhain*. Even after Christianity was spread by Patrick, Columcille, Bridget, Aiden and others,[54] much of the indigenous belief of Gaelic life and Druidism remained, often under other names. The festival of *Samhain* celebrating the Dead became called All Saints, All Hallows and All Souls. The Keens, loud and prolonged laments for the Dead, remained. The ancient harvest festival, *Lughnasa*, still celebrated the start of Autumn. Irish clans did not warm to changes to their customs and lifestyle.

Much of Irish life, culture and belief in the 16th century was heavy with fear, superstition and fervently held beliefs. Ignoring the rubrics and dictates that accompanied those beliefs, the Irish believed, could bring tragedy. Such fears were a constant part of Irish life. But the Gaelic world which had survived marauders, dodged Romans and barbarians, and survived the Vikings and the Normans, would encounter its worst fear under the Tudors.

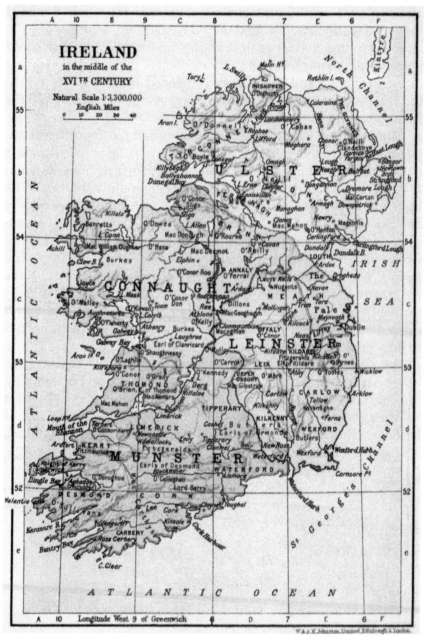

Ireland in the Middle of the 16th Century

WHO WAS IRISH?

Irish Enemies. The Native Irish who so concerned the Tudors were referred to in the 16th and 17th centuries as the "Irish enemies," a label used to distinguish them from the Old English who were called the "Irish rebels."[150] The "Irish enemies" consisted of the Gaelic Chieftains and captains who were the successors of the kings and who continued to resist Anglicization in every respect -- in language, custom, dress, religion and loyalty. "Irish enemies" and "Wild Irish" were official labels.[151]

Gaedhil and Gaill. The Irish designations of the peoples of Ireland after the arrival of the Normans have varied from one period to another. Those most commonly used in Irish were *Gaedhil* (for the native Irish), *Gaill* (for Normans and Vikings), *Sacsain* (for both English and the New English of Ireland), and *Eireanaigh* (for those born in Ireland among the *Gaedhil* or *Gaill*). The term Old English, a reference to Normans,[152] was more frequently an adjective usage than a noun. Ostmen continued to be the reference for Danish and other Vikings.

The Native Irish also comprised distinct groups within their own ranks.[153] There were clergy, judges, historians, peasants, kernsmen and even outlaw rapparees among them.[154] A relatively few lived in towns, burroughs or settlements of any size, while many more lived in the countryside[155] and in smaller settlements. They consisted of many separate clans who, relative to the rest of Europe, were less civilized and possessed an openly unruly character, traits which exacerbated the Tudors' concern. However valid or exaggerated the generalizations[156] about the Irish might have been, the resulting image that reached the eyes of the Crown was of native Irish who were unreliable, unpredictable,[157] untrustworthy, and violent.[158]

(continued)

(Who Was Irish?, continued)

The Irish clans had an almost godlike reverence for their native Gaelic leaders. Even the most confident King or Queen of England knew that this large segment of the Irish felt no loyalty to the English Crown that was worthy of comparison to the intense and fervent adoration they harbored for their own Chieftains.

The Five Bloods. By 1210 five chief Irish dynasties had, under royal grant, been regarded as freemen and law worthy. These native Irish became acceptable to the English in Ireland, and they were allowed the protection of the English common law and access to English courts to defend titles to their lands and to enforce other rights. These families became known through the following centuries as The Five Bloods, clans accepted as descendants of Irish Kings -- the O'Melachlins of Meath, the MacMurroughs of Leinster, the O'Connors of Connaught, the O'Briens of Munster and the O'Neills of Ulster.[159]

English Governors—The King's Lord Lieutenant

Royal officials were appointed to govern and they were given various titles. The early representative was a Justiciar addressed as Lord Justice.[56] Later there would be a secretariat headed by a Chancellor. The Chief Governor by 1462 was called the Lord Lieutenant; he was often a Prince or a Duke, and he wielded considerable power over Irish life though he lived in England. The King would name another official titled Lord Deputy to reside in Dublin and carry out royal administration.[55] In the absence of the Lord Deputy, Lords Justice would rule. A Privy Council of advisors and a Grand Council were a part of the government until 1600. Parliaments were called by the Deputy, but infrequently. By 1696 the Lord Deputy post fell to disuse and by 1767 the Lord Lieutenant began to reside permanently in Ireland.

In the mid-15th century, the power of the Crown extended only to the Pale surrounding Dublin. English law protected only the Palesmen and relatively few others in walled cities like Cork.[57] Irish lords still assumed that English Kings commanded stronger forces than any single clan[58] alone could ever muster, and collective action among the hostile fragmented Irish[59] clans and earls was an extremely rare and limited occurrence.[60] In the 15th century, however, there had been a serious deterioration in the power of England's Kings. Although medieval English Kings had been secure and occasionally as powerful as the Irish thought they were, the Kings who ruled pre-Tudor 15th century England were anything but secure. When Richard II left England briefly in 1399 to quell a disturbance in Ireland, Henry of Lancaster successfully seized his throne. The Crown then was contested for many years by Yorkists and Lancastrians, dynasties whose hatred of each other badly destabilized the Crown, and a distracted England had great difficulty dealing with a turbulent Ireland.

During the Wars of the Roses, Irish lords and chieftains could scarcely have asked for conditions more suitable for rebellion, yet none of them launched a strong rebellion. Then the Tudors came to power and established a singularly powerful dynasty. The lords of Ireland could see that any rising against Tudor England would be brutally crushed. Yet that is when the Irish rebellions began.

5

Ireland Reacts to the Wars of the Roses

[F]rom Ireland thus comes York to claim his right and pluck the crown from feeble Henry's head.[61]
— Shakespeare

The financial stress of thirty years of instability staggered England and made its grip on Irish affairs fragile, ready to be broken. During the Wars of the Roses a sustained revolt by 15th century Ireland might well have succeeded — that is, if there had been an Ireland, or even widespread unity among the clans, or even a widely embraced unifying intolerable grievance.[62] But even the Norman earls in Ireland were far from united; they simply chose sides between the two Roses.

Ireland and the House of York

Many Irish encouraged and supported York's challenge to the King. Dublin and the Pale marches were the perfect spot for York to regroup and then to prepare to renew his attack in England. York's strategic retreat to Ireland brought him into the midst of a tense political drama underway between the Irish earldoms.

York was well known in Kildare. He had visited Ireland while Lord Lieutenant, and his charisma had greatly appealed to the Yorkist noble families there. Now that he was back bringing with him the excitement of a challenge to an unpopular King, York reminded the native and Norman Irish that he was not just another English nobleman, but was also one of them — a Norman and a descen-

THE WARS OF THE ROSES

During the rule of the House of Lancaster and the House of York, England's nobility more than once abruptly shifted alliances and caused the overthrow of the English King. The English throne seemed constantly under challenge, and that contention spilled over into Ireland. The White Rose of York and the Red Rose of Lancaster have become vestigial symbols of two noble dynasties in the north of England, but Irish lords also divided between York and Lancaster. In England the competing forces were not neatly divided by the geography of Yorkshire and Lancashire, but in Ireland Kildare was Yorkist and Kilkenny, seat of the House of Ormond, was Lancastrian. In England the two dominant noble houses of the north — the Nevilles and the Percys — defined the combatants. The royal claims of both of these houses were virtually equal, both traced back to Edward III, and it was essential for a contender to display some claim of royal lineage to attract support for a claim to the Throne. During this thirty year dynastic struggle the Nevilles at most times supported the House of York. The Percys, along with the Woodvilles, the Beauforts, and others supported the House of Lancaster, but opportunism and old grudges led several nobles to switch sides.

The Wars of the Roses began with a widely supported challenge by Richard Duke of York against Henry VI. York was a leader of the noble faction in the English countryside who had been mistreated by the imperious Lancastrians. Charismatic and talented, York was a perceptive politician, and he could see that something was wrong with King Henry VI.

Henry VI had become King at the age of 8 months in 1422. The Lancastrians had a history even before Henry VI of

(continued)

(Wars of the Roses, continued)

mistreatment, high taxation, poor administration and poor politics. Among those mistreated at Court were Richard Duke of York and Richard Neville, Earl of Warwick. They began to rebel, at first reluctantly. For a while York dismissed the King's repeated slights and mistakes as ineptitude, but the King's speaking pattern began to unsettle those around him, and before long it became apparent that the King was having a mental breakdown. York began to receive encouragement to pull off a coup. Then Henry, already a weak King, finally went mad.

During Henry's first breakdown the ambitious courtiers jockeyed for position, and personal rivalries between York and John Beaufort, Duke of Somerset, and Somerset's supporter, Queen Margaret of Anjou, captivated the Court. Margaret, a strong personality, was hostile to York, but she was foreign born and such a Queen was in a poor position to outmaneuver York, and York succeeded in having himself named Lord Protector of the King, and he sent Somerset into the Tower. York seemed to be about to take the Throne through a political coup, but Henry VI recovered and York's power abruptly ended. Somerset was released and he turned his wrath on York. Henry's continued weakness and lingering instability and York's desperation due to his failure to gain the Crown erupted in dynastic war.

At St. Albans in 1455, York's troops defeated the forces of Henry VI, and they killed Somerset. The weakened Lancastrians sought a compromise with the challenger York. For the next three years Henry VI attempted conciliation, and at times the effort seemed to be having some success; at least it staved off a full civil war, but Queen Margaret assembled an army herself and she succeeded in driving York off to Ireland.

dant of renowned Irish families. He was a descendant of the great
Norman families of de Burgo, de Lacy and Mortimer, and also of
Irish Kings — indeed he claimed to be of the lineage of High King
Brian Boru (*Brian Bóruma*). The Geraldines' enthusiasm for him was
strong due to that panache of Anglo Irish nobility. York's substantial support in England, however, was wavering in his absence, and
he hurried his return. As promising as the Yorkist challenge to Henry VI had seemed when it began, when York returned to England to
launch his attack, it all seemed to end in a single afternoon.

York died in combat in 1460 at the Battle of Wakefield; his head
was placed on a pike on the walls of York. This would have ended
most rebellions.[63] However, York's son, Edward, rose up to lead
the Yorkists and within a year Edward defeated Queen Margaret's
army at Towton and he was crowned Edward IV, the first Yorkist
King. To the Geraldines in Ireland this seemed as though the world
had turned in their favor. Their House of Kildare had long controlled Leinster by the time of the Wars of the Roses. The House
of Desmond, also FitzGeralds, controlled most of the southwest
in Munster. Now that the Yorkists had come to power, the two
FitzGerald earls of Ireland expected great changes and a new and
wonderful era in Ireland. What they learned, however, was that to
an English King, Irish leaders in Dublin, Maynooth and Askeaton
were still merely Irish allies of modest importance. English nobility, even Yorkists, hardly valued FitzGerald earls as highly as they
did loyal English nobles, and the euphoria of Kildare and Desmond
over the Yorkist victory did not last for long.

The Norman Earldoms

Leinster, Munster and Connaught had by the Tudor era become
complex amalgams controlled both by Norman earls and native
chieftains.

The role models for the population of these areas were the
powerful wealthy Norman earls. The earls had large families who
were admired by the native Irish, and these feudal earldoms at first
seemed as if they would assure Anglicization of Ireland; but several
of them produced instead a new variety of Irish nobility.

For much of the first three centuries, the English devoted limited attention to Ireland. Richard II who came to Ireland in 1394 and

THE DEBURGO AND FITZGERALD NORMAN IRISH EARLDOMS

The first Irish noble title in Ulster was granted to Hugh de Lacy as 1st Earl of Ulster (1st creation). Later, Walter de Burgho was created 1st Earl of Ulster (2nd creation). Walter de Burgo's son Richard, the Red Earl, ruled from 1286 to 1320, and his daughter married Robert the Bruce who became King of Scotland. In 1270 Irish forces led by Aedh O'Connor, together with their Scots mercenary galloglass wearing coats of mail and wielding battle axes, defeated Normans led by Walter de Burgo and Henry III's Justiciar, Ralph d'Ufford, at the Battle of Athenkip. That battle was the watershed, the limit of Norman conquest in Ireland.

The Irish Geraldine patron was the Norman invader Maurice FitzGerald of Pembroke in Wales.[64] He came to Ireland with the original Normans and proved to be a major figure in the Norman successes in the southeast and in Leinster. Henry II named him governor of Ireland together with Hugh de Lacy. Strongbow granted him large tracts in Leinster. After Maurice died, his offspring prospered, controlling vast lands in Leinster and Munster. Soon there were two Geraldine dynasties, Kildare in Leinster and Desmond in Munster.

The FitzGerald Kildare earldom was conferred in 1316 as a reward to John FitzGerald for his service in the defeat of Edward the Bruce in 1318 at Faughart. Another son of Maurice FitzGerald was Thomas FitzMaurice of Shanid from whom the Desmond lines were descended and from whom their battle cry *"Shanid Abu"* derived. In 1329 Maurice FitzThomas FitzGerald was created First Earl of Desmond.[65] He expanded the Desmond lands by conquest and by marriage to Katherine deBurgh, daughter of the powerful Norman Richard deBurgh. The 1st Earl of Desmond became one of the most powerful men in Ireland.[66] To sustain his power, he introduced the burdensome practices for quartering troops on local landowners' property known as coyne and livery.

(continued)

(The Deburgo and Fitzgerald Norman Irish Earldoms, continued)

Earldoms were granted in Munster with names derived from Muma (Munster): Desmond (Desmuma or South Munster), Ormond (Ormuma or east Munster), and Thomond (Tuadmuma or north Munster). The earldom of Louth was conferred on John de Bermingham who had led the forces that defeated Bruce, but that earldom did not survive. Many other earldoms were created later – Clanconnell, Antrim, Clancarthy, Carrick, Clanrickard, Orrery, Inchiquin, Ossery and others.

The rights and powers of the earls were substantial. They were feudal lords to whom the King of England granted the right to rule the septs and the lesser lords within their earldoms. The earls' palatinate rights included the right to govern their subjects and to be paid rents in cattle and goods, which made the earls quite wealthy. The earls also had the right to demand the service of fighting men from the septs under them, which made them powerful-indeed fearsome-and as an earl's military strength rose, royal unease over his loyalty would rise even more.

again in 1399 was the only English King who set foot in Ireland during almost half a millennium, from 1210 to 1689, until James II and William of Orange came to face each other. The English provided only the most minimal forces needed to hold the turbulent colonial frontier in check. A few forts were established in the wildest areas, and they were bolstered by troops sent out from the Pale and by occasional forces of galloglass, kerne and horse provided by loyal Irish or Norman lords. More, however, was necessary to defend the fringes of the Pale, and far more would have been necessary to settle the Midlands.

The English lordship used two parliaments, one in England and another in Ireland, to legislate for Ireland, creating a fertile area for later disputes.

THE STATUTES OF KILKENNY

To steer Normans in Ireland away from the Irish lifestyle, to keep them English as they intermarried with the Irish, the Crown enacted the Statutes of Kilkenny in 1366. These laws denied fundamental rights to the native Irish and have been likened in their terms and their effect to modern day apartheid laws in South Africa.[67] They have been referred to by historians as the "outlawry[68] of the Irish race."[69] They ordered the Normans to cease living according to customs, language and style of the Irish. These laws were in part an effort to identify who was, and who was not, entitled to the protection[70] of English common law.[71] They were promulgated by Lionel, Duke of Clarence, son of Edward III, who became Lord Lieutenant in 1361. The Old English who did live among the Irish had become too fond of Irish dress, custom and religious ceremonies, after having plentifully intermarried with the Irish.

The Statutes of Kilkenny were also intended, however, to create a permanent barrier between the Gaelic and Norman races in Ireland,[72] for wherever they mingled,[73] the Irish lifestyle proved dominant. Alliance between the English and Irish by marriage was forbidden by the statutes; neither the English nor the Anglo-Irish were to use the Irish language. The Statutes of Kilkenny were not repealed until 1613.[74]

Competing Earldoms

Munster, site of the Desmond earldom in the southwest, was distant from the Pale, and Munster's heavily native Irish population was miserably poor, whereas the earldoms of Kildare and Ormond in the east were comparatively prosperous.

The Butlers of Ormond, descendants of Theobald Walter, the powerful Chief Butler of Ireland to Henry II, supported the Lancastrians. After the Yorkists defeated the Lancastrians at Towton, the Earl of Ormond, the leader of Lancastrians in Ireland, was attainted and executed. But Sir John Butler invaded and retook Kilkenny and Tipperary and the town of Waterford in early 1462. The Earl of Desmond, Thomas FitzGerald, handily put down the Butler revolt, winning the Battle of Pilltown, and Sir John Butler fled Ireland.[75]

Edward IV, the Yorkist King, overreacted to Desmond's success at the Battle of Pilltown. He appointed Desmond Deputy. But the Deputies' primary duty was to keep the Pale around Dublin secure, and Desmond in the far southwest had a difficult time protecting distant Dublin and the Pale.

King Edward at first devoted little attention to Ireland. He had appointed his brother George, the 12-year old Duke of Clarence, Lord Lieutenant, so Desmond felt he had a long leash. But the King began to be more attentive and concerned about Desmond's loyalty when Desmond failed to protect the Pale and appeared to assist the native Irish clans. Instead of expanding English control, Desmond virtually ignored the Pale.

Edward granted a loyal Anglo Norman, Roland FitzEustace, the Meath lands of Portlester, named him Baron of Portlester, and directed Desmond to follow the guidance of Baron Portlester in the hope that this would convert Desmond's followers to a path of loyalty, but Desmond did not improve. Edward hoped to see a loyal shift of all of the Desmond earl's followers to the policies and style of England.

Bishop Sherwood of Meath began a heated opposition to Desmond remaining as Deputy, and Desmond was called to London and barely succeeded in keeping his post temporarily; but King Edward soon decided to send a strong-minded Englishman as Deputy.

The Butcher and the 8th Earl of Desmond

In 1465 King Edward IV appointed John Tiptoft, the Earl of Worcester, as Lord Chancellor of Ireland. He also appointed as Deputy, Desmond's enemy, Bishop Sherwood. Desmond, however, chose to ignore these appointments. He continued to act as Deputy, and he appointed the 7th Earl of Kildare as Lord Chancellor. But Desmond, while fighting in the midlands, suffered a glaring embarrassment. He was taken prisoner by the local chieftain, the O'Connor Faly, and had to be rescued by a force of English from Dublin. Tiptoft

COYNE AND LIVERY

The Earl of Kildare, through his use of coyne and livery outside the Pale, in the marches and the surrounding Old English lordships loyal to him, was able to demonstrate a unique ability to discharge that prime duty of the Deputy – protection of the Pale from raids, rustling and black rents. He did it by turning the practice into a near continuous form of feudal taxation, thereby turning his loyal kerne and horse into the equivalent of a standing army. The distant Desmonds of Kerry were comparatively impotent, unable to sustain such a crucible of support by coyne and livery in the Pale marches where they had no loyal septs. An Earl of Desmond was, largely because of this, typically a far less satisfactory Deputy than an Earl of Kildare.

Why was coyne and livery so hated by the Tudors? Why so persistent? It was the essential source of the military power enjoyed by earls, lords and chieftains, and it was what enabled the earls to pose a credible military threat to the Crown. The practices were a menu of old Gaelic customs. They had originated as relatively rare, merely occasional occurrences. Coyne was the most oppressive and the most hated of the several related Gaelic impositions. It was customary to quarter a chieftain's or an earl's troops[88] on the land of his subjects at the subject's expense. Coyne was forbidden in the heart of the Pale, the maghery, but heavily practiced nearby in the contiguous Pale marches.

Both coyne and livery imposed by Irish on Irish and the comparable English practice of billeting English troops on lands of the Irish were far worse than just burdensome impositions. Both were oppression riddled with fraud and corruption.[89] The

(continued)

(Coyne and Livery, continued)

military officers would extract provisions and funds from the citizenry by transparent false troop counts. Theft and vandalism also accompanied the billeting of troops. Sir John Davies described coyne and livery as "extortion" and a "crying sin," and said the consequence of it could be that "when the husbandman had labored all the year, the soldier in one night did consume the fruits of all his labor...."[90]

Coyne and livery were among the many native practices that had been outlawed in the 1366 Statutes of Kilkenny, but the Kildare earls revived both practices and others in the 15th century without attracting retribution. In 1488 a statute was passed to outlaw coyne and livery in the Pale. The burden imposed by these combined practices – along with the obligations of summer oats for the earl's horses, bonnacht, cuddy and cosher – grew to be a heavy burden on those obligated to respond.

The full burden included hosting and feasting; it could throw a village into financial ruin when the earl's full entourage, sometimes hundreds, arrived demanding not only lodging, but banquets and money for all present. The mercenaries in the troop demanded bonnacht and the earl insisted on a feast called cosher. Cuddy was simpler, lodging and food for a night for the earl and his retinue. That it was invoked by Old English Earls and imposed by them on native Irish has a certain irony to it, since these practices were a native Irish tradition.

was ruthless.[76] He took control and ended any effort to appease the Irish. Desmond, however, continued to be unruly. In February 1468, on Tiptoft's demand, the Irish Parliament suddenly attainted Desmond and the 7th Earl of Kildare as well, charging that they had provided support to the King's Irish Enemies.

Edward IV was a disengaged ruler, and a lazy one, and he left the work of governance to Tiptoft. Tiptoft had already become known as the "Butcher of England"[77] for his summary executions of opponents of the King. Humanist scholar though he was, Tiptoft was notorious for impaling traitors. Tiptoft had Desmond beheaded eight days after his arrest. Portlester came to the rescue of Kildare and helped him escape. Kildare's followers, along with the Desmonds, O'Connors and MacMurroughs, rebelled, and attacked English settlers.

Edward IV was astonished. He had not been consulted by Tiptoft. Alarmed by the sudden rebellion, Edward attempted to bring peace by denouncing the charges against Kildare, and the Council withdrew them in exchange for Kildare's willingness to call for peace in Leinster and end the rising.

Meanwhile, in England the coalition with which the power of the Yorkists had been amassed began coming apart. Richard Neville, Earl of Warwick, leader of the Neville family, was the most powerful noble in England (called the "Kingmaker"), so powerful that he exercised royal prerogatives, including diplomacy with France, as though he had the right. In 1470 the opportunistic Neville suddenly abandoned Edward IV, threw his support to the Lancastrians, and the Lancastrians were back in power. Edward fled to the Netherlands. Tiptoft the Butcher, now without Edward to protect him, was executed.

But Edward IV regrouped. He invaded and regained the throne. Edward's quixotic brother George had realigned again and switched his support back to Edward. Neville, the powerful manipulator, was killed at the Battle of Barnet. With Edward back on the throne, George, Duke of Clarence, was again named Lord Lieutenant of Ireland.

He decided to grant the House of Kildare the chance to wield power in Ireland. He appointed the 7th Earl of Kildare Lord Deputy. This was a pragmatic choice. To enhance the Deputy's ability to carry out his duties to guard the Pale, Parliament established the Brotherhood of Arms of St. George, a force of horsemen and archers sponsored by thirteen prominent Palesmen, a standing army to protect the Pale.

6

The Rise of the House of Kildare

*The Dublin Council was "partly corrupted with affection towards
the Earl of Kildare and partly in... dread of him"[78]*
— State Papers of Henry VIII

The FitzGeralds of Kildare set out to capitalize on the opportunity mishandled by the FitzGeralds of Desmond, and to prove to King Edward IV and the Yorkists that they could govern Ireland, that Kildare political acumen combined with a powerful army in the Pale was England's solution to the Irish problem. The Kildares controlled the Council in Dublin,[79] but they had been forced to look over their shoulders at every point and to mollify the wishes of the Lord Lieutenant in London. Edward IV's brother George, Duke of Clarence, had twice been named Lord Lieutenant, and had more and more intruded into Irish government. Suddenly, in 1478, after one too many disloyal acts, King Edward IV personally prosecuted his mentally unstable brother and procured his execution. When news of George's execution reached Ireland, seven FitzGerald loyalists on the Dublin Council[80] decided this was their opportunity. They elected their own Justiciar to rule Ireland now that the Lord Lieutenant was dead. The Justiciar they elected was the 7th Earl of Kildare. Clever as their move was, it looked to be in vain — the 7th Earl died suddenly. The Council members, however, quickly took to themselves the prerogative of electing the Earl's 22 year old son, now the 8th Earl of Kildare, Garret Mor FitzGerald, as the new Justiciar.

Garret Mor FitzGerald (*Gearóid Mór MacGearailt*), called simply Kildare, was born an Irish aristocrat of Norman lineage, a direct descendant of the first Normans who had invaded Ireland in the 12th century. Now, at a young age, he was suddenly the heir to one of the ruling Norman earldoms in the ancient Kingdom of Leinster and also the holder of the fragile power of a Justiciar elected without the King's blessing.

Kildare, at 22, had been living the relaxed life of a wealthy heir-in-waiting, learning the lessons to prepare for the future, anticipating that in 20 years or so he may become the earl. There surely was no hurry, and he had anticipated that he could happily spend time riding and training his falcons. But that day in 1478 his life changed dramatically. Kildare found himself challenging the King.

Edward IV bristled at the extraordinary affront of the Kildare faction presuming to elect a Kildare as Justiciar. He promptly named his own Lieutenant and his own Deputy. The King announced his infant son George was the Lord Lieutenant and Lord Henry Grey was the Deputy. As for Kildare, Edward forbade him to convene a Parliament. Lord Henry Grey arrived in Dublin in September, 1478, expecting that the King's authority would be respected and that he would be accepted as Deputy. What he found instead was a direct challenge to his authority.[81] Young Kildare and his ally Viscount Gormanstown began to obstruct Grey's daily efforts to govern. Confused and out of his element, Grey tried to fight back; he convened a parliament to nullify the election of Kildare and to cut through the obstructionist maneuvers contrived by the Kildare faction.

But Grey and King Edward were witnessing an early modern flexion of Irish against the power of London. A political machine of some sort had come to life among the Anglo Norman nobility of Ireland, and the Kildare faction was out-maneuvering a King and perhaps about to achieve Home Rule. The political opposition tactics employed by the Kildares, as well as Grey's own lack of resolve, produced a mismatch. Lord Grey could not gain control, and Edward IV summoned Grey and Kildare to London. There, Kildare outshone Grey by a wide margin. He convinced King Edward himself to further marginalize Lord Grey. After three dispiriting months trying to gain stature, Lord Grey packed his bags and left Ireland, abandoning the deputyship. Exhilarated but anxious, Kildare awaited Edward's reaction. Despite the arrogance of it all, the King capitulated as well. In a face-saving stroke, Edward appointed Sir Robert Preston, Viscount Gormanstown, Deputy, but Gormanstown was succeeded within a year by the 8th Earl of Kildare.

The Irish had hardly been liberated by taking local administration of their homeland, but no blood had been shed and they had not bowed and scraped to gain power; they had taken it. The methods used were civilized and all moves were political. When it was achieved, there was no rebellion to be punished.

The Palesmen and marcher lords who witnessed this could see that they would benefit from the leadership of the young earl who had masterminded this campaign and achieved this unique détente with the Crown. He had shown them that he had the Irish spirit and the Norman temperament. Kildare was a large and agile Norman, a vigorous man and an excellent horseman. He loved falconry and was happiest hawking in the Curragh of Kildare. Though in his youth he had carried no burdens of office, he had often campaigned and fought alongside his father. During his youth he cultivated physical courage to a state of near fearlessness. Now, as Deputy, he would need not only political cunning and personal flair, but skill in battle. He immediately showed his great ability leading his men in skirmishes.

It was clear to the native Irish that he was not one of them. He looked foreign. It was not just his size, but his darker straighter hair. No portrait of him has survived, but he is described by the Four Masters of Donegal who compiled the Annals from prehistory to 1616, as tall, bearded and fiery when provoked.[82] A Hans Holbein portrait of his son, Garret Og FitzGerald, in his adulthood is the figure of a large Norman.

The Good Family

Kildare's relationship with the native Irish was perhaps the greatest evidence of his personal skills. The native Irish countryside of his era was home to a turbulent mix of restless chieftains and some vicious enemies. Though Normans were Irish in their own way by his time, the differences that persisted between the Anglo Irish and the natives were very clear – the larger size of the Anglo Irish, their

The 9th Earl of Kildare, Garret Og FitzGerald

clothes, speech, and Anglo Norman hairstyle. The wealthy Earl of Kildare wore an ornate chain of office, and he was well known for fine clothes and his large entourage. His Norman pronunciation of Irish marked him as different from them but his empathy for the people and his humor made him seem a friend and an equal. He would walk among the villagers, mingling in friendly fashion, and winning quite a few of the significant members of clans as personal allies. A man of unmistakable gravitas, he would speak to villagers as one of them, using their vernacular, chatting about their livestock and listening to the stories of their *seanachaí*.

A playful villager once approached Kildare and confided that he had accepted a dare from a friend that he could pluck a hair from the Earl's beard.[83] Kildare invited him to go ahead and take one, but promised him a poke in the jaw if he plucked more than

Ruins of Maynooth Castle

one. Unlike the Desmonds, the Kildares had not heavily inter-married with the Irish. Although they had thoroughly succumbed to Irish influence, it did not impair their aristocratic lifestyle at their Castle at Maynooth which was filled with Turkish carpets and beds of gold trim.

Kildare proved to be an intuitive star at politics. He won the support of the several Irish constituencies whose support would be necessary to obtain power and to wield power. Young as he was, he seemed naturally in charge. He did not bully or threaten. Instead, he displayed that most magical quality of a born leader — supreme confidence that people were happy to do his bidding. He had to prove to the English that he could be their leader and to the very different native Irish that he could be theirs also. He understood the native Irish wit. He saw that the Irish would use levity as a tool, not just for enjoyment. It helped them defuse tense situations. Clever repartee and humorous banter became a part of his persona and he used them very effectively.

He was a steadfast supporter of every aspect of religious culture in his earldom. Religion served his political goals as well since his open devotion helped to attract support from the clergy and Anglo Irish.

Dealing with opponents throughout Ireland, Kildare negotiated cleverly and fairly. He would reach accords. But when frustrated or insulted by the treatment he received, his geniality was gone in a flash of temper. He always found ways to underscore to his opponents the benefit of dealing cooperatively with him rather than making an enemy of him. He was quick to punish, even to execute enemies, and he was constantly marching against large and small clans who opposed his or his allies' interests.

He seemed to have no reluctance to serve England, and he set about to satisfy the desire of Edward IV to expand the peacekeeping influence of the Crown beyond the Pale marches and across the midlands. It helped greatly that Kildare was a Yorkist. Even after Edward's death in 1483, Kildare continued his service under Richard III. In most respects during these early years, Kildare could be viewed as a dutiful loyal Deputy, and as a wise choice to conduct the political bargaining and diplomacy required to deal with the Pale and the Butlers of Kilkenny. At the same time he proved himself an exceptionally capable field marshal with all the military skills needed of a Deputy charged with protecting the thorny frontier areas of Ireland. During the reigns of Edward IV and Richard III, he expanded and solidified his rule.

The events of June 1483 after Edward IV's death were as appalling as any in the Wars of the Roses or for that matter in England's long history. Edward made an historic mistake when he designated his brother, Richard, Duke of Gloucester, as Lord Protector of the young Edward V. Richard immediately set about to gather support to usurp the Throne from Edward V. He had Edward V arrested en route to his coronation. Edward's younger brother, Richard, was also seized, taken from his mother at Westminster and, along with Edward, disappeared into the Tower and one of history's saddest mysteries. The two youths were apparently executed, and their Protector, Richard, has ever since been a prime suspect. Some suspect complicity of his equally ambitious cohort, the Duke of Buckingham. By late June, Richard and his supporters manipulated and terrorized Parliament into petitioning Richard to take the throne as Richard III; and he of course acquiesced. Soon, however, Richard's ally, Buckingham, revolted against him, was caught, and by November he too had been executed. Edward IV's widow, Elizabeth Woodville, her young sons dead, brokered an historic marriage pact to wed her Yorkist daughter, Elizabeth, to the sole Lancastrian who had a claim to the throne — Henry Tudor.

Richard III was defeated at Bosworth by that Lancastrian, and the victory that day imprinted that obscure Welsh family name on a fashion of architecture, on a literary style, and on an era. Henry Tudor became Henry VII and, with great acclamation, he merged the warring peerages of the Red and White Roses by marrying Elizabeth, the younger sister of the two Yorkist princes in the Tower, and began the rule of the House of Tudor.

As comforting to the Crown as the Kildare performance as Deputy had been under the Yorkists, when the Lancastrian force slew Richard III at Bosworth in 1485, the world changed both for the FitzGerald Yorkists in Ireland and for the new Lancastrian Tudors in England. The ascension of the Tudors posed a challenge for Kildare for he was well known to be a fervent Yorkist and, despite the warm symbolism of the merger of the red and white roses of the Lancastrians and Yorkists in the new amalgam called Tudor, Henry Tudor had been on the side of the Lancastrians, and, at the outset, insecure and distrustful of Yorkists. Henry Tudor's grandfather, Owen Tudor, once a mere page at the Court of Henry V, ultimately fought at Agincourt. He also had later married Catherine of Valois, Henry V's widow and Henry VII's grandmother. Henry VII's claim to the throne was a weak one in the eyes of the Yorkist Geraldines of Ireland.

Henry VII's youthful Deputy in Ireland would one day be called the Great Earl of Kildare, but at Henry's accession, Kildare was still young and rough around the edges. He had lived through his father's experience with Tiptoft, the reversals of the Wars of the Roses, and he had witnessed the value of political and military strength rather than pliant obedience. At the dawn of the Tudor era, Kildare was young and imperious, and Henry VII was insecure and imperious. However, Kildare's contagious personality seemed to help them deal with each other. He was able to demonstrate for the new King and his new Court officials his value as Deputy, his political mastery and his popularity with the Leinster Irish. Unlike some who had merely bullied local septs into docile submission, Kildare convinced Henry that he had won the trust of the sept leaders, that his mystique spread throughout Leinster, then all across the land. Followers in Kildare, Munster and even Ulster supported him, and their loyalty afforded him the strength to deal with his enemies, the Butlers of Ormond, and with very different English Kings.

Henry VII had been extremely hesitant to embrace Kildare, but in time he came to realize that the surest way to maintain peace in Ireland was to retain Kildare as Deputy. Though cautious because the FitzGeralds were Yorkists, Henry became convinced that the suspicion and inflexibility that were the royal attitudes of old toward the Irish earls were useless with Kildare, and that he should be treated with respect. Kildare's political skills worked well as he pursued a distant cooperative relationship with the Tudors. Even when his actions appeared disloyal to the Crown, he would be excused, though not entirely forgiven. As the King's respect for him became evident throughout Leinster and the Pale, then ultimately all of Ireland, his stature grew beyond that of all earlier Deputies. Other leaders in Ireland began to court his friendship and alliance.

Kildare's relationship with the Tudors, however, was always edgy. Though he was not a habitual rebel, he was an irrepressible Yorkist, and to him the Tudors were merely a bunch of usurping Lancastrians. But when his personal dealings with Henry VII became tense, Kildare relieved the tension through his affability. The informality and humor he displayed in front of the King seems presumptuous and irreverent, but Henry apparently was not offended. Kildare spoke in an intimate enthusiastic manner. He would grab Henry's hand and unleash irreverent stories as rejoinders to the accusations others launched against him. When no less than the Bishop of Meath complained about Kildare and Henry VII summoned him to answer, the Earl leaned close to the King and whispered that the Bishop was in foul temper because he was yearning for a wench.[84] Henry roared with laughter. Such audacious familiarity dampened Henry's hostility and gave the concerned King a glimmer of optimism that Kildare's unruliness would never mushroom into treason.[85]

In the Dublin political arena as well, the Dublin Council, even some local Tudor officials, were taken with his geniality. They knew he might also explode at them, that he was easily provoked, but quick to be appeased, and that he would be decent to allies. The power of the House of Kildare is well framed by the later observation about his successor that the Dublin Council was "partly corrupted with affection towards the Earl of Kildare and partly in such dread of him that they would not oppose his wishes."

Kildare also had the vision to appreciate the value of bonds with the powerful chieftains in distant pockets of Ireland. He became one of history's authentic masters of strategic alliances. His large closely knit family was a natural resource for such relationships. He negotiated marriages of his daughters and sisters in ways that bolstered his power. His sister, Eleanor, married Conn Mor O'Neill of Tyrone (*Conn Mór O'Neill*), the eldest son of The O'Neill, Chief of the Name of that most powerful clan.[86] His daughter, Alice, married Conn's son, Con Bacach O'Neill (*Con Bacach MacCuinn O'Néill*). The O'Neill-FitzGerald marriages cemented a powerful alliance in early modern Ireland, and the Norman House of Kildare and the O'Neill Clan of Ulster each enhanced their power through the other.[87]

Hugh O'Donnell (*Aodh O'Domhnaill*), the ruler of the O'Donnells in the north from 1461 to 1505, also became a Kildare ally; he in turn was linked by marriage to the O'Neills. Calculated politics was at the heart of these romances and the political cunning they showed was never more evident than when the rival House of Ormond in Kilkenny was added to the Kildare network of alliances. The Butlers of Ormond remained fervent Lancastrians, and when the Lancastrian Henry Tudor gained power, Kildare's daughter Margaret was given in marriage to a Butler, the Lancastrian ally Piers Roe Butler, Earl of Ossory and later Earl of Ormond. With the creation of these many relationships among the FitzGeralds of Desmond, the Burkes of Connaught, the O'Neills and O'Donnells of Ulster, and many smaller septs, the FitzGeralds of Kildare were able to control the civil administration in Dublin, most Council members, and less directly a large percentage of the people in distant parts of Ireland. They could also gather a fighting force of clansmen who could, if push came to shove, overwhelm the English garrison. Thus, the House of Kildare had grown to be a political and military force to reckon with.

The Pretenders

Kildare's independence did, as Henry VII feared, ultimately turn to overt disloyalty. It happened when the first of two pretenders to Henry VII's throne came ashore in Ireland.[91] Though the Yorkist nobles had suspended going to battle to try to retake the throne after Bosworth, Henry VII found himself confronted with Yorkist impostors claiming the throne. These pretenders saw Ireland as fertile ground on which to enlist support. They actively courted Irish sponsors, tapped into the incorrigibility of the Irish Yorkists, and greatly heightened Henry's alarm at the threat that this strain of disloyalty running through the ranks of Anglo Irish posed to the Crown.

Lambert Simnel and Perkin Warbeck materialized several years apart each claiming to be one of the missing Yorkists from the tower murders. They came under very different circumstances, but the sponsors of both played on the same suspicions and fixation which gripped both England and Ireland over the mysterious disappearance of the two Yorkist princes and a Yorkist earl, the sons and a nephew of Edward IV.[92] Both pretenders' stories were seemingly preposterous, yet both acquired a level of credibility from those willing to swear to the truth of their identities. Verifying an identity in these times was often a process roughly equivalent to rumor passing for authentic evidence. With an already heightened national curiosity to play to, Edward IV's daughter Margaret and Yorkist priests recruited Lambert Simnel and schooled him to pretend initially to be one of the sons of Edward IV and heir to the throne, but they changed the pretense saying he was the Earl of Warwick, also an heir.[93] In response, in February 1487 Henry VII produced the real Earl of Warwick, who was a prisoner in the Tower, and paraded him before the public in London to destroy the myth that Lambert Simnel was the earl. Despite this, Simnel's claim was supported in Ireland by Thomas FitzGerald, brother of Kildare, and it was accepted in Dublin, and Lambert Simnel was crowned Edward VI at Christ Church Cathedral Dublin.

To the astonishment of the Tudor Court, Kildare accepted the post[94] as the dubious Edward VI's Lord Lieutenant of Ireland and summoned a parliament which confirmed Simnel as the new Yorkist King. Kildare named his brother, Thomas FitzGerald, Lord Chancellor, and Thomas accompanied an Irish force that invaded England in an attempt to place Simnel on the throne in England.[95] Some 4,000 Irish kerne sailed with the new Edward VI to invade England but they were defeated by a force led by Henry VII at the Battle of Stoke — the final battle of the Wars of the Roses. Thomas FitzGerald was killed at Stoke, and Simnel was captured.

After the defeat of the Simnel supporters, Ireland nervously awaited King Henry's response, sure that such an insurrection meant war, but Henry was surprisingly subdued. He had come to accept a sobering reality — it was his tenuous claim to the Throne that had attracted such a challenge. His unpopularity in Ireland had rendered him unable to control the Irish political structure. War, he concluded was not the answer to those unfortunate realities. The Simnel episode had confirmed Kildare's power in Ireland. Rather than attack the disloyal Irish, Henry sent Sir Richard Edgecombe to Ireland with a small force with authority to grant pardons, to extract bonds to assure future good behavior and to begin to build a base of loyalty.

When the Simnel treason failed, Henry VII could well have attainted Kildare and executed him. Had he tried, however, he would have had to catch Kildare in Ireland, since only Kildare's brother Thomas accompanied the invasion. It would have been difficult for the English to put an end to Kildare. It was more likely that Kildare would elude capture, call in all his debts of loyalty from The O'Neill, the Earl of Desmond and others. Had Henry VII forced Kildare into full rebellion after the Battle of Stoke, the House of Kildare may have emerged as a major force in Ireland then and there. With the network of fighters Kildare could muster all across Ireland, Kildare might have become the first in a line of modern Irish High Kings.

Instead, Henry invited Kildare and some of his supporters to London to explain their grievances. Though unapologetic, they were considerably relieved by such an invitation. Kildare delayed, avoiding the voyage to London for months, but he finally went. At a welcoming dinner at Greenwich, Henry VII took an impish delight in watching Kildare's startled reaction when he recognized Lambert Simnel (the once aspiring King Edward VI) sweating, hard at work as a helper in Henry's kitchen.

Before long, however, a number of Irish leaders were openly disloyal again when 17-year old Perkin Warbeck gained acceptance as Richard, Duke of York, another missing York prince.[96] Warbeck staged appearances wearing silk garments, an opulent costume viewed as evidence of royalty. In 1491, Warbeck's promoters were able to obtain Irish support for their scheme to place the youth on the English throne from the Earl of Desmond, the White Knight, the Knight of Kerry and the Knight of Glin, but no support at all from Kildare.

Henry lost patience with Irish self-governance over their support for this second pretender. Though Kildare was not one of those who supported Warbeck, Henry dismissed him as Deputy.[97] Black Butler (Sir James Butler of Ormond) claimed in a report to the King that Kildare did support "The French lad." Kildare learned of it and went to see the King in 1493 to deny it, but the King informed Kildare that he had decided to send a new Deputy, Sir Edward Poynings. Poynings, then the Lord Deputy of Calais, came to Ireland as the new Deputy with a substantial military retinue. His charge was to end the independent flare that had been developing under the House of Kildare. He had Parliament enact Poynings Law in 1494.[98] A poorly worded document, the statute was interpreted as forbidding the Irish to hold a Parliament without prior approval of the King, and forbidding that Parliament to introduce a bill without prior approval of the bill by the King's Council. It was largely an effort to prevent the festering Warbeck conspiracy from calling a Parliament, as had the Simnel conspiracy, as an effort to legitimize the pretender, but it set in place a repressive parliamentary process for Ireland.

Poynings' Parliament from 1494 to 1495, and subsequent parliaments, also passed laws declaring that the army was the King's army, forbidding artillery to be kept by anyone but the King and his Deputy, and declaring it treason to war against the state. Kildare did not war against the state thereafter or support Warbeck, but he certainly did work to stir political opposition to Poynings, and campaigns began in Dublin, Kilkenny and London to portray Kildare as an incorrigible, disloyal conspirator.

Henry VII himself was changing. He dealt with his courtiers in a different way. In 1495 he set up his Privy Chamber as a buffer keeping at bay the many nobles who sought access to him, dealing directly for most matters only with the few Privy Councilors he needed. He also behaved differently toward Kildare. Poynings' Parliament attainted Kildare for encouraging the Scots to send an army into Ireland. Assured of a pardon, Kildare went to Dublin, but was arrested and sent to the Tower of London where he was held for eighteen months. During his incarceration, his wife died and the Irish began limited insurrections. They raided towns in the Pale. Kildare's brother James seized Carlow castle, and the chieftains of the north, the Desmonds in the south and the Burkes of Clanrickard in the west all declared for Warbeck. With Kildare in custody in the Tower, Poynings found that he was powerless to restore peace in Ireland. With Poynings unable to keep order, in August 1496 Henry VII decided he would have to restore Kildare as Deputy, a painfully embarrassing concession that English control was proving impossible. When Kildare appeared before Henry's Council to go through what by then was the formality of demonstrating his innocence, he was told to choose a counselor to present his defense. Kildare said he chose the King to defend him. Henry, it turns out, was flattered by the compliment.

As for Perkin Warbeck (actually Piers Osbeck, son of an itinerant Picard customs collector from Tournai on the border of France), who was to have been Richard IV, he was not as fortunate as Lambert Simnel. Warbeck was sent to the Tower and later was publicly executed in London in 1499 after plotting to escape the Tower.[99]

Thereafter, however, Henry VII never believed for a moment that Kildare had become an entirely loyal Tudor; but he made concessions to Kildare hoping at least to stabilize the relationship. The restoration of the Great Earl of Kildare as Deputy after his support of a pretender to the throne was simply pragmatism, testament that Kildare had extraordinary power in Ireland and that Henry VII realized it. No comparable position of political strength against an English monarch was ever seen again in an Irish earl or chieftain.

Aside from his relationship with the English, Kildare's bond with the native Irish was always strong. Though a Norman aristocrat, Kildare became identified with the Irish. He encouraged Irish traditions and he reveled in Irish song and poetry, participating in the lifestyle which he had come to enjoy at a young age. He was accepted by the native Irish as their leader and he became an inspiration for, and he legitimized, Irish life and culture even though laws were in force that forbade virtually every aspect of it.

A visionary in education, he started building the college at Maynooth and it was completed by his son. He built and assembled a fine library in his castle at Maynooth.[100] The new printing press gave him the opportunity to have many manuscripts in his library printed. Most of his books were in Latin, but his collection included the lives of the saints and Irish annals. He spent many hours in his library and he could see the value that education might bring to the land he led. The FitzGerald's of Kildare became so highly regarded that they were called by the Irish "the good family."

The Kildare earldom was not, however, some panacea of an Anglo-Norman civilization, and the darling of all constituencies. While the English in the Pale approved of Kildare, Henry VII now only tolerated him. Kildare in turn only tolerated English rule. It had its unmistakable rewards, and Kildare had his doubts that he could overthrow the King and seize control himself. He liked to show the Irish that he was well connected to the King when it was beneficial to do so. Life, after all, was not entirely an us-against-them feud in 15th century Ireland. A Norman earl riding in the Pale marches enjoyed being able to tell the people about banqueting in London with one of the most famous men on earth. In Maynooth it was quite a life to be the representative of the King of England.

Even the "good family", however, had enemies and family problems. One of Kildare's worst enemies was his son-in-law, Ulick Burke. The Burkes of Clanrickard were of very mixed blood by Tudor times. The Burkes were Norman in name and origin, but became very Gaelic through intermarriage. They were also as warlike and rebellious as any of the chieftains.

Ulick Burke had married Kildare's daughter and mistreated her. Though what precise provocations occurred remains uncertain, Kildare was not a man who would tolerate insult or be hesitant to protect, retaliate and avenge. A bitter feud developed between Kildare and Ulick Burke. Ulick and his men had often stormed out of the Burke castle near Loughrea to conduct border raids, cattle raids and assaults virtually anywhere in Ireland, but a pitched battle was a rarity. However, such a battle was fought between Kildare and Ulick Burke and their assembled supporting septs on August 19, 1504, at Knockdoe (*Cnoc Tuagh*) near Galway.

The battle also included the expansionist Turlough O'Brien (*Toirdelbach Ua Briain*) of Thomond. Beginning in 1460, The O'Brien[101] had expanded his power east across the Shannon, forcing the payment by Limerick residents of a blackrent, a form of extortion. O'Brien was emboldened by overtures from Sir James Butler of Ormond who curried his support and tempted O'Brien to seek to extort blackrents even as far east as Kilkenny. Kildare's own forces at Knockdoe included troops led by his young son, Garret Og FitzGerald. Together they defeated Ulick Burke, the O'Briens of Thomond and the Butlers of Ormond. The battle was described as a frenzy of "slashing" and "hacking."[102] The Kildare force killed many of Burke's men and captured several of Burke's children, but Ulick himself escaped. Knockdoe demonstrated Kildare's ability to strike effectively even that far from the Pale.

By 1506 O'Brien had resumed hostility and constructed O'Brien's Bridge to facilitate his raids east of the Shannon, but in 1510 Kildare destroyed the bridge. While Kildare inflicted losses on O'Brien and MacCarthy Mor, this time, Kildare's men suffered heavy losses. His force weakened and his record of victories clouded[103] by such a setback, Kildare decided against invading Thomond.

After the coronation of Henry VIII, Hugh Oge O'Donnell and Kildare began to consider rebellion, including an alliance with Scotland against England. However, it all ended before any revolt occurred. History would have wanted a dramatic death in an important battle for so great a figure, but Kildare's end was almost ordinary, and it was ironic. Kildare has been credited with having introduced the gun to Ireland and, in 1513 he was in Laois campaigning against the perennially rebellious O'Mores. He paused to let his horse drink from the River Grease and an O'More shot him. Badly wounded, he was moved to Athy, then to Maynooth where the wound festered, and on September 3, 1513, The Great Earl died.

Kildare had seemed an inevitable king, yet he never rebelled to strike for clear, complete independence from England.[104] His support of a pretender, in retrospect, was a rebellion to put a different king on the throne, perhaps a carryover from the competition of Yorkists and Lancastrians, or perhaps a preliminary step to taking the throne in Ireland for himself. What he did create was Ireland's first early modern network of allies; thus he may be the archetype of the Irish political boss.[105] Kildare may well have been powerful enough to have taken total power in Ireland, but with the notable exception of his support of the pretender, Lambert Simnel, Kildare had exercised self-restraint.[106] That restraint did not reflect a lack of ambition, but an awareness that his own interests and his people's well-being may best be served by the limited independence they enjoyed with a strong Irish Deputy[107] rather than a cataclysmic break with the Tudors[108] and the prospect of executions, carnage and famine. He was well aware that the larger stronger kingdom across the Irish Sea might decide, if thoroughly provoked, to repeat the type of invasions that had been led by Richard II into Ireland in 1394 and 1399.

If Kildare was the perfect model for the Irish leader, his progeny were not. His son Garret Og was competent and intelligent, but began his lordship being suffocated by Henry VIII and Cardinal Thomas Wolsey. Kildare's grandson, Silken Thomas, was a swaggering scion given to an unbecoming flamboyance, capable of offending the elders a young leader needed to pamper.

The Irish resisted rule by English-born Deputies in Ireland almost without intolerable coercion in the time of Kildare. In the succeeding generations, they would be given abundant cause. They were about to be told by successive Tudor monarchs and Deputies to abandon their religion, their laws, their native chieftains and their way of life. This ominous turn in Tudor policy predictably met with violent resistance. When it did, the Tudors only turned up the heat and began the ambitious program of Anglicization and plantation of Ireland. They would bring English settlers, soldiers and adventurers to obtain Irish land and settle there. Such an advance of England into increasingly rebellious Ireland required that this land be forcibly and fraudulently taken from the native and Norman Irish and from the Irish clergy. England could foresee from the power displayed by the House of Kildare, that land confiscation would be fought not only by the native Irish, but by Norman earls in Leinster, Munster and Connaught, and that Ulster, lair of the mighty northern clans of O'Neill, O'Donnell, and Maguire, when its time came, would be the most difficult of all.

7

Wolsey and Cromwell Bring Down the House of Kildare

Thou that art so hollow to him wilt never be true to us[109]
— Lord Skeffington to Christopher Paris

It appeared that the sun rising to herald the dawn of the 16th century was smiling brightly on the House of Kildare and casting the warmest possible glow on its growing relationship with the House of Tudor. Until 1510, Kildare seemed virtually unbeatable in combat with any unruly clan even at the far end of the island, and his alliance with the O'Neills and O'Donnells in the north gave him a stature the envy of his competitors, the House of Ormond in Kilkenny.

The future seemed bright as well. Kildare's son, Garret Og FitzGerald (*Gearóid Óg MacGearailt*), was thriving in London, enjoying first rate English schooling, and he had grown very close to the royal family. Young Garret Og had been fostered to the royal Court and he became a close friend of Crown Prince Arthur. Soon, it seemed, Arthur would become the second Tudor King.

That bright sun seemed to fall out of the heavens for the Tudors and for the House of Kildare when Prince Arthur suddenly died in 1502. How different history might have been for Britain, Ireland, Christianity and the world if Arthur had lived to succeed his father. But his death changed everything. What might have been a half century of trust and cooperation became instead an era of intrigue, of scheming royal courtiers and of religious upheaval. No such close personal relationship ever developed between Garret Og and Prince Arthur's younger brother Henry, nor with Henry's powerful advisors Cardinal Thomas Wolsey and Thomas Cromwell.

Cardinal Thomas Wolsey

By 1513, the Great Earl was dead and his son Garret Og had succeeded him. Henry VII was dead and his son Henry VIII had succeeded him. It seemed that the well tested lordship, strained though it had been between the fathers, still might relax and blossom even under Henry VIII. An expanding England might at last include Ireland[110] in a peaceful union if these two talented sons simply became friends. The Great Earl had groomed Garret Og for leadership. He had learned that he could depend on him in battle. Diplomacy, however, often is unique to the temperaments of the individuals and to their interests. Henry VIII was less interested in the details of Irish government than his father had been.[111] Even in ruling England, he did so through a single chief minister, first Lord Chancellor Cardinal Thomas Wolsey, then Thomas Cromwell. Henry VIII was far more interested in regaining, as he saw it, the lost throne of France[112] than he was in Ireland, and it appeared that he might well leave administration in Ireland to the new Earl of Kildare.[113]

But one of history's most determined powers, Cardinal Thomas Wolsey, was becoming the man behind the throne of Henry VIII. Wolsey and his close advisor, Thomas Cromwell, seemed to discover what Ireland had really become – a lordship nominally under the English King, but a place that was home to a powerful coalition of Normans and Gaelic chieftains, and it was the House of Kildare in Ireland, not the House of Tudor in England, that appeared to run Ireland.

Thomas Cromwell

Wolsey's Wealth and Power

Wolsey coveted the great goal of Rome — the papacy, but Holy Roman Emperor Charles V stood in his way and Wolsey failed to achieve it. Wolsey did procure a cardinalate in 1515 from Pope Leo X. He took full advantage of Henry VIII's preference for hunting and other delights over government administration. Wolsey relieved Henry of all that and, blessed with high intelligence, he thereby controlled the government, and he presided over the Star Chamber. Wolsey was "vain, shallow, and greedy" as well. He was left free to enrich himself and he did. He was given to an unseemly "love of pomp and display" and an arrogance that drove him to take St. Albans, England's richest abbey, and Winchester, and then to flaunt his wealth. "No priest was richer or displayed the fact more proudly." Wolsey's corruption sat easily on him and "his income from improper bribes and patronage was large and notorious." Far from celibate, Wolsey had one son and several daughters. He arranged for his son to be ordained as a minor in order to acquire clerical benefices. Wolsey also became a papal legate and made himself the effective ruler of the church in England. Using his position as papal legate he dissolved abbeys, took the profits from bishoprics, removed lucrative court cases to his legatine court, and plundered wealthy probate estates.[114]

Wolsey was not about to yield the reins of power, or the wealth to be found in England or in Ireland, or the royal prerogatives he enjoyed. Although the Kildare earldom surrounding Dublin and the Pale offered rich cultural soil in which Tudor officials could harvest a new English world in Ireland, neither Henry VIII nor his advisors made the effort to court the new 9th Earl of Kildare. Instead they treated Garret Og and his family as vassals, then enemies, and finally as outlaws.

Ireland was under the lordship of a foreign ruler, but Henry VIII had a limited foothold, primarily in and around Dublin — the Pale. Even the Pale was insecure except the center, the maghery. The Pale marches were still frontier territories. The rest of Ireland was wild and unsettled, tempered only by a number of safe outposts guarded by walled cities like Cork, or by the castles of allies. For adventurers, these were the only comfort to be found among the "Wild Irish" clans.

Under Henry VII programs to settle or Anglicize Ireland had been rudimentary. The attention the English garrison gave to Irish lords was coercive, not diplomatic. The Crown depended on control from Dublin with a very small army under the direction of the King's Deputy. Little thought was given to forging a lasting alliance with those Irish leaders who might work the magic of leading the Irish people peacefully into full membership in English society.

Gerald the Great's son, Garret Og FitzGerald, became the 9th Earl of Kildare in 1513, just a few short years after the 1509 coronation of 17 year old Henry VIII. Garret Og was not unknown to Henry. He had spent 10 years, from age 6 to 16, being raised at the Court of Henry VII in exchange for the reversal of the attainder of his father. There, he received an English education and became such a friend of Crown Prince Arthur[115] that he played a principal role in the 1502 funeral ceremony for the Prince. But his years as Earl happened to coincide with the ascendancy of Cardinal Wolsey and then Thomas Cromwell, and Garrett Og's relationship with the Court of Henry VIII unraveled.

Garret Og and his supporters were far less the cause for the unfortunate change in Tudor/Kildare relations than were Henry VIII and his supporters. Garret Og was a competent and consistent successor to his father. Henry VIII's father had been an ultimate pragmatist in Irish matters, willing to defer Irish administration to the Earl of Kildare and even to forgive treasonous acts. Henry VIII was nothing like that. In England, while he was willing to delegate government to Cardinal Wolsey, Thomas Cromwell, Thomas More and Thomas Cranmer, he ultimately turned on all of them. He had fewer choices for governing Ireland and so began with allowing Garret Og to continue after the Great Earl's death. Soon Henry came to see Garret Og as less effective than his father whose many alliances and working relationships with local lords had been personal. Many of the nearby Gaelic lords had become discontented by the time Kildare died, and a number of the alliances disappeared soon after he died. Governing was more difficult for Garret Og because of the need to deal with those lords effectively and firmly. The Great Earl had suffered a pair of failed campaigns against Gaelic lords, notably the heavy casualties suffered against Turlough O'Brien near Limerick in 1510. Such unusual setbacks called Kildare military dominance into question by the time of Garret Og. While he was certainly not alone in failing to satisfy the expectations of Henry VIII, whose wives and once-trusted ministers were executed one after another, Garret Og ultimately failed as well.

Early Tudor Ireland had been run by the House of Kildare and its allies, the House of Desmond and the O'Neill clan, for a quarter of a century until the rise of Cardinal Wolsey and Thomas Cromwell. They appreciated what riches lay in Ireland and were not content with a distant lordship. They wanted that wealth for the English and they brought down the House of Kildare and ended that form of Irish-led local governance.

The competition between the Butlers of Ormond and the House of Kildare increased after the Great Earl died and ultimately became cutthroat.[116] And a competition among the Butlers of Ormond gave rise to problems for Garret Og. In 1516 Garret Og's fall to political doom began when Henry VIII placed him in the midst of a nearly impossible dispute over the succession to the Ormond earldom and its vast estates. The King ordered Garret Og to resolve the feud between the heirs of Earl Thomas Butler of Ormond who were locked in a bitter fight. On Earl Thomas Butler's death without a direct male heir in 1515, the Butler lands were left to the Butler sisters, Margaret Butler Boleyn, and Anne Butler St. Leger. Piers Butler considered himself the presumptive heir to the lands, while Margaret's son, Sir Thomas Boleyn, father of Anne Boleyn, considered himself the rightful Earl of Ormond. Garret Og, though never a friend of Piers Butler, supported him instead of supporting the sisters, and Thomas Boleyn, even though he had been ordered by the King to support the sisters. Garret Og seemed surprised that his disobedient choice was so important to Henry. What he failed to discern was that the dispute placed him on the wrong side of the seismic emotional issue of Henry VIII's wild craving for Anne Boleyn.

Garret Og and Piers Butler began to feud as well. They competed for the post of Deputy, and Henry VIII and others used their antipathy to control them. Piers Butler's wife, Margaret, was Garret Og's sister, but she was no ally of her brother. She had become intensely envious of his success. She became angry over any favor shown him by Henry VIII. Margaret FitzGerald, by now a Butler through and through, was jealous that the Kildare earldom was more prosperous and powerful and outshone the Butler earldom. Moreover, the House of Kildare seemed entrenched in its power. Especially frustrating, by virtue of the Kildares' strategic location within the Pale, was their ability to prevent the Butlers' passage to Dublin. Piers Butler came to hate Garret Og, and he reached out to Cardinal Wolsey for help. He accused Garret Og of sedition, of corresponding with the "Irish Enemies" and of other forbidden practices, and he found every malcontent and disgruntled landowner in or near the Pale willing to complain about Garret Og, and he brought their complaints to Wolsey's attention. In 1519 Garret Og was called to London to answer the charges.

Cromwell and Wolsey Turn on the House of Kildare

In London, Garret Og had an ugly, open clash with Wolsey. The Cardinal had become a great self-inflated ego. He had amassed wealth second only to Henry's, a household staff of 800, and he owned Hampton Court, so grand an estate that Henry ultimately took it as one of his royal palaces. Garret Og became Wolsey's target.

Unable to withstand the complaints that he was abusing his power, Henry removed him as Deputy. In July, 1520, after the June extravaganza at the Field of the Cloth of Gold at Guine, Cardinal Wolsey resumed compiling evidence against Garret Og. He presented it at Court, but the evidence was insubstantial and did not support Wolsey's accusations that Garret Og had enticed some Gaelic lords to attack the Pale and to cause trouble for any Deputy but himself. Nonetheless, Wolsey succeeded in removing Garret Og from office, and he convinced Henry to replace him, and to appoint Thomas Howard, Earl of Surrey as Lord Lieutenant. While Wolsey's main target was Garret Og, he was also delighted at the prospect of opening up a foreign post in Ireland to which he could banish his rival Surrey.

Garret Og was held in London, but in restraint so relaxed that he accompanied Henry to Guine in 1520 to the Field of the Cloth of Gold where Henry and an array of England's chivalry met with Charles V and Francis I[117] in opulent style in a lavishly tented jousting field. A year earlier, Francis had lost the competition against Charles V of Habsburg Spain to become Holy Roman Emperor, and at Guine all these rulers savored thoughts of empire, especially Henry VIII.

While Garret Og was away in London, Henry gave Surrey responsibility for the Tudor effort to subdue and then to Anglicize Ireland, to secure loyalty and tighten control over both the earls and the chieftains. Surrey campaigned energetically around Ireland, and his experiences convinced him that the Irish were incorrigible and untamable except by force. He recommended a major conquest. However, Surrey advised Henry that even if conquest succeeded, it would be necessary to send Henry's own natural subjects to live in the conquered land to assure that a conquest did not rapidly unravel. Surrey's advice to Henry in 1520 began the early planning for the plantation of Ireland that was later pursued by the succeeding generation of Tudors. At first Surrey was given only an army of 1,100 men. By contrast, the Irish chieftains' forces at the time were estimated at 22,000. Not surprisingly, Surrey made little headway.

Wolsey had been very successful in 1518 in arranging a détente with France, but by 1521, the détente had unraveled and war was on the horizon. Surrey, even at that stressful time, was still urging Henry to authorize a major conquest of Ireland. Henry's preoccupation, however, was France, and so he declined; moreover, he relieved Surrey. That seemed to make Garret Og virtually indispensable. Garret Og and Piers Roe Butler competed for the post, and they each did and said as much as they could to undermine the other. Garret Og refused to allow Piers, as Deputy, to employ coyne and livery to support his troops when in Kildare country, though Garret Og employed it when Kildare forces were in Butler territory. Piers regularly launched scathing reports about the House of Kildare, especially about Garret Og, and assured that his complaints got to Wolsey and Thomas Cromwell. Cromwell, moreover, was passing these complaints along to Henry VIII, emphasizing aspects that played on Henry's special anxieties. When anxious or inflamed, Henry was easily manipulated.

This time, Henry chose Piers Roe Butler as Deputy.[118] An Ormond Deputy, however, was even less effective in this era than before. When Butler tried to flex his new military authority as Deputy by taking Kildare castles, he only provoked a Kildare insurrection. Garret Og was named Deputy to replace Piers Roe Butler in August of 1524. As a show of his power and the extent of his influence, Garret Og arranged for the colossus of Ulster, Conn Mor O'Neill, to be his ceremonial sword bearer at the banquet celebrating his appointment.[119] Piers Roe Butler received the consolation of an appointment as Treasurer. Henry gave Garret Og instructions to quell the insurrection, but Garret Og instead assisted the Kildare allies rebelling against Piers Roe Butler.[120] Among those Kildare allies was Garret Og's cousin, James FitzGerald, 10th Earl of Desmond, who, it was suspected, was bent on treason. The Tudors believed Desmond was urging France to invade Ireland. Henry ordered Garret Og to hunt down and arrest his cousin, but Garret Og vacillated. He pretended to try, but Piers Roe Butler reported his vacillation to Henry and then went to London in September 1526 to make his case against Garret Og to Wolsey. The Cardinal was easily persuaded. Henry VIII summoned Garret Og and Piers Roe Butler to London again in 1526 and ordered them to explain their bothersome feud. Garret Og was not permitted to return for 3 years. Butler, too, was retained, but he was allowed to return earlier.

Wolsey finally commenced a proceeding to prosecute Garret Og, and Wolsey himself led the prosecution. Garret Og insisted in his defense that even now he had his men out scouring the hills and gaps of Kerry searching for his traitorous cousin, James the Earl of Desmond. This time Garret Og was held in the Tower. While he was jailed, Wolsey quietly issued a death warrant for Garret Og, and sent it to the Tower guard with an order that Garret Og be beheaded. However, Wolsey had been too high handed and his execution gambit failed when Henry learned of it and countermanded the order. Garret Og was spared, but Wolsey merely continued his campaign against him.

THE BUTLERS OF ORMOND

The storied Butlers of Ormond, perennial foes of the Geraldines of Kildare and Desmond, derived their family name from an actual butler. They were descendants of Theobold Walter, Chief Butler of Ireland, who died in 1206. This low sounding position was actually a high office. A descendant of a Norman Duke, Theobold was close to Henry II and served him in England, France and Ireland. He attended to Henry during the period of the king's lengthy public penance for his knights' murder of Thomas á Becket. Among the ceremonial duties of the Chief Butler was that of presenting the new king his first cup of wine at his coronation. In recognition of this wine privilege, the Butlers were given the prisage of wine in Ireland, the right to 2 tons of wine for every ship reaching an Irish port carrying 20 tons of wine. The wine prisage helped perpetuate the vast Butler wealth for the next six hundred years.

The Butlers were first granted a lordship by the King in 1185 spread over parts of both Munster and Leinster. Later the palatinate of Tipperary was added to their lordship. The Ormond earldom was bestowed in 1329. At the time, the family's principal castle was at Nenagh. A long string of healthy male progeny and their ready adoption of English law, custom and religion spelled a prosperous run in Ireland from 1170 to 1922 for the descendants of the Chief Butler to Henry II. Edmund Butler was raised to the lesser earldom of Carrick-Mac-Griffine in Tipperary by Edward II, but when the Lancastrians were defeated at Towton, James Butler, the Fifth Earl of Ormond, was executed and internecine feuding of the Butler family groups erupted, weakening the earldom for a time.

(continued)

(The Butlers of Ormond, continued)

The Earldom of Ormond flourished due to one daughter of an Earl of Ormond. When Earl Thomas of Ormond died in 1515, his rights and power were claimed by his grandson, Sir Thomas Boleyn, Earl of Wiltshire, the son of Earl Thomas' daughter, Margaret Butler (Boleyn). Thomas Boleyn was the father of Anne Boleyn whose noble credentials included two families of English nobility, Howard and Boleyn, and the Butler Irish nobility. And Henry VIII was smitten with her.

However, Piers Roe Butler (called Piers the Red by the Irish) also claimed the earldom of Ormond. Earl Thomas' daughter, Margaret, and her sister inherited the Ormond lands. The title dispute, however, was unsettling to Henry VIII. Twelve years later, in 1527, the year he started his affair with Anne Boleyn, Henry finally engineered a compromise. He settled the Ormond succession by forcing Piers Butler to resign as Earl of Ormond giving Henry a prize to lay at the feet of Anne Boleyn. He granted the earldom of Ormond to Thomas Boleyn and named Piers Butler Deputy and created him Earl of Ossory with a 30-year lease on a significant portion of the Ormond lands. Piers Butler and many like him were named to the Council in Dublin and to Church positions. Piers Butler later was reinstated at Thomas Boleyn's death as the Eighth Earl of Ormond and he is credited with re-starting the power of Ormond.

Piers' son, James, and grandson, Black Tom Butler, brought the earldom even greater strength. Later Butlers would more than match the resurgence started by Piers. The Ormond earldom eventually became a Dukedom and a Marquisate.

The Fall of Cardinal Wolsey

Many who had been victims of Wolsey rejoiced when Henry VIII turned against him — but none more than Garret Og. The fall of Wolsey in 1529, and his death that year, was especially dramatic because he had become such a many sided powerhouse. He had not only been Archbishop of York, but Archbishop of Canterbury as well. Most important to Henry, Wolsey could approve annulments on his own. He was blamed, however, for the failure to win approval of Henry's annulment, although Henry's interference alienated Pope Clement VI.[121] While Henry's motivation for the elusive annulment, of course, was his fervor for Anne Boleyn, the ravishing black-haired beauty of vast sex appeal who, for a time, had denied her favors to Henry, he offered a godly rationale for the annulment — his belief that his marriage to Catherine of Aragon was ecclesiastically improper and that God was punishing him for it by denying him a son and heir.

Henry VIII

In June 1529 Henry VIII sent Sir William Skeffington to Ireland as Deputy. Garret Og was ordered to return with him and to work cooperatively with Skeffington's administration. During 1530 and much of 1531 Garret Og and Skeffington cooperated reasonably well. Piers Roe Butler reported to Thomas Cromwell that Garret Og had Skeffington under his thumb. The Council, on the other hand, viewed Skeffington as a supporter of Butler.

Skeffington and Garret Og, however, gradually developed a contentious relationship and became opposing forces in the Dublin Parliament. All the affronts typical of political opponents were exchanged between them, but one was offensively personal. Skeffington was mockingly called "The Gunner" by Kildare Geraldines, a reference to the fact that he was a commoner and former Master of the Ordnance.

When Skeffington came to Ireland, the other Irish earldoms were offering little trouble. The Butlers were loyal. The Desmonds were again peaceful. The Earl of Desmond had died in 1529, and was succeeded by a *Tánaiste,* his uncle Thomas FitzGerald, who had a temperate style that put him on good terms even with the Butlers.

Trouble developed for Skeffington when a Kildare-led coalition protested to Crown authorities about his rule. In April 1532, Garret Og, without Wolsey to intimidate him, enlisted the support of James Butler, Viscount Thurles, Sir Patrick Bermingham, the Lord Chief Justice, and John Rawson, the Treasurer. They appeared before the Duke of Norfolk in London and convinced him to recommend that Skeffington be sacked. Surprisingly, with Wolsey dead and Henry now freed of his influence, Henry accepted the recommendation and replaced Skeffington as Deputy in July 1532 with Garret Og himself. However, the calm that produced was not merely temporary, it was momentary.

Thomas Cromwell's Ordinances for Ireland

Thomas Cromwell rose to fill the power vacuum left by Wolsey.[122] His power would grow from Master of the King's Jewels in 1532 to greater heights — Master of the Rolls, Chancellor of the Exchequer and Lord Privy Seal. It was said that Cromwell acquired "more credit with his master than ever the cardinal had" and that "now there is not a person who does anything except Cromwell."[123] By 1532, this all powerful man had become an implacable foe of Garret Og. Cromwell was largely in charge of Irish affairs, and he seethed at the spectacle of Geraldine power. When Skeffington returned to London, enraged by humiliations at the hands of the Kildares, he complained bitterly to Cromwell and plotted political and personal revenge against Garret Og. Piers Butler, too, had the ear of Cromwell and continued to lodge complaints against Garret Og. One complaint that struck home was that royal appointments to high positions in Ireland were being blocked by the Kildare faction. As such complaints increased, the peaceful infrastructure of the rare Butler-Geraldine balance came unglued, and fighting between the Geraldines and Butlers erupted again in late 1532, resulting in the death of Piers Butler's son, Thomas.

Others in the Dublin Council also spoke and campaigned against Garret Og, particularly Archbishop John Alen who was Master of the Rolls in Ireland. Alen had long enjoyed great stature and carried special weight in London, having been Cardinal Wolsey's chaplain. Archbishop Alen, however, lost all status after Wolsey fell.[124] He was removed as Chancellor and from the secret council. The Kildare opponents claimed that Ireland under Garret Og was in terrible shape, and urged the appointment of an English Lord Deputy to replace Garret Og.

After his break with Rome, Henry VIII grew skittish over the prospect of a Catholic invasion of Ireland from the Continent.[125] Charles V, the Holy Roman Emperor, had sent an emissary to Dingle to contact the Desmond FitzGeralds. Spain, France and Italy seemed ready to treat Ireland as engaged in a state of war over religion and to invade to reestablish Catholic control. Henry became sufficiently alarmed by Garret Og's usurpation of royal prerogatives that he issued a royal reprimand in August 1533. Garret Og sensed an ominous turn in these events, and decided to arm his own castles and fortifications with the powder and guns then in Dublin Castle. Henry summoned Garret Og to London, but he refused to go. Having twice before been detained there for years, he detested a third trip and he particularly dreaded the tone of this summons. He sent his wife to explain that Garret Og was suffering from a severe wound in his thigh received fighting at Birr in defense of the O'Carrolls.

HENRY VIII'S BREAK WITH ROME

Henry broke with the Vatican step by step, first in 1529, when he proclaimed himself Head of the Church of England. In 1527 Henry had sought from Pope Clement VII an annulment of his nearly quarter century long marriage to Catherine of Aragon. Henry believed he was owed this. However, the Pope's hands were tied. Charles V, a Habsburg, had captured Rome and placed the area under Habsburg control. Catherine of Aragon was his aunt. Thus, Charles V was unwilling to cooperate in her dismissal after 24 years of marriage.

Henry renounced the authority of the Pope hoping that his actions would advance not only his marriage and succession goals, but would help complete an English conquest of Ireland and bring about religious reformation. Henry had already cut a vicious laceration through the ranks of his top ministers while attempting to orchestrate the annulment of his marriage. Cardinal Wolsey was dismissed in 1529, charged with treason after failing to obtain Henry an annulment, but Wolsey died before his trial. Henry pushed the 1534 Act of Supremacy codifying his status as Head of the Church in England.

Thomas More, the former Lord Chancellor, was later executed for defying Henry's supremacy of the faith. Thomas Cromwell, for a time, became the power behind the throne, but Cromwell fell out of Henry's favor for various reasons including urging on Henry his disastrous marriage to Anne of Cleves, whose sagging breasts and guttural German speech and protruding stomach disgusted Henry. Cromwell was executed for heresy.

Henry, however, had become fed up with Kildare opposition, and he abruptly replaced Garret Og. Cromwell, as much as Henry himself, engineered the Kildare fall.[126] This was more than one of the periodic firings; none in the Kildare earldom mistook the significance. Cromwell issued "The Ordinances for the Government of Ireland" abolishing the liberty of Kildare. Worse yet, a new Deputy was named, and it was not the Duke of Richmond, as had been rumored, but Skeffington himself. The "Gunner" was about to return to govern Ireland and Garret Og.

The Succession

Garret Og's health began to deteriorate as his wound festered. He took the precaution of naming his 21 year old son Thomas, the Earl of Offaly, as Vice Deputy. Silken Thomas FitzGerald (*Tomaś Mac-Gearailt*), as he was called, had been born in England in 1513, the

Silken Thomas FitzGerald, Lord Offaly

year his grandfather, The Great Earl, was killed. He was exceptionally tall, and, with his fair complexion, quite good looking. Brave and generous, he was well spoken and he displayed the Kildare wit and added his own youthful swagger,[127] but he lacked discretion and his manner offended older men.[128] Silken Thomas, however, was simply amused by their anger. He would keep the Council waiting, then tease and taunt the Council members when they complained.[129]

Henry did not relent; he renewed his demand that Garret Og appear in London, and it was clear that the journey to London must occur. In March 1534 Garret Og appeared before the Council in London, feeble and defenseless. He knew that no political salvation was possible, and so he had given instructions to Thomas to ignore any order Thomas might receive to appear in London.

Though detained again, not jailed, Garret Og knew he was not there as a Tudor subject petitioning to be restored as Lord Deputy of Ireland. As the days wore on he could tell that this time his worst fears were to be realized. A summons ordering Thomas to London came in May, and Thomas knew that the time for action had come. He did not head for London, but for Dublin, to his historic encounter at St. Mary's Abbey.

The Silken Thomas Uprising

The epithet, Silken Thomas, was inspired by silken fringes on the garments and bridles used by Thomas and his men. The Kildare enemies knew that Thomas was volatile and easily provoked, but it was a surprise how easily they tricked or provoked him to start a violent revolt. One legend claims that the Butlers planted a story that Garret Og had been killed by Henry, and they let Thomas think he had intercepted a confirmation of the execution, but the document was a forgery.[130] James Delahide is said to have brought him a counterfeit letter that appeared to be a message intended for Skeffington reporting the "cutting short" (beheading) of Garret Og and recommending the same for Silken Thomas. Garret Og was actually confined in fairly comfortable quarters and was still hoping Cromwell would release him. The exact provocation is unknown, but Silken Thomas began the final chapter of the Kildare saga.

The Sword at the Council Chamber

In June 1534, over 100 Kildare horses and riders swept through Dames Gate en route to a "profound medieval drama." They stormed in to interrupt the meeting of the Council at St. Mary's Abbey in Dublin.[131] There, Thomas confronted the Lord Chancellor, Archbishop George Cromer of Armagh, resigned as Vice Deputy and discarded the sword of state. Stories of the event abound with flair and emotion. One story suggests Thomas was stirred to rebellion at the crucial moment by the song of his harper.[132] Whatever was the stimulus of the moment, Thomas declared Henry VIII was now his enemy. He announced, "I have more mind to conquer than to govern, to meet him in the field than to serve him in office, ..." He accused the King of "heresy, lechery and tyranny" and said "the age to come may score him among the ancient princes of most abominable and hateful memory."[133] Archbishop Cromer, reportedly in tears, begged Thomas to reconsider, but Thomas departed to begin the revolt.

It may have been intended only as a dramatic political gesture, and not as impetuous as depicted. Silken Thomas had not rushed headlong, but had taken the precaution in advance to enlist support of allies for what he intended to do. Though coupled with bombastic rhetoric, none of the Geraldines in the Council chamber actually drew swords. Silken Thomas' demands were, however, provocative to the Tudors. He demanded that he be made lord governor of Ireland for life. His insulting statements and unacceptable dictates would predictably outrage any monarch, and Henry VIII was one of history's least likely exceptions. Thomas and his family council had been mustering support among Dublin officials aligned with the House of Kildare, while also seeking support of the Desmond Geraldines, the O'Briens of Thomond, the O'Connors, and the O'Neills of Benburb, Strabane and Dungannon. Thomas' aim was to reestablish the FitzGerald claim to Irish rule, but his ensuing revolt would instead be used as the justification for Henry VIII's direct rule. Two weeks after Thomas stormed into St. Mary's Abbey, Henry ended Garret Og's stay in comfortable London quarters and locked him in the Tower.

Silken Thomas Fitzgerald Renounces His Allegiance to King Henry VIII

Thomas and his followers spread the word to their supporters that they served the Pope, were in arms against the King, and that they welcomed foreign Catholic intervention. But he suddenly ruined whatever chance of Catholic help he had. On July 28, 1534, his followers captured Archbishop Alen, still a supporter of Henry, near Artane. Alen, a hated Kildare foe, had been a commissioner of Wolsey's rapacious legatine court. Alen had tried to flee the FitzGerald revolt by ship but was driven ashore at Clontarf, captured at Artane; dragged begging before Silken Thomas whose soldiers killed Alen on the spot.[134] Foe or not, this was the murder of an Archbishop. Silken Thomas was promptly excommunicated by the outraged Pope, and his action effectively ended any chance of Catholic forces intervening to help him. But as summer wore on,

Thomas' campaign was becoming disturbing to Henry who was agitated by dissidents in England gathering forces to confront him over threats to their religious practices. Some of the dissidents, including Robert Aske who would soon lead the Pilgrimage of Grace, supported the goals of the Kildare revolt. As frustration grew, in August Cromwell's Commissioners contacted Silken Thomas and offered pardons to Thomas and to Garret Og for surrender. Thomas refused.

The Fall of the House of Kildare

Garret Og died in the Tower on September 2, 1534, probably done in by his wound. Silken Thomas, now the putative Earl of Kildare, was by then irreversibly in full armed rebellion.[135] This was not an insurrection flailing about out in the Pale marches; Thomas decided to attack Dublin Castle. His initial tactics, skirmishes with the Butlers to prevent them from challenging from the south, proved quite effective. He marched to the River Nore and won a battle at Thomastown and another when he took the Castle at Tullow. The Irish clans helped him hold the Butlers while he began to march on Dublin Castle where Kildare opponents took refuge. He burned and wasted farm land all around Dublin, and soon his army was at the city gates. The Commander of Dublin, Sir John White, agreed to surrender the city but not Dublin Castle — this despite the Castle's lack of powder and arms (both had been removed by Garret Og to fortify Maynooth). The Kildare siege of Dublin Castle lasted several weeks, but they failed to take it, and help was on its way for the Dublin Castle defenders. Skeffington and his army were en route. Skeffington was old, and he procrastinated, and the Castle came close to falling, until Piers Roe Butler invaded Kildare territory and Carlow, and on October 14 Silken Thomas felt he had to lift the siege of Dublin Castle to send his forces off to fight Butler.

When Thomas left Dublin to throw back the Butlers, frantic Dubliners closed the city, trapping the small Kildare force still holding the siege of Dublin Castle. Thomas returned part of his force to Maynooth to fight Piers Butler, and sent the rest to the shore to prevent Skeffington's arrival at Howth. Despite the Kildare force, Skeffington's ships succeeded in making shore at Dublin on Octo-

THE PARDON OF MAYNOOTH

In March, Skeffington marched on Maynooth. His siege of Maynooth Castle began on March 16, 1535, but it bogged down because the small cannons of the English artillery were confronted with the unusually dense walls of Castle Maynooth. However, after 2 weeks the castle commander, Christopher Paris, Silken Thomas' foster brother, contrived to betray the castle defenders in Thomas' absence. Paris used the elation over the success achieved by the castle defenders in a minor skirmish as an occasion to entice the weary Geraldines to celebrate. But that minor victory was a fake. Paris had conspired with the English to stage the capture of a small piece of English artillery. What seemed to the Irish a strategic victory was used by Paris to encourage a Kildare celebration, and Paris plied the garrison with liquor. Then he signaled Skeffington to send his troops to vault the low walls and capture the castle. "The Gunner," Skeffington, and his Constable, James Boys, discussed how to treat Paris. They had gladly accepted the perfidy of Paris and now were weighing how to treat the helpful Irish traitor. Skeffington knew that a politician would focus on the benefit their cause had received, but Skeffington was disgusted by Paris' treachery. Skeffington looked with contempt at Paris: "Truly, thou that art so hollow to him wilt never be true to us." Skeffington ordered Paris beheaded. The survivors of the battle, including two priests, were all executed by Skeffington in what has come to be called "the pardon of Maynooth."

ber 24, 1534. But when the English troops camped on shore, Silken Thomas attacked and badly weakened the force, and Skeffington was not able to be an effective opponent in the first several months. He also became very ill and was laid up for 3 of those months, but he had successfully landed some 2,300 men. While it was not yet apparent, any hope for a Kildare victory had ended when Skeffington landed his troops. He proclaimed Silken Thomas a traitor and sent his army into the Pale. In November, Skeffington had one of his first successes; he took Trim Castle before winter interrupted his campaign. Winter took a greater toll on the Kildare leadership. In December 1534, Thomas was attainted for treason, and he lost several of his top leaders to disease and two of his uncles by defection.[136]

After Maynooth, Thomas was relegated to hiding among the Irish clans who supported him, but his raids were having no serious impact beyond embarrassing Skeffington and Henry. The revolt was now seen as doomed. Thomas was exhausted and he finally surrendered. He sought a pardon from his uncle Lord Leonard Grey. The two met at the Bog of Allen and Thomas allegedly was promised that he would receive a pardon when he arrived in England, and he rode off in the custody of the English in August 1535. Henry fully intended from the first to execute Thomas, but was persuaded to wait a safe interval. The Duke of Norfolk urged Henry not to execute Thomas immediately since Lord Leonard Grey had pledged to Thomas that he would be spared, and a hasty execution would discredit Lord Grey.[137] The later arrest of Thomas' uncles, however, was a surprise, for they had opposed his rebellion. Henry, however, had decided to extinguish the Geraldine blood line.

The Execution of Silken Thomas

While Silken Thomas was in captivity, the large scale rebellion of supplicant protestors erupted in England. Robert Aske and the leaders of the "Pilgrimage of Grace" caused such turmoil, that it put Henry into a frame of mind to conduct a wave of executions to end the appetite for insurrection anywhere in his kingdoms. After the executions of Aske and the English Pilgrims, ultimately 178 of them, Henry had Silken Thomas and five of his uncles executed as well. The end seemed to have come to the House of Kildare.

The destruction of the House of Kildare removed from Irish dynamics the powerful force that had long kept at bay the more Anglicized House of Ormond, and that most-Irish of the Irish Earldoms, the House of Desmond. The crushing of the Kildares pleased those leaders yearning for the complete reformation and total assimilation of Ireland, and it gave vast leverage to Henry VIII, and he used it without restraint. He brought a large part of Leinster within the Pale and began doing with Ireland whatever he wished.

The Irish also had long endured excessive violence, but from the mid Tudor period they were "utterly devoured by it...."[138] Grey executed the women and children of Carrigogunnell Castle in Limerick in 1536, a total of 46 victims. At Bellahoe in 1539 Grey himself recounted killing many herdsmen, peasants and common people. In 1540, Grey beheaded the members of the Franciscan community in Monaghan, including the prior. The native Irish and Anglo Irish responded with violence and murder of their own, including the murder of non-combatants.[139]

Virtually all the major Irish lords submitted. The construction of new forts in the Kildare demesne did produce a modest reduction of tension. The historical restraint that had stayed the hands of Henry VII and Henry VIII, the fear that the Kildare earldom would serve as a rallying force for a major rebellion throughout Ireland, was gone after Geraldine supporters, a coalition later referred to as the Geraldine League, was defeated at Bellahoe in 1539. It has been said that the "utter extinction" of the culture of Gaelic aristocracy "was the declared colonial policy of England from 1541 forward."[140]

8

The Reformation and Land Confiscation in Munster

Cujus regio, ejus religio (Whose kingdom, his religion) [141]

Henry VIII had Parliament pass the Act of Supremacy in 1534 and set about spreading the Reformation of the Church[142] to Ireland with intensity. The reduced power of Catholic nobility like the Kildares seemed to enhance the chances of success of the Reformation. The Irish House of Ormond in Kilkenny was loyal to the Crown and Anglican. The Desmond Catholics in Askeaton were far less religious in their purposes and political agendas, and remote from the rest. The Irish, Henry justifiably thought, could now be reformed just as the English. The Church of England set out to change Christianity in Ireland and to tackle the traditional loyalty shown by Irish clans and the Old English progeny of the Normans to the Pope, and to transfer that loyalty to Henry VIII.[143] He anticipated the greatest difficulty in this endeavor would be with the native Irish. The Old English, as it happened, proved more resistant than some of the native Irish.

The Reformation was thrust more directly upon the Anglo Irish in the Pale and only to a far lesser extent, on the cities outside the Pale.[144] Only rarely did anyone, clergy or others, seek to carry the Reformation to the Irish living in distant villages and remote areas. This population outside the Pale was overwhelmingly Catholic. Most spoke only Irish, and the task of Reformation in Ireland as in England fell in actual practice entirely to English speaking reformers. Moreover, as the Counter Reformation became organized in Europe, the Jesuits and other friars pressed just as hard to restore Catholicism as the reformers did to eliminate it. The friars' Counter Reformation efforts in Ireland were welcomed both by the Old English and the Irish clans and septs, and ultimately proved to be the more successful of the two competing religious movements in Ireland.

The Act of Supremacy in 1534 had, however, brought Ireland under the Tudor Crown, and in June 1541, a parliament specially summoned for the purpose enacted the Kingship Act and conferred upon Henry the title King of Ireland.[145] The plantations and colonization which for many years had been desultory additions of New English, and had so far occurred without major resistance by the native Irish, began to accelerate and to display a hostile triumphalist momentum.

Surrender and Regrant

In 1534 Henry announced the "surrender and regrant" of all Irish lands. By this gesture, such chiefs as Hugh O'Donnell, The O'Neill (Con Bacach O'Neill) (*Conn Bacach MacCuinn O'Neill*) and McCarthy Mor (Cormac McCarthy) (*Cormac MacCarthaigh Mór*), surrendered their lands to Henry and immediately received a regranting of them, thereby confirming the king as their overlord and emphasizing their subservience to the Crown. Murrough O'Brien (*Murchad Ua Briain*) of Thomond, submitted under surrender and regrant and in 1543 he became the 1st Earl of Thomond and Baron of Inchiquinn.

Despite the ceremonial-sounding name, this technique seemed a trouble-free substitution of the King for the landlord's overlord. Many chieftains were already dissatisfied under the Irish system where they were beholden to a greater chieftain. Most were already required to pay their lord money and were obligated at any time to give service to him, so providing this same benefit to the Crown, often in a far smaller amount, was to most of them simply a trade. In many cases the change wrought by surrender and regrant could be done without any severing of old loyalties, and in some cases the severing was silently welcomed by an unhappy lesser chieftain and by his urraghs, vassals and churls, weary of what they considered abuse and injustice from the greater chieftain. That they had to accept some new English ways and English law seemed to some of the clan leaders an inconsequential point. There was, however, a major inconsistency between common law and Brehon law regarding who owns land. The concept of individuals owning documented interests in land conflicted with the Brehon law concept of control of clan land by the chieftain, and this conflict was soon to provide an opportunity for land fraud.[146]

The seemingly important notion of turning whatever loyalty could be found in Ireland toward the English monarch was often in actuality less a problem than might be expected. There was resistance in the clans based on tribalism and loyalty, but the Irish loyalty was to a way of life and to a clan or family group. By now these ancient clans had broken into many separate dynasties. The O'Neills of Ulster were so many and varied that by the 16th century they could be called a huge tribal grouping with common ancient ancestors. The O'Connors of Connaught were also spread widely into several lines of separate O'Connor clans: O'Connor Don (The Brown-haired), O'Connor Roe (the Red-haired), O'Connor Faly, O'Connor Sligo and O'Connor Kerry.

The O'Briens of Thomond had descended from King Donough O'Brien who, prior to his death in 1242, had been granted the territory of Thomond by King John. The O'Briens had won the battle of Dysert O'Dea defeating the Norman forces of Thomas de Clare and they stopped further Norman acquisition of land in Clare. But the O'Brien clans often battled among themselves. Even the smaller, historically more unruly clans of Wicklow, the O'Byrnes and O'Tooles, were relatively quiet except for regular cattle raids and occasional kidnapping of traveling government officials. In the central west, though Irish clans abounded, the Normans held a territorial edge in the 16th century. In the far west the MacWilliam Burkes ruled Mayo and the Clanrickard Burkes ruled Galway.

Piers Roe Butler, Leader of the Reformation

Piers Roe Butler led the religious Reformation in Ireland. Lord Leonard Grey, the Deputy, was at least equally charged to do what he could to make the Reformation succeed. Grey convened the Reformation Parliament which oversaw the passage of religious laws. Symbols and relics were targeted for destruction. St. Patrick's Crosier was burned publicly in Dublin at the new Archbishop George Browne's direction. The abbeys of Ireland were dissolved, many of them were wrecked and their properties were usurped by Henry, bloating his long depleted coffers with the wealth derived from the monastic land he took. In the process he eliminated these centers of learning. The giddy infusion of wealth from monastic lands in Ireland and England made Henry one of history's richest kings until he squandered it all on expensive military adventures and vanities.

Piers Roe Butler and Archbishop Browne and other Reformation leaders did their best, but reformation of the Irish did not take. In July 1540, Sir Anthony St. Leger[147] replaced Lord Grey, as Deputy. Grey, Kildare's uncle, was executed at the insistence of Cromwell on suspicion arising from his failure to capture his young nephew, Silken Thomas' younger half-brother. With the loss of the abbeys, many of the activities which before had fallen to religious establishments — education, health care, tending to the infirm and the poor — had to be taken over by others, often by the colonial government, and they were inadequately financed and poorly staffed. It was no simple matter for the reformers to replace Catholic educators with an entirely new staff of Protestant clergy educators. Many Irish who could find the resources to send their children to obtain Catholic education on the Continent did so. Thus, the two societies grew even further apart in Ireland. The Old English[148] and the native Irish remained Catholic, and continued living by Irish custom, language and dress. Their refusal to abandon loyalty to the Pope, a foreign ruler, made them like aliens. The New English embraced the new religion and the King of England as its leader, and it bolstered their colonial garrison mentality and highlighted the separation of the societies.

The most substantial number of native Irish conversions to the new Church of Ireland came at the urging of chieftains who, to preserve their power and lands and to remain in the good graces of Henry VIII and the Lord Deputy, decided to renounce the Pope. Some lower clergy also agreed to accept Henry and reject the Pope. Even a few Bishops did, but Archbishop Cromer of Armagh and some others did not. Finally, the dwindling Reformation efforts in Ireland stalled completely, leaving the overwhelming numbers of the Irish people still Catholic.

By the time of Henry's death in 1547, he had succeeded, through the efforts of his Deputy, Sir Anthony St. Leger,[149] in obtaining submission, and surrender-and-regrant of the lands of virtually all of the greatest Gaelic chieftains throughout Ireland.[150] Henry's son Edward and his daughters, Mary and Elizabeth, were left with Ireland as an overwhelmingly Catholic country amid a European religious landscape of hostile Catholic countries. Ireland's Catholicism made Henry's children fearful that Ireland and England itself were terribly vulnerable to conquest by Spain and France. Those in Ireland who posed a risk of rebellion were now a greater source of concern for they had, by virtue of the Reformation, been given that unifying religious cause that earlier Irish rebellions had lacked.

This precarious position was being guarded by a monarchy that had recently enjoyed vast wealth but was spending heavily on wars. Henry VII had accumulated great wealth by sequestering valuable land of nobility who became his enemies. Henry VII had the instincts of a bookkeeper and kept careful account of what he was owed. The result was, by the accession of Henry VIII, that the previously strapped English Crown was flush. Henry VIII added greatly to this wealth through the Reformation and his confiscation of the vast lands of the abbeys. Wolsey and his protégé, Thomas Cromwell, added even more wealth as they mastered the legal procedures for obtaining bills of attainder which disenfranchised heirs and families of political opponents, and used the Star Chamber to collect major fines. But all this wealth proved too tempting to Henry VIII. By the time of his death, Henry had spent much of the wealth on three French wars and had produced runaway inflation while Ireland, so very near, provided the perfect staging area for a successful French or Spanish invasion of financially distressed England.

Henry VIII had made a lasting imprint on the world, and he left a story that has amazed and bewildered those affected by his rule. The split with Rome and the Act of Supremacy were feats beyond the bounds of arrogance. Yet it was the almost incidental policy that accompanied the Act of Supremacy, the process of surrender and regrant, that set in motion the policies and practices of confiscation, plantation and extirpation of the Irish population which spawned the seminal rebellions.

Edward VI

At his death in 1547, Henry VIII was succeeded by his nine year old son, who reigned until 1553 as King Edward VI. The child King's affairs were controlled entirely by his uncle, Edward Seymour, Duke of Somerset, his first Regent and Lord Protector. Little ambiguity existed in this brief period in the policy of royal governance of Ireland. Seymour replaced the more tolerant Anthony St. Leger in 1548 as Ireland's Chief Governor with Sir Edward Bellingham, who was determined to pursue Reformation and to take military action to deal with Ireland. Seymour, however, was thrust aside as Regent by John Dudley, Earl of Warwick (later Duke of Northumberland). Warwick was able to exercise even greater control over the sickly royal youth whose ailments were growing increasingly ominous.

Edward died at age 16, a victim of the effects of medicine prescribed by his physicians, but not before a hasty marriage was arranged to Lady Jane Grey, a Protestant who, it was hoped, might block the ascent to the throne of Edward's Catholic half-sister, Mary. Although Edward formally designated his wife (and cousin) Lady Jane Grey to succeed him, Henry VIII had already provided for the successors to Edward – his half Spanish daughter Mary and then his daughter Elizabeth.

Bloody Mary

Mary Tudor, the daughter of Henry VIII and Catherine of Aragon, refused to abide the ascent of Lady Jane Grey to the throne. Despite Mary's Catholicism, she received an outpouring of popular support, and she arrived in London enjoying widespread acceptance as the rightful heiress to the throne.

Edward's designation of Lady Grey had done little more than assure Lady Grey's beheading. Mary I reigned as Queen from 1553 to 1558. To the dismay of the many Protestants who accepted or welcomed her, Mary quickly proved as inflexible a Catholic Queen as Edward had been a devotedly Protestant King. She saw no hope of salvation outside Catholicism for anyone, and she was ruthless in her faith and her reign.

THE LADY JANE GREY CONSPIRACY

When Edward VI died, John Dudley, the Duke of Northumberland led a scheme to rig the succession and steer it to Lady Jane Grey, granddaughter of Henry VIII's sister, Mary, Duchess of Suffolk. Lady Grey had quickly married Dudley's son, Guildford Dudley.

Lady Grey was crowned Queen in July 1553, but she lasted all of 9 days. Within 4 days the people of London and the Catholic gentry rose; soon even the peasants were rising up to Mary's side, and finally the Council gave up and recognized Mary I as Queen at age 37.

Centuries of conventional wisdom held that Lady Grey's assumption of the throne lacked any legitimacy. However, Edward VI, though only 16 and quite ill had endorsed her as his successor. He had by then become extremely Protestant and he well knew that his half-sister Mary was extremely Catholic and that Lady Grey would preserve England as a Protestant nation.

Edward Courtenay became a central figure in the maneuverings to guide the succession to the throne as young Edward VI weakened and slipped toward death. Stephen Gardiner, the Bishop of Winchester, urged Mary Tudor to marry Courtenay, but she was more receptive to the recommendation of her cousin, Emperor Charles V, that she obtain a papal dispensation from the bar of consanguinity and marry his son, Prince Philip, her cousin.

Conspiracies to block Mary's ascension began: first the audacious usurpation by which Lady Grey was crowned; next, the rising of Thomas Wyatt in Kent and the loose plot to marry Elizabeth to Courtenay and place her on the throne. When these plots unraveled, Lady Grey and her new bridegroom, Lord Guildford Dudley, and his father, Northumberland, were executed. Elizabeth and others, including Robert Dudley, Northumberland's younger son, were locked in the Tower and sharply interrogated, but lacking evidence that Elizabeth was anything but a pawn of others, she was sent to close quarters at Woodstock and Robert Dudley was spared and lived to form his historic lifelong close relationship with Elizabeth.

"Bloody Mary," as she became known, burned almost 300 at the stake in an effort to purge them, save their souls, and force the return of England to Catholicism. She married Philip II of Spain and together they waged war against France during much of her five-year reign. She too saw the need to have Ireland firmly under control of the Crown. Under Mary, England returned to Catholicism but not to the papacy; it remained a schismatic Church until 1555 when, through the efforts of the returned Cardinal Pole, the English Church became reunified with Rome. Though she authorized the Catholic Mass to be celebrated openly in Ireland, and decreed that the clergy should return to the Catholic faith, she did not enforce these changes. As Queen of Ireland, however, she ordered the first substantial plantation in Ireland.

The Earl of Sussex

Mary returned Anthony St. Leger to the office of Deputy until 1556 when she sent a new Deputy, Thomas Radcliffe, the Earl of Sussex, Barron FitzWalter,[160] with a new policy. Mary's return of England to Catholicism came at a crucial time, and it broke what little momentum existed toward conversion of Ireland to Protestantism. With the added force of the friars' active opposition to Reformation in Ireland, Catholicism survived in 16th century Ireland. Anglicization of Ireland, as opposed to religious conversion, however, was a separate goal toward which there was no letup under Mary.

The Kildare Restoration

Young Gerald FitzGerald, the 11th Earl of Kildare, had eluded the English and had gone into hiding after the Tyburn executions of Silken Thomas and the Kildare uncles. He was taken, smallpox and all, to the Continent.[161] The Geraldine League,[162] an informal coalition of O'Donnells, O'Neills and others, bonded together to urge the royal administration to restore the Kildare earldom. Their goal was to preserve its unifying value. After Cromwell's efforts to capture young Gerald proved fruitless, and diplomacy with the French and the Holy Roman Emperor to render him to England failed, a pardon was negotiated. After the fall of Cromwell, the pardon was granted and in 1549 the putative 11th Earl of Kildare returned and swore loyalty. He became known as the Wizard Earl. He was pardoned during the protectorate of Henry's son and heir, Edward VI, and the attainder brought about by Silken Thomas was withdrawn. In 1552 he was restored to the manor of Maynooth and several other manors. After Mary ascended the Throne, he was restored in 1554 to the full title as 11th Earl of Kildare and Baron of Offaly.

A Tudor program for Ireland called the New Departure led by Sussex commenced in 1556 and Sussex believed that a loyal Kildare would be a valuable presence. Sussex welcomed, as did Queen Mary, the restoration of the balance between the Irish nobility brought about by the restoration of the House of Kildare. But Mary and Radcliffe had no appetite whatever for the return of the Kildare dominance of old. Thus, they were vigilant to prevent it. However, the restored 11th Earl, like his predecessors, coveted the power of the Deputy, and never stopped striving to obtain it. When Lord Deputy Sussex withheld liberty jurisdiction in the manor of Kildare, the Earl formed an alliance with Shane O'Neill. Theories have abounded that the 11th Earl of Kildare encouraged Shane, or even directed him, in Shane's disruptions in Ulster in order to display to Sussex the Kildares' power to cause disturbance and the consequences that ensued when a Kildare was not in control.

Kildare, to be sure, would benefit from having Sussex and his program fail. Kildare believed that a Sussex failure would very likely lead to a royal decision that it was once again necessary to look to Irish nobility to provide governance. He knew, of course, that to become Deputy, particularly with the historical question and the cloud of attainder remaining over the Kildare earldom, he would have to compile an unambiguous record of loyal action. That in turn would require that he offer military support for royal incursions against the Gaelic septs. He did weigh in when needed to fight to guard the Pale. Finally he came to be viewed as loyal and he was given martial law powers in 1559. In 1560 when Sussex was elevated to Lord Lieutenant, Kildare was made Captain of the Kildare territories during the absence of the Lord Lieutenant. Yet despite the gestures and improved stature, Sussex distrusted him.

Plantation – The Beginning

In the mid-16th century Edward VI's handlers, and Lord Deputy Edward Bellingham had been far more inclined to finish the conquest, but they did not have the resources to wage the fight. Their attempts to encourage English to settle in Ireland had little success. Queen Mary chose to begin what seemed a more affordable solution to the Irish predicament — plantation.

The Laois Offaly Plantation

East Ulster, Offaly and Laois, were Mary's selected targets for plantation. Long dominated by Gaelic chieftains and their clans, those clansmen found that they had new neighbors, hordes of immigrants transplanted from England, and many New English brought out from the Pale. In 1556 the plantation in Laois and Offaly took land from the O'Mores of Laois, the O'Connors of Offaly, and the O'Dempseys of Clanmalier, lands forfeited by juries of inquisition and annexed by the handlers of Edward VI.[163] They became Kings and Queens Counties. The clans were outraged by the confiscations[164] but stopped short of open revolt. The practices surrounding plantation then became even more offensive. Many confiscations were accomplished by assertions of treason, sometimes true, often entirely false, against barons and large landowners. Most confiscations held up against legal challenges, but Owney O'Dempsey succeeded, after years of desultory revolts by local chieftains and tribes, in obtaining a re-grant of his lands. The O'Connors were not as fortunate; nor were the O'Mores. As the plantations became commonplace, the population occupying some of Ireland's finest lands was now heavily English. However, the English people brought in as planters were very uncomfortable themselves, they found that they had to endure living among hostile O'More and O'Connor clans.

A Butler Descendant on the English Throne

On Mary's death in 1558, Elizabeth I, daughter of Henry VIII and Anne Boleyn, and great-granddaughter of Margaret Butler Boleyn (daughter of the 7th Earl of Ormond), succeeded Mary as Queen. Elizabeth ascended the Throne determined to return England to Protestantism, but to forego coercive measures against Catholics and recusants. She would not repeat Mary's fanatical Smithfield burnings.[165] For Ireland, she began with only the vaguest aim to colonize it with English settlers, to impose royal administration and then to attempt to extend Protestantism throughout.

When it was that Elizabeth first contemplated armed conquest, is uncertain, but Elizabeth would in time be the Tudor who decided it was necessary to conquer, rather than merely plant, pacify or reform, Ireland. Until the Desmond rebellion, her policies were marked by an absence of the financial stamina needed to wage a transforming war in Ireland. None of those policies ever reflected a willingness to tolerate native self-government.

Unrest in Munster and Ulster

Elizabeth, Sussex, Sidney, and the entire Tudor apparatus, would be called upon to deal with the Munster uprisings of James FitzMaurice and the Rebel Earl of Desmond in the distant south of Ireland while they were also distracted by trouble caused in the north by Shane O'Neill, the disinherited son of The O'Neill.

Sir Henry Sidney, the Lord Deputy in 1566, had difficulty trying to conduct peacekeeping operations in two provinces at once. He would march through the south, then suddenly find that he needed to take his limited troops north into Ulster in an effort to put down violence there. The Munster unrest turned to widespread rebellion, first under James FitzMaurice and then under the Rebel Earl of Desmond, but fortunately for Elizabeth and her Deputies, the Ulster chieftains did not rebel until some 7 years after the Rebel Earl of Desmond's rebellion ended in 1585. By then, Munster had been beaten, coerced, and infused with many New English planters.

Queen Elizabeth I

ELIZABETH

Elizabeth was born at Greenwich, and inherited her father's red hair and his temper. She was relegated to bastard status after her mother's execution and banished from court, but she made repeated efforts to insinuate herself into the favor of her father, seeming to ignore his role in Anne's death. She was befriended by Catherine Parr when Henry remarried, and with Catherine's intercession, was restored to Court, a reconciliation with her father that seemed to bring her great joy. After Henry's death, Catherine married Thomas Seymour, but soon Seymour took to behaving inappropriately with the young Elizabeth, flirting with her and tickling and kissing her in her bedroom. After Catherine died in 1548, Seymour proposed to Elizabeth.

When her half-sister Mary achieved the throne, Elizabeth was under a heavy cloud of suspicion, believed to have encouraged the Lady Jane Grey scheme to keep the Catholic Mary from the throne. Once cleared, Elizabeth curried favor with Mary. (Neither of them had a bit of success attempting to befriend Edward VI). She feigned sympathy with Catholicism with sufficient credibility that Mary did not attempt to bar Elizabeth's succession. She was living at Hatfield when she received the news in 1558 that Bloody Mary had died and she, aged 25, was Queen. As Queen, Elizabeth held Court at several palaces, including Hampton Court, Whitehall, St. James, Nonsuch, Hatfield, Richmond and others. Her mottos were *semper eadem* (always the same), and *video et taceo* (I see and stay silent). The once rich Tudor dynasty was financially strapped in 1558, and bold economies had to be made by Elizabeth, including reduction of the standing army to less than 2,000. Early in her reign she had her attention drawn to unruly Irish leaders. She ordered forays into Ireland to deal with the Earl of Desmond, Shane O'Neill, and one or more of the Butlers, including the Earl of Ormond himself.

(continued)

(Elizabeth, continued)

Once Elizabeth became Queen, by the Act of Uniformity she returned England to Protestantism and readopted Edward's Prayer Book. While tolerant of Catholics for a time, Elizabeth cracked down after the papacy declared her a heretic. Ultimately some 200 Catholics were executed during Elizabeth's reign for displays of Catholicism. In 1563, tempted by the pleas of the beleaguered Huguenots of Le Havre, Elizabeth sent troops to relieve them; but the English were routed.

Her romances or loves have given rise to novels, plays and crass gossip. Speculation and rumor place many lovers in Elizabeth's bed -- Robert Dudley, Christopher Hatton, Thomas Butler, and Robert Devereaux among them, but evidence, even after 400 years, is lacking. Elizabeth may truly have been a virgin.[166] First in her affection, however, was Robert Dudley. He was her "Robin" and "Eyes." When Elizabeth contracted smallpox in 1562, in her feverish ramblings, Elizabeth professed her love for Robert Dudley and her wish that he be named Lord Protector.[167] The turmoil that such a royal endorsement created -- heightened jealousy and intensified competition -- was palpable even at that moment. But when the young Queen miraculously recovered, the fear that she would arrange somehow to marry Dudley left his rivals nearly crazed. Though she would not marry him, when his wife died mysteriously, Elizabeth broke off her relationship with him fearing it would jeopardize her popularity and power, and before long, he secretly remarried. When Elizabeth found out, she was furious, considering it a court affront. Dudley died in September, 1588 after sending his last letter to Elizabeth.

(continued)

(Elizabeth, continued)

Whatever may have been their history, she was inconsolable at his death.[168] Christopher Hatton died in 1591 with Elizabeth personally feeding and ministering to him. Many royal proposals from European suitors spurred by the obvious power of an alliance came to naught. The Pope too had once mused that if he could marry Elizabeth, their children would rule the world. The Archduke of Austria was another potential suitor, but he would not come to England without assurance of a marriage. Even Philip II of Spain, her brother-in-law, proposed to Elizabeth after the death of Mary.[169]

Her attitude toward the Irish was hostile and uncompromising, but she lived long enough to realize the long-term consequences of her campaign of conquest. She described Ireland in her correspondence as "that rude and barbarous nation." By the end, she admitted that the price of conquering rather than cultivating Ireland had been the alienation of the Irish people. More lamentable, the alienation seems intact in Ulster 400 years later. Perhaps most curious, two of the preoccupations of her life were Mary Queen of Scots and Ireland, and she never saw either of them.

9

The Woman Who Loved
Two Warring Earls

[A] man void of judgment to govern and will to be ruled[170]
— Sir Henry Sidney about the Rebel Earl of Desmond

Two earls, both powerful personalities, controlled Munster in 1562. In the east was the 10th Earl of Ormond, in the west was the 14th (or by some counts the 15th) Earl of Desmond. Neither was promising as a loyalist surrogate who could galvanize Irish support for the Crown. Gerald FitzGerald, Earl of Desmond,[171] was loyal but only reluctantly. He was overwhelmingly Irish and his personal style was hostile and imperious. Thomas Butler, Earl of Ormond, though entirely loyal, was Protestant and therefore unable to deliver to the Crown any widespread support outside of east Munster.

"Black Tom" Butler the 10th Earl of Ormond

There was a grating condition that inflamed the tension between the two earldoms in Munster — the Tudor favoritism of the Butlers of Ormond. Elizabeth's favoritism was flagrant and both the Butlers and Desmonds knew it. Thomas Butler, 10th Earl of Ormond, named Duff, or "The Black" and called "Black Tom," was a lifelong friend of Elizabeth[172] and even her reputed lover (her "Black Husband" as Elizabeth called him).[173] Black Tom was cultured, talented, and Anglican. The great Butler home, Kilkenny Castle, and other Butler castles at Cahir and Carrick on Suir reflected the vast wealth of the Ormond earldom. His refinement is evident from the modern mansion he added onto the castle at Carrick on Suir. It was natural that a loyal earl would become an ally or confidante of the

"Black Tom," the 10th Earl of Ormond, Thomas Butler

Deputy, and Black Tom and Thomas Radcliffe, Earl of Sussex, became especially close allies. The Butler army regularly accompanied Sussex and the royal troops on their marches through Ireland. In exchange, Sussex invariably supported the Butlers' claims and interests at Court.

Black Tom Butler sported an aggressive style and it usually paid off. Not only would Elizabeth always side with him, but she flaunted her willingness to retaliate against his Desmond opponents, particularly his western rival, Gerald FitzGerald (*Gearóid MacGearailt*), Earl of Desmond. Emboldened by the secure position Elizabeth's support gave him, Black Tom pushed his rights and his claims to the limit. But when he tried to capture Desmond lands at the site of a recurring boundary dispute, he learned that, in the eyes of the Earl of Desmond, he had exceeded that limit.

Ormond Castle, Carrick-on-Suir

Gerald Fitzgerad the 14th Earl of Desmond

Gerald FitzGerald of Desmond, was the son of a renegade. Though very wealthy, Gerald acted more like a wealthy warlord[174] than the Anglo-Irish aristocrat that he was. The Desmond earldom controlled the far southwest of Ireland, now Counties Kerry and Limerick, and the Earl commanded 50 subservient lords and barons and all of their followers. The Desmond castles at the time were at Askeaton,[175] where Gerald lived, and at Limerick, Tarbert, Newcastle, Shanid, Dingle, Castleisland and Castlemaine. The Askeaton castle was built on a small hill surrounded by the River Deel. Gerald loved its comfort and its refreshing views. The lavish hospitality at Askeaton included abundant drink — beer, whiskey (*uisge beatha*), sack (a Spanish wine), and ale. To eat the meals heavy in medium

Askeaton Castle, County Limerick

cooked meat, the guests reclined on couches. Askeaton's comfort would make it exceedingly difficult for its wealthy owner to choose the path of a rebel, the hardships of a fugitive's life and prison.

Succession issues, however, complicated Gerald's hold on the earldom. His father, James FitzJohn, had married the daughter of Maurice Roche, Lord Fermoy, and they had a son, Thomas Roe FitzGerald. But that son's right to inherit was contested from birth because his mother injected a tainted lineage. To resolve his own rights of succession to become the Earl, James FitzJohn divorced Lord Roche's daughter and married the daughter of Lord Ely O'Carroll. To them, Gerald was born in 1533,[176] followed in the ensuing years by John, James and five daughters. An early sign that the Desmonds were separating themselves from the English was James FitzJohn's refusal of the offer to have Gerald fostered to the English Court, preferring to foster his son, the heir to an Anglo Irish earldom, to the O'Moriartys of Kerry — and the snub was not lost on Henry VIII.

The Irish lords in southwest Munster, Gerald included, were worried by growing demands of the Dublin administration that they demilitarize and cease coyne and livery, all the while knowing the Crown was increasing its own military presence. Munster Geraldines, moreover, had never developed any appetite for English control.[177] Gerald's father, in fact, had once harbored ambitions of an independent kingdom of Munster, a Catholic land backed by Pope Paul III, but he had died young before the plan ever advanced. Gerald was too young to have been a serious collaborator with his father, and he never renewed James' precise plan, but his father had clearly influenced Gerald's attitude toward the Crown. Nevertheless, he spent his younger days in a considerably more reactive mode defending his rights and the borders of his earldom. Gerald's claim to the earldom was contested in 1558 when his half-brother Thomas Roe launched a contest at Court, but Gerald succeeded in establishing himself as the Earl of Desmond.

With his black hair, dark eyes, and pale skin, Gerald was strangely handsome; he grew to be a dashing womanizer at a young age, despite being somewhat frail and slightly hunchback.[178] Gerald was variously called the Black Earl, and the Pale Earl. After wounds produced a chronic ailment in his hip requiring help on and off his horse, he became known as the "Crippled Earl." His close supporters praised him as ingenuous, upright, a man of character, and even a talented poet. Only one of Gerald's poems survives to demonstrate this — "Against Blame of Women" which featured the progressive refrain "Speak not ill of womankind." But to his subjects he was domineering and vindictive. He was by most standards a very poor earl, notoriously insensitive to the conditions in which his tenants and followers lived. As a field general he was brave enough to bear personally the brunt of battle, but slow witted and woefully ineffective as a tactician. Yet he could be effective in the talentless aggressive techniques of the Desmond style of warfare – burned crops and villages, reprisals and executions of those seeking pardons from the English, bodies mutilated to spread terror of the fearful fate that awaits a Desmond adversary. In serious warfare, however, he was indecisive, undisciplined and a poor strategist, causing some to call him the "Mad-brained Earl."[179]

Like many Irish leaders, Desmond's arch rival was a fellow

Irishman, a hated foe, the Earl of Ormond, and these two earldoms shared a contentious border. The disputes between the two earls over control of the border towns and control of the border septs led to frequent skirmishes and at last to one serious battle.

The enmity between Butler and Desmond was more than one hundred years old by the time of Gerald's ascent, but by 1560 the Desmond earldom's support was declining. Gerald had to rule his subjects by force and by distraint. Not surprisingly his most powerful enemy, Black Tom Butler, Earl of Ormond, realizing the Desmond's declining strength, flaunted his own power and provoked territorial disputes. The flashpoint with Ormond was the boundary dispute over the Deices, the eighth century lordship in Waterford granted to the Desmond FitzGeralds, where the contentious boundary at Clonmel had become a border between Desmond and Ormond lands — a line in the sand between the two prickly earls. The FitzGerald lords of the Deices often sought protection from the Ormonds to temper the stiff demands made on them by the Desmond FitzGeralds.

Gerald was claiming that rent from Kilfeacle, Kilsheelin, and Clonmel was due him from Lord Maurice FitzGerald of the Deices as a dowry and he decided to take the rents by force. When he did, the Butlers invaded Desmond. Gerald then blocked the Butler's access to the wine ports of Kinsale, Youghal and Cork,[180] cutting off a good part of the financial lifeline of the Earldom of Ormond. Gerald's men also began pirating the wine shipments. Despite Elizabeth's warnings that battles on Irish soil were an affront to her, the two Earls began to muster their forces. Soon their armies were facing each other.

In 1562 Gerald, with his sizeable army, marched to confront the Butler army ready to do battle over the tense dispute. The battle was to be fought at Bohermor on the border of Limerick and Tipperary. Gerald was in command of the Desmond force and Black Tom Butler was in command of the Butlers. But suddenly a woman rode in as a self-appointed peace-maker. Her name was Joan. She galloped back and forth, pleading with the two volatile commanders. Joan was Gerald's wife, and she loved Gerald dearly, but she also loved Black Tom Butler.[181] She was Black Tom's mother. Despite the earls' animosity, Joan carried the day. The battle was called off.

JOAN – A BUTLER AND A FITZGERALD

Gerald was 29 years old, Joan his wife was 52. The May-December marriage of Joan and Gerald, when it occurred years earlier, had been especially distressing to Black Tom Butler.

Joan was a Desmond FitzGerald who had earlier married James Butler, Earl of Ormond, but James died in 1546 after she bore Black Tom, Edmund and Edward Butler. She married again but just as quickly she began an affair with the young Gerald, her second cousin, then barely 18. Nevertheless, they married in 1550. Eight years later they had become the Earl and Countess of Desmond.

Joan Butler and Gerald FitzGerald were as unlikely a pairing as Munster could produce. Among Joan's appealing features were royal access as a confidante of Elizabeth. She was nobility, a strong personality, lusty and attractive. As immature as Gerald is described, Joan by contrast was mature, intelligent, cultured and wise.

The alliance of Joan with a Desmond was less startling than the Butler/Desmond contention would suggest, since Joan was a FitzGerald and a descendant of the Roches of Fermoy. Her father was James FitzGerald, 10th Earl of Desmond. Her marriage to a Butler had many obvious attractions, but after the death of James of Ormond, marriage to the youthful Gerald, making him the stepfather of his staunchest enemy seemed a baffling act. What is chronicled about the personalities of Gerald and Joan suggests that she had enjoyed the role of wife of a powerful earl too long to become at age 40 a quiet dowager in the shadow of a dynamic son like Black Tom Butler. Joan quickly perceived the opportunity to seduce the rather slow, poetic Gerald. Gerald was laconically alluring and may have proved irresistible. She pragmatically sized him up as the only noble catch in Ireland, and went right after him. He responded enthusiastically and a passionate genuine and lasting love affair was launched.

Word that the confrontation between the two earls had come that close reached London and infuriated the Queen.[182] It triggered the start of events that brought about the final undoing of the Tudor-Desmond relationship.

Though no battle occurred at Bohermor, Elizabeth demanded that Gerald and Black Tom both come immediately to Court to explain their conduct and resolve their disputes. Gerald temporized, then he and his lordly assemblage appeared en masse before Elizabeth, where Gerald gave full display to his haughty and contemptuous demeanor. Gerald knew nothing firsthand about the Queen, and even in 1562 she knew little about Gerald FitzGerald of Desmond.[183] An unfortunate clash of two harsh personalities was about to occur. Desmond arrived in London, confrontational and headstrong.[184] He railed against the Butlers, and he addressed Elizabeth in rude and defiant tones. Elizabeth was astounded at the effrontery. She became so angry she spat, and she abruptly ordered Gerald into the Tower.[185]

More as a result of Gerald's attitude than the battle that had not happened, Elizabeth detained him, requiring him to stay at the Tower of London for two years. While obstinate for a brief time, Gerald found that he was unaccustomed to incarceration and paupery. When his health began to deteriorate, he entered into a treaty and promised to resolve his disputes with Butler. He agreed to remit to the Crown the exactions Elizabeth demanded, to return Desmond to order, to abolish the Brehon law in favor of the common law of England and to abolish bards and rhymers. For these assurances that he would begin deconstructing the Irish life and system, he was freed, remanded to Ireland in 1563, but required to remain in Dublin for a year to be retaken and questioned from time to time.

Released from Dublin in 1564, Gerald returned to Askeaton where his wife lay dying. Joan died on January 2, 1565.[186] A scant three weeks after Joan's death, Gerald was courting Eleanor Butler, the 19-year old daughter of Lord Dunboyne, a cousin but an opponent of Black Tom Butler. If Elizabeth or her Justiciars and Deputies thought that the Earl of Desmond was now reformed, they would soon enough learn otherwise.

As these events temporarily calmed Munster, the Crown already had its hands full elsewhere. A violent clan chieftain was cre-

ating disturbances all across Ulster and having great success elud-
ing the forces of the Deputy.

10

Elizabeth Struggles to Humble Shane the Proud

I am O'Neill, King of Ulster[187]
— Shane O'Neill

In 1562 Elizabeth still seemed to have a modicum of patience and tolerance when faced with local disturbances and disorderly conduct among the Irish. Even so, the Earl of Desmond's arrogant confrontation with the Queen at Court was startlingly presumptuous coming from an Irish lord.

The other great Irish spectacle at the Tudor Court in 1562, the high drama of the appearance of Shane O'Neill (*Séan O'Néill*), was much different. This O'Neill was a clansman, a chieftain of Gaelic followers, and his disturbances targeted Irish, Scots and even the English in Ulster. The increasingly perceptive young Queen showed her Court during the appearance of this reputed wildest Ulster clansman that she was capable of discerning differences between unruly Norman Earls and native Irish chieftains, and was astute enough to devise different programs to try to reform them.

Shane O'Neill was variously viewed as Shane the Proud and Shane the Contemptuous, but when he stormed into the royal Court, he coupled his bellows and boasts with some candid admissions of his transgressions and with welcome gestures of obeisance. While he was politely detained in London, Shane was not jailed. Elizabeth was well versed in the back story of Shane and of the assassinations of his own family members that had brought him to such prominence in the large and powerful O'Neill clan of Tyrone, tales which had made him universally feared by the other clans of Ulster.

Though the Kildare overthrow had made the south and east of Ireland weaker, more vulnerable to English expansion and domination, Ulster was another matter. Tudor officials had always thought that the great obstacle to English control was Ulster, a remote, impenetrable land few English had ever seen. The less accessible north remained so inhospitable that the few settlers who ventured there with the support of Henry VIII abandoned in short order the effort to establish permanent colonies.[188]

It was still the ancient clans who ruled 16th century Ulster. No single clan in Ulster had an earl or chieftain with the military resources of The Great Earl of Kildare, but all were powerful enough to intimidate. From the Glens of Antrim in the northeast to the peninsulas of far northwest Donegal, large well-armed clans led by powerful chieftains were poised to hurl back any foreign challenger who dared show his face in their ancient territories. The O'Neill, O'Donnell and Maguire chieftains of Ulster kept fit fighting each other. The Scots clans of the South Isles and Western Highlands had crossed into eastern Ulster and claimed lands in the northeast. Frequent raids by the Irish clans against those Scots led to fierce battles. Rarely would the clans join forces unless out of utter necessity to resist encroachment by the Scots or the Crown. All the Ulster clansmen were serious warriors, but it was the O'Neills who, by the 16th century, had become the most powerful, and in 1519 the O'Neills elected one of their mightiest chieftains, Con Bacach O'Neill, Chief of the Name.

Con Bacach O'Neill

The O'Neills were descendants of *Niall Glundúb*, High King in 919. They dominated the ancient kingdom of *Tír Eoghain* (now County Tyrone). In the 15th century the O'Neills had become part of the grand political alliance when Eleanor FitzGerald, the daughter of the 7th Earl of Kildare, had married into the O'Neill chieftain's family.[189]

For twenty years Con Bacach O'Neill had built up his own power in Ulster, warily assessing Henry VIII's ineffective reformation attempts in Ireland. In 1539 the O'Neills, led by Con Bacach, together with the O'Donnells, led by Manus O'Donnell, decided to join forces and invade the Pale in response to an appeal from the Pope to rise up to resist the Reformation and preserve Catholic Ireland. Geraldine supporters hoped this might restore the House of Kildare under Silken Thomas' half-brother, Gerald. Such cooperation had been a rarity with the combative northern clans; the centuries of grievances and grudges that had grown among them were a major obstacle to teamwork, even against their common royal opponent. Though spurred to action by religion, the O'Neills and O'Donnells gladly snatched any valuables they laid their hands on in the course of their venture. Pleased by the success, they were nevertheless quickly reminded that cooperation of this kind was essential against the Crown. Returning toward Ulster, the forces of the two chieftains separated, and when they did, the pursuing English forces under Lord Deputy Leonard Grey and Sir William Brereton struck back successfully against one group of the Ulster clansmen.

The powerful alliance between the O'Neill Clan and the House of Kildare was badly weakened by the attainder of the Kildares and the surrender and execution of Silken Thomas. During the decade after the Kildare executions at Tyburn, efforts to restore the House of Kildare came to naught, and Con Bacach came to appreciate how costly the defeat of the House of Kildare had been to him. Whether in fights between Ulster clans or clashes with Crown forces, Con saw that without the Kildare alliance to help him, his effectiveness, particularly against the Pale, was badly diminished and his power and prosperity began to slip away. Though royal officials continued to fear his wild reputation, by August 1542 Con Bacach, like many others, was offering to go to London to accept surrender and regrant.

Con Bacach took the Tudor pledge before Henry VIII himself. He swore loyalty and promised to abandon The O'Neill title, to accept the English title, Earl of Tyrone, to speak English and adopt English habits for himself and his heirs. But his capitulation provided the first evidence that even the wilds of Ulster might be Anglicized by means less bloody and expensive than military campaigns into its hostile bogs, thick woods and treacherous glens. For that reason, Con's 1542 treaty with Henry was heralded by the Crown, and Henry saw to it that Con's submission was extravagantly staged and widely publicized. So much was made of it that French diplomats reported to the French Court that they had just witnessed the greatest of the barbarians surrender to Henry VIII.[190]

If by this time Henry had any hope of bringing a segment of the Irish into the embrace of England by diplomacy rather than by divisive combat, he missed his opportunity when he declined to reach out boldly to Con Bacach O'Neill. Though he rewarded Con with the valuable prize of the first earldom of Tyrone, Henry and his circle of deputies and courtiers considered Ulster too wild and Con Bacach too unruly to be the Tudor surrogate for all of Ulster. The matchmaker who could lead Ulster into the English fold was yet to be found, and while Henry listened carefully, he rejected Con's lobbying to be given full control of the north as the Earl of Ulster. At the time, the earldom of Ulster seemed the most important of Con's demands, but it was a different, seemingly trivial request by Con which proved momentous. He asked to be allowed to designate his successor.

Euphoric over Con Bacach's submission, Henry saw little reason to refuse this gesture of appeasement, and he quickly agreed to the unorthodox request that Con Bacach's son, Mathew (*Feardorcha O'Néill*), be designated his putative successor as Head of the Name. It was unorthodox because Mathew was a bastard. Henry agreed to allow Con Bacach to pass over his legitimate sons, one of whom was Shane, as successors to the lordship of Tyrone. This offhand concession was to have an exorbitant cost for Ireland and England in the years to come.

The O'Neill Succession

Clan violence in Ulster was not only one clan attacking a rival clan; some of the worst occurred within a clan. The rifts within the O'Neill clan were especially bitter. The O'Neills of Benburb, the O'Neills of Strabane, the O'Neills of Dungannon and the Clandeboye O'Neills were less a family than a group of competitive fiefdoms of their own. Turlough Luineach O'Neill of Strabane, and Shane O'Neill of Benburb and Dundrum, seemed to share little but the O'Neill name with Mathew O'Neill of Dungannon. Each was an avowed opponent of the other two. The intra clan violence that was about to result from Con naming Mathew rather than Shane his successor would eventually engulf Ulster.

At the time of Con's treaty with Henry VIII in 1542, Shane O'Neill was just a 12 year old. It was unusually self-indulgent that Con would arrange that the succession as Earl should descend to Mathew, but Mathew was Con's favorite son by his favorite mistress, Allison O'Kelly, and Con proudly claimed Mathew, as he had claimed other bastards.[191] Marriage was not the exclusive arrangement in late medieval Ireland that it is in the modern world. Keeping company with mistresses was so widespread a practice that many men made no effort to keep their dalliances secret. Siring bastards was open, common and comfortable. Many bastards were acknowledged by important fathers and treated very well. Shane O'Neill was, ironically, not the oldest legitimate son of Con Bacach; he was likely the fourth oldest son. Shane, however, as he grew, set out to challenge this bastard, Mathew, by claiming that Mathew was actually not Con's son, but the son of O'Kelly, the local smith.

Con's submission to Henry helped assure peace in Ulster for over a decade while Shane was a youth. Other great and lesser chieftains followed suit. The O'Donnell, Ulick Burke, Murrough O'Brien and others became English Earls, and some like the Desmonds renewed earlier pledges of loyalty. *Taoisigh* and tanistry began to look as though they soon would be titles and institutions of the past. But peaceful conditions would not last in Ulster once Shane O'Neill came of age. He refused to acquiesce in the loss of a lordship. Shane had been reared in the medieval tradition when fosterage of children of major families was common. Shane's mother died in the year of his birth and he was fostered to the O'Donnellys. He bonded with the O'Donnellys more closely than he ever bonded with his father or his brothers. The gulf was such that he was called *Sean Donnghaileach* (John of the O'Donnellys).[192] By the time he was a young man in 1551, Shane O'Neill was already volatile. He became openly hostile to the Crown, his father, his brothers and most O'Neill leaders.

Shane gave them abundant reason to distrust and malign him and to contribute to his dark legend. They told stories of Shane burying himself to the neck in hot ash or cold sand to cure his hangovers, and whispered tales of sexual depravity and cruelty.[193] Whatever may be the truth of all the Shanian legends,[194] his mistresses, not wives, were his favored company. *Séan an Diomáis* (John of the Ambition), often imprecisely Anglicized as Shane the Proud, was to label him more arrogant, incorrigible and vain than proud.[195] But whatever its emotional root, his unruliness was the provocation that drew Tudor forces to suppress the clan territories of Ulster.

By 1551 Con had soured on Mathew and let him know that he was going to name Shane as his heir. When Mathew learned that, he turned on his father and on Shane. He decided to secure the support of the Tudor officials. Mathew passed along to the new Deputy,

Sean an Diomais (Shane the Proud)

James Croft, assertions of disloyalty of his brothers, John, Hugh and Shane. However, he added accusations about the loyalty of Con Bacach as well.[196] Mathew suggested to Croft that Con Bacach was planning to return the clan to tanistry and the Irish system.

Croft had Con Bacach brought to Dublin where he was imprisoned for several months. Shane realized Mathew had turned on him. With Con out of the way, Shane decided to launch an attack against Mathew at Dungannon. However, Shane's attack was against the named successor approved by the King and that was an affront to the Crown. The English garrison at Carrickfergus under Marshal Nicholas Bagenal, charged with maintaining peace in east Ulster, was ready to enforce the approved succession and prevent violence. In 1552 Shane enlisted the help of the Scots and, in a ferocious night attack at Dungannon, he routed Mathew's forces. Shane burned Con's castle at Dungannon, but the English garrison hurried to the site, saved the castle and captured some 700 of Shane's men. When Shane's forces fell back, the English withdrew, and then Shane's attack resumed. Some 200 were killed in the attacks at and around the castle at Dungannon. It became clear that this was not merely a feud reflecting pent up fraternal hostilities; it was a campaign to determine who would decide clan succession and who would dominate Ulster.

It took Shane until 1558 to kill Mathew. Con Bacach O'Neill went to Meath to stay with the Bishop. He died there shortly after Mathew was killed.[197] To secure his claim to control, Shane knew he had to complete the job, to eliminate all other potential successors to Con Bacach. So Shane's men were periodically attempting to hunt down Mathew's children. A few years later, in collusion with Turlough O'Neill of Strabane, Mathew's son Brian was caught and murdered by Turlough's henchmen. Shane intended to complete this grisly process to assure that he could not be challenged by Mathew's elusive son, Hugh. To that end Shane and his henchmen would search the woods around Dungannon for young Hugh O'Neill. However, try as they might, they just could not find him. Hugh O'Neill had already been found, but by the English. Sir Henry Sidney had hoped to preserve the approved succession to the earldom of Tyrone and to keep Tyrone out of the hands of the violent Shane O'Neill. Sidney found and rescued Hugh, a horseboy living in the woods. Not only did Hugh, survive but before the century was over, he would become a legend and the leader of the clan whose men had murdered his father and his brother.

Shane — The Chief of the Name

Despite the O'Neill clan's and the Tudors' consternation over the assassination of Mathew the designated heir by Shane's men, they could see that Shane would never stop. The O'Neill clansmen, some with trepidation and some intimidated by Shanes' violent bent, elected Shane The O'Neill. Shane increased his skirmishes against the O'Donnells and began near constant battles against other Ulster clans. Shane as the O'Neill chieftain was seeking to renew the Tyrone O'Neill claim to lordship over all of Ulster, and he launched many attacks to achieve it.

The Ulster Earldom that Henry VIII refused to award to Con Bacach O'Neill had once been a reality, but in 16th century Ireland it would remain an elusive prize. In 1205 King John had taken Ulster from John DeCourcy, the Conquistador of Ulster. It was the Norman Knight DeCourcy who had successfully invaded Ulster as the Norman expansion approached its height. King John conferred the Earldom of Ulster on Hugh de Lacy the younger. Richard de Burgo, among others, had also held the great northern earldom in the 13th century and Roger Mortimer had held it in the late 14th and early 15th centuries. King Edward IV had once been Earl of Ulster, and the title thereby passed to the Crown. A belief within the O'Neill clan was that this meant that, absent a new Earl of Ulster, it was The O'Neill who should rule all of Ulster as the mesne lord of the King. Such O'Neill dominance, however, was not acceptable to the O'Donnells or the Clandeboye O'Neills. The O'Neills fought with every sept around them, but most persistently with the O'Donnells of Tyrconnell, the Clandeboye O'Neills, the Maguires of Fermanagh and increasingly in the 16th century with the growing influx of Scots who settled in the Glens of Antrim, principally the ferocious MacDonnells. The O'Neills were also pestered by the need to fight rear guard battles in the southern fringe to deal with smaller clans in Louth and Cavan.

Once Elizabeth focused on the need to settle and Anglicize Ireland, however, her focus fell on Shane O'Neill. His power grab in Ulster had to be ended. The increasing flow of Scots into Antrim only heated the debate in the London and Dublin Councils over the need, now being seen as urgent, to send the Deputy north with a force strong enough to put down all lawless and disloyal leaders. Strong military action in Ulster was a policy that well suited Elizabeth's Lord Lieutenant at the time, Thomas Radcliffe, Earl of Sussex. Sussex was a tough and aggressive mainstay of the Tudor circle. He served as Lord Lieutenant from 1556-1564, and was the first to institute systematic martial law. He did so in parts of Munster and Connaught, but for untamed Ulster, martial law was not an effective tool. To Sussex, only an invasion could have an impact on the two disruptive forces in Ulster — Shane O'Neill and the Scots.

Shane O'Neill presented a special challenge among chieftains; he had greatly increased the military power of the clan. Shane conscripted ploughboys and soil tillers, churls, unfree peasants, people called billeted men.[198] He enlisted Scots mercenaries, even when he was fighting other Scots. But the O'Donnells of Tyrconnell were his special enemy.

Attacking the O'Donnells in 1559, Shane captured Calvagh O'Donnell. In one of his greater outrages, he consorted with Calvagh's wife, a grotesque affront because Calvagh's wife, whom Shane used as a concubine, was Catherine MacLean, the Scottish step-mother of Shane's own wife, Mary.[199] Shane simply did whatever he wished. He held Calvagh captive, impregnated Mary's step-mother, and the traumatized Mary was overcome and died.

Shane decided to try his hand at international diplomacy, and at that he was equally outrageous; he offered to make Charles IX of France King of Ireland. He tried to play all sides at once. He pursued anti Scots diplomacy with his English contacts, but simultaneously explored a Scottish alliance through the Earl of Argyll.[200] He offered the Crown of Ireland to Mary Queen of Scots in exchange for help from the Scots.[201]

Elizabethan Court Politics

Sussex weighed all the risks of attacking this warrior prince, and reached the decision, despite the danger, that it was high time that he send English troops north against Shane O'Neill. Elizabeth, however, wanted a less expensive plan. She decided to see if Shane could be bought off; to see if he would agree to end the three Scottish threats — Mary Queen of Scots, the Scots clans settling in Antrim, and the Scots ally, the French. The price she was willing to pay was a low one – a poorly defined relationship with the Queen. Elizabeth at first instructed Sussex to discuss with Shane O'Neill the possible earldom of Tyrone. Elizabeth concluded that was the prize that might save her the expense of the costly war that would ensue if she attacked Shane in Ulster. Sussex grudgingly set out to do so, but he went with a total absence of enthusiasm to parlay with Shane. Sussex, however, found Shane so repugnant upon meeting with him that he simply could not bring himself to make the offer. Instead he returned to London and succeeded in talking Elizabeth out of offering the earldom to Shane.

Shane meanwhile, saw that his tactics were meeting with no success on any front. He felt he was blocked at Court by Sussex' opposition to any royal concessions to him, so he resumed warring with the O'Donnells. The English were duty bound to react because the O'Donnells were considered loyal[202] at the time despite their own frequent incursions against some of the loyal septs in Connaught. Sussex marched to the north against Shane, and he enlisted Sorley Boy MacDonnell and the Scots to try to box in Shane and prevent his elusive movements. Sussex penetrated into Ulster as far as Clogher, but to little avail. Shane, meanwhile, had grown impatient and frustrated; he had become tempted by the benefits of a deal with the Crown and he put out feelers to the Wizard Earl of Kildare about making peace with Elizabeth. Just as a showdown in Ulster seemed imminent, the Earl of Kildare, having earlier been restored by Queen Mary, aiming to display loyalty to her sister Elizabeth and to demonstrate his influence, brokered a controversial deal between Tudor and O'Neill — the submission of Shane O'Neill to Queen Elizabeth.

Elizabeth Meets Shane

Shane requested safe passage to London to submit to Elizabeth. Though Sussex had become certain that a military campaign against Shane and the Scots was inevitable, he acquiesced to the urging of Elizabeth's trusted Chief Secretary Sir William Cecil, later Lord Burghley; he reluctantly set aside his war plans, and watched as Elizabeth granted Shane's request for safe passage. Sussex now could only lobby against Shane O'Neill at the Tudor Court, but Sussex had too many enemies at Court. They included two of the powerful favorites of Elizabeth, Robert Dudley, Earl of Leicester, and William Cecil. Both Dudley and Cecil would now have a hand in the diplomacy of dealing with the submission of Shane O'Neill. These two enemies of Sussex were also, however, enemies of each other as well. Like Shane, Cecil was also dealing with the Earl of Argyll, seeking Scots support and Scots forces to fight Shane and the Ulster chieftains. Others at Court were working the opposite side of the field; they supported Shane's anti-Scots agenda and sought to join forces with Shane to drive the Scots out of Antrim.

This wild clan chieftain packed up and came to London with a contingent of dozens of his men. They appeared in lavish clan regalia before the Queen, draped in animal skins, looking like a pack of Ulster wolves. Shane O'Neill's men are described in colorful terms, performing a well-choreographed drill in Elizabeth's presence, waving their weapons about, bellowing in Irish, then abruptly dropping in lockstep to one knee, crashing their battleaxes on the floor with a resounding single clang.[203] The Queen loved the unruly spectacle.[204] She gave Shane O'Neill royal approval of sorts and confirmed him as the Captain of Tyrone. Elizabeth also agreed to the earthy Shane's request that she find him a noble wife who could somehow bring herself to share his spectacular existence.

Shane's visit to the royal Court, outlandish as the raucous appearance and howling in the presence of the Queen was, did not take place under an ominous summons of the type some others had received. Instead a relieved Elizabeth welcomed the submission; she was happy this would be inexpensive. But Sussex calculated that Shane would demand unpalatable concessions, and he lobbied against all of Shane's demands and marshaled all the political resistance he could.

Dudley served as Shane O'Neill's champion; and this alone was enough to have made Shane the enemy of Chief Secretary William Cecil. Things were that complex and that personal. But Cecil's hand in negotiating with Shane was strengthened by the ace card he held — he had the Scots' support if he wanted it. With Scots' support in his pocket, Cecil raised a firm opposition to Shane's demands, to the great irritation of Dudley, Kildare and Shane O'Neill himself. This palace intrigue, the Tudor Court's attempts to withstand Shane O'Neill's outrageous personality and brash style and Shane's demands for royal support to grant him power over other Ulster septs, riveted all of official London and made 1562 a tense year at the Byzantine Court.

Shane, however, was well treated; indeed he wound up spending half the year in London. None at Court seem to have been won over to him or to have warmed enough even to trust him; but Sussex more than others was totally repelled by Shane's arrogance, entirely unconvinced by Shane's claim to submit, and he made these beliefs clear. Sussex, of course, agreed to align with Cecil in the effort to deny Shane the earldom, but Sussex wanted an end to Shane. Dudley was less a convinced supporter of Shane than he was a bitter foe of Sussex, but it was his advice which Elizabeth followed in accepting Shane's submission and granting him rights which, after all, had been accorded many others. She drew the line, however, at the earldom, and, after some vacillation, she declined to make Shane the second Earl of Tyrone. She agreed to make him Captain of Tyrone.[205]

Still Sussex remained incensed that Elizabeth would reach any accord at all with Shane. Indeed the whole affair humiliated Sussex. The rejection of Sussex' highly visible pleas to reject Shane had the effect of undercutting Sussex' stature and it was exquisitely galling that the contemptuous Shane benefited from Sussex' political defeat. Sussex held the Wizard Earl of Kildare to blame, and as his irritation grew, he became a receptive listener to new rumors that Kildare and the Earl of Desmond were planning rebellions in Munster and the Pale.

Shane believed that Captain of Tyrone also showed that he had been accepted by Elizabeth as The O'Neill. [206] That she did not make him Earl of Tyrone may have been due to Sussex' protests. If Shane were to be believed, it was a product of his own ambivalence toward the title. Raised in the tradition of Irish chieftains, the title Earl of Tyrone, to some among the clansmen, was less than the

Gaelic title, The O'Neill, the venerable title that in Ulster still inspired reverence. Shane at least made an effort to display a dismis-
sive attitude toward the title, Earl of Tyrone, when the opportunity
was hinted at by Elizabeth's Commissioners:

> If Elizabeth your mistress be Queen of England, I am O'Neill
> King of Ulster; I never made peace with her without having
> previously been solicited to it by her. I am not ambitious
> of the abject title of earl; both my family and birth raise me
> above it, ... my ancestors have been kings of Ulster; ....[207]

But Shane, like Con Bacach before him, certainly did want the
earldom of all Ulster.[208] Failing that, he very likely did want the
earldom of Tyrone. His own demands were not satisfied, though
what broke down the London negotiations with Elizabeth and her
Court may be impossible to say. Conditions in Ulster required that
he return. Back in Ulster the turmoil was increasing in his absence.
Turlough Luineach O'Neill procured the murder of Brian O'Neill,
Mathew's son, while Shane was in London.[209] But Shane departed
London abruptly in May;[210] and he was lucky to get away. Though
he left in disgust, and pretended that was the reason, he had ample
cause to fear the growing animosity of the Tudor Court.[211]

Shane failed to obtain any earldom, and he returned to even
more trouble than he expected in Dublin and Ulster. The Dublin
administration refused to accept that Shane had the rights or the
powers of The O'Neill.[212] Back in Ulster, the opportunistic Scots
sought an alliance with him, but he was no longer ready to make a
pact with them. He resumed his disturbing attacks on other clans.
He attacked Fermanagh and Tyrconnell, and conducted raids on
the Pale and the Armagh garrison. He caused enough disturbance
that within less than a year Sussex again urged that it was necessary
to attack Shane in Ulster. Elizabeth, who made the final decisions,
was still not persuaded to invade Ulster and go to war, particularly
the expensive all-out war that would be needed to topple Shane
O'Neill. As usual, she was more focused and financially committed
elsewhere — to saving the Protestants of France — and much more
influenced still by her Robin (Dudley) than by Sussex or even Cecil.

Shane, no fool, deflected royal action by sending loyalist messages and new proposals promising he would resume loyal conduct, enough that he, and separately Dudley, successfully undermined Sussex yet again. When Sussex laid out plans to begin a campaign into Ulster in 1563, he aroused little support, obtained few supplies, insufficient troops and meager funds. Dispirited, he proceeded anyway, and his raids in 1563 accomplished very little.[213] Weary and frustrated, Sussex tried to orchestrate an inexpensive assassination of Shane by sending Nele Gray to slip poison into Shane's wine goblet. That plot failed as well.[214]

Unable to decide the best course of action with regard to Shane O'Neill, Elizabeth began dangling the earldom of Tyrone before him, a reversal inspired by little more than Shane waging cattle raids on his favorite victims, the O'Donnells and Maguires.[215] Once Elizabeth saw that Shane's deportment did not improve after he returned to Ulster, she sent her emissaries to offer him virtually all that Sussex had opposed. Shane was delighted, and Sussex was again humiliated.

A Prescient Warning

It took a new intermediary, former Lord Chancellor, Sir Thomas Cusack, to negotiate terms with Shane and the Peace of Drumcree was signed in 1563.[216] Cusack's advice to Elizabeth was emphatic that it was essential for England's own benefit that a peaceful settlement be reached by diplomacy and that Ireland should not be reduced to submission by force. Cusack had made a thoughtful evaluation of the long evolving Ireland problem and he gave Elizabeth a very sobering warning as to the consequences of a war with the O'Neill clan; the risk he emphasized was not military defeat. Rather, Cusack's prescient message was that winning such a war was a thing to be feared in itself, that a catastrophic legacy of hate[217] would be born if Ulster were taken by force rather than won by diplomacy.[218]

The Tudor officials agreed to most of Shane's demands and reluctantly acknowledged that they accepted him as the Captain of Tyrone. When this happened, Sussex was all but finished. By September 1563 Shane O'Neill and England had agreed to the unprecedented accord, one which, with the right chieftain, could have formed the cornerstone on which to build a consensual peaceful union with the Crown of England. Shane was to be called the Lord O'Neill, a sound Sussex could never bring himself to utter. But here Elizabeth was performing at her pragmatic best. She had begun to appreciate that these Irish she often called beasts, savages and a barbarous nation were, in strategic terms, being sought by her as her prodigal loyal subjects. The deal made with Shane in London was abandoned, Hugh O'Neill's ultimate succession to the earldom was to be extinguished by an Irish statute, the Armagh garrison was to leave, Shane was empowered to resolve Ulster disputes with the authority of a commissioner, the assassin who had tried to poison Shane's wine was to be brought to justice, and Elizabeth agreed to find him a noble wife.

The Peace of Drumcree sounded like a solution, but it collapsed completely when the English failed to perform. They did virtually nothing but call Shane Lord from time to time. He waited in vain for an invitation to the castle of a noble woman who would have him. During 1563 Sussex remained as Deputy and it fell to Sussex to interpret and administer the agreement, but Sussex and Shane O'Neill were incapable of agreeing on anything. They repeatedly disagreed on the import of the indenture; Sussex then resumed forays against Shane. However, the three attacks he launched were entirely unsuccessful. Shane finally became impatient; he decided to take military action himself, to improve his leverage. He was not ready to rebel, so he carefully chose a target that would serve his purposes but not provoke Elizabeth — he chose the Scots.

Sussex virtually collapsed from his total humiliation at the hands of Shane and his opponents; he appeared exhausted or worse.[219] Sir Nicholas Arnold was named Lord Justice and took over from Sussex in 1564.[220] In 1565 James MacDonnell of the Scots Clan Donald brought a major force to Ireland and Shane knew he had to challenge him. Shane asked for an assignment to help drive the Antrim Scots out of Ulster purportedly to show his loyalty. Cecil and Dudley agreed to Shane's request that he be authorized to attack the MacDonnells. Neither of them was fooled by Shane's insistence that this initiative was a show of loyalty, not done for his own advancement. Elizabeth, nevertheless, approved and Shane swung into action.

In 1565 at Glenshesk near Ballycastle, Shane and 2,000 of his men defeated the MacDonnell force and killed 700. Shane captured their leader, James MacDonnell, and then tolerated the neglect of MacDonnell's wounds, leading to his death. James had a charismatic brother, *Somhaile Buide* (Sorley Boy) MacDonnell, who was to be James' successor as the new clan leader. Shane, however, also captured Sorley Boy at Glenshesk, and he held the new MacDonnell chieftain hostage for 2 years.

War Between the Clans

Shane O'Neill proved useful to Elizabeth in her efforts to drive the Scots out of Antrim, but he remained incorrigible, and he eventually resumed attacks against the O'Donnells and other Ulster clans. Before long Shane had ravaged Tyrconnell killing some 4,500 O'Donnells and their followers.[221] As his assaults on the O'Donnells worsened, the Maguires threw their support to the O'Donnells and war between the Ulster clans was underway. In London, this was seen as an intolerable threat to Elizabeth's plans for peaceful Anglicization.

Elizabeth sent Sir Francis Knollys, her Vice Chamberlain, north with a special commission to investigate the state of affairs in Ulster, to appraise anew and objectively report whether the clan war and increasing excesses of Shane O'Neill were finally making war with him, as Sussex had all along told her, inevitable.[222] Tales of Shane O'Neill's horrendous personal habits were taking on new life. Calvagh O'Donnell had been released by Shane for a ransom payment. Calvagh went to Whitehall after his release was purchased by the Cenel Connell and gave first hand reports about Shane. There, he would tell anyone who would listen what a degenerate Shane was and what this monster had done to him.[223] Knollys was also directed to assess the need for forts, particularly the feasibility of establishing a fort on the Foyle at Derry. Knollys' report to Elizabeth confirmed the accuracy of all of Sussex' warnings. Knollys left no doubt that Shane had heated Ulster to a cauldron and that Shane would now not relinquish any of his power.

It was then that Sir Henry Sidney was sent to Ireland as Lord Deputy.[224] Sidney endorsed Knollys' recommendation that military action against Shane should be commenced immediately. Elizabeth accepted the Knollys report she had commissioned, but as usual she sliced the budget for the coming campaign in the north.

The fort at Derry was authorized, and Sir Edward Randolph led an operation by sea[225] in 1566 to land a garrison there, while Sidney set out with an expeditionary force from Dublin to march north.[226] Sidney coordinated his campaign to trap and kill Shane O'Neill with the O'Donnells. But first Sidney had to find Shane. Sidney marched his army from Dublin to Armagh, Benburb, Derry, Donegal, Sligo and back to Dublin, but could not find a trace of Shane O'Neill. Soon after Sidney's departure, Shane appeared as if from nowhere and brutally attacked the 700 men under Randolph at the Derry fort and they killed Randolph. The English at the Derry fort somehow held the position and did not surrender the fort, demonstrating for the moment their ability to hold this most crucial northern Ulster site as a secure place for future landings by sea. The Irish, with no organized navy, were powerless to blockade it.

DERRY

Edward Randolph's 1566 garrison at Derry, after the attack by Shane O'Neill, lasted only a few years. Another garrison would return under Sir Henry Docwra but not until 1600. Modern Derry stems from the small trading settlement that began in about 1603 and thereafter acquired the legal status of a city. When the trade guilds of London were granted the colonization of the area that is now County Londonderry, the new fortified city as well as the county were renamed Londonderry. The walled city was built in 1633 and St. Columb's Cathedral was added afterwards.

Shane O'Neill Decides to Conquer Ulster

Shane decided the time had come for the O'Neill clan to invade Tyrconnell in full force and finally conquer the ancient O'Donnell kingdom. The combined forces of the O'Donnells and Maguires were being led at the time by Shane Maguire, but Shane Maguire died in 1566, and the Maguires accepted the leadership of Hugh O'Donnell, Shane O'Neill's nephew.

Shane O'Neill had burned the Cathedral at Armagh[227] to prevent its use to house an English garrison and he was excommunicated. He asked for absolution for hanging a priest in Tyrconnell, but was refused. He could later be heard saying that the enemies he hated most were the Queen and Archbishop Creagh of Armagh.

Shane Is Beaten at Farsetmore

In 1567 Shane attacked the O'Donnells and caused them to retreat, but other clans rallied behind them. The O'Donnells and Maguires found Shane's camp at Farsetmore (the ford of *Fearsat Suibhle*). They waited near the camp until help arrived in the form of several hundred MacSweeneys, and the combined O'Donnell, Maguire and MacSweeney force launched a major attack on Shane's camp.

Many of Shane's men were killed in the battle, and many more were drowned in the River Swilly. The tide had flowed into the *Fearsat*, making the ford hard to pass just at the height of the O'Donnell's attack. Shane may have lost as many as 3000 men at Farsetmore. Among those killed was Dubhaltach O'Donnelly, Shane's foster brother and closest friend, one of the men who in 1558 at Shane's direction had helped assassinate the Baron of Dungannon, Mathew O'Neill. Despite the rout, Shane himself survived and escaped with the remnants of his force.

The end of this hard chapter of Ulster's history, Shane O'Neill's downfall, was brought about not by Crown troops, but by the Maguires, the O'Donnells and the Scots MacDonnells who all knew the terrain far better than the English. Elizabeth saw that she now had in hand the chance to rid herself of Shane O'Neill. She authorized Sidney to push forward and finish what the O'Donnells, Maguires and MacSweeneys had at long last made possible. Sidney's greatest contribution to the demise of Shane O'Neill was to help put Shane on the run and then simultaneously to reach out to Shane's three enemies urging them that Elizabeth now agreed completely that Shane's time had come. O'Donnell, Maguire and the Scots, from the west, the south and the east, all began to close in on Shane.

With Shane desperate and on the run, even Turlough Luineach O'Neill also sent his forces to attack Shane. With the net closing, Shane guessed that his array of pursuers would never dream that he would dare set foot in the Glens of Antrim, stronghold of the Scots. Desperate, or tricked by his captive, Sorley Boy MacDonnell, Shane did the unimaginable — he walked into the camp of the Scots MacDonnells at Cushendun.[228] Whatever may have been his plan, it amounted to a very risky test of the theory that the Scots could forgive and forget what Shane O'Neill had done to them.

Shane had by now paraded Sorley Boy MacDonnell around for almost two years, showing him off as a prized hostage. He had come to think that he had pacified or charmed Sorley Boy. Based on these rank miscalculations, or with no other route available, Shane sought a truce with Alexander Og MacDonnell, now head of the Clan Donald of the Scottish Isles. The Scots from the Isles and western highlands would regularly come to Ireland to help Scots in Antrim when summoned by signal fires set on the cliffs of Antrim. Alexander Og MacDonnell was called to Cushendun from Scotland, either by Shane or by Captain William Piers, the Constable of Carrickfergus. Shane arrived at Cushendun with his small force, hoping to negotiate an alliance some Scots had earlier suggested to him. Shane also appears to have failed to appreciate that his dynamic personal style, close up, triggered all the wrong reactions in the MacDonnells. The MacDonnells met with Shane for two days at Castle Carra at Cushendun, and suddenly they pounced on him, slashing Shane and his small entourage to death, likely with their double bladed claymores, and dragged him to a hasty burial in a nearby pit.[229]

Sidney, through Captain Piers, may have encouraged Alexander Og MacDonnell to kill Shane.[230] Official assassinations were common in Tudor Court politics.[231] Sussex, after all, had sent one assassin to poison Shane's wine only a few years earlier. Piers is reported to have met with Alexander Og before the MacDonnell parley with Shane at Cushendun, and Piers arrived back at Cushendun to deal with the MacDonnells only days after Shane was killed. It was Piers who instructed that Shane's body be exhumed, and it was Piers who delivered Shane's head to Dublin Castle and may have pocketed the bounty.[232] Despite the MacDonnell's useful service to Elizabeth in killing Shane, no lasting benefits accrued to the Scots for putting an end to him.[233] Instead, Sidney promptly renewed his efforts to drive the MacDonnells from the Glens.

SHANE'S LAST SUPPER

One legend claims that Shane O'Neill was slain by the MacDonnells after a drunken dinner held to celebrate an alliance between the MacDonnells and the O'Neills, but that the Scots became provoked by Shane bragging of his sexual prowess and making lewd references to Mary Queen of Scots. That, it is said, led the MacDonnells to hack him and others in his tent to pieces. History suggests this story was contrived to portray the Scots as considerably wilder than they were. The oft told fact that they sent his head to the Lord Deputy also seems to suggest that this grisly trophy was a gesture of alliance toward the English. In fact, Shane had been dumped in a grave before the MacDonnells realized there was a price of £1,000 offered for his head. Told of this prize, they returned and rummaged through the makeshift grave until they found it. It is uncertain and endlessly debated who gets the credit for engineering Shane's end. The theory that Sorley Boy duped a near desperate Shane to run to the Scots in the first place is persuasively articulated by Ulster historians, but still only a theory.

Sir Thomas Cusack's wise warning to Elizabeth suddenly was less relevant. The most troublesome native Irish chieftain of Ulster lay dead and defeated without the need for England to conquer Ulster or Ireland. Perhaps that malignancy of hate would never materialize in Ireland.

Elizabeth extinguished the name on Shane's death. The attainder of Shane O'Neill led to confiscation of O'Neill lands and the grant of those lands and lands in the Ards and South Clandeboye to Thomas Smith and later to Walter Devereaux. Sizeable lands were also declared appropriated from Sir Brian MacPhelim O'Neill of Clandeboye. After Shane O'Neill's death, the O'Neill clan chose Turlough O'Neill of Strabane to succeed Shane as The O'Neill. The queen approved. Turlough had no appetite for the adventurism Shane had practiced, and he submitted to Elizabeth. Under Turlough, Ulster calmed considerably and would remain calm.[234] This long peaceful period was not seriously broken until 1593 when Hugh Maguire attacked the English in Sligo and the northern clans began the fights that would become the Nine Years War.

The Murder of Shane O'Neill by the MacDonnells at Cushendun, County Antrim, 1567

During the long peace in Ulster, Sir John Perrot, a later Lord Deputy, was given the chance by the Queen to reorganize the balance of power in Ulster between the chieftains and the Bagenals, and to set a course for bringing English governance of all of Ulster to reality. In 1584, Perrot instituted a power balance among the clan leaders and the English officials in Ulster. Perrot delegated some power to Nicholas Bagenal, but also granted certain power to The O'Neill, the elderly Turlough, and another share to the much younger Hugh O'Neill.

This relative stability cleared the way for Sir Humphrey Gilbert to be appointed governor of Ulster, and Gilbert set in motion a long planned colonization of Ulster through plantation. Chief Secretary Cecil approved a plan to carve up Tyrone and to divide it among various O'Neill sub-groupings. He also approved plans for the construction of over a dozen Ulster forts to protect the New English planters who, he hoped, would be pouring in to Ulster. Elizabeth, however, in typical fashion authorized funds for only a few of the forts, scarcely adequate to control the wild Ulster of the 1560s. But with Shane dead, quiet descended on Ulster, and Turlough Luineach O'Neill, though occasionally disruptive, remained loyal to Elizabeth for the next 25 years.

Young Hugh O'Neill, Shane's nephew and Con Bacach's grandson, was granted part of the O'Neill lands with the title, Baron of Dungannon. This far in life Hugh O'Neill was a Tudor disciple, and a grateful friend of Sir Henry Sidney's family. The alliance would continue to grow between Hugh O'Neill and the Crown, and despite the attention drawn by Shane and the Scots, Ulster was considerably less demanding of Crown attention after 1567. A refreshing calm during this period permitted the Dublin Council and the royal Court to believe Ulster might, at long last, have become susceptible to peaceful colonization. The isolated threats that did continue to arise from time to time from the Scots, the Maguires and the O'Donnells presented no urgent need for a heavier royal investment of troops, forts or planters.

Even before Ulster under the lordship of Turlough O'Neill had calmed, trouble had arisen again in Munster. What began as a renewed Desmond disruption in Munster was already commanding attention from Elizabeth and her Lord Deputy and it would try to consume their available military resources from 1565 to 1585. The hatred of the Earl of Desmond for the Earl of Ormond had begun to threaten civil war in the south. That would make Anglicization of Munster nearly impossible; at the least, it would necessitate the heaviest repressive measures. The measures Elizabeth approved to calm the beautiful lands of Kerry and Limerick would be the ugliest form of martial law Ireland had ever seen.

11

Munster Begins to Come Apart

To an impartial 16th century Englishman in Ireland the Irish were a people of "strong and able bodies, proud hearts, pestilent wits, … lovers of music and hospitality … light of belief … extremely superstitious"[235]
— Sir John Harington

The saga Elizabeth and Sir Henry Sidney had endured in dealing with Shane O'Neill in Ulster was difficult enough, but in the midst of it she learned of a violent eruption in Munster at Affane. In 1565 the same two earls who had come toe to toe at Bohermor three years earlier, had begun a local war against each other and fought a major battle over their rights to the Decies. Gerald, the Earl of Desmond, claimed that he had a rightful claim to the Decies in Waterford despite Joan's death. But Maurice FitzGerald of Decies rejected Gerald as his overlord and refused to pay him rent. He protested that the Decies was now under the feudal lordship of Elizabeth, and he enlisted the protection of Ormond. In 1565 Black Tom Butler rose to defend the Decies, and Gerald called a Desmond rising. He assembled his MacSheehy galloglass to fight Butler's MacSweeney galloglass.[236] Without the intermediary skills of Joan, this time the armies did attack[237] and a major battle was fought.

GALLOGLASS

Galloglass were foreign soldiers, a name derived from the Irish word *gall*, meaning foreigner. Most were from the Scottish Isles where many families for generations raised their sons to fight as mercenaries. For centuries they found opportunities for service all over Ireland. There were three forms of mercenaries – Galloglass (original Scots), Albanachs (Scots highlanders), and Bonnaghts (locals).

Battle at Last Erupts Between Desmond and Ormond

Affane was no minor skirmish. Two small armies fought a pitched battle which produced hundreds of fatalities, a rout[238] of Gerald's troops and complete outrage in the Queen. Gerald was badly wounded, shot in the thigh and hip by Sir Edmund Butler. He was captured by the Butlers and they jailed him in deplorable conditions at Clonmel, then hauled him about in public in bondage. The Butlers taunted the wounded Desmond: "Where now is the great Earl of Desmond?" He yelled back at them: "Where he belongs, on the necks of the Butlers." Both Gerald and Black Tom were again ordered to London immediately.

The Earl of Leicester, Robert Dudley

Wounded, crippled and quite subdued, Gerald was carried into Elizabeth's presence, splayed in pain on a litter. Butler's champion was Sussex (Thomas Radcliffe) while the Earl of Leicester, Robert Dudley, and Sir Henry Sidney argued in favor of Desmond and they sounded more effective than Sussex. But Black Tom Butler knew when to make a personal plea directly to Elizabeth and when he did, it was hardly a fair fight between her lifelong favorite and the despised Gerald. Black Tom Butler had more champions at Court than Gerald and this affair portrayed the precarious conditions created by the Butler-Desmond running disputes and focused Elizabeth's attention upon it. The spectacle convinced Elizabeth that the solution in Munster was that Butler should prevail in all of their disputes. The two were now repeat offenders, yet Elizabeth could scarcely incarcerate Gerald for this offense without also incarcerating her close friend, and Gerald this time benefited from her leniency to Black Tom Butler.

Both were interrogated in London but then released under a bond obligating them to keep the peace. Fortunate as he may actually have been to be permitted to return, Gerald was not reformed or appeased, but even more bitter after the palpable favoritism shown by Elizabeth to his face, helping the person he hated most in the world. Gerald's outrage at this galling humiliation gnawed at him and he became even more truculent.

The Leicester (Dudley) faction at Elizabeth's Court was also displeased. Dudley had a personal motivation in supporting Gerald of Desmond against the handsome, charming Black Tom Butler. Dudley wanted to marry Elizabeth. But when the Affane standoff reunited Elizabeth with Butler, Elizabeth urged Butler to stay for a while in England. As he did, it became clear to Dudley that she had grown quite fond of Butler.

Sir Henry Sidney Marches to Munster

In 1566, Elizabeth determined to get to the bottom of the disputes pitting Ormond against Desmond and to deal with the sorry state of affairs in Desmond. She was still frustrated at her inability at that time to catch or subdue Shane O'Neill in Ulster, but she instructed Sir Henry Sidney to investigate and determine what was at the root

Sir Henry Sidney

of the recurring disputes between Butler and Desmond and then to extend English administration into Munster.[239] Both Black Tom and Gerald were to be dealt with, but only Gerald was about to have his independence sharply curtailed.

An Earldom Set Adrift

The Earls of Desmond, however, were used to living and ruling as potentates, feeling secure from interference due to the remoteness of their lands from Dublin. Many retainers protected and served them, including seneschals, galloglass, marshals, physicians, brehons, tradesmen, bards, clergy and rhymers. Eight fortified castles guarded this great ancient kingdom ruling the far southwest of Europe. Despite all this, Gerald sensed the end of his power approaching and grew defensive.

When Sidney was appointed Deputy in 1565, he had already served a provincial presidency in Wales. He seized on a plan he thought could inform English administration. His plan, however, was about to collide with the independence of the earl and provoke Gerald's anxiety.

The Desmond earldom drew suspicion when Elizabeth was told that Gerald had begun helping the O'More and O'Connor clans. She knew that Rory Og O'More was no trivial rebel; he was already a legend, the Robin Hood of Ireland. Elizabeth hoped to find evidence on which to arrest Gerald. When she ordered Sidney to investigate the Ormond/Desmond disputes, her purpose was to use the inquiry to obtain enough evidence to prove that Desmond had become disloyal, and her instructions to Sidney left no doubt as to the outcome she wanted; Sidney was to find in favor of the Butlers. Equipped with the preordained outcome, Sidney embarked to conduct the inquiry.

To appraise conditions in Munster first-hand the politically beleaguered Sidney marched south in late January 1567. He began in Butler territory[240] and his first pacification steps surprisingly were against Black Tom Butler's far less loyal brothers. He arrested them and held both of them for trial for engaging in coyne and livery. He then arrested Lord Dunboyne and Dunboyne's brother to end a troublesome feud. Next, Sidney headed south and west into Desmond lands, and Sidney's own attitude began to change. He was treated to firsthand accounts describing the abuses by the Earl of Desmond, and, as he progressed, he saw with his own eyes sights of famine, evidence of Gerald's reprisals, charred remains of abbeys and communities sacked and burned by the forces of the Earl of Desmond. Bones and skulls of murder and famine victims were plentiful as Sidney penetrated into the Desmond lands. What he saw revolted him, and, before long, he concluded that the Earl he had been defending at Court was not merely incompetent; he was a brutal tyrant to his own followers. Sidney wrote London reporting that the Earl of Desmond was "a man both devoid of judgment to govern and will to be ruled."

Sidney learned that Earl Gerald and Eleanor were staying at Youghal after the birth of their daughter, Margaret, and Sidney marched to Gerald and confronted him.[241] Gerald's reaction ended any chance to retain the support of Sidney. He showed no sign of remorse or appreciation that what he had done was wrong. Rather, Gerald was highly agitated and complained to Sidney about the many royal affronts to which he had been subjected. He said he was insulted by the Queen's June 1565 creation of MacCarthy Mor as Earl of Clancare; she had carved a new large Earldom out of Gerald's own Desmond Earldom.[242] Sidney's genuine disgust, more than his orders to side with Ormond, turned the inquiry into a series of stinging rebukes to Gerald. Gerald grew even more incensed; and his pugnacious tone provoked Sidney. When Sidney decided the Kilsheelin Castle controversy and awarded the castle to Black Tom, Gerald exploded. He upbraided Sidney and challenged his authority. Sidney, unsure how much armed support Gerald could call up right there in his own land, bit his tongue and endured Gerald's intemperate lectures; but he held fast to his ruling.

But finally Sidney had enough; he decided he had to take preemptive steps to end Gerald's power before Munster got completely out of hand. Sidney went behind Gerald's back and negotiated the surrender and submission of Gerald's *uirrithe*, subordinate lords of Munster who owed fealty to Gerald. When Gerald saw Sidney's success in weaning away some of the support he took for granted, he knew every sept in Munster would be called on to choose sides. He could see that the mistreated inhabitants of his troubled Desmond earldom were no longer responding to old loyalties; they were intensely dissatisfied with the conditions of life, and had come to feel that all those in power were to blame. Sidney, however, concluded that the animosity of those sublords of Munster was primarily against the Earl, and he expanded his cautious efforts to insinuate himself between Gerald and his vassals and sublords. Concluding that he might even drive a wedge between Gerald and his brothers, Sidney gave Sir John of Desmond a commission as a Seneschal of Desmond while he put Gerald on trial for misconduct.

Some of the underlords were only too happy to gain Sidney's ear to complain about their mistreatment and to describe in lurid detail the poor administration of the earl. Still others, however, hurried to Gerald's side, and his still loyal supporters were near enough to assemble as a fighting force. Fed up, Gerald called a "rising out" of those lords willing to side with him against the English. That Sidney was the Queen's Lord Deputy was no longer sufficient to intimidate the irate earl or restrain him from a show of armed resistance. Sidney, however, beat him to the punch; he arrested Gerald.[243]

Gerald was put on trial in the 1567 assizes at Waterford, found guilty of misconduct, and Sidney declared Gerald's earlier peace bond forfeited. When Gerald protested the forfeiture of the bond on slim evidence, Sidney raised the charge to treason and had him transported to confinement at Dublin Castle. When the news reached Elizabeth, the fact that there was little evidence to support a charge of treason was of little concern. She took comfort from the fact that the source of the charges against Gerald was Sidney, the one man who had historically sided with the Desmond cause at Court and who had provided assistance to Dudley in Dudley's spirited defense of Desmond against Black Tom Butler. Thus, to her, the presumption of Gerald's guilt was now very strong. Moreover, contrasted with the huge trouble she had endured with Shane O'Neill in Ulster, she welcomed the pre-emptive arrest of Gerald. Elizabeth ordered Gerald removed from Ireland and brought to the Tower of London. There he would await trial for treason.

Gerald's Long Confinement

Gerald's brothers John and James were also arrested in order to forestall a Desmond rising, and all were taken to London, escorted under guard by Sidney and his young aide, Hugh O'Neill, Baron of Dungannon, who in 1567 was still one of her majesty's loyal soldiers. The Desmonds were thrown in the stark but bearable political prisoners' quarters in the Tower of London. A large contingent of loyal Desmond supporters, family, servants and bards came to London to hover nearby. But with little evidence of treason to present, the Tudor officials did not bring the case on for trial. As the wait dragged on, the cost of Gerald's entourage soon shrunk them to a handful.

Martial Law in the Desmond Lands

Without the fist of the earl to control Munster, lawlessness became widespread. Elizabeth cranked up the pressure in Munster, and Sidney lashed out at the disorder they encountered and invoked martial law. Lord Deputy Sussex had earlier introduced martial law to parts of Ireland back as early as 1556, but had not actually used it widely. Sussex, like Sir Anthony St. Leger before him, had been particularly careful, however, to be tolerant of the Anglo Irish aristocracy.

Sidney's New System

Sidney's instructions from the Queen were to impose English law and custom with no exceptions in Munster, and he did. His parliament introduced what was termed the New System, and it enacted legislation to achieve it.[244] Central to the New System was a monstrous office — the seneschal, an English captain in charge of a band of soldiers with unchecked power to confiscate and kill. These were English surrogates appointed to preside over districts. Those the seneschals assumed were traitors were allowed to be hanged without trial. The seneschals received a despotic form of judicial power, explicit authority to summarily execute anyone who was merely unemployed or a vagabond, and the choices they made were not subject to question. Their assignment included "extirpating those who were 'masterless.'"[245] The seneschals were also given a base motive to kill – money – the legal right to confiscate the goods of anyone they branded a traitor, unfettered by any practical requirement that there be reliable evidence of treason. The result was a series of small conquests in areas where the seneschals took over all the property they coveted and left a local group of survivors standing in horrified disbelief at the executions by which property of their neighbors was appropriated.

The number of victims grew rapidly as seneschals[246] saw that their unsupervised killings under the pretext of legal executions produced no Tudor disapproval. Larger and larger numbers of distrusted Irish were selected for destruction. Indeed the Tudor officials posted to Ireland during the New System happily took the spoils that flowed from the upheaval. Even lowly offices — Edmund Spenser's post as Clerk of Decrees and Recognizances in the Irish Chancery Court where he merely certified state documents — were "lucrative" jobs.[247] Senior English officials such as Peter Carew, John Perrot and Humphrey Gilbert, all put rebels and those they merely labeled rebels to death. In 1570 an unprecedented draconian coercion bill was enacted by the Irish Parliament; accused traitors were, under this bill, to be attainted if they merely failed to come forward promptly and respond to the charge.

Historian James Anthony Froude describes in terse style the evolution of British policy and tactics in Ireland from its well-intentioned outset to the awful reality that eventually fell upon the Irish: "England's first desire was to give to Ireland in fullest measure. The temper in which she was met exasperated her into harshness and at times to cruelty; and so followed in succession alternations of revolt and punishment, severity provoked by rebellion, and breeding in turn fresh cause for mutiny, till it seemed at last as if no solution of the problem was possible save the expulsion or destruction of a race which appeared incurable."[248] Elizabeth concluded it may be necessary to expel the Irish entirely[249] to some distant West Indies or American location and replace them with civilized English.[250]

Froude also describes the viciousness of some English soldiers posted to Ireland: "Elizabeth's soldiers ... lived almost universally on plunder. Placed in the country to repress banditti they were little better than banditti themselves ... too few to take prisoners or hold a mutinous district in compelled quiet, their only resource was to strike terror by cruelty. ... [T]hey came at last to regard the Irish peasants as unpossessed of the common rights of human beings, and shot and strangled them like foxes or jackals. ..."[251]

The sobering reality that English soldiers received no pay for extended periods — two years from 1571 to 1573 – reveals an awful truth – that the Crown was aware and tolerant of the widespread plunder of the Irish. For what else were the Tudor soldiers living on? Murder and corrupt executions went hand in hand with the Tudor officials' encouragement of flagrant theft of the lands of the Irish. Elizabeth and her Court were told the stories[252] of the plunder and corruption; official complaints about it were filed by some whose consciences and good sense made them gag at it, but the

Queen tolerated it because it made the monumental problem of Ireland she so poorly understood seem cost effective.[253]

Efficiency soon demanded more than isolated executions. Among the most appalling events amid the excesses of this period was the slaughter of 50 members of the O'More clan of Laois Offaly at Mullaghmast in Kildare, killings arranged by Francis Cosby, Commander of the Queen's Troops. The O'Mores had waged a lengthy campaign against Queen Mary's attempts to colonize Laois and Offaly.[254] Cosby enlisted a rival clan, the O'Dempseys, to carry out the killings. The Rath of Mullaghmast was chosen as the site of a friendly conference where the trap was sprung and the O'Mores were slain. Only one, Henry Lalor, fought his way out to tell the story. The episode was authorized by a March 18, 1577 order signed by Sidney. Cosby was knighted for arranging these killings.[255]

The murderous rampage of martial law would continue unabated for 15 more years until finally Elizabeth despaired of its effectiveness and instructed the Deputy that martial law was to be ended completely. While it lasted, it amounted to one of mankind's most despotic periods, 35 years all told during which a succession of scoundrels were turned loose with official power as seneschals and commissioners and licensed to put the native people to death with only the most subjective arbitrary basis for executing them. Lord Grey de Wilton was an especially bloodthirsty practitioner of martial law killings.[256] He boasted of executing 1,500 during his years as Deputy. This gruesome tally, he said, counted only the "chief men and gentlemen" and did not include the innumerable churls he killed.[257]

Even Tudor sympathizers concede that the great number of these executions as well as their callous cruelty was a product of the attitude most English still harbored about the Irish. In the first half of the 16th century, the New English view of the Irish was imperious and condescending. They were taught to assume the native Irish were uncivilized, irreligious and barbaric. Edmund Spenser and others wrote unflattering first hand characterizations of the Irish that permeated thought at the royal Court. Bias against the native Irish was strong among Tudor officials and they entertained the least favorable assumptions about the Munster Irish. At the base of this was the Tudor belief that these Munster Irish in particular had little potential to accept civilized prodding toward reform or Anglicization.

These attitudes gave rise to policies less suited to reform than to devastate the Munster Irish, and it was inevitable that such policies would inflame ethnic and religious hostilities. The destruction of revered shrines and holy wells produced a special revulsion among the Irish. Some courtiers wanted to expel all Irish clergy, but one cleric sent to Ireland directed it be done gradually: "For it is necessary that we eradicate them little by little and by stages."[258] The sense of relief that passed through the Tudor Court in 1567 on the death of Shane O'Neill in Ulster did nothing to temper their coercion policies. The small group of men who had experience in the political and military governance of Ireland knew that native leaders would not willingly submit. How close Munster was to rebellion, however, seems to have been badly underestimated by Tudor officials. Desperation over the outrageous land confiscations, and revulsion at the random executions, had Munster, site of a once loyal earldom, finally ready for total rebellion.

A Countess Enters the Tower

The one place on the planet Tudor subjects wanted to avoid was the Tower of London; it was as feared then as modern legends suggest, and to be summoned there was akin to the call of the Prophet of Doom. Eleanor of Desmond astounded her family and her ladies and requested permission to enter the Tower to live with her jailed husband in his cell.

Her reasons grew out of the complex affairs of the Desmond earldom and her acute awareness that the once haughty and powerful Earl desperately needed her with him.[259] Gerald was a needy person and Eleanor was drawn to him. She knew that without her steadying influence and far more gracious way with the Elizabethan Court, he would provoke even worse treatment for himself, their children and the earldom. Less astonishing, but still surprising, her request was granted by Lord Deputy Sidney. Her own existence in Munster had become intensely stressful as she tried without success to collect rents in the absence of the intimidating earl, and to endure daily life in the deteriorating lands of Munster.

By 1570, Eleanor left Munster to travel to join Gerald in the Tower.[260] Once there, Eleanor lived with him in his Tower chamber, but she lobbied, bribed and begged to have them released to return as rehabilitated prodigals to quiet the disorder in Munster. Failing in that ambitious plea, she asked that Gerald be released from the Tower and moved to the home of Sir Warham St. Leger. In the summer of 1570, Elizabeth permitted Gerald, Eleanor and Sir John and over a dozen servants to move from the Tower to Sir Warham's Leeds Castle in Kent.[261] In this comfortable home of the son of the late Lord Deputy Sir Anthony St. Leger, and with a very modest allowance, Eleanor continued to work for Gerald's release. Though the confinement in the St. Leger homes was not exactly jail, it was penury. St. Leger wrote the Council that Gerald and Eleanor did not have money to buy even a pair of shoes. Later that year, strained by the financial burden of caring for the Earl and his retinue, St. Leger moved himself and the Desmonds to his town house at Southwark in London across the Thames from the Tower. This simple move, however, created the environment for an entrapment plot that set in motion one of the triggering causes of the Munster rebellion.

The Frobisher Sting

In June 1571, James FitzGerald was born to Gerald and Eleanor, but James was a sickly child and only added to their despair. Gerald became desperate; he milled around the docks of London seeking help, but found only thieves and government informants, one of whom, Martin Frobisher contrived an historic sting[262] and, set up Gerald for a charge that threatened his life. Frobisher sought out Gerald at a bankside tavern and presented him with a plan to hire a ship to take Gerald and his contingent to escape to Ireland. Frobisher, of course, was a well-connected Tudor sea dog acting as an informant, and Gerald was charged with treason,[263] but he was assured he would be spared if he agreed to give up his palatine rights to his earldom, and he did. Thus, began the Munster plantation.

An English President Is Handed The Munster Reins

Elizabeth found difficulty everywhere in her attempts to subdue and colonize Munster. No two areas seemed susceptible to the same solutions. Each locality was evolved from a different 8th century Irish kingdom or 14th century Norman earldom. As she contemplated the maps of Munster, Leinster, Ulster and Connaught, Elizabeth saw in common only resistance to usurpation and change, but from one province to another it was waged by greatly differing peoples.

The Tudor officials who were commissioned to travel to Ireland with the task of Anglicization were stepping into several different ancestral societies occupying small tribal homelands. Villages, towns and camps as near to each other as across a river, over a single hill, or further up a coast, presented very different problems and often called for different tactics.

By Elizabeth's reign, the geopolitical terrain of Ireland was a product of centuries of warfare between clans, a legacy of competing clan ambitions, styles, and personalities. Although unabated clan warfare had never fully prevented travel, only the adventurous, careless or militant had ever ventured far from their small communities. Without diffusion and commingling, the most distinctive and peculiar characteristics of Ireland's insular societies had yet to be erased. This insularity made the O'Connor Don clan, for example, different even from the O'Connor Roe clan, and any Earl of Desmond ruled a populous different in style and attitudes from the subjects of the nearby Earls of Thomond or Clanrickard.

The Tudor Court that planned the Anglicization of this complex land was, to make matters worse, limited by a lack of experience and little talent. Development of wise policies flexible enough to deal with the variety encountered throughout Ireland, or the skill to carry out such policies was beyond the experience of the Tudor era officials posted to Ireland. Despite solid military experience, the Tudors did not have a nucleus of the types of mature foreign affairs strategists or talented colonial governors needed in Ireland.

The Provincial Presidency

Elizabeth's resolve to subdue and Anglicize Ireland, nevertheless, had become irreversible. In 1570, recognizing that the royal governor had a history of weak and troublesome control, she asked the Irish parliament to establish a new executive form, the Presidency, one in Munster and another in Connaught, an office which was to organize the government in each of these provinces and to provide an English official as the replacement for the earls and chieftains. The Presidents were to be military commanders who would have standing armies. They would be financed not by Gaelic coyne and livery or by English cess, but by a composition rent. The Presidencies were expected to usher in gradual, peaceful responsiveness to the Crown and spare Elizabeth the cost of the rebellions that a more hostile attempt to radically restructure Ireland would surely spark.

Heavy turnover of Deputies and Chancellors had contributed to instability. The turnover was seldom for the better because it resulted from increasing tensions and from the competition[264] among the small group of Tudor officials. These appointments continued to rotate among the favored few, many of whom were related. Robert Dudley's sister was married to Sir Henry Sidney who in turn was Sir William FitzWilliam's brother-in-law, and Sir Walter Raleigh was a half-brother of Sir Humphrey Gilbert, President of Munster.[265]

Sidney chose Sir Warham St. Leger to be President of Munster and installed him as a special commissioner pending Elizabeth's confirmation. The Ormond/Desmond contention was not only about border disputes; there were also controversies over royal appointments and patronage in Ireland, and Butler did not like the appointment of St. Leger. Butler and his champion Sussex both knew that Warham St. Leger was sympathetic to Desmond, so they lobbied aggressively against St. Leger's appointment. Elizabeth acceded to the objection and withdrew St. Leger; but her decision only intensified the controversy in the English Court. Elizabeth, uncharacteristically on the defensive, criticized Sidney's selection of St. Leger charging that it showed favoritism by Sidney to Gerald. She insisted that Black Tom's lobbying against St. Leger had not in any way influenced her withdrawal of St. Leger's name. The brunt of the criticism was left to fall squarely on Sidney. He came in for stinging attacks for his earlier historical support of the Earl of Desmond; and the criticism got to him. He became so offended that at one point he erupted and challenged Sussex to a duel before they were both subdued.

Sidney, for all his military, administrative and diplomatic talents failed, as had all others, in the great adventure of Anglicizing Ireland, and he was recalled in 1571. Sir William FitzWilliam stayed as Justiciar, and was quickly elevated to the position of Lord Deputy. He was anxious to do so, despite the odds against political success; he was in debt and he knew Ireland was the place where he could line his pockets. FitzWilliam, as Deputy from 1571-75, dabbled in graft and corruption to a far greater degree than even some of his other crooked predecessors.

12

Corrupt Courtiers Spark
the FitzMaurice Rebellion

What a slippery seat they sitte that govern that Kingdom[266]
— James Perrot

Tudor officials rarely enjoyed a lengthy respite from trouble in the fragmented frontier landscape of Ireland; even when things would quiet in the north, there was often no such peace in the south. The English belief was that the native Irish of Munster were perennially incorrigible; that was nothing new. But there was in the south that special cause for alarm — the Anglo Irish of Munster, the once loyal Old English. They were becoming as worrisome a source of disloyalty as the native Irish. The Norman influence, once the cure for the wildness of this far Gaelic frontier, was now itself becoming the disease.

Long before the Statutes of Kilkenny were written in an attempt to halt the assimilation of the Normans by the Irish, the early Norman Desmond FitzGeralds in Munster based in the west at Askeaton had already become more Irish than most Irish. They were called "degenerate English." That sobriquet was applied by New English to Normans who adopted Irish speech, dress and customs. In Munster this description fit not merely the general Anglo Irish population, by the 16th century it fit even the Earl of Desmond and his household.

Desmond Munster was the scene of local conflicts, the types that occurred continuously throughout most of Ireland. Raids on royal troops, cattle raids and skirmishes among the clans were common everywhere outside the Pale; but they were isolated events. Prolonged conflicts were interrupted by the winter and by long truces, and they did not warrant the massing of a royal attack force. Elizabeth, however, was no longer content with the partial stabilization of Ireland. That seemed to her to be the most that had been accomplished by her father's program of surrender and regrant. She felt the time had come to Anglicize this troublesome island, and, in 1566, she began a campaign to extend the full reach of English administration to Munster and Connaught.

Ireland Seen as a Honey Pot

Many English officials had their sights set on Irish land, but few were brazen enough under ordinary circumstances to take it. To do so they would have had to risk the outrage of the Irish they displaced, the strong disapproval of Elizabeth and the retaliation of the earls. The danger from the native Irish clans, particularly the so-called "Wild Irish," was also a reason for restraint. Even royally approved efforts in Ulster had led only to the deaths of settlers. Munster, however, was seen as more promising,[267] and the opportunists among the English still had hopes for an interest in the land grabs in the fertile south.

The opportunity to take Desmond lands had fallen into the laps of English willing to risk revenge by the Munster clans once the Earl of Desmond was charged with treason and forced to forfeit certain rights over his earldom to Elizabeth on July 12, 1568. English opportunists rushed to make fake claims to some of the finest Desmond estates — Arthur Chichester, Peter Carew, Richard Grenville, Warham St. Leger, Humphrey Gilbert, Walter Raleigh and others all took land in Munster, promising that their noble purpose was "to carry England to Ireland." Much of Ireland was still forests, bogs and hillsides, but these were not the areas the planters coveted. They wanted the finest properties, but those manors were owned and occupied by Irish. Turning a blind eye to a series of provocative frauds, Chief Secretary William Cecil approved their land grabs and Queen Elizabeth did as well.

The FitzMaurice Rebellion

The process of surrender and regrant had injected the contagion of a legal and a historical paradox into land ownership, one which would give New English opportunists "a legalistic validity to much stylishly justified theft."[268] The use of dubious old documents became rampant. Some large land holdings were also taken by abuse of government coercion; land was taken by the government as a "penalty" for "misbehavior" of an Irish chieftain. The land of the chieftain was then given to English planters or developers who re-sold it to another English investor. The legal gambits[269] used to take the property and to title it in the hands of the English were shameless. "A sanctimonious and rather unreal preoccupation with legal niceties contributed a last element to the piece." They needed an Englishman "who could put up an adequately plausible claim to a land title in Munster.... One presented himself almost immediately. Sir Peter Carew.... had more rough edges than most....He was physically tough, as ruthless as any Gaelic or Norman Irish Chief, ... and he had a good lawyer."[270]

The lawyer, John Hooker, was adept at using "illegible deeds" that Hooker argued gave Carew, a distant descendant of one of the Normans invaders, "hereditary right to the ownership of large expanses of the forfeited Geraldine lands."[271] Hooker presented the foggy deeds he dug up to the Queen, and she approved Carew as the owner of these prized Irish lands.[272] Word spread of lawyer Hooker's success, so the other hungry courtiers followed suit.

Carew sealed his land confiscation by presenting his hereditary claim to the Dublin Parliament headed by Sir Henry Sidney,[273] and the Parliament quickly approved it.[274] It confirmed that Peter Carew and his family were now the rightful heirs to the Barony of Idrone, not the Kavanaghs who had farmed it "immemorially." Grenville, St. Leger and others followed suit in Cork and around the River Blackwater and "the cycle followed by all these communities was identical: eviction of the Irish, distribution of land, construction of the first buildings, clearance and cultivation."[275] This amounted to "armed confiscation of the source of the [Irish] race's wealth."[276]

In response, "a murderous opposition accumulated among the dispossessed Irish," and they began to ambush and attack Carew.

The Roches, Barrys and Muskerry McCarthy's decided to launch such attacks before the Carew program had the chance to fall upon them. Then a "formidable soldier" emerged as their leader – James FitzMaurice FitzGerald (called FitzMaurice).[277]

The Disloyal Butler Brothers

When Carew took the land in Idrone from the Kavanaghs, he also took land of the Catholic branch of the Butlers in Idrone, as well as lands in Meath, Waterford, Cork and Kerry. As a result, FitzMaurice was able to enlist allies among the Catholic lines of the displaced Butlers, Edward and Edmund Butler. The Butler lands at Idrone had once been occupied by a Carew ancestor who was driven out long ago by the 14th century chieftain, Art MacMurrogh. But Carew also laid claim to Butler lands west of the Barrow. That land, however, was controlled by Edmund, the least loyal Butler, a Catholic and a leader of parliamentary opposition to the English. Edmund and his brother Edward joined with FitzMaurice in June 1569 in open rebellion in[278] and around the palatinate of Kilkenny, and they drove the Idrone settlers to seek refuge in Youghal and Cork.

The Butlers raided cattle on Carew's new land, and in response Carew invaded Kilkenny itself and "destroyed, looted, burnt and raped" in the process.[279] Carew and his men overran Kilkenny Castle where "the rape victims included Sir Edward Butler's wife," and they captured Sir Edward. Carew went on to take Sir Edmund Butler's Clogrennane Castle and slaughtered the garrison and their men, women and children. Guerrilla ambush and assassination was not new in Munster, but it increased once Elizabeth sent Earl Gerald to the Tower. There were increasing attacks against English leaders, even shots at Sidney and Perrot. Tudor encroachment continued, however, as if widespread rebellion was only a remote risk. Oblivious to the rage that was building in Munster, Tudor courtiers just continued to seize land;[280] on one occasion, however, they seized land from the wrong owner[281] and he plunged Munster into years of widespread rebellion.

Sir Warham St. Leger and Sir Richard Grenville confiscated land from James FitzMaurice[282] and the FitzMaurices maneuvered to elect FitzMaurice as Captain of the Geraldines, and FitzMaurice set out to take Munster into a fight against the English and to end their threats to the Desmond lordship.[283]

The Confiscation of Kerrycurrihy

The land confiscation that drove FitzMaurice to seize the Geraldine leadership in Munster was an especially naked affront. Sir Richard Grenville and his followers wanted to seize enough land in Cork to establish an English colony[284] in the cantred of Kerrycurrihy on the south coast, the demesne of the FitzMaurices.

Outraged, FitzMaurice, one of the major Irish personalities of the 16th century, called for a Munster revolt. FitzMaurice summoned a meeting of the Munster chieftains in Kerry and bluntly warned them that they all faced confiscation[285] or annihilation if they failed to join together now in full rebellion. If they did, he said, Spanish help[286] would arrive and the Catholic rebellion[287] would spread even to England. The Desmond leaders agreed at his urging to offer the Crown of Ireland to a Spaniard to be chosen by Philip II.

The FitzMaurice rebellion began in earnest in 1569, and soon was more widespread than any of the eruptions in the previous century in response to the earlier provocations committed by prior Deputies. Some of those had merely been the last gasps of the Wars of The Roses, not efforts by the Irish to throw off the lordship of England or royal rule. This rebellion was of a different kind, and it was different to a sobering degree. This was not merely an irate native Irish chieftain in the mold of Shane O'Neill, but a full blown mutiny led by Anglo Irish gentry.

FitzMaurice was a longtime ally of his imprisoned cousin Gerald, and at the outset Gerald sent a warrant endorsing FitzMaurice's presumptuous grab for Desmond leadership during his absence.[288] Eleanor FitzGerald, Gerald's countess, however, was strongly opposed to a Munster rebellion and she became a determined critic of FitzMaurice and his rebellion. She saw it as an invitation to Elizabeth to increase martial law, and a reason to establish forts and an excuse to seize castles in Munster all in the name of protection. Eleanor had to endure the ravages of the FitzMaurice rebellion knowing that many English and many Irish attributed it to Gerald as well as to FitzMaurice. She herself strongly disapproved of everything about the FitzMaurice rebellion and considered it ill-advised in every respect and entirely counterproductive. She also distrusted FitzMaurice[289] and believed this was a coup attempt;[290] a plot to topple Gerald, not at all a genuinely religious crusade. Eleanor also saw that the rents which should have gone to the earl were being expropriated by the Crown to subsidize the martial law forces abusing Munster. Despite Eleanor's disapproval, what began as a fairly disorganized revolt of the earl's followers, soon gained momentum. As the rebellion caught hold in Munster, FitzMaurice sought support from other leaders in Ireland, and then from foreign Catholic powers in Italy and Spain. The peaceful colonization Tudor England hoped for had suddenly degenerated into major bloodshed.

Attacks Against the New English Colonists

Several Old English in Munster, Lord Maurice Roche, Lord Barry and Lord Deices, refused to join FitzMaurice in the early days of his rebellion in June 1569, but he obtained the support of Donal McCarthy Mor, Earl of Clancarthy, the White Knight (the title of the FitzGibbon hereditary Anglo Norman knighthood)[291] and the Seneschal of Imokilly (another hereditary manor). He launched a surprise attack on Grenville's colonists and drove them out of Kerrycurrihy into the town of Cork. He then went on to attack Tracton and Carragaline Castle in Cork.[292]

FitzMaurice's attacks were sharp and very effective against small sites, far less so when he attacked fortified towns, but even his successes came at great cost. Sidney retaliated[293] against the Munster areas that had been spared by FitzMaurice because of their presumed loyalty to his rebellion, and the devastation by both sides produced conditions in Munster that became increasingly horrific.[294]

That the rebellion lasted several years surprised everyone because FitzMaurice's coalition was a loose one[295] and it began to disintegrate. The Butler alliance in particular created stress at a very personal level. FitzMaurice's wife had a flirtation or worse with Edward Butler, and FitzMaurice divorced her. However, he remarried quite well to the widow of The O'Connor Kerry, and thereby acquired the O'Connor's Carrigafoyle Castle.

Sidney proclaimed not only FitzMaurice, but also the Butler brothers' traitors. Black Tom Butler was still loyal to the Crown and he was acutely embarrassed by the Butlers' participation; he demanded that Edmund give up the rebellion, and in 1569 Edmund submitted. Black Tom's embarrassment led him to accuse Carew and Sidney of provoking the revolt by permitting and participating in the fraudulent land confiscations. This accusation helped him win leniency for his brothers, and it seriously tarnished Carew and Sidney.[296] Nevertheless, some blood had to be shed to repair the damage the Butler rebels had done to Black Tom's loyal stature, so Black Tom executed more than 100 of the Catholic Butler followers who had rebelled. Black Tom also abolished coyne and livery, ending a transgression he had often allowed. Edmund and his younger brothers, however, were merely attainted, and only for a short time. Once Black Tom had offered expiation of a sort and safely deflected the criticism leveled by his enemies, he quietly negotiated pardons for his troublesome brothers.

Others, however, also began to abandon FitzMaurice. In December, 1569 MacCarthy Mor abandoned FitzMaurice, leaving him such thin support that he had no option but to resort to intermittent guerrilla warfare. The rebellion received a last boost giving it a religious tone[297] when Pope Pius V excommunicated Elizabeth as a heretic in 1570, yet it became increasingly apparent that the rebels, though still tenacious, were too few and were achieving little lasting success by their attacks on the settlements.

President Perrot

During the FitzMaurice rebellion Sir John Perrot was appointed President of Munster in 1571, succeeding Sir Humphrey Gilbert.[298] When Perrot took up residence at Limerick, it was as though Henry VIII had come to Ireland. Perrot,[299] a soldier from Wales, was brave, blunt and irascible.[300] He was also a reputed bastard of Henry mainly because he was Henry's spitting image.[301] Worse, he had Henry's temper, and it was sorely tested by the FitzMaurice rebellion.

As the years of rebellion wore on, FitzMaurice's dwindling rebel force kept hoping for Spanish help, but the Netherlands revolt against Spain in 1572 had become the overwhelming preoccupation

Sir John Perrot

of King Philip II. That revolt imposed increasing financial and man-power demands on Spain, and those demands made effective Spanish help for Ireland impossible. The Pope also failed to respond; Pius V simply had no interest.

As the rebellion grew weaker, in the summer of 1572 FitzMaurice attempted to relieve a siege of Castlemaine with Burkes and Scots mercenaries, but the castle surrendered before he could succeed.[302] Most disheartening of all to FitzMaurice was that the other provinces of Ireland declined to join him. Ulster did not merely fail to help; several clans from Ulster and Connaught even sent troops to fight for the Crown.

FitzMaurice's unpredictable tactics, nevertheless, constantly surprised and infuriated Perrot. Perrot could not catch him. As Perrot tried to "hunt the fox out of his hole," FitzMaurice eluded Perrot in the woods, glens and bogs.[303] FitzMaurice also ambushed Perrot's forces and came very close to killing Perrot. Perrot came to the sobering realization that FitzMaurice's bothersome guerrilla tactics continued to pose real danger and might preoccupy his forces and stall the Anglicization of Munster. To end it, Perrot proposed a duel between twelve knights chosen from each side. FitzMaurice suspected treachery and, when the day came, FitzMaurice did not appear, but sent a messenger who simply arrived and called off the duel while Perrot stood there on the dueling ground, plainly embarrassed before his men. These skirmishes, and the spread of the story of Perrot forced to wait for FitzMaurice's messenger, plus Perrot's near death experience, all were wearing on the Munster President and on his men.

FitzMaurice Surrenders

In 1573, Elizabeth offered FitzMaurice his freedom to end it all and leave Ireland, and FitzMaurice surrendered. The terms approved by Elizabeth were generous. Both were weary, and FitzMaurice came out of hiding, knelt in the Church at Kilmallock, and submitted to a relieved Perrot. FitzMaurice was dealt with in a style more like the reform measures for a wayward youth than the sanctions inflicted on a defeated rebel. FitzMaurice and his supporters, the White Knight and the Seneschal of Imokilly,[304] laid down arms in exchange for their agreement to leave for the Continent. When FitzMaurice finally departed, those who knew him well realized he would be back. True to form, once he was safely in exile in a Catholic country, FitzMaurice immediately resumed his campaign to secure military support for a religious invasion of Ireland, an invasion he intended to lead, and one he hoped would be under the banner of the Pope.

The FitzMaurice upheaval had kept Munster unstable and agitated for several years, leaving Munster unreceptive to Tudor rule. However, the attitude typical among the Munster sub-vassals was not innate hostility to the Queen, but rather hostility to anyone who camped soldiers on their land, took provisions, and slaughtered their cattle under coyne and livery. They had come to fear and thoroughly hate the royal seneschals for the arbitrary executions they carried out. Earl Gerald FitzGerald was about to discover that FitzMaurice's rebellion had so agitated Munster that it was no longer amenable to Desmond rule either.

The Earl and Countess of Desmond had waited long and apprehensively for an answer to Eleanor's persistent pleas that they be allowed to return to Askeaton. Elizabeth wearied of the lack of success flowing from the costly confinement of Gerald, Eleanor and Sir John. Their confinement in London had plainly had a destabilizing effect on Munster for it allowed the disloyal elements to run unrestrained. Elizabeth summoned Gerald, Eleanor and John before her. She lectured them and extracted from Gerald and Eleanor assurances that they would help extend English law into Munster and find a way to end the Butler-Desmond disputes. She also directed that their two-year old infant be left in the fosterage of the Court, entrusted to the Earl of Leicester. Thus, after 6 years in England, in March of 1573, Gerald, Eleanor and Sir John were being released, allowed to return to Ireland.[305]

Though Elizabeth herself had ordered their release, when Gerald arrived in Dublin, the Deputy, Sir William FitzWilliam, unexpectedly made additional unauthorized demands on him. When Gerald rejected them, he was held at Dublin Castle. Eleanor and John were allowed to continue on to Munster. Nearly crazed at this new incarceration, Gerald ranted and shouted at the Dublin officials, and spouted blunt treason. Though he was kept in easy restraint, it was made clear to him that he was forbidden to return to Munster. His obstreperous protests, however, were offensive and there was a danger that he might be committed back to the Tower of London at any moment.

On her return to Askeaton, the Desmond overlords filled Eleanor with tales of England's alarming encroachment. She sent those same stories to Earl Gerald in Dublin and Gerald began to look for an opportunity to escape. Gerald was being allowed a long leash in Dublin. He was periodically permitted to join hunting parties. As his concern about his earldom got the best of him, one evening in November 1573 he simply failed to return from the hunt. He had decided to risk escape, and by nightfall was off to Kerry and home after an absence of six years.[306] Little if any effort was made to rearrest Gerald, since the new impositions on him on which his Dublin confinement had been based were completely unauthorized, and FitzWilliam would be hard pressed to explain a substantial investment to enter Desmond lands and fight to recapture an earl who had been released by Elizabeth.

Gerald's homecoming was a warm event, almost triumphal. At Lough Gur in Limerick, faithful crowds greeted him. He repeated his old promises never to allow English rule or to allow sheriffs to exercise authority in Desmond territory. After Lough Gur, he headed toward the Shannon and finally back to his beloved Askeaton.

Unlike the emotional and impulsive Gerald, Eleanor, remained fearful. She had shrewdly sized up Elizabeth and concluded that English intrusion into Munster was inevitable. She saw Anglicization as Gerald's only hope, and she began a careful campaign to persuade him to write Elizabeth. She started slowly, and soon had convinced Gerald to promise loyalty, and offer apologies and excuses for his escape.[307]

Sidney's Return

Sir Henry Sidney returned as Deputy in 1575 to oversee the shiring of Connaught into Mayo, Roscommon, Sligo and Galway. He had wanted to return and he needed a source of wealth to support his expensive estates.[308] To earn the chance to return to Ireland, Sidney promised not only to pursue the entire Tudor plan of Anglicization, but to make Ireland self-supporting as well. He planned to do it by imposing widespread rents. He returned, however, to find Dublin and the Pale racked by Plague and bad harvests, all of which made the rents formulated by Sidney and his secretary, Edmund Tremayne, unaffordable. However, Sidney, aided by commissioners of martial law, resumed tackling the power of the Irish lords, intent on finally ending the lordship style the Tudors were referring to as bastard feudalism.

Sidney worked to improve the composition rent on Connaught and Munster. In 1575 and 1576 he traveled around Ireland negotiating composition agreements with the ruling chieftains and earls, but his effort met much greater resistance than expected, and the small rents he could collect in many areas were insufficient. He remained committed, however, to making all of Ireland loyal, profitable,[309] and no longer a potential staging ground for a Spanish or French invasion of England, but Irish acceptance of the great new solution, the composition rent, was clearly going to take considerable time. Even the previously loyal Palesmen rejected the rents, and, try as he might, Sidney could not make the rent system work or achieve peace.

By 1578, Munster was a society on the brink of collapse, but finally Sidney's efforts to deter further insurrections began to show promise. His many years of experience in Ireland had finally taught him enough to make him a Deputy who could understand what worked where in Ireland. Ironically it was the English nobles of the Pale[310] with whom he would have the final difficulty that would cost him his office, and it happened while he was still heavily in debt with little left of Irish spoils of his own. The Palesmen loudly complained about Sidney's use of cess (the English equivalent of the Irish coyne and livery). The Palesmen saw these practices as a hated protection racket. Sidney, nevertheless, billeted the troops he needed on the lands of Palesmen. While his use of the practice was not especially heavy, the complaints to the frugal Elizabeth harmed Sidney, and she recalled him,[311] thereby removing from Ireland the only man who had seemed capable of intimidating Earl Gerald of Desmond, and deterring him from leading a full rebellion.

President Drury

To govern Munster, Elizabeth replaced Perrot with a seasoned but aging field marshal, Sir William Drury. Named President in 1576, Drury presided over the composition rent in Munster, but he too found repression necessary, and he imposed martial law with full force on Munster. Drury carried out widespread executions, including uncontrolled executions of masterless men, some 400 of them in Munster between the summer of 1576 and the end of 1577.

13

Massacre at Smerwick

To Their Queen, the Irish were "ravening beasts"[312]
— Elizabeth I

The foreign intervention hoped for by the Desmond rebels and constantly feared by Walsingham, William Cecil (by 1571 created Baron Burghley), Sidney and by Elizabeth herself, had so far amounted to nothing. Spain and the Papacy, the two chief allies of the rebellious Irish chieftains and barons in this era, had provided no effective assistance to the Irish at the crucial moments of the 1570s. Although Pope Pius V had issued a widely disseminated 1570 Papal Bull proclaiming that the Irish need give no allegiance to the Crown, he did little else besides recognizing Philip II of Spain, Elizabeth's brother-in-law, as King of Ireland. Spain too did little until 1578 and not much then.

When foreign military support finally did arrive in 1579, it was less than robust. The exiled FitzMaurice had been away for five years and had convinced Pope Gregory XIII to authorize a papal force to land in Ireland. FitzMaurice returned leading a small advance force in preparation for a larger papal force having applied to the Pope and Philip II for 6000 armed soldiers and a papal nuncio. He had called on France as well but without success, doomed by the French hope that an alliance between France and England by marriage was imminent. King Francis' brother, the Duke of Alençon, was about to marry Elizabeth, or so the French Court believed. Philip II was sympathetic to the Irish, but he provided no men and no ships; he even denied FitzMaurice an audience. Pope Gregory did respond to FitzMaurice's pleas, but he granted only 2000 troops to Ireland to challenge the "heretic Queen." FitzMaurice, however, pestered the pontiff; he convinced the Pope to pardon scores of Italian robbers and highwaymen languishing in Roman jails, increasing the potential invasion force to 4,000, still far short of the force he needed.

To brand the invasion as a holy crusade, key clergymen joined FitzMaurice. Foremost among them were Nicholas Sander (sometimes called Sanders), an English Jesuit, and Cornelius O'Mulrian, the Bishop of Killaloe. Sander, a professor of theology at Louvain, was well known to the English as a provocateur and polemicist. Thomas Stukeley, yet another reputed bastard of Henry VIII, was placed in command of 2000 men and sent to Portugal, but there King Sebastian commandeered his entire force. King Sebastian forced them to join him in an ill-fated invasion of Morocco. There, at Alcazar, not only were Stukeley and most of the Italians killed, King Sebastian was killed as well. Nicholas Sander and Bishop O'Mulrian made it back to Rome to brief FitzMaurice on the loss of a substantial part of the force he had accumulated.

FitzMaurice, however, pressed on, hoping instead to attract support from the Irish nobility once he reached Ireland. His cousin Gerald, the Earl of Desmond, had returned from London confinement and was back in his castle at Askeaton. FitzMaurice gambled that Gerald was willing to support a full rebellion. With his force now down to barely 700, FitzMaurice put to sea from Coruna and arrived on the Kerry Coast.

Sir Humphrey Gilbert was brought south from Ulster to help defend Munster. Walsingham ordered Gilbert's ships to patrol the Kerry coast and to intercept the expected invasion force, but they failed to find the papal ships at sea. The invaders first put into Dingle, set it on fire, then sailed to Smerwick.

FitzMaurice and Sander wrote of the invasion as a holy war, a military extension of the Counter-Reformation. They landed at Smerwick on July 18, 1579 with only a fraction of the soldiers FitzMaurice had sought. They dug breastworks, set up headquarters and began to fortify *Dun an Oir* fort, chanting their war cry, *"Papa Abu"* (The Pope to Victory), proclaiming war in the name of Pope Gregory and starting the second Munster Rising. Helping Nicholas Sander, the fervent crusader, was Bishop Mateo de

Lord Burghley, Sir William Cecil

Oviedo, a Spanish friar, later to become Archbishop of Dublin and a key strategist for Spanish military aid. This second FitzMaurice revolt at its start was more spirited, more effective and better organized than the poorly organized first FitzMaurice rebellion, but it lost steam even more quickly than the first, and Earl Gerald of Desmond provided the invaders' their first disappointment.

Now 46, Gerald and his Countess Eleanor were back living peaceably at Askeaton when FitzMaurice landed at Smerwick. Gerald wrote with unctuous sympathy to Elizabeth lamenting the FitzMaurice invasion, and proclaiming to her his steadfast loyalty. Whether he was actually choosing loyalty, keeping his options open or seeking to deceive her is hard to know. Gerald rode to Smerwick with a modest force of galloglass and musketeers, where he found the Tudor Constable, Sir Henry Davells, in charge. Davells pointed out the vulnerable defenses and urged Gerald to attack the invaders. Gerald, however, vacillated and expressed doubt that he could defeat the trained soldiers FitzMaurice had brought.

Davells perceived what was happening; he observed from an elevated site near shore that the empty invasion ships had already begun to set sail, and he realized that the only ships which might have offered the rebels a sea escape had obviously planned to depart. He concluded that they left because the rebels viewed Gerald as their ally who, they believed, would join with them. Davells decided that Gerald was untrustworthy; indeed that he was aligned with FitzMaurice.[313] Gerald continued to insist that he would expel the traitor FitzMaurice, but he sensed that Davells was not buying it.

A Geraldine Murder

Within a matter of days the suspicion of Gerald exploded into open accusations when Davells was found murdered. A double political assassination occurred in the heart of the Desmond earldom and the murders were easily laid at the feet of the Desmonds. Constable Davells, together with Arthur Carter, both official emissaries of the acting Lord Deputy, Sir William Drury, were decapitated just days after Gerald declined Davells' request that he attack FitzMaurice. They were killed in their room in a tavern at Tralee. The murders fueled the growing suspicion of Gerald since it was Gerald's brothers, Sir John FitzGerald[314] and Sir James, who killed Davells and Carter, probably with the connivance of Sander. Gerald gave his brother James a silver bowl one week after the killings and this was seen as an apparent reward for the murders; it also cemented the belief that Gerald was a covert rebel conspirator, an ally of FitzMaurice. Word spread rapidly that a second Geraldine rebellion in Munster was underway. The slaying of Carter and Davells, brutal killings recounted throughout the English world, ended any vestige of trust in Gerald's pretensions of loyalty.[315] Still Gerald did not take the lead of this new rebellion; he was leaving that to FitzMaurice. The following month, however, FitzMaurice was killed, not by the English, but by other Anglo-Irish.

FitzMaurice's Fatal Skirmish

In August 1579 near Barrington Bridge (*Beal Antha An Bhorin*) James FitzMaurice and his, by then, small band, having parted ways and parted company with the hot-headed and newly notorious Sir John FitzGerald, was confronted by a loyal Burke, Lord Theobald Burke of Castleconnell. Burke, a Protestant landowner, was an opponent of the rebels and he became outraged by the by the rebels' trespasses on his land. FitzMaurice's forces took a plow horse from one of Burke's farmers, and Burke chased after FitzMaurice. When he overtook their group, Burke recognized FitzMaurice by his yellow coat and confronted him. They argued briefly and one of Burke's men shot FitzMaurice. Mortally wounded, FitzMaurice was able to gallop across a shallow stream and spear Burke, killing him with a single thrust of his sword through Burke's neck, before FitzMaurice himself fell dead from his own horse.

The English discovered FitzMaurice's body in late August and hung it in the marketplace in Limerick where, over several weeks, it was gradually shot to pieces. Queen Elizabeth sent Theobald Burke's father, William, a letter of gratitude for their show of loyalty, and she expressed her condolence for his loss. The rebellion, however, did not end with the death of FitzMaurice. By then, other rebel forces in the south already had begun to weigh in to support what had become a second Munster rebellion.

The Reluctant Rebel

After FitzMaurice was killed, John FitzGerald effectively took charge,[316] but Gerald resisted the pressure from his brother John to rebel. Relations between the two were strained; John had a particular disdain for Gerald's wife, the Countess Eleanor, and she for him. Gerald was conflicted, and he was made even more indecisive by the recurring memories he had of the consequences of failure in these endeavors, years of poverty and confinement in London. He would genuinely have preferred to find some way to avoid being backed into that fateful corner from which rebellion was the only escape.

Eleanor wanted to avoid rebellion even more than Gerald. She shared those same recollections of the Tower and the humiliating poverty that followed. It was Eleanor, then, who had taken the lead in the begging, bowing and scraping it took to extract them from the Tower and later to free them from the crushing boredom of confinement at the home of Sir Warham St. Leger. But the main focus of her concern was their son, James, an heir to the earldom, and their daughters. She was nearly insane with fear that James would be enslaved or killed to extinguish the succession. Eleanor helped push Gerald, during the late summer and early fall of 1579, toward the Crown. In an effort to show the Crown officials that he and Munster were stabilized, Gerald assisted in royal military strikes against the rebels. Though they were only minor military actions, they did not seem to be mere feints or empty pretense.

Malby Provokes the Earl

What eventually turned Gerald, or provoked him into rebellion, or simply removed all options, was the political maneuvering of Sir Nicholas Malby, a strident puritan whose course was guided more by religious zeal than by Elizabeth's policies.[317] Elevated from temporary governor of Munster to Lord Justice, Malby saw that the spoils of Munster were unlimited if he could but topple the earl. Malby decided to push the reluctant Gerald into rebellion, and he attacked Gerald's garrison at Askeaton. Gerald rejected an ultimatum to surrender and the Desmonds fought back against the attack. As Gerald watched, Malby vented his puritan hostility against the Catholic Desmond shrines. Malby burned the abbey and defiled the Geraldine tombs, including the grave of Joan FitzGerald. He had his men exhume the bodies and throw them along the river bank. Gerald's garrison abandoned Askeaton, blowing up a part of the Castle as they went. Gerald fled, and the combined forces of Malby, Lord Justice Sir William Pelham and Black Tom Butler pursued him. However, when even this provocation failed to push Gerald into aggression and open rebellion, Malby did the next best thing and unilaterally directed Pelham to proclaim Gerald a rebel.[318] On November 2, 1579, the Privy Council publicly proclaimed Gerald a traitor on the motion of Pelham, and without consultation with Elizabeth's Court, for Lord Burghley, as Malby well knew, was sympathetic to Gerald. Malby then enlisted the willing support of Black Tom Butler to close in for the kill.

Eleanor saw what Gerald had been too stubborn to grasp — Malby had decided to kill him. She began a desperate lobbying effort. As Gerald and his assembled forces retreated from Askeaton Castle, she tried to get a plea to Elizabeth to stop Malby, but her messages were blocked by Malby. Unable to reach Elizabeth, Eleanor had no alternative but to make her pleas locally to Malby and Pelham. Both, however, declined to help; they simply placed their own arguments before Elizabeth. Desperate to save her children, Eleanor believed she could trust Sir William Drury, and she placed James in the protective custody of Drury. Drury, however, was on his last legs and the young James wound up languishing in Dublin Castle. Gerald and Eleanor's daughters were far less threatened; they were sent to hide with Eleanor's half-brother, Donal MacCarthy of Carbery, and with her brother-in-law, Owen MacDonagh MacCarthy.

After many attempts, Eleanor finally succeeded in delivering a letter to Elizabeth pleading with her, assuring her that Gerald had joined the rebellion only because he had been falsely labeled a traitor and, once accused, he was overrun and thus had no choice. Elizabeth had already received similar information from other more objective sources making her skeptical both of Malby's version of events and of his treatment of Gerald. Though her detestation of Gerald had not dissipated in the slightest, she apparently saw through the machinations of Malby and Pelham and was furious that their personal ambitions were going to cost her a small fortune in military action, whereas a capture or a pardon of Gerald at the right moment might have eliminated all resistance to colonization, plantation, and Anglicization of Munster. Elizabeth demanded to know why Gerald had been proclaimed a traitor before he was caught.

Desmond Sacks Youghal

But Gerald had been alone without Eleanor for weeks, exposed instead to the mesmerizing influence of Nicolas Sander, the captivating Jesuit. He had become a mirror image of FitzMaurice. He went from inspired to near messianic in his fervor to return Ireland, even England, to Christ. Just as the pendulum of Tudor favor seemed as though it might swing in Gerald's favor, precisely as he himself had earlier wanted, Gerald went over the edge and into open rebellion. His war cry was no longer the Desmond cry "*Shanid Abu;*" it became "*Papa Abu.*"[319] In late 1579, Gerald suddenly attacked and sacked the walled City of Youghal.[320] Why he did it can best be explained by the need for supplies or the influence of Sander, but precisely what he and his rebels did was another matter. His attack on Youghal made little sense; Youghal had little value other than as a source of victuals or as a landing site. Worse, was the rebels' conduct; they spent four days sacking, pillaging, and plundering. They raped, stole, burned and executed many in the city.[321] When the news reached Elizabeth, all thought of pardoning Gerald vanished.

Gerald was now The Rebel Earl in truth; his rebellion was to last for five years. His rebellion may have started with hostile forces pushing him, virtually forcing him, into rebellion, but, by the attack on Youghal, he had embraced rebellion himself and there was no going back. Eleanor was horrified when she learned of it and she pitifully begged Pelham, but he refused to allow her access to Court to plead for Gerald. Philip II, Gerald's only real hope, sat in Spain weighing, contemplating, rethinking and temporizing, as was his wont, but he would never send Gerald the help needed to prevent catastrophe. Thus, the strange Desmond rebellion was under way at long last, but it could hardly hope to transform itself into a campaign that would bring down the Queen. When Sir William Drury, the ailing Lord Justice, died at Waterford, Sir Nicholas Malby was placed in full command, and the attacks on the sprawling Desmond kingdom began in earnest.

Carrigafoyle Castle Falls

The O'Connor Kerry's Carrigafoyle Castle at the mouth of the Shannon had long been the protector of Munster. Its aging defenses had recently been enhanced by an Italian engineer. But in 1580 English forces commanded by Sir William Pelham, Sir William Winter and Black Tom Butler began an assault on the fortress. Winter's ships came up the Shannon to attack with powerful siege guns and Pel-

Carrigafoyle Castle

ham began shelling it with small cannon. On March 29, 1580 the combined assault breached those thick walls that the people of Kerry had thought made it an impregnable fortress. Carrigafoyle fell and its inhabitants were executed. The capture of this strategic bulwark instantly exposed all peninsulas south of the Shannon. Desmond supporters were suddenly vulnerable, and those in the Kerry peninsulas, McCarthy Mor and the O'Sullivans of Berehaven, saw defeat was inevitable. Many of them sought immediate pardons, and many threw in with the English completely.

Pelham and Butler increased their attacks and quickened their pursuit hoping to catch and kill Gerald and his brothers. They drove Gerald from Tralee and Castleisland where he and Eleanor narrowly escaped, forced to hide in the mists of a nearby bog. When he failed to catch Gerald, Pelham would burn the crops and kill the cattle wherever Gerald had been. His brothers were hunted as well. In the late summer of 1580, Sir James of Desmond was wounded in a raid and captured by the Sheriff of Cork, then tortured for two months before being executed in October.

Glenmalure – Baltinglass and Lord Grey de Wilton

One of the most relentless of the Tudor Pantheon of brutality, Sir Arthur Grey de Wilton, was named Deputy in September 1580 and, as the efforts to take the Rebel Earl of Desmond continued in Munster, a separate rebellion erupted in the Pale. This was not a spread of the Desmond rebellion. James Eustace, Viscount Baltinglass, and Feagh MacHugh O'Byrne of the Wicklow glens went into rebellion in and south of the Pale. Lord Grey de Wilton was determined that he would be the sword of extirpation who would put down the Baltinglass revolt and put an end to the rebel O'Byrnes and O'Tooles. Grey chose to attack in the Wicklow Mountains, an unfortunate spot in which to try to display his military leadership to the high command in Ireland. Grey lead his troops in the Fall of 1580 in pursuit of the Baltinglass and O'Byrne rebels to Glenmalure, a steep and treacherous ravine in the Wicklow Mountains, held by Feagh Machugh O'Byrne. Grey brought with him to Glenmalure Henry Bagenal and Nicholas Malby so they could see firsthand the ferocity of his campaign against the rebels.

Climbing in the slippery, steep, wooded glen where the Irish kerne and galloglass of the Wicklow clans were hiding, Grey's troops found their armor a weighty, exhausting burden. The troops under the field command of Sir Peter Carew (a cousin of the Peter Carew who claimed the Idrone lands), Captain Audley, General Francis Cosby, and Master of the Ordinance, Jacques Wingfield, tried to navigate the bogs, push through the thick woods and traverse the slime-covered rocks of the steep glen, but they were repeatedly ambushed by the Irish kerne. Many of Grey's men and officers were hacked to death with battle axes appearing suddenly from behind the trees. The river in the steep glen became clogged with fallen bodies. Cosby, Audley, Moore and Peter Carew were all killed at Glenmalure.

Irish Kerne by Albrecht Dürer, 1521

The Baltinglass rebellion spawned a subsidiary Nugent rebellion that implicated the House of Kildare. Christopher Nugent, Baron of Delvin, the 11th Earl of Kildare's brother-in-law, was implicated in a conspiracy to join the Baltinglass revolt. Suspected as a conspirator in the Nugent conspiracy, Kildare was sent to be confined in the Tower and was held there from 1575 to 1580. He was tried for conspiracy in connection with the Baltinglass and Nugent rebels but acquitted, and before long was restored.[322]

The Pacification of Turlough O'Neill

The widely heralded Irish rebel victory at Glenmalure briefly roused and emboldened the Lord of Ulster, Turlough Luineach O'Neill. A notorious drunk, Turlough O'Neill was, for an O'Neill, comparatively easy to appease, but no one in the Dublin government, indeed none at Elizabeth's Court, ever for a moment took their eyes off the O'Neills of Ulster where, in 1580, Turlough, drunk or sober, could command as many as 5000 men. After Glenmalure,

THE NUGENT CONSPIRACY

In this conspiracy the Old English and native Irish gave the New English ample opportunity to eliminate competitors for the spoils so lavishly being plundered. The New English, however, falsely accused many Old English nobility who had not been participants in either the Baltinglass or the Nugent conspiracies.

Lord Christopher Nugent, Baron of Delvin, an Old English Oxford graduate, was arrested. As efforts to learn the identities of all involved continued, one conspirator, John Cusack, arrested in 1582, implicated a number of Pale gentry. Native Irish were also participants, notably Turlough O'Neill of Strabane, the O'Rourke and the O'Reillys, but evidence against a number of them was thin. Many who were caught were executed. Some 45 accused conspirators were hanged; some fled. William Nugent, the brother of Sir Christopher, fled to Rome, returning later to Ireland and to a pardon. Baltinglass also fled to the continent. In one "utter travesty of justice" Cusack falsely implicated Chief Justice Nicholas Nugent, and the Chief Justice was executed based on Cusack's accusation. Lord Grey de Wilton succeeded in blocking Ormond's efforts to extend leniency or amnesty to many other rebels in Leinster and Munster. Elizabeth refused amnesty for the Rebel Earl of Desmond, the Earl of Kildare and Viscount Baltinglass.

Turlough alarmed Elizabeth when he went to battle against forces under Sir Hugh Magennis south of Lough Neagh, and then began proposing new demands to increase his power and rights among the northern landholders of Ulster. Lord Grey de Wilton, stunned by the defeat at Glenmalure, was even more alarmed by Turlough O'Neill's southward reach and Grey decided to travel personally to Drogheda to pacify Turlough.

Had this still powerful northern chieftain decided to weigh in and help Eustace in the east and Desmond in the south, a strong Irish opposition might have developed to overwhelm the forces

Submission of Turlough Luineach O'Neill to Sir Henry Sidney

that the Crown was able or willing to devote to Ireland at that difficult moment. A northern rebellion did not develop, however. Once again the old Turlough was able to be appeased or bought off. Shane the Proud was by then long dead in an overgrown cairn at Cushendun. The Great O'Neill, Hugh, had not yet had his breach with Elizabeth. Indeed the still young Hugh O'Neill, given a prized cavalry command, actually fought on the English side during the Desmond rebellion. Thus, as Turlough turned his forces to saunter back to the North, Munster and Leinster were left on their own as the seats of rebellion, and theirs were to remain fragmented rebellions.

As the encroaching presence of the English in Munster took its new shape, with a presidency, several captains, forts and many martial law commissioners, the drain of support and revenue away from Earl Gerald of Desmond increased. He had been relentless in enforcing and collecting feudal and Gaelic exactions, leaving his feudal Old English tenants and historic Gaelic followers hard pressed, and making them more hostile to the Earl of Desmond than other parts of Ireland were to their lords. The unpaid arrearages owed him from tenants and monasteries and the forfeiture

Rocky Cairn Grave of Shane O'Neill at Cushendun

of amounts owed him because of other Crown actions, placed his valuable earldom under extreme financial stress. The Earl's outrage at the confiscation of most of his land and wealth, his inherent disloyalty, his reaction to Elizabeth's overt hostility to him, provoked him and had him lashing out against the intolerable growth of all these threats.

The Royal Audit of Black Tom Butler

In 1580, Black Tom Butler fell from grace when he drew the attention of Elizabeth's auditors. Put onto him by Anthony St. Leger,[323] the auditors succeeded in fueling enough suspicion to damage Butler at Court, but they proved nothing that would support serious charges. Elizabeth, nevertheless, instructed the Deputy, Lord Grey de Wilton, to terminate Butler's tenure as Lord Lieutenant of Munster. By then, however, Munster was in the midst of famine.

Colonel San Giuseppi Lands at Smerwick

With famine eclipsing other conditions, with threats from the north and the west, indeed from every part of Ireland, Tudor officials had their hands full in 1580. An invasion of Ireland from abroad was the last thing the Tudor administration would tolerate. And then an invasion came. But it was a small, ineffective band that came ashore; what awaited them was a vengeful Tudor commander ready to inflict horrifying reprisals.

The fortunes of the Munster rebels briefly appeared to rise in October, 1580, when the second Catholic invasion force arrived under Colonel Sebastiano di San Giuseppi; however, the invaders numbered only seven hundred. This eclectic group was seen by the British as another Spanish invasion, and there actually were a few Basques amid the force of Italians and varied prisoners who landed at Smerwick. They were quickly trapped by the forces of the brutal Lord Deputy Arthur Grey de Wilton in the *Duń an Óir* Fort FitzMaurice had once prepared on the Kerry coast. When San Giuseppi's force landed, Earl Gerald started to go to their aid; he went to the high ground above Smerwick, this time openly siding with the invaders. But again, he inexplicably failed to support them with any form of attack, leaving the besieged invaders, after days of heavy shelling, with no option but surrender. Many such surrenders occurred before and after Smerwick, but the merciless slaughter that followed was recounted with shock throughout Ireland. The tale was so graphic that it repelled those who learned of it, fueling hatred of Tudor Deputies for generations.

Grey's own report and Edmund Spenser's report both recount Grey ordering the breaking of arms and legs for torture and the slaughter of the 600 after they had surrendered at Smerwick.

Elizabeth did not denounce the massacre, instead she applauded the carnage at *Dún an Óir* fort and expressed her "joy", writing to Grey and extolling his action as helping "the hand of the Almighty's power" so as "to make men ashamed ever hereafter to disdain us."[324] She asked him to thank his men for their work and awarded Sir Walter Raleigh a large estate. But the Smerwick landing also added an element of desperation to the resolve of the Desmond rebels. This was the grim fate if they failed.[325]

GREY'S PROMISE

After it appeared certain that Grey's continued shelling of *Dun an Óir* Fort was making it indefensible, the Italians and Spaniards at the besieged fort sent a succession of negotiators, Alexander Bartoni and others, to plead for terms. They endeavored to convince Grey they had been misused and misled into joining the invasion. Naively, they told Grey that it was an invasion authorized only by lower than royalty – by the Governor of Bilbao, not by Philip II or the Pope. Grey then decided to treat them as mere pirates.

Sebastiano di San Giuseppi and his senior officers, and Oliver Plunket, his translator, came out to try one last time with Grey, before dawn on November 8, 1580. Grey, weeping, refused to grant safe conduct. The emotional exchange was virtually impossible to translate calmly and accurately. Afterwards, both sides evidenced confusion over what exactly had transpired. But on one central point, the Irish remain firm -- that Grey promised the Italians mercy if they surrendered.

After brief fire on the morning of November 8, a surrender flag was hoisted. What followed has become known as *Graia fides* – Grey's promise (literally Grey's faith). The few Irish women with them were hanged. Oliver Plunkett, William Walsh and Father Lawrence Moore were taken to the blacksmith where their arms and legs were broken in three places each. They were left to suffer for two days and were then hanged, drawn and quartered. The Italians were herded inside Dun an Oir Fort and stabbed with pikes and swords. Captain Walter Raleigh and Captain Humfrey Mackworth commanded the company of men who carried out this final grisly execution murdering all 600 after their surrender.

The Munster Famine

The rebellion took a terrible toll on south Munster; food had become very scarce. Famine and disease spread to the east and north and finally engulfed all of Munster. Horsemeat began to be eaten, at first only very reluctantly, but before long horses were sought for sustenance and gladly eaten.

In 1581 Lord Grey de Wilton issued orders for a ruthless assault on Munster.[326] That assault even by the diminished army, coinciding with the Munster famine, traumatized the people of Munster. No one was immune from the inevitable diseases that were always the worst horror of famines.[327] Father Nicholas Sander was one of them; he died of dysentery and starvation in April 1581 at Kilmore.

Lord Grey de Wilton as Deputy swept through Munster. He was "ruthlessly severe, and yet not successful." This was so, "in spite of the thousands slain, and a province made a desert."[328] Grey boasted almost 1,500 killings. Ormond followed suit; he boasted killing over 3,000. The Deputies prowled the country with their troops and there followed in their wake many tales of the Deputies and their soldiers hanging the Irish that were so awful that they bore "sometimes a touch of the grotesque."[329] Warham St. Leger reported that "Munster is nearly unpeopled by the murders done by the rebels, and the killings by the soldiers; 30,000 dead of famine in half a year, besides numbers that are hanged and killed."[330]

The Killing of Sir John Fitzgerald

In January 1582, Sir John FitzGerald, the leader of the FitzMaurice rebels and instigator of many other Desmond rebellion adventures, met his end. At Aherlow he and his men happened upon an English armed party led by John Zouche that was out in search of the rebels. Zouche, through skill or luck, recognized Sir John on the road and killed him. He sent Sir John's head on a pike to Dublin Castle and his body to hang from the great portal in Cork.

Lord Grey had as his secretary the poet Edmund Spenser,[331] who chronicled many of the events of this era. Spenser's horrific description of starved and craven Munster Irish crawling ghost-like and emaciated from the woods stands as one of history's most graphic depictions of the multiple horrors of real famine.[332]

Faced with such inhuman conditions, all Tudor officials at the royal Court and in Dublin were insistent that the war simply had to be brought to an end. But there were few options available to Elizabeth short of tracking down and killing the Rebel Earl of Desmond. A well- developed plan to end the war was presented by Archbishop Adam Loftus in a letter to Lord Burghley. It involved pardoning Earl Gerald as a way to bring him in before the famine and pestilence worsened; but the Loftus plan was rejected.[333]

The Countess Seeks Mercy

The greatest desperation was, perhaps, that of the fugitive Desmonds themselves. In May 1582 Eleanor appeared at Dublin Castle as if from nowhere, exhausted and in rags, throwing herself at Lord Grey's feet and begging for mercy. But she was simply sent back to rejoin Gerald. Eleanor, however, refused to stop trying to save them both. She made perilous sporadic visits to Grey and other government officials, encouraged by nothing more than vague assurances of safe conduct. In June she surfaced again, still exhausted and emaciated. She met again with Grey at Maryborough, but this time Grey took Eleanor captive. She was held in Dublin, but there she had the opportunity to visit her 11 year old son James who was held at Dublin Castle. Elizabeth, her patience with the efforts to capture Gerald gone, directed Grey to instruct Eleanor that mercy would be shown Gerald if he surrendered, but Grey ignored Elizabeth's order.[334] Instead he dismissed Eleanor to rejoin Gerald and resume her miserable stealth existence, living only to elude capture – and a wretched existence it was. They lived the life of hunted renegades in the woods and hills, sometimes sneaking into freezing rivers to hide while soldiers beat the bushes nearby in search of them.

The Earl Stays a Rebel

These hardships and rejections spurred Gerald to gather his remaining supporters and resume his attacks. Somehow reinvigorated, he and his uncle, the Seneschal of Imokilly, plundered Tipperary and Kerry. During the Summer of 1582, Gerald built up his troop strength at Aherlow and commenced successful attacks in Tipperary, the Rock of Cashel and finally Cahir Castle on the River Suir where he executed many Butlers. He proceeded on to Carrick on Suir and badly damaged Black Tom Butler's castle. On to Fermoy, he slaughtered the English garrison and many of the villagers. On November 13, he attacked Youghal again.

Ormond and Pelham burned the villages and lands that might help the Rebel Earl. In Dublin, Lord Grey's administration was becoming increasingly tense over Gerald's surprising ability to carry on the rebellion. Grey's anxiety was rising for he was publicly failing in his orders to end the Desmond Wars. He tried to stamp out the flame of the final rebels by burning crops to spoil the harvest and drive away the cattle. English forces elsewhere had used these tactics, but only as an emergency measure. Grey, however, used scorched earth in an intentional effort to spread and to worsen the famine. Much of Munster was devastated by the rebellion, with scores of castles and lands destroyed or badly burned and vast acreage confiscated. Contemporaries wrote that the lowing of a single cow could not be heard anywhere from the Dingle coast to the Rock of Cashel.

The Queen Sends the Earl's Worst Enemy to Get Him

Hearing of the desperate state of Munster crumbling under the spreading famine, Elizabeth re-commissioned the demoted old stalwart Black Tom Butler to bring it to an end. She appointed him Lord General with pardon power. Weary of famine, pestilence and privation caused by the Desmond War, pardons were quickly accepted by several lords whom Gerald had to depend upon if he were to survive. Butler in his campaign to bring the war, and not coincidentally, the Desmond earldom to an end, pardoned lavishly wherever he and his men ventured, and the tactic eroded the last vestiges of Geraldine support. Lord Maurice Roche, Lord Barry, the Baron of Lixnaw, the Seneschal of Imokilly, and Patrick Condon and 300 of his followers accepted pardons. But for Gerald, Black Tom and the Dublin administration continued to demand unconditional surrender. Lord Grey bristled even at Ormond's other pardons despite the progress they appeared to bring. Privately Grey remained deeply concerned that Black Tom might pardon Gerald as well.

By early 1583, before the occasion for a pardon could present itself, many around Gerald had already deteriorated to near starvation and Gerald was not much better.[335] It was now easily seen that Gerald, if found, would have no support and no leverage to demand terms. The powerful magnate who had once stood toe to toe with Elizabeth, barking with outrage, unapologetic, defiant, was now a broken, terrified fugitive. Deputy Grey took steps to assure that Elizabeth refused any plea any official might make to include the Earl and the Countess in any amnesty. Neither Grey nor those around him wanted mercy for the Earl. They wanted him dead because that was how they could confiscate Munster.

Near the end, Eleanor capitulated; she sought a meeting with Ormond in Cork to plead for mercy for herself and Desmond, but Ormond rejected her pleas. He forwarded her petition to Grey who purported to be affronted by the arrogance he saw in Eleanor seeking mercy for Gerald who had, as Grey believed, enticed the Smer-

The Death of the Earl of Desmond

wick force into Ireland. But in June 1583, a desperate Eleanor simply surrendered while Gerald remained hiding in the mountains. She did so after seeking terms for Gerald one last time, but Butler could see the end was at hand, and he saw no need to endure the criticisms at Court and in Dublin Castle which a pardon of Gerald would unleash.

The Final Hiding Place

Gerald knew the consequences of surrender. He and a small band of close followers continued in hiding, starving and desperate. The end that finally befell the once proud and wealthy Earl of Desmond was a miserable one. He died near the comfortable Desmond estate at Tralee, but hiding in the woods in a bare hut, close to where he had been fostered and raised by the O'Moriartys of that area. His life had come full circle. It was the O'Moriartys who slew him.

For five months, the earl had prowled the woods of southwest Munster, hiding in the Slieve Mish Mountains, until November 1583 when Maurice O'Moriarty, a farmer who had been robbed by the Earl's ragtag followers weeks earlier, discovered the cabin in the Glenageenty Woods where Gerald had taken refuge. O'Moriarty and a small group, a posse of sorts, quietly surrounded the cabin, waited until dawn and burst in. There Gerald lay on a mat. As they attacked, he seized upon his last desperate hope that he was close to the land of friendly clans and cried out, "I am the Earl of Desmond. Spare me." But O'Moriarty responded: "Thou hast killed thyself long ago."[336] They dragged him away and beheaded him. When they presented the head of the Earl to Sir William Stanley at Castlemaine, the O'Moriartys received 1,000 pounds silver. The head of the Earl of Desmond was sent to Black Tom Butler at Kilkenny Castle who, too old to gloat, forwarded it to Elizabeth who triumphantly impaled it on London Bridge.

With the death of Gerald FitzGerald, Earl of Desmond, the Gaelic society in south Munster, the most Irish of the Irish Earldoms, passed into a new phase of history, in which Munster was finally vulnerable to being taken and shaped by English in their own style. The confiscation of the Earl of Desmond's vast lands by the legal process of attainder took 3 years. It gave the Crown "the largest expanse of land in Ireland held by one man,..."[337] It was given out as a reward for services to the Crown and to English developers. The biggest shares of the Desmond lands were doled out to the British military commanders – Sir William Herbert, Sir Edward Denny, Sir Warham St. Leger and even Lord Grey de Wilton's secretary, Edmund Spenser. The displaced Irish were destined to be uprooted "flying to the mountains or the forest to die by starvation, or to live as savages or as robbers."[338]

Gerald, for all the upheaval his troublesome tenure as an earl had caused Elizabeth, had achieved very little. His leadership was poor and his military strategy uninspired, though his daring once in actual combat was not to be discounted. However, his losses at Carrigafoyle, Castleisland, Askeaton and Castlemaine, coupled with his failure to relieve San Giuseppi's Italian force at Smerwick at a crucial time, have left his legend branded with stains of lack of initiative and indecision.

Perrot and the Plantation of Munster

Once the Rebel Earl of Desmond had been slain, the final rebels were quickly taken.[339] Archbishop Dermot O'Hurley[340] was publicly executed in Dublin.[341] The Desmond rebellion, however, did not educate Elizabeth about Irish conquest. She continued to believe that she could plant English settlers in Munster and eventually Anglicize the hostile south. When the solution to the Irish problem was eventually fashioned by Queen Elizabeth and her courtiers, it was "a solution that was shrouded in enormous slaughter, suffering and devastation."[342]

Lord Deputy Perrot

Sir John Perrot[343] lobbied the Queen harder and more persistently than any to be named Deputy,[344] flooding her with ideas for subduing and governing Ireland. He was warned by those close to him not to seek or accept the post, but he paid them no heed, and in 1584, Perrott was elated as he began his tenure as Lord Deputy, but he would live to regret this stroke of good fortune.

Perrot would oversee the Plantation of Munster following the Articles of Plantation for the Desmond lands that had been approved in June 1582 when Plantation of Munster had actually begun after the attainder of the Earl of Desmond and his family.[345]

To do so, however, vast areas of Munster were confiscated by the Crown and offered for plantation. Perrot summoned a parliament which voted to take new acreage due to the attainder of Gerald's rebel followers — their lands were confiscated and awarded to English adventurers chosen by Elizabeth. By June 1586 a half million acres had been divided into plots and granted to English planters. Some 40,000 acres in Youghal went to Sir Walter Raleigh alone for his valuable service, including his services in the slaughter at Smerwick.

To solidify control and enforce English law throughout Ireland Elizabeth established the Court of Castle Chamber in Dublin, a parallel to the infamous Star Chamber in London. It was clear to Elizabeth, however, that martial law had been divisive and had provoked hatred and rebellion. Hoping for improved relations, she ordered martial law gradually curtailed starting in 1586.

However, there was little success in the new plantation. By 1589, only 10,000 New English settlers had actually taken over land in Munster. Ultimately only 210,000 acres, less than half of the confiscated lands, were planted by the undertakers and their tenants and the exasperated Queen gave up on the idea of plantation of the rest of Munster, leaving the Desmond lands dominated neither by native Irish, Anglo Irish or by planted English.

14

Connaught — The Pirate Queen Meets the Virgin Queen

They "think no man dead until his head be off"[346]
— A description of Ulick Burke ("The Beheader") and his men.

The increasing Tudor coercion and executions like those that had outraged the earldom of Desmond, provoked muffled discontent in the west of Ireland among the Burkes of the historically more loyal Clanrickard earldom of Connaught. The Burkes' muted reactions to encroachment from Lord Grey deWilton and later President Edward Fitton were not due to their peaceful nature. The Burkes were quite unruly, but the Clanrickard Burkes were heavily dependent on royal support in maintaining their power base. Despite political and military moves against them, the Burkes held their powder and endured encroachments. But even the Burkes would only endure so much.

The Clanrickard Burkes of Galway and the MacWilliam Burkes of Mayo were very different constituencies by the time of Elizabeth's attempts at Anglicization. During her father's reign, Lord Deputy Leonard Grey, on his first visit to Galway in 1536, had concluded that the Burkes were disrupting his efforts to complete the pacification of Galway. Back then, Grey decided to support Ulick Burke as the new leader in Galway to secure cooperation. Ulick Burke was known as "The Beheader." This attention-getting sobriquet was earned by the dozen galloglass who always accompanied him. It was said of them: They "think no man dead until his head be off." Grey decided to support Ulick when he realized that Ulick was easily bribed to stay loyal. Through various enticements, Ulick was

THE TWO BURKE CLANS OF CONNAUGHT

The name Burke that was so dominant in the Connaught leadership in the 16th Century came from the early Norman de Burghos, descended from the powerful Norman William de Burgh and his offspring. A junior branch of the family became the Burkes of Connaught.

William de Burgh, came with the early Normans in 1185, and conquered Connaught. His descendent, Walter de Burgh, became 1st Earl of Ulster (2nd creation). Those Burkes in the west became very Irish as Normans go. But the Earldom of Ulster reverted to the English royal family for want of a male inheritor when the Countess of Ulster, Elizabeth de Burgho, married the son of King Edward II, Lionel Duke of Clarence, and Lionel became Earl of Ulster. The Connaught lordship of the Burkes was divided into the two separate lordships of Galway (the Clanrickard Burkes) and Mayo (the MacWilliam Burkes).

The Burkes of Connaught fought an internecine civil war among themselves in the 1330s. Two Edmund Burkes fought against each other and against an early Ulick Burke. The war resulted in the three Burke clans of Galway, Mayo and Limerick. The titles of the Clanrickard Burkes of Galway and the MacWilliam Burkes of Mayo title is MacWilliam Iochtar meaning lower MacWilliam (though Mayo is north), and the Galway title is MacWilliam Uachtar meaning upper MacWilliam (though Galway is south). In Limerick a lordship called Clanwilliam held the lands of Castleconnell.

The two sons of 14th century William (Liath) (the Grey) Burke founded the two major Connaught families which became the rulers of the two Burke earldoms in Connaught. His son Ulick took control of Galway and his line became the Clanrickard Burkes. Ulick's brother Edmund (Albanach) took control of Mayo. The Mayo Burkes have most commonly been called simply MacWilliam Burkes and their leader The MacWilliam.

After Ulick Burke established lordship over the Galway Burkes, under the Tudor re-grant, Ulick's son Richard Burke became the Earl of Clanrickard in 1544, calling himself William Uachtar MacWilliam or simply William of Clanrickard.

To the south of the lands of the two Burke clans, Thomond (Clare) in Munster was ruled by The O'Brien. Sligo to the north of the Burkes was ruled by the O'Connor Sligo, and Leitrim by the O'Rourkes under the O'Donnells.

persuaded to agree to surrender and regrant, and to abandon his army. After Lord Grey was recalled, Ulick embarked on fulfilling his submission commitments. As he did, he realized that it would be difficult to spread the English language as required when he could not speak it himself, or to pay the agreed taxes when he had no funds, or to remain loyal when he was incorrigibly rebellious. Ulick also found that whatever benefit English succession rights offered others, for him their value was somewhat elusive since he had no readily identifiable heir. With him, marriage, mistresses, legitimate children and bastards were casually mixed without clear understandings and record keeping; to him, a right to designate an heir hardly seemed a great prize. As O'Neill and others had aspired to be named Earl of Ulster, Burke aspired to be more than Clanrickard. He wanted to be the Earl of Connaught.

Ulick Burke traveled to London in 1543 to receive the title of 1st Earl of Clanrickard, but he became ill and died during his trip back to Ireland. At his death, Ulick left at least two legal wives as well as several concubines, most of whom had produced children. The Earl of Ormond chose the second Earl of Clanrickard from among Ulick's legal and quasi-legal offspring. He selected Richard Burke who was yet a boy, and he appointed a protector of sorts to rule during Richard's early years, an appointment that merely provoked contention and bloodshed when the protector later refused to step aside.

The Sassanach

The successor, Richard Burke, 2nd Earl of Clanrickard, was far more willing to Anglicize, and he readily became a royalist. He took to wearing English clothes and displayed distinctly English ways. The Connaught population was quick to scorn any who converted to English ways and they took to deriding Richard Burke as the "Sassanach" (the Englishman).[351] The Sassanach had six wives and so many dalliances and concubines that it was said his practices "recall those of the poultry yard…." He fathered sons who were brothers, half-brothers, and mere bastards. He developed a host of enemies, and among the most serious were two of his sons, John and Ulick, who refused to join in his English conversion. They refused even to speak English or wear English dress.

President Fitton of Connaught

As the century progressed, Richard Burke's worst nemesis, however, was Sir Edward Fitton, a ruthless Tudor courtier who became President of Connaught in 1569. Fitton began destroying homes and tower houses and killing the inhabitants of abbeys, concluding that was the easiest way to empty them. The Tudor plan was to shire Connaught and the other provinces and create the organizational backbone for English administration, the framework for extension of the common law, and the crucible in which to create loyalty to the Crown. A President would govern each province and Sheriffs would collect taxes and enforce law and order. Henry Sidney was the chief proponent of shireing. To achieve, reform, however, this had to work. They had to come up with a financial model by which Ireland itself could generate the financial support for English public administration — they chose a composition rent. This rudimentary wealth taxation began as an experiment in the east and the south. But soon it was being touted as the foundation of modern public finance — prematurely it turned out.

The rents were a failure. The British imposed rents unilaterally; they were excessive and gratingly uneven; and they were widely condemned as grossly unfair. Worse, the system itself was fragile and when a poor harvest impaired the stability of the local economy, the rent system failed. Early programs charging rents of this type in Leinster and Munster had met little success, but, once the early lessons were learned, the English believed that a far more thoughtful program of negotiated rents in the west, in Connaught would be more successful.

Peace in Connaught, however, was Fitton's top priority. Religious reformation was also still a Tudor goal, but conversion would have to be preceded by elimination of the secular practices of Gaelic life. Nevertheless, when Catholic clergy were discovered, Fitton expelled them to pave the way for reformation.

Pacification of Connaught, however, proved to be a turbulent process. Violence erupted in Connaught over the same kind of outrageous land confiscations as in Munster as land titles perfected under the Irish system were under a cloud with the advent of the English legal system. In addition, there were the perennial boundary disputes, protests over the right to wear Irish dress, quarrels over replacing the Brehon Law, fights for leadership confused by the abolition of tanistry. People who knew no English demanded the right to speak the Irish language. The Connaught Irish challenged many other Tudor initiatives. As Fitton went about wholesale dismantling of Irish life, trouble spread in northern Connaught and Thomond. Conor O'Brien, the Earl of Thomond, and Brian O'Rourke of Leitrim both rebelled. Fitton called on Black Tom Butler to help with the most immediate trouble — the Burkes of Clanrickard and the O'Briens of Thomond. The anger smoldering in both of these recently created earldoms came to a head when it came time for a Sheriff to be appointed.

The Sheriff was to wield great power including martial law authority in a Tudor shire, and a loyal earl had a right to expect that he would be the Sheriff. However, the Tudor Presidents wanted just the opposite. They saw that appointing an Earl's strongest rival as Sheriff would be an effective power balancing tactic; that it would help erode the power of the earl, and help entrench the President. Other steps to undermine the earls were also not overlooked in this escalating chess game. Tudor officials openly supported the earls' discontented sub-lords, vassal chiefs and sept heads; the officials gave them freehold status and assurances of support from the provincial council and protection against coyne and livery. With these stratagems, Anglicization of the far west of Ireland finally began to gain momentum, but it was done at the cost of alienating the Connaught earls.

Conor O'Brien, the Earl of Thomond, expected to be named Sheriff, but Fitton instead named the Earl's worst enemy, a candidate from another O'Brien faction, Sir Tadhg MacMurrough O'Brien, but Conor O'Brien would not tolerate the encroachment. He began arresting English officials, including the new Sheriff. Conor O'Brien also boycotted Fitton's assizes at Ennis and denied cattle, food and crops to Fitton's army so that the army could no longer be billeted in Clare. This confrontation proved far easier to quell than others. Black Tom Butler was called to intercede, and he marched to Thomond and convinced Conor O'Brien to stand down. In April 1570 Conor O'Brien abandoned his Irish dress and hair style, and made his submission at Court in London, receiving a pardon and pledging loyal behavior.

CLARE - THE O'BRIENS OF THOMOND

In 1543, Thomond and Clanrickard had been granted earldoms, Clanwilliam was granted a lordship, and McNamara and O'Shaughnessy in south and central Connaught were made knights. The Earls of Thomond and Clanrickard were more receptive to Anglicization than the Earl of Desmond because they historically had received more government support to hold the local lords of the west at bay.

O'Brien succession disputes in Thomond had never been mild family quarrels. Donal O'Brien had murdered the heir designate to the Thomond earldom. The decedent was no distant enemy; it was his brother, Donough. Donal, nevertheless, was elected as The O'Brien, but his dead brother's troublesome son, Conor, was the Tudor choice to succeed Donal as Earl. Donal resisted the selection of Conor as Earl of Thomond, and in 1564 Earl Gerald of Desmond had marched to Thomond in support of Donal, but they were overwhelmed by Earl Conor O'Brien's supporters, the Earl of Clanrickard and the Earl of Ormond, Black Tom Butler.

Trouble continued, and Fitton imposed martial law in Connaught from 1570 to 1572. He arrested and jailed Connaught earls and clan leaders at the first pull on their swords. Fitton was even wary of the Sassanach, despite all of the Earl's trappings of loyalty, so in Galway, as he had in Thomond, Fitton appointed an opponent of the Earl as Sheriff, in the process shattering any hope of calm in Galway. When Fitton named John Burke as Galway Sheriff, the once stable Clanrickard earldom exploded.

Jolted by Fitton's ham-handed display of political control, and outraged at Fitton's draconian martial law punishments, the Clanrickard Burkes began with open protests. Thinking it might head off the growing signs of rebellion, Fitton arrested the Sassanach and imprisoned him in Dublin Castle. Though much of the province detested the Earl of Clanrickard as much as his sons did, many followed the sons when they began to foment retaliation throughout the province. Ulick, John and William Burke, were all born of different mothers and could scarcely tolerate each other let alone their father. However, the arrest of the Sassanach was to them that final intolerable slap added to the kick they had received from the boot heel of martial law. This was too flagrant a challenge to their own future power for them to tolerate. When word reached Clanrickard's sons that their father was imprisoned, Burke blood (or the threat of their own capture) proved thicker than their hatred of their father. Their embarrassment at his Sassanach sobriquet was pushed aside by their outrage at his incarceration, and in 1572 the Burke sons rebelled.

Elizabeth was irate when she learned of the Earl's arrest. She saw it as a byproduct of Fitton's quarrels with the Deputy, his nemesis, Sir William FitzWilliam. She knew that Clanrickard was loyal and that it was his sons who were not. Though tempted to intervene, she succumbed to indecision, failed to countermand the arrest, and the Earl languished in prison for six months. As he did, John and Ulick Burke assembled a rebel army. Heavily supported by galloglass, they proceeded to burn Athlone, Athenry and its abbey (where Church of Ireland clergy now lived), and they began to threaten Galway.

Fitton was withdrawn first to Dublin, then to London. He was soon allowed to return, but in a position akin to membership in a triumvirate. He was restyled as Vice-Treasurer and province commissioner with the Earl of Thomond and the Earl of Clanrickard. Government by these enemies was impossible and the Deputy repeatedly asked for the appointment of a skilled and acceptable President.

President Malby of Connaught

Due more to her own disgust with Fitton than to a desire for a pre-emptive solution to the Clanrickard rebellion, Elizabeth recalled Fitton in 1573. Within three years the Clanrickard Burkes rebelled again and Captain Nicholas Malby, the driven Puritan colonel, was named President of Connaught in 1576. Malby became heavily occupied, as had Fitton before him, with the incorrigible Burkes. The Sassanach's sons, John and Ulick, were arrested, but they escaped within months and burned Athenry a second time. Malby was ordered to track them down, and when they eluded him and refused to surrender, Malby decimated the lands of John and Ulick Burke, destroying homes and killing young and old alike among their followers.

The Clanrickard Burkes were supported in their uprisings by the Mayo Burkes. But Malby finally put down the latest Clanrickard revolt in brutal fashion, killing many Burke followers and forcing them to submit.

Sir Henry Sidney returned as Deputy and he released the Sassanach upon his promise to subdue his sons, and they relented temporarily. Sidney put the sons under close supervision for a time in Dublin, but when released, they raced back to Connaught throwing their English clothes into the Shannon and restarting the revolt. Sidney blamed the Sassanach for not controlling his sons and he arrested the Earl again, sent him to the Tower of London and seized Clanrickard's Castle at Loughrea. The sons attacked Loughrea, but the rebellion then stalled. The Sassanach's son, William, surrendered, but was hanged in Galway. This time the Sassanach remained six years in the Tower, until in 1582, wasted and dying, he was sent home.

The Sassanach's death spurred a cutthroat competition between his remaining sons, John and Ulick, and they each petitioned Elizabeth to be allowed to succeed him. Ulick won and became the 3rd Earl of Clanrickard. His half-brother John was given the consolation prize of Baron of Leitrim. Soon after becoming Earl, Ulick and his followers stabbed and killed John to prevent a challenge.[352] With his father dead and his brother assassinated, it became clear to Ulick Burke that fortune lay with the Crown and he became steadfastly loyal. The relieved English administration in Ireland pardoned him for the murder of his brother, conveniently treating it as a legal extermination. Nevertheless, Ulick Burke continued to refuse to speak anything but Irish.

The Mayo Burkes

The Burkes who dominated Mayo were another story. Called the *Mac Iarlas* (the MacWilliam Burkes), they were a different line than the Clanrickard Burkes, but Fitton's army had trouble subduing this Burke clan as well. The MacWilliam Burkes of Mayo had fought Fitton at Shrule Castle in 1570, and when Fitton was removed to London in 1573, the temperament of the MacWilliam Burkes had seemed to improve for a time.[353]

When Malby succeeded Fitton in 1576, he promised the Connaught landholders protection. He assured them he would set them free from the burdens of coyne and livery, cess charges and other costs of billeting troops. In exchange for rents, Malby promised the local lords protection from the MacWilliam Burkes and from each other. Despite the tone of a protection racket, the sublords found Malby more convincing than Fitton. They came to believe that Malby was interested in putting an end to the power the earls and lords had used to coerce their lesser lords into supporting them.

Malby also divided the power of Mayo's rival clans. At the time, Mayo was dominated by Shane MacOliverus MacWilliam, known as the MacWilliam Iochtar and his tanaiste. "The Iron Burke", Richard-an-Iarainn Burke,[354] the MacOliverus tanaiste, rose against his rival, Richard MacOliverus, in 1580, and Malby felt he had to intervene to stop the fight. To display his power over them, Malby executed a castle garrison at Donamona. Then he accepted Richard-an-Iarainn as the MacWilliam Iochtar, but diluted his power by appointing the competing claimant, Richard MacOliverus, Sheriff.[355] As notable as the "Iron Burke" was,[356] it is his wife who captivated the attention of the history of Mayo like no one before her, or since she disappeared into the mists – she was Grace O'Malley.

The Pirate Queen of Clare Island

Grace O'Malley (*Gráinne Uaáile NíMháille*) forged a unique life in this male dominated world of 16th century Ireland with her extravagant bold persona, her array of talents, her gravitas and fighting style. Scores of men were willing to follow her as their leader in preference to other men. She is often called a man's woman;[357] she was attractive and appealing to men and noted for foregoing the modesty of some women of the day. Her exceptional charisma apparently came from physicality, strength, fearlessness, the best qualities of a boatswain and a sea captain, badges of honor including massive callouses from handling sails, oars and hawsers, and a lusty freedom with men.[358]

She decided quite young that she would simply not take a back seat to the men. She refused to leave tough and intimidating tasks to the clansmen around her. Grace O'Malley could do it herself, all of it. She loved her men and they her. Her clan followers set aside any embarrassment and followed her as their leader. The other clan leaders were fearless, strong, lusty and earthy, and Grace was all of that. In the exceptionally long life she lived, she would need all those traits, and she used them to great effect.

They called her a Pirate Queen, sounding at first like a one eyed, with a peg leg who lived on the high seas, but she was very appealing to men and campaigned mostly on land. She led the O'Flaherty's of Connaught and the MacWilliam Burkes of Mayo in raids and plunder on land far more than all the nautical raids. Two husbands and some lovers gave her a robust love life, but the murders of her lover and her son and the deaths of her husbands sorely tested her, but she always held on and she always struck back. She was bold enough to confront politicians and royalty face to face at Council and Court and did so with great effectiveness.

Much of Grace's life was high drama. She married young, to Dónal O'Flaherty (*Dónal an Chogaidh O'Flaithbheartaigh*), an authentic warlord who was constantly in battles with his rivals, the Joyces. He was killed by them in 1560.[359] Grace captured Cock's Castle in Lough Corrib to retaliate. Grace was then 30 and bold and ambitious, but she was ineligible under Brehon or English law to be elected Chief of the O'Flaherty Name. She had nevertheless succeeded in establishing herself as a commander of fighting forces on land and on sea and many O'Flahertys and other clans' members followed her when she decided to move back to Clare Island.

She took a young lover, a seafarer who had washed ashore on Achill Island. He was much younger than Grace. Grace tended to him and likely saved him. But O'Flaherty feuds with the nearby MacMahons lead to her lover's end when the MacMahons encountered him and murdered him.[360] Grace set aside her mourning and her outrage took over; she went after the MacMahons, caught and killed the murderers with the help of her men, then took the Mac-Mahon, Doona Castle.

Grace entered into a second marriage, initially calling it a trial marriage. Her new husband was the "Iron Burke," Richard Fitzdavid MacWilliam-an-Iarain Burke. During the era of the uprising in Galway by the Clanrickard Burkes, Grace continued to lead raids at sea against opportunistic targets for booty and she sailed to west coast Irish ports to raid there as well.[361] In March 1577 Lord Deputy Henry Sidney came with his army to Mayo, but there he found a friendly and cooperative Grace O'Malley. Among Sidney's officers was his son, Philip Sidney, and Philip and Grace O'Malley became friends.[362] She agreed to submit to Sidney, and she pledged the aid of her ships and her seamen. Nevertheless, afterwards, she continued to launch the occasional raid when she felt the need.

In one such raid in March 1578 in Desmond lands she was caught by the Earl of Desmond and jailed at Limerick, then at Dublin Castle, but she was freed when her husband began a revolt. A year later, when the Earl of Desmond was proclaimed a traitor, Grace's husband, "Iron Burke", went to the aid of The Rebel Earl

Sir Philip Sidney

and launched raids in Connaught. But Richard came under attack by the forces of Sir Nicholas Malby and he was forced to back down and in 1580, Richard, the "Iron Burke," submitted. When a succession dispute arose after The MacWilliam died in 1580, Malby helped settle the dispute and supported "Iron Burke" in becoming the MacWilliam. Malby, however, was grudging as to continued use of the Irish title by the Burkes who had adopted Gaelic custom and the Brehon law. Malby extracted commitments that the Mac-William Burkes would be subject to English law, and to balance power, Malby appointed "Iron Burke's" opponent as Sheriff.

President Bingham of Connaught

Malby died in March of 1584, and Sir Richard Bingham was named to succeed him as President of Connaught just as Perrot arrived in Dublin as Deputy. Perrot brought with him the same volcanic temper he had displayed in Munster, and that temper erupted repeatedly at Bingham. Where Malby and Sidney had seen eye to eye, Bingham and Perrot were very public opponents, and the policies of Bingham in Connaught badly conflicted with Perrot's plans.

By the time of Bingham's arrival, the leadership of the Connaught lordships had also changed. Ulick Burke in Galway was loyal. Donough O'Brien, also loyal, succeeded in 1583 to the Earldom of Thomond. With peaceful Earls in Connaught, the stage was set for Perrot to formalize control of Connaught, the scheme that became known as the Composition of Connaught[363] (see table on page 195).

With peace and the promise of a healthy financial base for English governance, New English immigration toward the west of Ireland began. However, only desultory small groups of English came as far as Connaught; large scale plantation of Connaught failed to develop. Yet the *Taoisigh* and *Tanaisti* who would have succeeded under the old system had now been made to feel insecure in their future rights. They also developed a rising fear of land confiscations, and, as feared, more Connaught lords' estates were confiscated.

Sir Richard Bingham

The MacWilliam Burke Rising

In 1586 The MacWilliam, "Iron Burke," Richard MacOliverus, died and Edmund Burke, the Gaelic law successor, claimed the banned title. Bingham, however, intervened, as had Malby six years earlier when Shane MacOliverus died. Bingham decided to end the MacWilliam Burkes' Gaelic customs. Bingham awarded the Mac-

William land to the very young William MacOliverus instead of the Gaelic law successor, Edmund Burke. Bingham also seized Hag's Castle on Lough Mask and that further infuriated Edmund Burke, so the MacWilliam Burkes called a rising, and the Joyces, Clandonnells and O'Malleys all rallied to the Burkes' side. Bingham caught and executed the Burke leaders and 70 of their followers in Galway, extinguished the rebellion, and expunged the MacWilliam Burke name. Bingham also put down revolts in Mayo and Leitrim with brutal thoroughness and, in the process, proved himself as ruthless as any.

Sir Richard Bingham, as President of Connaught, began to enforce the Composition of Connaught with inflexibility and brutal tactics. To enforce compliance by the MacWilliam Burkes, he apprehended Grace O'Malley's younger son, Tibbot,[364] and sent him as a hostage to serve the Sheriff of Sligo, his brother, George Bingham. Far worse, in 1586, Bingham and his brother John and their men captured and murdered Grace's son, Owen O'Flaherty. Bingham also hanged a number of Owen's men with no more basis than unproven accusations made to disguise what was a brazen confiscation of all their cattle and horses.[365]

Bingham's corruption was matched by his casual, offhand murder habits. He seemed to lack the patience to remit prisoners his men captured to custody. That took time and effort. Death was a quicker solution and it eliminated any bother that attended taking a captive, and he used death as the penalty for even minor infractions. Happening into his presence while being Irish was very risky. To him, every random arbitrary hanging was a royally ordained execution despite the complete absence of evidence of guilt or any adjudication by a tribunal. Bingham could seldom even assign words to justify why he executed Irish as readily as any man of his era. His attempt to recount why he abruptly executed Grace O'Malley's son Owen was especially vague.

There came a day when he finally caught Grace herself. She, along with a number of her men, were arrested by Bingham's men and brought to face punishment, and true to form he had the men executed. He decided to stage a grand finish for Grace herself, and ordered a delay for the erection of an elevated scaffold, better for staging the hanging. Once the gibbet was built to suit his dramatic taste, Grace was brought forward for the show, to face the scaffold and the spectators. One report says she was ascending the stairs when a commotion arose. A warrant arrived ordering Bingham to stop, and he did.[366]

Such a command was foreign to Bingham's typical treatment of prisoners and his usual bent. Thus, the warrant likely came from a powerful person, and for some important reason. One theory is that her life was spared by order of the Spymaster himself, Sir Francis Walsingham. Grace is thought to have been a valuable intelligence asset on Atlantic maritime threats and shipping. The other reason for Bingham's abrupt cancellation was that Grace's tough and unruly son in law, Richard Burke, known as "The Devil's Hook,"[367] agreed to reform and become peaceful in exchange for Bingham sparing her.

Massacre at Ardnaree

In 1586 the Mayo Burkes enlisted the support of a large contingent of Scots for their Connaught campaigns. The Scots arrived at Ardnaree, bringing their women and children with them; but Bingham's men captured them, then proceeded to hack to death "every man, woman and child of them just over 1,000."[368] One English captain complained of fatigue from hacking and stabbing so many.

The Final Clash of Bingham and Perrot

Bingham and Perrot could not get along.[369] Their disputes, both policy and personal, were incessant, but as their hatred continued to deepen, Perrot finally marched with troops to Connaught to confront Bingham. The Irish and the English in the west were suddenly treated to the spectacle of two Tudor leaders in a very public quarrel; at the height of it, Bingham was replaced. He was sent to the Netherlands leaving his cousin, Sir George Bingham, as Vice President of Connaught.

After all this repression and numerous arbitrary hangings by Bingham, Grace had the daring to travel to Dublin when Bingham was removed as President of Munster, to seek the ear of Lord Deputy Perrot, and turn the tale on Bingham. It was in May, 1587 that

Bingham was recalled from office and ordered to serve in Flanders. As soon as Grace learned that he was gone, she raced to Dublin to plead with Perrot and lay out the details of her mistreatment by Bingham, knowing how Perrot loathed Bingham. Perrot granted a pardon to Grace and to her sons as well.[370]

However, Perrot was then replaced in 1588 by Sir William Fitz-William, and FitzWilliam allowed Richard Bingham to return as President of Connaught. Bingham was delighted that Perrot was gone and that under the new Lord Deputy FitzWilliam he could now resume his harsh military rule in Connaught. Bingham was eventually charged with corruption and with committing a serious breach of the Composition of Connaught, but he was tried for this in Dublin in 1590 and was acquitted.[371]

The Meeting of the Queens

The inevitable historical crescendo finally sounded in 1599. Grace petitioned for an audience with the Queen. This gamey Pirate Queen came together with the Virgin Queen and the two talked and assessed each other and made peace.[372] The Queen first called for a report from Bingham and he sent one continuing his claim that Grace was the nurse of all rebellions in that part of Ireland,[373] but the Queen was not persuaded.[374] She ordered that Grace's son should be released[375] and she granted Grace the right to an income from clan lands.[376] Not long afterwards Bingham died of natural causes in 1599.

Grace's end was most theatrical. She disappeared.[377] What became of her is a mystery. The belief is that Grace O'Malley died at about age 73 in 1603 and may be buried in the Cistercian Abbey on Clare Island.

Perrot and the Poisoned Chalice

Perrot had joined the others who failed to please[378] the demanding Elizabeth.[379] He became another casualty[380] of Tudor Irish service, culminating in a failure of his 1585 parliament.[381] Perrot had also created many enemies, including Adam Loftus.[382] Even after Perrot was withdrawn,[383] the spiteful and vindictive FitzWilliam continued to seethe about him, and to fear that Perrot would expose FitzWilliam's corruption. He kept after Perrot until he had accumulated enough support to have Perrot convicted of treason.[384] To do so, FitzWilliam used forged evidence and vouched for stories fabricated by a criminal priest.[385] The false evidence fit the agenda of Lord Burghley, however, and Perrot was convicted. Elizabeth was never willing to execute Perrot, perhaps because the charges were suspicious, or perhaps because she believed the stories that he was a bastard of Henry VIII and her half-brother. Although this was doubtful, she knew that Perrot himself had claimed that he was. If so, killing him would have been another Tudor family political execution of sorts. In any event, she kept Perrot a prisoner in the Tower until his death.

In 1596 accusations against Bingham drew the attention of Lord Deputy William Russell and Bingham was removed again, charged with extortion and other infractions and brought to Dublin, but he left for London without leave and, for doing so, was thrown in the Fleet prison.[386] There he stayed, until the need for officers in the fight against O'Neill and O'Donnell grew severe and he was sent to Ireland. Bingham was replaced by the far better Sir Conyers Clifford who quickly made substantially better progress making peace with the chieftains in Mayo.

**MODERN TAX POLICY—
THE COMPOSITION OF CONNAUGHT**

In 1585, a province wide Composition agreement was established in Connaught, a scheme far more similar to a modern system of taxation than the imposed rent of 1577. Though based on the limited precedent of the composition rent that had worked earlier in parts of Connaught under Malby, the 1585 Composition of Connaught, unlike the earlier scheme, was a negotiated agreement. The land tax was payable only to the Crown. No other payments were required and those who paid were to be defended against all enemies, including local lords. It covered more of Connaught than earlier plans and, while expensive, the local lords saw it as a fair exchange for the freedom and protection that accompanied it. Gaelic titles such as *Taoiseach* and *Tanaiste* and Gaelic succession rights and forms of land ownership were to end. The 1585 Composition of Connaught appeared to be the perfect financial model for the peaceful Anglicization of a substantial part of previously ungovernable Ireland.

15

Ulster—Massacre on Rathlin Island

the rude magnificence of ancient Ulster[387]
— Edmund Campion

By far the most difficult challenge in Ireland for the English was always going to be Ulster,[388] and central and western Ulster would be difficult even for the English to enter.[389] Scots were coming in ever larger numbers to settle in the east of Ulster in Antrim and Down, and the idea of troublesome Scots in troublesome Ulster was profoundly disturbing to London. Though Scots in Ulster were viewed by the Tudor Court as intruders, in the 16th century these particular Scots were not without legal claim to Ulster lands. The MacDonnells came to Ulster because the Scottish monarchy had grown hostile to their clan; the MacDonnells' hold on the Scottish Isles of Islay and Kintyre had become very insecure, but they had a legitimate claim to large tracts in the northeast of Ulster. Marjorie Bisset, who inherited the Glens of Antrim, was the granddaughter of the King of Ulster, had married John More MacDonnell of the Scots Clan Donald and the MacDonnells thereby succeeded to her hereditary claim to the Glens of Antrim.[390] They also made their position there more tolerable by intermarriage with the clan aristocracy and by negotiating alliances with the O'Neills and O'Donnells. The MacDonnells' leader, Sorley Boy MacDonnell, had arranged the marriages of his sister and his widowed sister-in-law to two leaders of Ulster, Hugh Dubh O'Donnell (*Aodh Dubh U Domhnaill*) and Turlough Luineach O'Neill (*Turlough Luineach U Niall*).

Elizabeth, however, feared the Scots. She had developed serious anxiety over Mary Stuart and her allies in France, the Catholic nobility of the House of Guise. The specter of hostile Scots joining with rebellious Ulster Irish clans was unsettling. She gave orders to challenge the MacDonnells' expansion into Antrim at every opportunity, and to colonize the northeast with New English.

MARY QUEEN OF SCOTS

Mary Stuart, Mary Queen of Scots, was briefly Queen of France (1559-60) and of Scotland (1560-68), but despite her many efforts, and despite her lineage which provided her the claim as Elizabeth's most likely successor, she was never Queen of England. Mary, as the great granddaughter of Henry VII, was a blood heir to the English throne and heir apparent to the childless Elizabeth until Mary's execution.

Mary Stuart became Queen of Scotland at one week of age on the death of James V in 1542. Despite her Catholicism, she may well have succeeded Elizabeth absent a designation of a new successor. Her mother was Mary of Guise. In 1543 the Treaty of Greenwich bound her as a child bride to wed Prince Edward. Scots nobles, however, refused to accept an English king, and, in 1544, the Scots breached the Treaty. The English retaliated with the "Rough Wooing" of Mary Queen of Scots -- two years of brutal raids in the Scots borders.

In August 1548, Mary went to France and married the Dauphin, Francis of Alençon, who would later take the throne as Francis II. She was still only 6 years old. Mary's departure for France would seem to have ended England's urge to conquer Scotland, for war with Scotland now meant war with France. She became Queen of France in 1559 when Henry II took a fatal lance in his eye in a joust leaving the young Dauphin as King Francis II and Mary as his Queen. The two main threats to the royal Anjou dynasty were a powerful family of French Catholics, descendants of Charlemagne, the Duke of Guise and his family, and the reformed Protestant House of Bourbon. More threatening from England's perspective were the French alliances, the traditional alliance with Scotland, and a prospective major alliance with the papacy through the Duke of Guise' brother, the Cardinal of Lorraine, a potential Pope.

(continued)

(Mary Queen of Scots, continued)

England decided to invade Scotland and the English drove out the French, resulting in the Treaty of Edinburgh of 1560. When the French troops departed from Scotland after the Treaty of Edinburgh, the auld alliance between France and Scotland appeared broken.

As abruptly as Mary had become Queen of France, she moved back to Scotland only two years later. In December 1560 young King Francis II died and his 18 year old dowager, Mary, returned to Scotland in August 1561. In 1562, Elizabeth, herself only in her 20s, consented to invite Mary for a meeting. Elizabeth had received flattering notes from Mary but was envious and curious over comments from ambassadors and tactless intermediaries extolling Mary's beauty.[392] But in France the Duke of Guise attacked a Huguenot colony, civil war erupted, and Elizabeth abruptly cancelled the meeting with Mary, apologizing in part due to a growing fatigue and fever -- it proved to be smallpox.

In 1565 Elizabeth refused to send aid to support the Scottish Earl of Moray, James Stewart, in his campaign against Mary. The Earl of Argyll was supporting Stewart, and, upon England's refusal to support Stewart, Argyll switched his support in the Irish competition to Shane O'Neill. Mary married Lord Henry Darnley, a nephew of Henry VIII, in 1565. This marriage strengthened the case for her claim to the throne. In 1566 Mary gave birth to James[393] who 37 years later, would ascend the throne of England as James I. His father would not

(continued)

(Mary Queen of Scots, continued)

fare as well -- Mary fell in love with the brutish Earl of Bothwell. Soon Lord Darnley was murdered and the suspected mastermind of the murder was Bothwell. Documents called the Casket Letters[394] implicated Mary, and she and Bothwell were tried as murderers. Though acquitted by a stacked court, Mary was deposed, and in 1568 fled to England.[395] Mary's complicity or lack of it remains debated.[396] What is known is that she promptly began to live with Bothwell to the outrage of all who contemplated their shocking alliance.[397] Once in England Mary Stuart began to treat with the lords of the North, and conspired with them to gain the throne of England.

Her suitors were many. The Duke of Norfolk sought to marry Mary, but he was implicated in the Wyatt conspiracy to overthrow Elizabeth. The northern English earls of Northumberland and Westmoreland also rose in 1569 after their ally, Norfolk, was arrested, but their revolt was quickly put down, and Norfolk was executed. In 1570, Leonard Dacre, a marcher lord from the north, led another brief rebellion of his tenants, but Dacre was attainted and fled to Scotland.

Adding to the great color of the age, by 1576 Mary Queen of Scots was being enthralled with thoughts of marriage to Don Giovanni, Don Juan of Austria, victor over the Muslims at Lepanto. But her end was not to be victorious or romantic.

Colonize or Conquer

Ulster had appeared quiet after the Shane O'Neill years ended in 1567, and various English adventurers succumbed to Elizabeth's encouragement to colonize the northeast. The first was a group led by Sir Richard Grenville. Though little came of Grenville's at-

Lord Darnley and Mary Queen of Scots

tempt, Elizabeth continued to support efforts to settle English into Ulster, especially into the Scots territory. Her successive Deputies provided her with plans to subdue the unruly chieftains, but her own indecision hampered their efforts. She had typically vacillated, always economized, and too often temporized. The plans she approved rarely were what Sussex, Sidney or Lord Burghley had recommended to her. Even with Shane O'Neill dead, the risks of adventuring into Ulster were now so well known that only a brave few would try. One who did, Sir Thomas Smith, a Privy Council member and vice chancellor of Cambridge, soon regretted it. Smith sought and obtained from Elizabeth the rights to lands in Clandeboye where he planned to establish a colony and a firm English foothold. Smith's son Thomas led a hundred English settlers to Ulster in 1572, but they were attacked by the Clandeboye Chieftain, Sir Brian MacPhelim O'Neill, and the entire colony fled to the protection of the garrison. Young Thomas Smith was then killed by his own Irish servants.

The First English Colony

In 1573 Elizabeth became more expansive; she agreed to a proposal by Walter Devereaux, 1st Earl of Essex, to entrust the colonization of eastern Ulster to him, granting him a commission to subdue and colonize the entire area, and, with her full approval to exterminate entirely the more unruly clans. Devereaux had an ambitious confidence as a proven general that he could colonize most of Antrim and acquire great wealth in the process. He convinced Elizabeth not only to grant him the authority, but to lend him the money for the venture. He mortgaged his lands to the Queen and amassed over 1,000 troops to support his daring private enterprise, promising Elizabeth he would drive out the Scots and create a western Tudor domain. In August 1573, named governor of Ulster, Devereaux landed at Carrickfergus, determined to begin the dangerous work, but lost many of his men even before landing.

Devereaux first tried to establish a colony in Clandeboy, but encountered great opposition from the Clandeboy O'Neills. He began a futile attempt at diplomacy to win the cooperation of their leader, Sir Brian MacPhelim O'Neill, but it became apparent that the Clandeboy O'Neills would never put up with an English settlement in Ulster.

Devereaux met stiff resistance both from the Scots and the other Irish septs of Ulster, and by 1574 word had spread that Elizabeth was about to revoke his authority, so Devereaux' tactics became more urgent. To kill their leaders, he launched a campaign against the Clandeboy O'Neills, and in the process engaged in treachery and committed atrocities that still remain a part of the hostility of some in Ulster toward the British Crown. After accepting the hospitality of Sir Brian MacPhelim O'Neill for a large dinner at Belfast in 1574, Devereaux' forces slaughtered 200 of Sir Brian's followers, and arrested Sir Brian and his wife and brother and took them to Dublin to be executed.[391] Yet Devereaux was still unable to conquer eastern Ulster, and his efforts became even more extreme. Fearful that he was about to fail completely in his great adventure, he attacked Rathlin Island, a refuge of the MacDonnells to drive them out of Ulster.

Walter Devereaux, 1st Earl of Essex

The Hill of Screaming

On the *Cnoć a Screidliń* (the Hill of Screaming) on Rathlin Island, on July 26, 1575 some 500 of the MacDonnell clan were slaughtered by Devereaux' men. The women, children and elderly had been left unprotected on the island as their leader, Sorley Boy MacDonnell, went to the nearby Antrim mainland with his men. Rathlin Island is barely three miles off the Antrim coast and visible from there. The clan warriors had arrived on the cliffs at Ballycastle when one of them spotted the Earl of Essex' ships approaching Rathlin Island. John Norris and Francis Drake led the raiding party on the orders of Devereaux. Sorley Boy and his fighting men on the mainland could see the looming slaughter, but they were powerless to help. At least a hundred Scots were caught and killed at the Castle on Rathlin.

The men at Ballycastle could only wail as the English searched for Scots hiding in the caves and cliffs of Rathlin Island, horrified as four hundred more were pulled out and slaughtered. Again, Elizabeth voiced no disapproval of the massacre of her subjects by her courtier. They were Scots and she wanted them gone from Ireland.

Sorley Boy had to wait many years to avenge Rathlin Island, so long that the Earl of Essex escaped his revenge. Devereaux died (or was poisoned by his wife) in 1576 in Dublin. Devereaux' efforts had only made the Scots in Antrim more rebellious, and made all the clans of Ulster more determined to resist, and in 1575 Elizabeth removed a third of her army in Ireland and suspended all efforts at planting an English population in Ulster.

Sorley Boy eventually struck in 1580 plundering Carrickfergus Castle. In 1583 at Bonamorgy he burned an abbey and killed the English living there. Then he took Dunluce Castle on the cliffs of Antrim. The MacDonnells went on to conquer the Irish MacQuillen clan in the Route. Elizabeth's resolve to stop Scots from settling in Ulster finally weakened and she grudgingly recognized the MacDonnells' rights in Ireland. But Scots in Ulster would never be a phenomenon that would be acceptable to the worried Queen while her Scot-centered fears lived.

Mindful of the failure of the Earl of Essex' brutal attempt to settle Ulster, still weary from the years spent battling Shane O'Neill, Elizabeth concluded that a military solution was needed in Ulster. But Elizabeth failed to appreciate how wide, deep and permanent was the hatred born of the atrocities in Ulster and the martial law abuses by her deputies and seneschals in Leinster, Munster and Connaught. She now saw the full hostility of native Irish and Scots in the brutal responses they unleased against even small English troop incursions. Ulster, already ripe for rebellion, was about to be boiled over as never before. This separated region housed the archetype of clans. Their heritage was laced with epic stories; they immortalized every fallen leader; and demonized the invaders who killed them. Over the next 20 years the Ulster tales would cause disloyalty to spread and grow, and those legends would spawn there in the wilds of Ulster Ireland's greatest rebellion.

As the dawn of the 17th century neared, Elizabeth had even more cause than usual to fear Spain and equal cause to fear France.

Ruins of Dunluce Castle on the North Coast of Antrim

The Spanish, she felt, were intent on using Ireland or the Netherlands to launch a conquest of England, and she became convinced that Philip II had finally successfully courted the Irish.

A widely accepted slogan of the day was, "He that would Old England win, must first with Ireland begin." But who would that be — Spain or France? And from where — the Netherlands or Ireland? Elizabeth knew how Spain and France would benefit from an Irish alliance, through manpower, funds, logistics, assistance in other military campaigns, and protection against rearguard battles.[401]

The Armada

Each time the Tudors sought parity with Spain, the embarrassing question hung in the air — how could Elizabeth and England be a legitimate threat to Spain's empire if they could not colonize, Anglicize or even control Ireland? Was there not an increasing danger during her reign that Ireland, if not assimilated soon by England,

THE EXECUTION OF MARY STUART

Anxiety over the Scots seemed at times personified in the tension between Elizabeth and Mary Stuart. In 1585 Francis Walsingham led a second effort to put an end to Mary Stuart's claim to the Throne. He had Mary transferred to Chartley Manor where she was convinced she could communicate safely with France using letters smuggled to her in beer barrels. All her letters were intercepted, however. She became part of a plot led by Anthony Babbington. The plot included a plan to execute Elizabeth. This time Elizabeth was presented with clear documentation of conspiracy. After considerable temporizing and vacillating, Elizabeth finally signed her cousin's death warrant on February 1, 1587, and on February 7 Mary was executed at Fotheringay Castle. Elizabeth's reaction to the actual execution was rage, well beyond anything seen before by her advisors. James VI, however, adopted a composure quite unusual for an orphaned son; he cautiously bided his time.[398]

The execution of Mary, however, had a powerful galvanizing effect on Catholic Europe. It served to bond Spain and the Guise faction in France, and justify Spain's decision to begin the ultimate attack on Elizabethan England. The Vatican supported Spain's invasion plan, though Pope Sixtus V was a strong counter-reformation Pope, he was highly skeptical of Philip's motivation, believing it was Spanish empire Philip sought and not the return of Catholicism to England. Philip had indeed been heard to claim, on Mary Stuart's death, that her son James was a heretic and could not inherit, and that he, Philip, would assert his own claim to the throne of England. Philip claimed, among other things, that his wife, Mary Tudor, had bequeathed the throne to him. Though skeptical, the Pope gave his blessing,[399] and perhaps equally important to the financially stressed Spanish, the Pope gave his financial assistance to Philip,[400] and the Spanish Armada began its voyage north hoping to conquer England and Protestantism.

FRANCE AND THE IRISH

To Irish rebels, Catholic France seemed a more natural partner than Spain, and its channel ports were closer to the Irish coast. To French royalty, however, a peaceful alliance with England was more valuable than joining with Irish rebels. Accordingly, the royal families of France sought to broker a wedding with Elizabeth, and that slow moving enterprise made France's plans about Ireland inscrutable to the Irish from the time of Elizabeth's youth well into her early middle age.

The medieval wars between England and France had often been quieted by the need, which both appreciated, for strategic alliances and treaties with several European rulers. During the Hundred Years War, the French and the English usually struck such alliances not with each other, but with rivals of the other. There were times, however, when trouble from their mutual enemies also led to alliances between the ruling French and English monarchs. In the late 15th century England still held its last remaining French trophy, Calais, and in 1492 Henry VII invaded France from there. But peace and trade flourished once the Treaty of Etaples ended that campaign and reestablished trade between England and France. Marital alliance flirtations also became more frequent. War, however, was always just around the corner. Henry VIII waged three wars against France during his reign. Indeed, Tudor England and France would be at war from 1512 to 1514, from 1521 to 1525, from 1542 to 1547, and from 1557 to 1559, during which France won back Calais, ending England's continental toehold.

England and France had common foes, particularly Spain and the states of the Italian north, and the threat of these enemies spurred England and France to seek a closer, friendlier relationship with each other, and to arrange royal marriages to solidify the bond. However, the marriages seldom brought lasting peace.

(continued)

(France and the Irish continued)

Henry VIII's sister, Mary Tudor, married Louis XII, King of France, in 1514. The marriage was cut short by Louis' death the next year, but when Francis I succeeded Louis as King in 1515, Francis I and Henry VIII became allies, even wrestling each other with gusto in 1520 at the summit meeting at the Field of the Cloth of Gold. But religion became a polarizing presence in 16th century Europe, and when the Pope excommunicated Henry VIII in 1539, Francis I signed a treaty of alliance with the Habsburg Holy Roman Emperor, Charles V.

Tension among England, France and Spain also grew when Spain pursued its 16th century campaign to control the Netherlands, posing a terrifying threat to England. The once peaceful English-Spanish relationship, symbolized in the marriage of Philip II and Mary, was soon gone. After Mary was succeeded by Elizabeth, England was back to Protestantism and heavily engaged in repression and execution of Catholics. Spain was chasing and killing Protestants and heretics against Catholicism with the Spanish Inquisition. In addition, Elizabeth chose to infuriate Spain by challenging Spain's dominance over the slave trade and by pirating from the Spanish ships the spoils they had taken from the Spanish Main. With Spain thoroughly provoked, the Netherlands now looked as though it would be the launching site for an invasion of England by Spain. This risk made it essential that England and France align against Spain and provide strong support for the Dutch insurrection against Spain.

But France too posed a threat to the firmly Protestant Elizabeth, and Ireland and the Catholic Stuarts of Scotland could be seen as allies who could combine with France to conquer England. Moreover, the Stuart threat was clothed with legitimacy since Mary Queen of Scots had a claim to the English throne. And

(continued)

(France and the Irish continued)

when King Francis II married Mary Queen of Scots, the risk that France would conquer England never seemed higher. But just as quickly, the "auld alliance" receded from its height in 1560 when an car infcction claimed the life of young Francis II and the widowed Mary returned to Scotland.

The net result for Ireland of the ebb and flow of relations with France was that Catholic France, during the reign of the Tudors, failed to help Catholic Ireland. It was not until the Stuarts that Ireland received French help when James II was assisted by his cousin Louis XIV in the late 17th century Jacobite wars by Louis sending French generals to aid the Irish troops against William of Orange.

would instead be taken by Spain? Could anyone conceive a greater disaster for England? Spain was the catalyst for Tudor urgency. Midway in her reign, Elizabeth made the emphatic choice that Ireland must become English. This blossom of English imperialism mimicked Spain's own moves toward empire. Elizabeth had been watching with envy as Spain plundered the riches of the Spanish Main and Hispaniola. Her envy led to competition and to English piracy against Spanish galleons, to battles at sea, raids on Spanish ports. Ultimately the combination of her aggressive actions would provoke the 1588 attack by the Spanish Armada. When, in 1585 Pope Sixtus V urged Philip II to take action against England, Philip was reluctant, but the decisive provocations of Spain were the execution of the Catholic contender, Mary Stuart, and Essex' and Drake's great attack on Cadiz in April 1587 destroying some of Spain's finest ships.

The Spanish Armada was to be led by Don Alvaro De Bazan, the Marquis of Santa Cruz, a highly skilled naval leader. Spain's tactical goal was to win the English Channel and then safely transport 3,000 troops under the Duke of Parma from the Netherlands across the channel to invade England. For two years, 1586 and 1587, on the west coasts of Spain and Portugal the vessels of the vast Armada were stocked and readied. But the Marquis of Santa Cruz died, and Philip chose as his replacement Alonzo Perez de Guzman, Duke of Medina Sidonia, an undistinguished, inexperienced commander.

On the English side, the Lord Admiral, Lord Howard of Effingham, commanded England's renowned captains, Sir Francis Drake, John Hawkins and Martin Frobisher. Each was a skilled and courageous naval officer. It was their collective judgment to sail south to attack Spain, but the prevailing winds were pushing north. Their attempts to fight their way southward to Spain brought only frustration. The Spanish Armada, on the other hand, was to benefit greatly from those same winds when it sailed north toward the English Channel.

When the Armada arrived at the west entrance to the Channel, there were some fifty fighting ships and eighty support ships on each side. The Spanish ships were stronger in short-range bombardment. Despite heavy illness on board the Spanish vessels, they were still loaded with Spanish troops. But the English vessels were swifter, more maneuverable and far superior in long-range bombardment. The Spanish shot was brittle and could not penetrate ships as well as the English shot could. The Armada believed, however, that it could depend on its seemingly invincible crescent formation.

The orders of the Duke of Medina Sidonia, as the fleet commander of the Armada, were to make for Calais and the Netherlands, take aboard Spanish troops fighting in the Dutch rebellion and take them across the Channel to England. When the Armada sailed up the channel, the faster smaller English ships positioned themselves to secure the advantage of the wind. They were quick and nimble and able to fire effectively from a distance and avoid the Spanish efforts to come alongside, fix grappling hooks and board the English ships. For nine days a battle raged moving up the Channel at a speed of three knots with commanders Effingham on Ark Royal, Drake aboard Revenge and John Hawkins on Victory.

On July 27, the Armada arrived off Calais, and formed a very tight crescent, but on July 28th, the English sent their fire ships. Eight old ships filled with flammable material set afire were launched toward the Spanish fleet.402 They caused great confusion among the Armada and broke the crescent formation of the Spaniards and caused the Spanish fleet to scatter. The Armada managed to reassemble the next day, but by then the Spanish were already on the run. The Duke of Parma's troops assembled at Calais but decided not to try to board the ships because their route to the anchored Armada was blocked by Dutch fly boats. The principal battle was fought off Gravelines where the Armada suffered heavy losses and decided to flee north toward Scotland.

Much of the Armada escaped destruction by sailing north. The Duke of Medina Sidonia decided to lead the remnants of the Armada up the east coast of the British Isles and around Ireland. Then came horrific weather. The damaged vessels fell prey to the "Protestant Wind" — the worst storms any of them had witnessed. Many perished. Some made it home to Spain. The rest barely made shore in Scotland and Ireland.

Survivors of the Armada

The English fleet commanders could not determine whether enough Spaniards survived to land somewhere, regroup, and attack again. Of the 25 shipwrecks around the coast of Ireland most of those who made it to shore south of Ulster were killed, some by Irish natives, others by martial law commissioners under Sir George Bingham, Vice President of Connaught. All told over 6,000 were lost in or off the coast of Ireland. Many were killed or handed over for execution, and these killings would for years to come dampen Philip II's enthusiasm to send troops to aid Ireland.403 Several thousand, however, were sheltered in Ulster and Connaught by the chieftains and their followers. The O'Donnells gave refuge to some of the Spaniards and helped them recover and escape to Spain. These acts of mercy put Spain in O'Donnell's debt. But in Tudor Ireland, aid to Spaniards was viewed as a telltale sign that loyalty to Elizabeth was doubtful, and her ministers would later cite the aid to the Armada survivors to prove their suspicions of O'Neill and O'Donnell when doubt of their loyalty increased.

Armada survivors also came ashore in Mayo. Lord Deputy Fitz-William and George Bingham presided over the search to extinguish the Spanish survivors. George Bingham caught and executed 700 Spaniards. Richard "Iron Burke" of Mayo, Grace O'Malley, Brian O'Rourke of Leitrim and several other Irish chieftains helped Spaniards survive and escape to Spain. Once it became known that the Burkes and O'Rourkes had aided the Armada survivors, Bingham's strongest measures were turned on them. He sent John Browne, the Sheriff of Mayo, to retaliate, but Browne was killed by the Burkes. Bingham himself eventually invaded O'Rourke's Leitrim lordship causing O'Rourke to flee to Scotland. O'Rourke was handed over to the English, and in 1591 his Leitrim lordship was confiscated and O'Rourke was executed at Tyburn.

Elizabeth launched a retaliatory attack against Spain in April 1589, led by Sir Francis Drake and supported by John Norris. The troops on board were commanded by Robert Devereaux, 2nd Earl of Essex. This expedition was as great a failure as the defeat of the Armada had been a victory. After a fleeting raid on the Azores taking only a single port, Corunna, in northern Spain, then losing many lives, the small English fleet, in virtual shambles, sailed quietly back to Plymouth.

ELIZABETH'S MARRIAGE NEGOTIATIONS

As plentiful as are the stories of Elizabeth's romantic entanglements, her attempts to marry for strategic purposes provide stories of another kind. When Elizabeth was 28 years old in 1560, negotiations began to have her marry a ten year old -- Charles IX, King of France. Charles, however, would not suppress his Catholicism and Elizabeth would not tolerate the lad attending Catholic Mass.

Marriage negotiations between the Tudor and Valois dynasties became more serious in 1570 with a plan to have Elizabeth wed Henry, Duke of Anjou. The Anjou marriage negotiations progressed far enough that Elizabeth notified the Council in 1571 that she would marry Henry, but the French insisted that Henry be permitted to attend Catholic Mass, and that proved even more unpalatable to Elizabeth than his request to be King. Henry rebuffed the English terms, offending Elizabeth; but his mother, Catherine de Medici, then offered her youngest son, the 17 year old Francois of Valois, Duke of Alençon, as a groom to the 38 year old Elizabeth. If Alençon's age and Catholicism were not problem enough, he was also small and badly pockmarked from smallpox. Yet Elizabeth rather liked Alençon. The religious incompatibility that had stopped the courtship with Henry was less a problem with the rather indifferent Catholic, Alençon. Elizabeth encouraged intermittent negotiations that would begin, languish, end, then restart abruptly. Lord Burghley supported the marriage plan, but Elizabeth's Privy Council did not. Nevertheless Alençon visited Elizabeth frequently.[404] The Ridolfi plot of 1572 alarmed Elizabeth enough to spark her interest in a treaty with France, and a marriage again seemed imminent. France and England signed the Treaty of Blois in April 1572. Cooperation in the

(continued)

(Elizabeth's Marriage Negotiations, continued)

Netherlands was a key feature of the pact. On July 23, 1572 the Queen wrote to Walsingham that she was inclined to accept the French offer to marry the Duke of Alençon. But in August 1572 on St. Bartholomew's Day it all fell apart when rampaging Catholics in Paris began a several week rampage and massacred 5,000 or more Protestant Huguenots. The French Crown tolerated the slaughter, and Elizabeth's attitude toward a French marriage turned sour.

Marriage prospects rose again in 1573 when Charles IX granted religious freedom to Huguenots, causing Elizabeth to agree a year later to meet once again with Alençon. Before they could meet, however, Alençon was arrested for plotting against Charles. Then Charles died in May 1574, succeeded by Henry, Duke of Anjou, now King Henry III. Alençon somehow eluded his loose surveillance and became a wanderer around the capitals of the continent. Alençon's odd behavior, plus a slight improvement in relations with Spain, seemed finally to dash any prospect of a wedding. An exasperated and somewhat relieved Elizabeth notified the French that she was unavailable to wed Alençon. The courtship seemed over -- or at least it would take a Don Juan to revive it. And he did. In 1578, Don Juan of Austria inflicted a major defeat on the Dutch Protestants. Elizabeth quickly renewed marriage overtures to Alençon out of fear that Alençon might intervene in The Netherlands. Her concern increased when Philip II sent Alexander Farnese, Duke of Parma, to subdue the revolt in The Netherlands after Don Juan died.

Alençon had become the Duke of Anjou by 1578. This time he sent his courtier, Jean de Simier, Baron de St. Marc, to

(continued)

(Elizabeth's Marriage Negotiations, continued)

negotiate the marriage agreement, but Elizabeth appeared to fall for Simier (her "monkey"). The negotiation became a huge pretense with public professions of great fondness for Alençon, at least largely intended by Elizabeth to keep Philip II off balance. This too came to naught. When Alençon finally died of a fever in 1584, Elizabeth publicly professed grief. But feigned or genuine, the protracted courtship was at long last over.

Ultimately a near perfect French husband appeared when a French Protestant, Henry IV, became King. His predecessor, Henry III, last of the Valois, was driven out of Paris and the French nobility was set to place the Duke of Guise on the throne when Henry had the Duke and his brother, the Cardinal of Lorraine, assassinated. But Henry III was himself assassinated by a fanatical monk, and Henry of Bourbon, King of Navarre, a Huguenot, succeeded to the throne as Henry IV. But no marriage to Elizabeth occurred, even when she sent English troops into France at the request of Henry IV to help him fight off a challenge from the Catholic League. Henry IV, however, changed his religion in 1593. He became a Catholic and French Catholic opposition to him ended. So did the urgency of France's need for a royal wedding

In the end, Elizabeth's nuptial diplomacy would amount to little more than an interesting source of insight into her mind, a revelation of her steel will and cunning, her coyness, and her susceptibility to charm and flattery.

16

The Great O'Neill

Thou carest for religion as much as my horse [405]
— Essex to O'Neill

Hugh O'Neill had become Earl of Tyrone in 1585[406] and he had different ambitions than Red Hugh O'Donnell (*Aodh Ruadh O'Domhnaill*) Chief of the O'Donnell Name and leader of the O'Donnells. O'Neill was more reluctant to rebel against Elizabeth than was O'Donnell. O'Donnell was often focused on revenge against the English. After the murders of Hugh's father, Mathew (*Ferdorach*), Baron of Dungannon, and Hugh's brother, Brian, Hugh did long for revenge, but against members of the O'Neill clan. Hugh was said to have caught and hanged one of the murderers, Shane's son, Hugh Gaveloch (*Aódh Geimhleach*) (the Fettered), from a thorn tree with his own hands in 1590. Hugh denied hanging him in that fashion, but did admit to ordering his public execution for theft and murder.[407]

Hugh O'Neill, however, was virtually unique among Ulster chieftains for the good relationships, even genuine friendships he had with some of the Tudor officials. O'Neill's credentials as a Tudor ally were still impeccable in 1585. He also enjoyed clan loyalty and respect despite Turlough's stature; his Irish credentials as an Ulster clansman devoted to his own kingdom of Tyrone were also solidly intact. Ironically, those firmly rooted Irish credentials made him all the more valuable to the Tudor community. However, Hugh was torn by the competing tugs of those two allegiances.

In 1559 when Hugh was a 9 year old boy,[408] and was being sought by Shane's men, he was rescued and fostered to the English for his own safety. Sir Henry Sidney[409] was said to have sent him to England where, for the next 9 years, Hugh, many believe, lived intermittently with the households of Sidney and his wife, Mary, at Penshurst Place in Kent.[410] Sidney in his memoirs described taking in "young Baron of Dungannon" "whom I had bred in my house from a little boy, then very poor of goods."[411] Hugh also was said to have been fostered jointly to the family of Elizabeth's reputed lover, Robert Dudley, Earl of Leicester,[412] at various places, including Holkham in Norfolk and London.[413] He came to know Dudley's stepson, Robert Devereaux, who would become the 2nd Earl of Essex. He was also said to have spent time living in the Pale, under the patronage of the New English family of Giles Hovenden.[414] Some historians of this period conclude that the references to O'Neill being bred in Sir Henry Sidney's house, and other contemporaneous references to O'Neill as a youth being raised among the English, do not prove that he was raised in or educated in England, but suggest he was raised in the Pale by the Hovendens.

Wherever his time was spent, young Hugh O'Neill's experience being taken as a boy to be educated and trained in warfare replicated an ancient Irish tradition, one found even in the *Tain's* account of Cuchulainn being sent to a shared fosterage among the wisest at Conchobar's Court. Despite the indelible impressions created by Hugh's rebellion, there seems little doubt based on his reluctance to rebel that whatever families took him in after his father's murder were very kind to him. They surely appreciated the trauma endured by the young boy suddenly separated from his father by

Penshurst Place

forces that bewildered him, a tragedy that would one day recur in O'Neill's life in different, even more painful fashion. When he left them in June, 1568, at the age of 17, to return to Dungannon, he took with him genuine lifetime affection for the patrons of his youth,[415] one that conflicted him until he became the last chieftain to join the final conflict against Elizabeth.

But Hugh O'Neill also had a fiery temperament and it seemed to govern much of what he chose to do. His arguments were loud and lengthy, and often he would begin weeping even in the midst of argument. He was also a man of guile. He kept Tudor courtiers guessing and revealed little to his clansmen. He would as fit his needs and his plans apologize to Crown officials with a great show of remorse for his periodic disloyalty to Elizabeth. He would then fervently promise the Tudor officials one thing or another and do absolutely nothing to carry out the promise. He would seek truces and pardons, all the while girding privately for war. Though Hugh was volatile like Shane, he did not match Shane's uncivilized viciousness. Like Shane, he was given to open dalliances with mistresses, as was customary among clan leaders.

During the time he served in the English cavalry, he learned well from the British military's insistence on discipline and precision march, and he had shared the pride that English troops derived from handsome uniforms. O'Neill was Irish when among Irish, but he spoke and acted with all the patina of Tudor English when that suited him. Despite his years with the Sidneys and the Hovendens, Hugh's ambition to secure recognition and control of his lands and subjects was great, and he was certainly motivated by an ambition to gain extraordinary personal power. Whether he achieved it as an English earl, as Chief of the Name, as governor of Ulster, as a Spanish colonial ruler, or perhaps, as leader of his own nation, seemed secondary to achieving it somehow and soon.

O'Neill's English Friends

As Earl of Tyrone, an emphatic English title and a bright stamp of English approval, Hugh O'Neill took a seat in Elizabeth's Irish Parliament in Dublin.[416] There, he became familiar with all of the English hierarchy in Ireland; indeed he thoroughly won over a few influential English. A number of English leaders in Dublin had the prescience to appreciate, as the Munster rebellion taught them, that they must find ways to contain the hostility which the Gaelic clans of Ulster harbored against English control. Most of them could also see that Hugh O'Neill was the obvious key. Those who became O'Neill allies among the English in the Pale were Sir Edward Moore, Viscount of Drogheda, his son and eventual successor, Sir Garrett Moore, Sir Patrick Barnewell of Swords, Sir Warham St. Leger, and Mr. Justice Robert Gardiner. Sir Edward Moore, a soldier adventurer, came over to Ireland during Elizabeth's reign and, like Nicholas Bagenal who was awarded the Newry Abbey, Moore was allowed to settle at spacious Mellifont Abbey. His son, Garrett Moore, was a contemporary of Hugh O'Neill and became O'Neill's true friend. Although he had formed strong personal bonds with the Sidneys, Moores and others, several New English were far from his friends. Hugh developed his most complicated relationship with the New English Bagenal family of Newry Abbey.

As O'Neill wrestled with the conflicting demands for rebellion on the one side, and loyalty to the Crown on the other, he was in a quandary for several years in the 1590s. On a purely personal level, the role of a rebel did not come easily to the Earl of Tyrone. He knew first-hand the power, the resolve and the ambitions of Elizabeth and her Tudor disciples. He feared the wrath of England, and he also thoroughly enjoyed the stature, power and vast wealth of his earldom.

The Gaelic Chieftains of Ulster

Although O'Neill had friends among the New English in Ireland, his people were in Dungannon, and the Irish chieftains of the North, like the Desmond Geraldines in the South, considered themselves rulers of frontier kingdoms that had never been subdued in the first place. The Tudor effort to subdue and colonize[417] the northern chieftains, was proving even more challenging than defeating the Earls of Kildare and Desmond. And in 1590 the tension with the O'Donnells, O'Neills and Maguires of Ulster was growing worse. Elizabeth's confrontations with the chieftains provoked them,[418] and they in turn provoked her, until she decided that as difficult and expensive as conquest would be, she had no choice. She was certain that Spain would steal Ireland if she did not conquer the northern clans.

Even by Hugh O'Neill's time England had not been able to make progress in its campaign to tame Ulster. Protestantism had not reformed Ulster; the Elizabethan system of shires, sheriffs and other state officials had not penetrated Ulster; and nothing of England had displaced Ulster's Gaelic ways. Irish was spoken everywhere. The music of Ulster was Irish music. The Irish way of life was as it had been for over a thousand years. Tyrone and Tyrconnell remained Irish, Catholic and highly independent. As one Deputy put it, Ulster was "as inaccessible to strangers as the Kingdom of China."[419] But the encroachment by the Crown against them and their way of life was growing. Concerned at the approach of Tudor hoofbeats, the Gaelic north of Ireland finally headed toward organized revolt.

The Ulster chieftains had seen the pattern, and knew their clans faced extinction if the New System of the English took hold. It was not only their language, dress, customs, culture, religion, outdoor life, and their system of Irish law that would all entirely disappear. On a more epic scale, the Tudor colonization of Ulster threatened the end of self-governance over their civilization – the end of their freedom. Governance would instead be placed in the hands of English people who hated the Irish, and were bound intensely to a very different way of life. The northern clans were as unique as any; their life was born of centuries isolated together on a mystical, beautiful part of the island, sheltered by natural barriers from unwanted contact even from the southern half of the island. Anglicization would be the end of everything they and their ancestors had always been.

Tyrone

The lands in Ulster derive their names from ancient O'Neill chieftains, from three sons of High King *Niall Noigiallach* (Niall of the Nine Hostages). Three of his sons conquered land in Ulster. Their names were Conaill, Eogan and Enna. The land of Conaill (*Tir Conaill*) became Tyrconnell (Donegal), the land of Eoghan (*Tir Eoghain*) became Tyrone, and the land of Enna became Enniskillen.

THE O'NEILLS OF TYRONE

These O'Neills of the Cenel *Eoghain* were descendants of the 919 High King Niall Glundubh. The O'Neills had won the Battle of Caimeirge in 1241 securing power over the MacLoughlins in *Tir Eoghain*. Control over the northwestern sector of Ulster, however, eluded them even as they consolidated control over southern and east Ulster. Hostility between the northwestern O'Neills and the southern O'Neills persisted, causing a long history of civil war in the O'Neill tribe. The northwestern O'Neills' border fights often amounted to attempts to control *Tir Conaill* and dominate the O'Donnells. Throughout the middle ages the O'Donnells held their own in *Tir Conaill*. When *Tir Eoghain* was divided between the MacLochlainns and O'Neills by the last Ard Ri, Rory O'Connor, in 1167, *Aed O'Neill* was Chief of the Name. His son, also *Aed O'Neill*, defeated the Normans in Ulster in 1212 and became King of Ulster. However, his nephew Brian's effort to re-establish the High Kingship ended with his death at the Battle of Down in 1260.

The Clandeboy O'Neills (*Clann Aodha Buidhe*) held the Clandeboy lands in East Antrim. They were descendants of King *Aodh Buidhe O'Neill*. The Clandeboy O'Neills became allies of the O'Donnells and together pushed, pulled and pecked away at the O'Neills of *Tir Eoghain* lying between them. They declared themselves independent of the O'Neill dynasty and refused rents, tribute or hostages. The Clandeboy O'Neills thereby became a lodestone attracting all enemies of the Dungannon O'Neills.

The chieftains had their own individual motives to resist the Tudor incursions of the late 16th century — they faced the loss of personal power and immense wealth. O'Neill and O'Donnell were, before the Tyrone war, in charge of kingdoms of sorts.[420] Those kingdoms coexisted in a tense fragile peace with the Dublin administration, the royal Court in London, with bordering rival chieftains, with very ambitious subservient chieftains, with impatient *Tánaistí* waiting to succeed them, and with the growing number of Scots settling in Antrim.

O'Neill's New English Competitors — The Bagenals of Newry

The Moyry Pass, just southwest of Newry, through the Gap of the North, was the only feasible land route along the east coast an army could follow to march north into Ulster. The early Norman, Maurice Fitz Gerald, built the first castle at Narrow Water to secure a crossing of the River Clanrye and thereby complete the land route into Ulster. Another castle, Greencastle, was erected to secure the area at the northeast point of Carlingford Lough. The other break in the hills and drumlins historically used to access Ulster was far off to the west at Ballyshannon. The Moyry Pass lead to the site of the fabled "yew tree at the head of the strand" (*lubhair Cinn Tragh*) — the tree, as legend has it, planted by St. Patrick at a site that became Newry Abbey.

Henry VIII's split with Rome, codified in his 1534 Act of Supremacy, caused considerable upheaval on many fronts. The surrender and regrant of the Irish chieftains established a new style of overlord. In Ireland, as in England, the Tudors confiscated the Catholic religious houses and this decimated the Irish Catholic clergy when those fine properties were taken away and given to Tudor loyalists. The Abbeys were the most highly coveted; most were handsome structures built on lovely demesnes. The Abbeys north of Dublin at Mellifont, Baltinglass and Newry were ripe for the taking.

Newry Abbey was especially grand. It had been a Cistercian Abbey, but a Dominican, Maurice MacBruin from Dromore (County Down), became abbot in 1378. Though religious in their origins, the Abbeys in Ireland had gradually become exceedingly worldly and actively political. The native Irish dominated the Abbeys and that was a source of concern to the governing friars in England who nominally were the overseers. Even the Anglo Normans, determined to spread their unique influence, chafed at the control of influential Abbeys by native Irish clergy.

Newry Abbey was dissolved and taken by Tudor edict, and by 1550 it had become home to a recently arrived Englishman named Nicholas Bagenal, a loyal Tudor disciple.[421] Nicholas Bagenal arrived in Ireland in 1539[422] and served as a member of the royal army. He also acquired a powerful friend among the Gaelic leaders

– The O'Neill, Con Bacach O'Neill. When Con Bacach O'Neill was created Earl of Tyrone in 1542, he used the occasion to ask Henry VIII to grant a pardon to Nicholas Bagenal. The need for this favor was due to Bagenal's role in a murder. He was said to have been in the company of certain "lyght persons" while still in England when one of the king's subjects was slain. Bagenal was one of those charged in connection with the murder, and he fled to Ireland. Once in Ireland, he proved to be of service to the King. While the details are not known, Bagenal apparently also rendered some significant service to Con Bacach O'Neill. Bagenal was rewarded; Henry VIII granted Con Bacach O'Neill's request to pardon Bagenal, and he went on to serve for some time in the King's army, distinguishing himself to such a degree that, by 1547, Henry VIII appointed Bagenal Marshal of the King's Army in Ireland.

The one acre estate of Newry Abbey consisted of a chapter house, a church, dormitory and a hall, but the Abbey's additional landholding included another 5,500 acres containing dozens of one and two story cottages, an orchard and gardens. The Abbey also enjoyed the right to receive the customs of the weekly Thursday market held at Newry. Bagenal was awarded the Abbey as well as the old Newry Castle and the castles at Greencastle on the point of Carlingford Lough, and the castle at Mourne, and all the rights enjoyed by the monks. Henry VIII originally awarded the Abbey for Bagenal's use for a period of 21 years for a modest rent, but later Henry's son, King Edward VI, conveyed it all to him as a fiefdom for life. The King's goal was to use such grants to extend the reach of English influence and law and some level of stability and protection beyond the maghery, the heart of the Pale, up the coast at least to the northern extreme of the Pale at the southern entrance to Ulster. Bagenal seemed the perfect Englishman to accomplish this since his loyalty and his military credentials were both solid. Not only did he serve both the Tudors and Con Bacach O'Neill in Ireland, he also returned to England to perform military service against the French as well.

Nicholas Bagenal also sired a promising family, a new generation of English men and women who might succeed him in securing English governance of Down and Mourne. Newry, at the time, was bordered by a thick population of native Irish. To the north of

Newry across Lough Neagh was The O'Neill, Con Bacach O'Neill, in his castle at Dungannon. Con's son, Shane O'Neill, had his own castle at Benburb. Turlough Luineach O'Neill of Strabane led another O'Neill sept. Each of the O'Neills captained a substantial retinue of kerne and horse.

The installation of men like Nicholas Bagenal in strategic homes was a prelude of sorts to the large scale planting of Ulster by Scots and English settlers who were to arrive in Ulster after the turn of the 17th century. The Tudor strategy in 1550 was to depend heavily on a handful of loyalists like Nicholas Bagenal to stabilize, defend and pacify pivotal frontiers like Newry beyond which, in the minds of the English in London, lived fearsome Irish savages.[423]

Con Bacach O'Neill, though a patron of the young Nicholas Bagenal, on a few occasions would cause trouble in the Pale and in the area around Newry. When it suited Con to surge south toward Dublin, his raids could finish with a retreat back through the Gap of the North. The English forces in Dublin would pursue him only as far as the dangerous ambush sites.

When at last the aged Con died, and the bloody O'Neill succession fratricide erupted, he was replaced by his most ferocious son, Shane O'Neill. By 1562, Ulster was in unprecedented turmoil stirred up by Shane O'Neill's campaign of cattle raids, ambushes and disruption. Nicholas Bagenal tried his best to subdue Shane O'Neill, but he failed, thereby branding himself a disappointment to the youthful Queen Elizabeth. By 1563 Shane erected another castle of his own a mere two miles south of Newry at Fathom.

Despite her disappointment at Nicholas Bagenal's lack of effectiveness, with no clear alternative at hand, in 1565 Elizabeth again made Bagenal Marshal of Ireland, but Nicholas had become apprehensive about his ability to stop Shane O'Neill, and soon after his reappointment, he attempted to negotiate a sale of the Marshal's post to Thomas Stukely. His concern was justified; in 1566 Shane O'Neill took Newry itself and drove Bagenal's garrison out. But after Shane O'Neill was killed by the MacDonnells at Cushendun, Nicholas Bagenal won a new chance to stabilize Down, and Elizabeth had her opportunity to extend English rule into Gaelic Ulster.

O'Neill's Nemesis – Henry Bagenal

Nicholas Bagenal had been redeemed. The ensuing long peace with the Ulster Clans was seen as a success partly attributable to him. Nicholas used this success to attempt to make Newry a commercial capital with himself as chief beneficiary, and to solidify power for the Bagenals for the future. Elizabeth refused Nicholas' requests to be permitted to hold fairs and other commercial events, but she did approve Bagenal's request that his son, Henry, be made Marshal in 1583, allowing this key position to stay with the Bagenal family. And by the time Nicholas Bagenal died in 1590, he had secured lasting prosperity for his family and succeeded in transferring the remainder of his status and power to his son, Henry. Henry Bagenal's rise destabilized Hugh O'Neill's world, and the family complexities increased.

Though Con Bacach O'Neill had once been an ally of Nicholas Bagenal, after Con's death, as Hugh rose in stature, Nicholas Bagenal became his competitor and an obstacle to Hugh O'Neill's rise.[424] And after Nicholas' death, there was certainly no love lost between Hugh O'Neill, and Henry. These two contemporaries were bitterly hostile, openly antagonistic and extremely jealous of each other. Henry Bagenal was exceptionally hostile toward the native Irish, and he viewed Hugh O'Neill, for all of Hugh's English style and connections, as nothing more than the leader of those natives. And to Hugh, the O'Neills and Bagenals were the opposite poles of two societies pitted against each other, competing for power,[425] riches, territory and religious vindication in the rapidly changing world of Tudor era Ireland. One Bagenal, however, won the favor of Hugh O'Neill.

As perfect as the Capulets and Montagues seem as the protagonists for the tragedy of Romeo and Juliet, Shakespeare might well have used for the framework of a play a comparable plot occurring right under his nose — the contemporaneous romance between the widower, Hugh O'Neill, and Henry Bagenal's beautiful young sister Mabel. That Hugh and Mabel would even attempt a courtship in the face of the hatred between Hugh O'Neill and Henry Bagenal seems highly unlikely; but they did.

Hugh was handsome, dashing and quite charming[426] and in

1591, even at 45, still impetuous. Mabel was just 16 years old but she was smitten; she saw in Hugh a great, mature leader.[427] Hugh had divorced his first wife, Alice, in 1574. His second wife, Joanna O'Donnell, a daughter of The O'Donnell, had died in early 1591. Hugh fell hard for the young Mabel Bagenal, and, as he usually did when he wanted something, he went right after her. Well aware of the difficulties they faced, both still felt a relationship could work. After all, Hugh O'Neill was also a Tudor earl, a friend, it was said, of the Queen, a protégé and former ward of the former Lord Deputy, Sir Henry Sidney, and a man of wealth and power, who looked and sounded as English as any Irishman in the Pale. Moreover, Henry Bagenal was merely Mabel's brother, not her father. By the time of this star-crossed romance, Mabel's father Nicholas had died, and she was willing, if it came to that, to defy her brother.

Defying the Queen, however, was quite another matter. Mabel as a young subject of Her Majesty fretted over how she might try to obtain Elizabeth's consent to her marriage to this 45-year old earl. Hugh, however, knew they would easier gain royal forgiveness than advance consent. So, when Henry Bagenal evaded O'Neill's request for Mabel's hand in marriage, O'Neill convinced Mabel to elope.[428]

They needed help for an elopement, and Hugh enlisted his friends; he made arrangements for Mabel to stay as a guest of Sir Patrick Barnewell, a friend of Hugh's, whose home was Turvey House near Swords in the Pale. Hugh enlisted another friend, William Warren, to ride to Turvey House where, after a dinner one evening, Warren and Mabel slipped away on horseback. Hugh followed, and on August 3, 1591, Hugh and Mabel were married at Drumcondra in Meath. Hugh was indifferent to religion except as a political element, and they were married by the Protestant Bishop of Meath, Thomas Jones. Later, however, at Hugh's insistence, Mabel converted to Catholicism.

Though youthful, Mabel Bagenal was a cultured, sophisticated and wealthy English woman with refined tastes. Mabel tried to bring a civilizing influence to O'Neill, but with only mixed results. He allowed her to furnish Dungannon with imported fineries as lovely as one might have found in London or Paris.[429] Afterward, Dungannon has been compared to English estates and said to be almost of the quality of Penshurst Place in Kent.[430] However, O'Neill was set in his earthy ways, and those ways included mistresses. Moreover, he did not conceal them, and Mabel was publicly humiliated by his obvious cavorting.

Mabel proved to have an independent spirit. She would not follow Hugh's every whim nor tolerate his behavior. Their harmony came unglued amid their Gaelic life in Dungannon. Hugh persisted in his philandering, and it became the talk of Dungannon that he had impregnated two mistresses. When this became obvious, Mabel was bold enough to challenge Hugh publicly. She moved out on him and lodged a complaint against him in the Council in Dublin for his infidelity with the two women.[431] However, she also made an attempt to reconcile with him and even returned to live at the O'Neill Castle in Dungannon.

But then in late 1595, after three and a half years of marriage, Mabel suddenly died, still at odds with the flagrantly unfaithful O'Neill, and still estranged from the Bagenal family. The circumstances of Mabel's death are not known. No illness is named, nor an injury. Likewise, however, nothing chronicled reveals suspicious circumstances. Her death did occur in the winter when illnesses often lead to pneumonia and were very often fatal. Suggestions that she died of a broken heart seem merely dramatic speculation.

Hugh remarried quickly after Mabel's death. He wed Catherine Magennis in 1596 and they remained together during the remainder of Hugh's life.

Tyrconnell

In 1588 the O'Donnells, were led by Hugh O'Donnell and were more actively hostile to the Crown than to the O'Neills, in part because President Richard Bingham had taken north Connaught and the town of Sligo from them. Hugh O'Donnell's dynamic young son, Red Hugh (*Aodh Ruadh O'Domhnaill*) O'Donnell, became specially revered among the O'Donnells. He was believed to be the fulfillment of an ancient O'Donnell prophecy – that a Hugh O'Donnell matching his ancestry would lead the O'Donnell clan to greatness.[432] Red Hugh had caught the attention of Hugh O'Neill, and his potential was about to rise because he was to marry Hugh O'Neill's daughter.

The O'Donnell Castle at Donegal with 17th century windows and towers and a modern addition

Among the northern chieftains only Hugh O'Neill of Dungannon had been viewed as reliably loyal to the Crown, seemingly content with his exalted Tudor status as 2nd Earl of Tyrone, though several of Elizabeth's ministers were becoming increasingly concerned about Hugh as hostility to the Crown increased throughout the North.

In 1587, the Lord Deputy, Sir John Perrot, was very suspicious of the O'Donnells and he suspected that Red Hugh might become a rebel. Goaded by this anxiety, Perrot committed one of the most significant of the several Tudor mistakes that sparked the great Tyrone Rebellion. He decided to send his men to find and kidnap Red Hugh O'Donnell. They captured him in 1587 at Lough Swilly and imprisoned him in a bleak cell in the Bermingham Tower of Dublin Castle. Perrot also feared Shane O'Neill's progeny, so he imprisoned two of Shane's sons, Art and Henry, along with Red Hugh O'Donnell.

THE O'DONNELLS OF DONEGAL

The descendants of the ancient Cenel Conaill, the O'Donnells of Tyrconnell, were a pure bred Gaelic clan living in the most remote sector of the Irish mainland. The Chief of the Name O'Donnell was a potentate. Even the rite confirming The O'Donnell held at Doon Rock was a mystical ceremony with the new O'Donnell surrounded by his chieftains, brehons and seanachies turning around slowly as dictated by ancient rubric, viewing the entire circumference of the horizon from the elevated mound topped by the crowning stone, where he could view the vista of the great lands of Tir Conail he now ruled.

The renowned O'Donnell of early modern time was *Aodh Ruadh O'Domhnaill* who had such power, that in 1498 he was instrumental in having his choice, *Domhnaill O'Neill*, named as The O'Neill. Succession to the Chief of the O'Donnell Name often passed smoothly to a *tánaiste* designated by the incumbent O'Donnell, but in many cases succession was contested, particularly as the progeny grew and dispersed, and The O'Donnell was sometimes overthrown. Calvagh O'Donnell deposed the Gaelic poet scholar Manus O'Donnell in 1555, just as Shane O'Neill was approaching his era of disturbance.

Shane O'Neill captured Calvagh O'Donnell and held him as his prisoner and used Calvagh's wife as his mistress. Calvagh negotiated his freedom from Shane in 1564, and he also negotiated an earldom, but Calvagh died in an accident in 1566 just prior to his investiture.

The O'Donnells had several opponents in addition to the O'Neills, mainly lesser lords. The O'Doghertys and MacSwineys in Tyrconnell constantly fought with the O'Donnells over tribute and concessions. But when the O'Donnells engaged in a sustained dispute against the O'Neills, The O'Donnell would receive aid from dissident O'Neill clans -- from the Clandeboye O'Neills and the O'Neill clan from Omagh, known as the *Slioght Art.*

After four miserable years of imprisonment, on Christmas Eve, 1591, Red Hugh O'Donnell escaped. He led a daring breakout from Dublin Castle and brought both Art and Henry O'Neill with him through a very distasteful route, privy holes they had arranged to leave open. The January cold made the moat into which they escaped freezing. When they made their way south, a blizzard was raging in the nearby Wicklow Mountains just south of Dublin, but they were assisted there by the O'Hagans, a Wicklow clan. The O'Hagans helped them escape Dublin and led them to the safety of the camp of one of the "Spoilers of the Pale," Feagh MacHugh O'Byrne, the Wicklow clan chieftain.[433] O'Byrne, together with Rory O'More of Leix and Brian O'Connor of Offaly, were the Spoilers, so called because they were the leaders of the native clans in the area surrounding Dublin, who would attack the Pale by daylight with loud bagpipes, and would torch English villages. In the bitter cold, Art O'Neill froze to death. Red Hugh O'Donnell and Henry O'Neill survived, but Red Hugh lost his frozen two big toes to a painful amputation.[434]

The harrowing escape brought instant fame to young Red Hugh O'Donnell, making him the apparent successor and an instant legend. But the Irish in Ulster believed that much of the credit should go to Hugh O'Neill for arranging O'Donnell's escape.[435] The escape clothed O'Neill with the aura and mystique of one who could pull off anything, even against the English and their impregnable Dublin Castle.[436] Hugh O'Neill had every motive to be instrumental in O'Donnell's escape. He was well aware Perrot had arranged the capture of O'Donnell in part for the purpose of gaining leverage over O'Neill by holding a captive who could be used to stymie any O'Neill rebellious inclinations. Many also believed that O'Neill had helped his historic O'Donnell enemies in part so that he could capture Art and Henry O'Neill. It was well known that Hugh had never achieved the revenge he craved against Shane O'Neill for murdering Hugh's father and brother, and these two sons of Shane were his last opportunity for revenge.[437] When Henry O'Neill made it back to Ulster alive, Hugh O'Neill immediately found him and took him prisoner.

The O'Donnell clan united as never before around Red Hugh. All of Tyrconnell was energized by the return of the young man they had virtually given up for dead. In May 1592, the elder Hugh O'Donnell, enfeebled, resigned as The O'Donnell in Red Hugh's favor. After his crowning day at Doon Rock, Red Hugh O'Donnell promptly formed the very pact Perrot had feared, an alliance with Hugh O'Neill of Dungannon and with Hugh Maguire of Enniskillen (*Aodh Mag Uidhir*), Chief of the Maguires, lord of Fermanagh, a son-in-law of Hugh O'Neill, and cousin of Red Hugh O'Donnell. The connections of the great Ulster clans had finally all come together.

O'Neill, O'Donnell and Maguire had tolerated many actions by the Tudor officials that would be an offense to the sovereignty of a true king because, at worst, they perceived that toleration of these individual intrusions was necessary to avoid invasion and an end of the vast power they enjoyed over their very substantial demesnes. Surrender and regrant had been accepted and shrugged off as a sop to the Tudors so long as the life and power of the chieftains remained largely undisturbed. Forbearance by royal surrogates was giving way, however, to visible intrusions of a more immediate and alarming type.[438] These imperious men upon whom the English were advancing were accustomed to being feared and watched with awe. They were also violent people, reared in combat and quick to attack. As Tudor encroachment into Ulster increased, the discontent of the chieftains who surrounded the O'Neill lands also increased. O'Neill firmly believed that peace in Ulster required his leadership, but the willingness of O'Neill's vassal chiefs to continue to embrace his loyal posture began to diminish. O'Neill's own bitterness over the treatment he was receiving from the Tudor courtiers then began a dramatic rise.[439]

What the Ulster clans were seeing were more sporadic small plantations, isolated outrages in the name of martial law, embellished with increased forays of royal troops into Ulster. O'Neill, Maguire and O'Donnell all knew that they as leaders of their clans had only a single last option short of rebellion – some form of royal appointment. One or all of them would need to obtain some type of commission as a Tudor representative that would equal their vast power as *Taoisigh*. But their fear of slaughter was also very real. The recent history of Tudor slaughters in Ulster, the killing of Sir Brian MacPhelim O'Neill's family, the slaughter of the MacDonnells on

Rathlin Island, following on the heels of the slaughters of Anglo Irish and Scots in Connaught and the recent utter devastation of the Desmonds in Munster, was enough to tell O'Neill that the same might be in store for the rest of Ulster.

Of the several Ulster chieftains, only O'Neill made a serious overture to compromise after 1592. Only O'Neill had the cultural predisposition to see a certain cachet in Anglicization of Ulster and think that might be a tolerable change. Despite his signs of willingness, however, the Tudor Court and the Dublin administration pushed even the loyal Earl of Tyrone to the brink.

By 1592 O'Neill's complex agenda had become downright Byzantine. He was alarmed that President Richard Bingham of Connaught was pushing northward and that the Crown intended to extend the Composition of Connaught to Tyrconnell, then to Tyrone, and to colonize the west coast all the way up and along the north coast. O'Neill privately told Hugh Maguire and other chieftains to resist the encroachment of Bingham while O'Neill gave the appearance to Tudor officials that he was trying his best to convince Maguire to stop fighting and to submit. By slowing his course toward open rebellion, O'Neill planned at least to avoid war until the English were lulled into reducing their troop levels in Ireland or until Spanish help materialized.

O'Neill portrayed himself to the Dublin administration as Elizabeth's loyal pacifier of the Ulster clans. The sincerity of his loyal stance was becoming a subject of growing skepticism in Dublin and London. Whether he had enough control to pacify unruly men like O'Donnell and Maguire, the dangerous chieftains any loyal Ulster earl would be obligated to Anglicize, was also in doubt. Clan politics injected great uncertainty into the appraisals of O'Neill. He had links by marriage to the other clans, but each chieftain had a rival within his clan. Red Hugh O'Donnell's chief rival was an O'Donnell clan aspiring leader, Neill Garbh O'Donnell, who sided with the Crown. Maguire's rival was Connor Roe Maguire, called "the Queen's Maguire."[440] O'Neill's efforts to bridge the gap between these chieftains and the Tudor officials lasted for several years; his efforts appeared for the most part convincing and persistent. Some Tudor officials, however, came to believe that O'Neill's promises to pacify the others was entirely a pretense to bide time. O'Neill

THE MAGUIRES OF FERMANAGH

Much of Fermanagh was ruled by The Maguires (*Mag Uidhir*). Even after the Norman invasion broke their control, they reacquired the lordship of Fermanagh.

The legendary Norman knight, John DeCourcy, the "Conquistador of Ulster," had conquered eastern parts of Ulster in the assimilation period that followed the early Norman conquest. Richard DeBurgh, the Red Earl of Ulster and lord of Connaught, a descendant of a branch of the DeBurghos, became Earl of Ulster and conquered much of Ulster including the Maguire lands.

Donn Og Mag Uidhir, until his death in 1302, had ruled *Feara Manach* (Fermanagh). The Maguires were a particularly brave, loyal and learned clan. They regained their independence from the De Burgh Earls in 1333 when Earl William DeBurgh, the Brown Earl, died without a strong successor, but by the late 14th century, the Maguires were forced into a subordinate alliance with the O'Neills of *TirEoghain* (Tyrone).

Two lines of Maguires ruled in Fermanagh, *Clan Pilib* and *Clan Tomas*, one descended from *Pilib* "the *Tanaiste*" Maguire, who died in 1470, and another line descended from Pilib's older brother, *Tomas Og Maguire*, who died in 1480. *Clann Pilib* became the dominant clan. Its most famous descendant was "The *Coarb*" -- Cuchonnacht Maguire. After The Coarb died in 1537, his grandsons, *Aodh Maguire* and Connor (*Cuchonnacht Og*) Maguire and their sons shared power in Fermanagh. By 1591 *Hugh Dubh Maguire*, the son-in-law of Hugh O'Neill, had become The Maguire. Hugh O'Neill was himself a Maguire descendant; his mother was Joanna Maguire of Enniskillen.

has been described as a "consummate liar"[441] in pretending loyalty during the run up to his rebellion. These suspicions were hard to sustain once O'Neill was seen willingly and aggressively in deadly combat on the side of the Crown against Ulster clans, but some courtiers urged the Deputy to confront O'Neill and O'Donnell.

In August 1592 the Deputy FitzWilliam called O'Neill's hand and demanded that he appear before him, and that O'Neill bring what he called the fugitive Red Hugh O'Donnell and Hugh Maguire with him. O'Neill decided to comply. As O'Neill and O'Donnell rode into the redoubt of the Tudors to assure the Deputy of their loyalty, they knew how vulnerable they were to arrest or assassination.

O'Neill brought O'Donnell to a church in Dundalk and he vouched for O'Donnell, whose English was very poor. Both bent humbly and performed the rituals of swearing obedience and making submission. The Deputy did, however, take note of O'Neill's inability to convince Maguire to join them and do the same. However, O'Neill's efforts to win support of Tudor officials in Ireland faced an obstacle that was beyond his persuasive personal powers — the ambitions of the Dublin officials. At bottom, they were unwilling to cede their power over the control and the wealth of Ulster to O'Neill. Even after this precarious visit, nothing was accomplished — instead the Deputy made a simple passive mistake. He let O'Neill and O'Donnell, vulnerable and ripe for arrest, walk out the door and return unmolested to Ulster free to light the powder keg of rebellion.

The O'Donnells, O'Neills, and Maguires of Ulster, together with the O'Sullivan Beares of Munster, were about to forge the strongest military alliance the Gaelic chieftains would ever field in combat against the Throne. The great Tyrone Rebellion was about to begin.

17

The Nine Years War

You and the traitor spoke half an hour together without any-body's hearing[442]
— Elizabeth I to The Earl of Essex

Connaught may have seemed calm, but that was due only to the greater tension in Ulster. The upheaval in Ulster that began in 1592 had allowed Connaught the comfort of feeling insulated from the threat of raids by northern chieftains. For the first time in England's long history with Ireland, the wild frontier lords who inhabited Ulster were no longer a major threat to spill a rebellion down into Connaught. The main western path to and from Ulster was the route by Ballyshannon, which controlled the ford across the river at the western end of Lough Erne providing access from Donegal into Connaught. Sligo Castle, a string of other castles, and a new fort, now served as bulwarks against the O'Donnells' and Maguires' forays into Connaught.

Sir Richard Bingham, President of Connaught and Roscommon, had entrusted Sligo to his cousin, Sir George Bingham, ostensibly to help with the pacification, settlement and resolution of land disputes, and to secure the Ulster border. George Bingham was hardly a source of unification — he was one of the Tudor's most incorrigible land confiscators and he took abundant territories belonging to The O'Connor Sligo lordship and others. He took the entire inheritance of Donough O'Connor Sligo, the *Tánaiste,* even after it had been guaranteed by the English. Donough traveled to London to plead his case at Court. The Leitrim lands of Brian O'Rourke were taken as well. George Bingham did little to appease these displaced lords; he remained settled comfortably and confidently in Ballymote Castle, which he had confiscated in 1584 from the Mac-Donaghs. Bingham began new settlements of English in Sligo from 1590 onward, and the nervous New English huddled around the safety of Sligo and Bundrowes Castles. Other spoils in Sligo and Connaught, including prizes from the Spanish Armada, were also being grabbed by relatives of Bingham and their allies. The anger from the Binghams' maladministration, confiscations and corruption was aggravating the clan disputes, exacerbating the inequities of the Composition of Connaught, and making extremely dangerous enemies for the Binghams.

President Richard Bingham sought to strengthen the border by constructing another fort at Ballinafad in the Curlew Mountains and by seizing other strategic castles near it to secure Connaught against the Ulster Chieftains. To him the passage south from Ulster finally appeared secure. However, all these efforts of Bingham were being seen in Ulster not as a defense of Connaught, but as encroachment toward Ulster, as a threat aimed at Maguire and O'Donnell.

Bingham had begun attacks on rebels in north Connaught as early as 1589, and by 1593 he began to strike periodically at the Ulster chieftains. He authorized raids into Fermanagh and Donegal. The English came to believe they could now extend this promising military campaign and begin stabilizing west Ulster, so Bingham started raids against the Maguires and war began. Hugh Maguire and Hugh O'Donnell were forced to head southward, to defend against these attacks and to retaliate, in the process reopening the western passage between Ulster and Connaught. Thus began the events that erupted into the Nine Years War and the great Tyrone Rebellion.

The Maguire

The Maguire became the first chieftain out in the Nine Years War, and at the start, Hugh O'Neill was on the side of the English. The fight over control of the entryways to Ulster began in earnest in 1593. English troops under Captain Willis were driven from Donegal Friary by Red Hugh O'Donnell, but then Willis attacked the Maguires in Fermanagh, provoking Hugh Maguire to attack the

English at Sligo in May 1593. At that moment Hugh O'Neill, still the Earl of Tyrone, was obligated to actively support the English effort to subdue Ulster. Maguire, however, son-in-law of O'Neill, was his own man, and he was not willing to become a mere underling of O'Neill. He pursued his own path and his own timetable. Hugh Maguire, after all, had no place at Court. None of the Tudors served as his advocate, and when Maguire attacked in 1593, with no promise of Spanish aid, his actions were contrary to O'Neill's interests and disruptive to the way O'Neill was pursuing those interests before the Tudor Court. In the attack on Sligo, Maguire's force suffered a notable loss, but one that would empower the broader cause. Archbishop Edmund MacGauran of Armagh was killed during Maguire's attack. MacGauran had become somewhat of a celebrity. He had been central to efforts to create a Catholic confederacy of O'Donnell, O'Neill and Philip II, and his death was a great loss to that effort, but it soon became clear that an Archbishop killed in battle would help brand the whole campaign as a war of religion more emphatically than rhetoric ever could.

Despite the developing momentum toward a northern rebellion, O'Neill refused to join Maguire. Instead he fought on the side of the English against Maguire. Whether O'Neill was optimistic about an alliance with the Crown in 1593, or whether the events precipitated by Maguire's attack left him too little time to choose, it stands as the great paradox of this period of the war that O'Neill first went into battle in the Nine Years War on the side of England. When Maguire attacked the British garrison in Monaghan in September 1593, the English counter assault against him in October was led by the combined troops of the two powerful field generals, the brothers-in-law — Marshall Henry Bagenal and the still loyal Earl of Tyrone, Hugh O'Neill. Together they killed hundreds of Maguire's men as they routed Maguire at Belleek. Nor did Maguire's musketeers and foot soldiers fail to fight back; at Belleek they stabbed a lance into O'Neill's thigh.

Suspicion of O'Neill was warranted. He was a very convincing chameleon, crafty, secretive, willing to deceive both sides to facilitate a plan known only to himself. However, there is little that would support a belief that O'Neill's actions in this battle were mere charade. O'Neill and his forces joined aggressively in the fight, and

Enniskillen Castle of the Maguires

Belleek was a deadly battle. When Bagenal and O'Neill combined their two armies to defeat Maguire at Belleek, none of them knew that this was the beginning of a war that would not end for 9 years. Nor did anyone but perhaps O'Neill himself foresee that this could well be the last battle in which Bagenal and O'Neill would be allies.

With Maguire weakened, on February 2, 1594, Bingham and Connor Roe Maguire (the "Queens Maguire") and Captain Dowdall seized the Maguire Castle at Enniskillen. O'Neill's wound at Belleek had forced him into recuperation, but O'Neill's brother, Cormac MacBarron O'Neill, now openly supported Maguire, intensifying Tudor suspicion of Hugh O'Neill. Cormac O'Neill's open break had a significant effect on O'Neill's own fortunes, for O'Neill's many political opponents were now able to gain the upper hand in Court debates, and were able to defeat O'Neill's champions' efforts to win power for O'Neill in order to preserve his allegiance.

Morale among the Irish clans began to take great swings.

Illustrated Siege Map of Enniskillen

O'Donnell and Maguire had been euphoric over the early successes of the rebellion. O'Donnell was still burning over his miserable jail term, and Maguire was now burning over the seizure of his ancestral castle, whereas O'Neill was, by comparison, so far relatively unmolested and his lands undefiled. And O'Neill, more than any other chieftain, well appreciated what lay in store for Ulster and perhaps all of Ireland. He saw that Irish success would only draw more English troops, and that a rebellion would take years of casualties, famine and unrelenting misery. A considerably older O'Neill knew what his younger chieftains had yet to appreciate — victory could come only if the Catholic countries would send a major invasion force to Ireland — and that is precisely what they had perennially failed to do.

To this point it was younger chieftains who commanded the Irish forces in the field. Each had only modest experience in clan skirmishes and no experience in battle array against an army in the field. Neither O'Donnell or Maguire was steeped in English military formations or tactics. Hugh O'Neill alone among the chieftains knew English military maneuvers. He had learned the basics in the Pale, and had fought on the English side in the Desmond Rebellion. He alone had experience as a Tudor cavalry commander, a firsthand taste of the value of discipline and tactics. He saw too, as only uniformed soldiers could, the energy exuded by a well-equipped army and the surge of a uniformed force's confidence upon seeing that the native troops were intimidated by their swagger.

O'Neill was still being viewed in two different ways by London. He was perceived by some as a genuine ally of England. He had not only professed loyalty but had shown loyalty to Elizabeth, Lord Burghley, Walsingham, Hatton and Dudley. Others harbored great suspicion of O'Neill and refused even to conceal their hostility. At Court, Elizabeth herself, Burghley and Walsingham were wealthy and above the crass political and spoils competition. While Dudley was not, he still supported O'Neill out of trust; and he calculated that an alliance with O'Neill would serve England's long range interests.

But the lower Tudor officials had motives that pitted them squarely against O'Neill. Raleigh, FitzWilliam, St. Leger, Perrot, Bingham, Bagenal, Carew and many others had always seen Ireland as a target for corruption and a festival of graft. Each wanted the spoils of Ireland and several of them were in desperate need. Raleigh like Sidney had fallen into dire financial straits and FitzWilliam was in debt. There were no ready opportunities for wealth waiting for these ambitious men in England. They had to make their fortunes off the back of Ireland.

At least two of them, if not more, genuinely hated O'Neill — and O'Neill knew it. FitzWilliam and Bagenal were unrelenting; they opposed any proposal favorable to O'Neill and both were vicious in defaming him. O'Neill was repeatedly enraged at false reports about him that his friends in the English ranks attributed to FitzWilliam and Bagenal.

After Belleek, O'Neill grew increasingly furious with Henry Bagenal. O'Neill had played a crucial role in the victory at Belleek, yet his contribution was all but ignored in Bagenal's reports of the great victory. The Dublin Council heaped praise on Bagenal, and seemed oblivious to O'Neill. To the proud clan leader this underscored the Council's larger insensitivity to O'Neill's singular importance as the one person whose alliance with or alienation from the Tudor English could well determine whether Ulster could become peacefully Anglicized. O'Neill was trying hard to demonstrate his loyalty and to make the Council see his importance. However, his display of loyalty by fighting the native Irish at Belleek was offered to an unreceptive Council whose members were hopelessly influenced against O'Neill by Bagenal and FitzWilliam and by O'Neill's other detractors who wanted Ulster free of O'Neill so that they themselves could grab the spoils.

This treatment by Bagenal and FitzWilliam may have been what finally pushed O'Neill off his loyal stance. They were unrelenting in condemning him as treacherous. O'Neill was too proud to endure it, yet unable to rebut their accusations. He made several requests to Elizabeth to require her Irish surrogates to treat him with the respect he deserved and to reward him with a commission to exercise an increased level of governance over central Ulster. He proposed that she make him Chief Governor of Ulster. At his most conciliatory he even offered to allow a sheriff to rule in O'Neill lands so long as Armagh and Tyrone were not separated as shires. But his proposals came to nothing. Much of the mystery and confusion that persists as to the intentions of O'Neill at these times flows from the changing dynamics of the Tudor Court itself, as a result of which the options available for Ulster and the personal goals attainable by O'Neill also were changing.

None could doubt that O'Neill's actions were heavily based on his personal ambitions. If King of Ireland may have been only a very distant possibility for O'Neill, Earl of Ulster or President of Ulster was surely a more realistic one. What is quite unlikely is that his entire early life as a Tudor disciple had been a decades long facade; rather he saw his alliances with Sidney, Essex and Elizabeth as a political path to wealth, and to the power that Shane O'Neill could never have acquired but by combat. Aspirations for acceptability, for mainstream English nobility, also motivated O'Neill. Upward social mobility was an ambition whose delights he had tasted; nor was he the first of his clan to succumb to it. Even the primeval Shane O'Neill had yearned for a noble wife.

Hugh O'Neill, however, was now in the grip of a tightening vice of royal policies, a relentless Tudor push to end the Irish life he lived. He had seen ever more frequent military expeditions into Ulster. Just south of Dungannon a garrison of English troops was stationed at Armagh — then another garrison built a fort, even closer, at the Yellow Ford on the Blackwater. Mindful of the defeat and pitiful death of the Earl of Desmond, weary of the unfulfilled flirtations of Spain, distressed at what a chimera the promise of a meaningful papal invasion had become, he was still very hesitant to rebel. When the 1st Earl of Essex failed in his attempt to settle Ulster, O'Neill thought of himself as the man to whom Elizabeth should turn to bring wild Ulster into the Tudor realm. Yet who should turn up armed with Elizabeth's blessing, one after another, but a parade of O'Neill's most hated foes — especially Henry Bagenal and William FitzWilliam.

Overtures to the Tudors

During FitzWilliam's second tour as Deputy from 1588-94 the bribery that had been occasional became rampant. FitzWilliam enlisted cronies to demand bribes, and lesser officials correctly assumed that their own petty bribery would be met with approval by the new Deputy. FitzWilliam also continued to undercut O'Neill, making any O'Neill political progress with Dublin and London impossible. FitzWilliam and Bagenal had strong influence in the Dublin Council and O'Neill was encountering increasing difficulty having his voice heard in London. In the spring of 1594 O'Neill sent a plea to London spelling out FitzWilliam's misconduct and renewing his own assurance that he could help the Tudor program more than any other man in Ireland.

It was a very different face, however, that O'Neill showed to his followers and allies in Ulster. To them he presented a striking contrast to the loyal O'Neill who made private entreaties to Elizabeth. To the Irish, he demonized the heretic Queen and cursed all tyrannical English. He pledged to his Irish septs that Ulster would remain theirs forever and that the Pope, Spain and others would soon arrive at their side to drive the detested English from Ireland.

Little wonder that O'Neill's overtures to Elizabeth were furtive, witnessed by only a few trusted allies, and mostly by his English allies. He would arrive virtually alone to deal with English officials and do so in English. Few riders would accompany him. No other chieftains came along unless he brought one for a purpose. None of the Irish whom he allowed to accompany him likely even understood what was being said.

O'Neill was quite adept at keeping his finger on the pulses of London and Dublin. Several close to the Tudors routinely passed messages to him. Among them were two especially strong friends of O'Neill, Tom Lee and Garrett Moore. O'Neill's foster brothers, the Hovendens of Laois all served O'Neill in this period. They and others, including Sir Robert Gardiner, and even Black Tom Butler, on occasion provided O'Neill valuable inside information, seeing to it that he learned of important developments promptly — and from them rather than others.

His close confidante, Garrett Moore, the prosperous nobleman from County Louth, had long befriended O'Neill and he was considerably closer to O'Neill than those numerous English serving in Ireland who maintained proper but distant relationships with their Irish counterparts. Many such English who had come to live or spend time in Ireland played both sides to a degree without treachery to the Crown.

Tom Lee was a New English officer raised in Ireland, a son of Sir Henry Lee, and a storied warrior in battles against Irish kerne. Lee was one of the undertakers who had followed Walter Devereaux, 1st Earl of Essex, to Ireland. After Devereaux' failure, Lee stayed, helping suppress the Baltinglass and the Eustace Rebellions, then he married a Eustace widow who owned considerable property in Kildare. Lee inhabited the castle of Reban and used it as a base to fight against the turbulent O'Mores and other rebel clans. But Lee was an odd sort, lacking constancy or discipline. In 1595 he fell into melancholia and killed MacPhelim Reagh, for which he was briefly imprisoned in Dublin Castle. Later, in a gruesome attempt to resurrect his standing, he delivered some 17 rebel heads to the Castle, ending with his most foolish act, the presentation of the head of the rebel Feagh MacHugh O'Byrne to Elizabeth. The Queen was strangely tolerant of the affront, sending Lee nothing stronger than a message of disapproval.

Lee and O'Neill had become friends and trusted each other.[443] On occasion they even engaged in the Gaelic practice of sleeping in bed together, a bond-forming practice, not a sexual one. Like O'Neill, Lee too had difficult clashes with FitzWilliam. Lee had difficulties also with Black Tom Butler whom he had publicly criticized for failing to catch and kill Feagh MacHugh O'Byrne. His understanding of the Irish and their goals and the English and their goals convinced him that an Irish alliance was good for both. O'Neill cultivated his relationship with Lee and others among the English. Well out of the earshot of his Irish followers, he would make his case to the English over and over, convincing several of them that with O'Neill as lord of Ulster, the chronic problem of Ireland would be converted into one of England's greatest strengths.

After the English took Enniskillen Castle in February 1594, O'Neill received a blunt order from FitzWilliam to come again to Dundalk for talks and to bring O'Donnell with him. He was mindful of the danger he had sensed when they summoned him there in 1592. By 1594 O'Neill had virtually despaired of political success at the Tudor Court. Walsingham, Leicester, and Christopher Hatton, his sponsors and defenders before Elizabeth, had all died. O'Neill knew his enemies at Court now had a completely clear path to block his ambitions. He balked, especially at a summons from FitzWilliam.

Lurking in the Hills

In March, as tension mounted, the Commissioners tried to convince a reluctant O'Neill to meet at a home near Dundalk to appear before Lord Chancellor Loftus, Sir Warham St. Leger, the Master of the Rolls, and Sir Robert Gardiner, Chief Justice of the King's Bench.[444] Gardiner was instructed to ride out of the town to calm the wary O'Neill, to assure him that no arrest would occur. O'Neill brought O'Donnell with him and they both confided to Gardiner their great concern about the hostility of FitzWilliam and Bagenal. Gardiner urged them to meet with Loftus for dinner, but O'Neill and O'Donnell came only to the nearby hills.

But a night or so later, accompanied by many relatives and followers, O'Neill and O'Donnell came down to speak with Loftus and Gardiner. O'Neill in most moods was a man who spoke sparingly — but when speaking of the Queen, O'Neill would suddenly grow emotional. He began to weep, conceding or bragging that Elizabeth had always been very kind to him — then he lashed out at the government's mistreatment of the Irish clans. He said he was under great pressure from his supporters to return to Ulster and end his dealings with the Tudor administration.

O'Neill knew that Tom Lee and Garret Moore were advocates who would support his grievances and vouch for his claim that he sought a lasting partnership with Elizabeth. Most important to O'Neill, they would both confirm that only Bagenal's hateful gossip against him and FitzWilliam's corrupt administration were obstacles to a solution to the Ireland problem. Now O'Neill asked Gardiner[445] to send Lee and Moore back with him to help him deal with the other chieftains, and the two of them rode out to meet with the clansmen camped in the hills.

But that night in the hills near Dundalk, all of Moore's and Lee's efforts to convince O'Neill to continue dealing with the Council were to no avail, and Moore and Lee turned and slowly rode back to Dundalk without him. O'Neill's refusal had all the earmarks of the turning point. No one's entreaties, not even Gardiner's assurances of safe conduct, were any longer sufficient even to coax O'Neill to come down to Dundalk. Instead, he sent Harry Hovenden, his foster brother, to Dundalk to tell the Commissioners that O'Neill and O'Donnell feared arrest if they came themselves. There now seemed little cause for hope that O'Neill would choose the Tudor side since he was offered nothing, but still the graver question remained — would he rebel?

Just as O'Neill seemed about to rebel, Spain offered help, and O'Neill's hopes turned once again to a foreign champion. Maguire, O'Donnell, and the Archbishop of Armagh, reported to O'Neill that their appeals for Spanish assistance had been granted. Spain wanted an Irish invasion to serve Spain's own needs. Though O'Neill had already accepted with dismay the reality that rebellion was his only choice, he now could harbor the hope that Spanish help might make success possible, but time was needed for Spain to mobilize.

The Ford of the Biscuits

Spanish aid would come, but it was a long way off, and until it arrived, the fighting would continue. On August 7, 1594 Maguire ambushed Sir Henry Duke and Sir Edward Herbert's troops at *Bel Atha in Briosgadh*, the Mouth of the Ford of the Biscuits. Duke and Herbert had led an English relief force headed for Enniskillen. Maguire and Cormac O'Neill attacked and killed 56 English soldiers, a modest battle by military standards but one that emboldened Irish clans anxious for a rallying point. Cormac O'Neill's small force of 400 chased the British troops of horse and soldiers until, at a spot on the River Erne, which that day became named the Ford of the Biscuits, the English troops dropped their supplies, including biscuits, and fled.

Exciting as this isolated victory was, most Irish knew that the English troops fielded in that early part of the war were untrained conscripts and plowboys. The relatively few capable English volunteers in these troops found themselves serving in ranks composed only of a handful of trained soldiers and many more ill-clad novices inadequately equipped. Regardless, the trumpeting and jubilation which followed this small rout of the English gave the Irish a great story to recount.

But conditions continued to be changed by new developments. O'Neill received a message that FitzWilliam had abruptly been recalled by Elizabeth. Sir William Russell was coming to Ireland as the new Deputy; O'Neill's chief detractor had been discredited and whisked away. The promise of eventual Spanish aid suddenly seemed far less the perfect solution than this immediate opportunity. Emotional and decisive, O'Neill burst toward the opening. The obstacle of FitzWilliam's venomous reports was gone; Bagenal alone might be unable to prevent an O'Neill/Tudor alliance. He rode to Dublin, throwing safety to the wind, invigorated by the belief that Bagenal could not block his proposals.

On August 15, 1594 O'Neill stood before the Council in Dublin assuring them that he was a loyal earl and a friend of the Elizabethan Court, complaining as always of the wrongs done him by FitzWilliam and Bagenal. O'Neill professed that his hands were clean, that he had no role whatever in the attacks by Maguire and O'Donnell.

He offered to educate his son in England, to drive the Scots out of Ulster, to pay a composition rent, and, if allowed to govern Ulster, to secure loyalty for the Crown in Ulster. The proposal he made was no less than an offer to take full responsibility for a peaceful Ulster. O'Neill hoped that his belief that only he could bring peace to Ulster would finally be obvious to the new Dublin administration.

O'Neill Offers Peaceful Anglicization

O'Neill assured Loftus and the Council members that Hugh Maguire was willing to surrender if pardoned. He assured the Council that he would ride with their men to relieve the siege of Enniskillen Castle. He claimed he could lead the social as well as the political transformation in Ulster and do it peacefully. O'Neill believed this was the hour of a momentous breakthrough. Gone was the powerful Deputy who saw O'Neill as antithetical to his own graft and a threat to Tudor plans. Now, only Bagenal seemed to stand in his way; Bagenal, whose personal grudge was obvious to all, came to the Council and interrupted O'Neill and recited a list of his offenses. The Dublin officials were impressed by O'Neill's bold arrival, but their personal interests conflicted with O'Neill's ambition. As a result, he received no encouragement from them and barely escaped arrest. O'Neill's friends on the Council — Gardiner, Butler, Loftus, Dillon and St. Leger — were opposed to arresting O'Neill, but later they would all hear of Elizabeth's anger that they let him get away.

In these few days, O'Neill presented history's most unique opportunity to solve the chronic Irish problem. The Council, however, was more inclined to arrest O'Neill than to forge the alliance that could have led to a lasting peace. Neither the new Deputy, Russell, nor the Council displayed even a conciliatory attitude. They gave O'Neill curt orders to control his subjects, to withhold any support from O'Donnell and Maguire, and to send one of O'Neill's sons to Dublin to be held for assurance. By the time O'Neill made his last proposal to bring about a loyal Ulster, the English courtiers were a new breed of adventurers who were well aware of the rich Irish lands that had been parceled out to their predecessors, Carew, Raleigh, Perrot and others, and that these rewards had been made possible only by displacing the Earl of Desmond. The English administrators of 1594 were thus not at all inclined to embrace the Earl of Tyrone and thereby help secure his hold over the very lands of Ulster they themselves coveted.

O'Neill's visit to Russell did not — as such a visit could — mark the beginning of the end to the century of strife. There was a reservoir of support for him among the English. A very few Dublin officials had for some time seen merit in much of what O'Neill claimed. Gardiner and St. Leger had gone so far as to recommend to the Privy Council that Bagenal and others have their commissions revoked. Even Elizabeth approved of efforts to make peace with O'Neill. She had sent a message with Russell that Bagenal was to be forbidden to take any action against O'Neill. The Queen had given Russell a conciliatory message from her to convey to O'Neill. But Russell never delivered the message. Instead, O'Neill's visit with Russell was thrown off balance by Bagenal who claimed that O'Neill had been a supporter of Archbishop McGauran and thus a part of the conspiracy to turn Ireland over to Spain. With conflicting presentations laid before him about O'Neill fresh upon his arrival, Russell neither embraced O'Neill's submission, nor acted on Bagenals accusations. He made a calculated guess that O'Neill was too Anglicized to join the Irish rebels. After four days making no headway with the Council members, a confused and dispirited O'Neill received a warning by some friend close to the government, and fled. Russell's inaction had just become another of the seminal mistakes that spawned the ensuing centuries of Irish conflict.

The Final Straw

O'Neill left Dublin determined to join the rebellion. He recognized that finality had come with the failure of this overture, and he spent the next year fortifying and training troops and enlisting galloglass and highland Scots. Russell dispatched several more directives to O'Neill throughout September and October, but O'Neill either ignored or toyed with them. Through the winter of 1594, O'Neill continued to write Russell purporting to explore pardons for the other chieftains, as though nothing significant had happened, all the while denying his own involvement with the rebellion.

O'Neill's proposals were now merely diversions, offered with scant expectation that anything would come of them. Yet O'Neill remained riddled with doubt, uncertain whether the course of rebellion was more dangerous than cooperation. He had also become convinced that Elizabeth's purpose was not merely to extend her power, but to eliminate his. He listened to the demands and threats of Ulster chieftains in Tyrconnell and Enniskillen. It had fallen to him and his Ulster allies to be the final caretakers of the Irish world and all its tradition, the final defenders of an ancient civilization. If England ended that heritage, history would record that he had been the final bulwark and that it was Hugh O'Neill's hands from which the English had taken Ireland.

O'Neill began to spend heavily; he bought arms from lowland marauders in Scotland, and concentrated on smuggling arms and supplies. Then he began making gunpowder. He knew that Dungannon would become the focus of Tudor England, so he moved the powder and stores from Dungannon to several crannogh to protect them from attack. He increased his troop strength, using bonnaghts as soldiers as Shane had. Soon many of them were trained and equipped with shot, arquebuses and calivers. O'Neill also began drilling these Irish troops as Irish had never been drilled before. It was the power of England they would face, and O'Neill decided to assure that his men were the equals of the English in skill, tactics, equipment, and even dress.[446] By early 1595 he was ready. His cataclysmic break with Tudor England was imminent, and he urgently renewed calls for help from the Pope, from Spain and from Austria. But he decided, with or without them, he was going to war.

Art O'Neill, another of Hugh's brothers, attacked the English Fort on the Blackwater on February 16, 1595. Despite O'Neill's months of professing loyalty and offering peace, it was obvious that O'Neill had put his brother up to the attack. When other clans attacked Cavan, Louth and Drogheda, the Tudor administration was all but certain that O'Neill was out, and that the final war of the Irish people against England was underway and unstoppable.

Tullaghoge – O'Neill's Choice Is Made

O'Neill now accepted that he was not to be the Tudor royal Ulster governor; he was ready to cast away all remnants of his English demeanor. In the midst of these events the aged Turlough Luineach O'Neill relinquished the leadership of the clan to Hugh, and O'Neill took the forbidden title. The once Earl of Tyrone went to the O'Neill coronation stone at Tullaghoge[447] and had himself crowned The O'Neill, fully reverting from Tudor gentleman to the image the Tudors now hated above all others — the wild Ulster clan leader.

Clontibret

In May 1595 O'Neill's brother Cormac helped Maguire retake Enniskillen Castle, and soon the O'Neill clan laid siege to the town of Monaghan. To fortify her deteriorating position in Ulster, Elizabeth sent Henry Bagenal 4,000 fresh troops. Bagenal set out from Newry in June with a force of nearly 2,000 men to relieve Monaghan. On Bagenal's return journey from Monaghan his force was attacked at Clontibret by an Irish force. What Bagenal's shocked troops saw was not the ragtag Irish of old,[448] but a serious military force, a well-organized, well dressed, regiment of riflemen and light cavalry, the likes of which had never before been seen in Ireland outside English ranks.[449] And they saw that its commander was Hugh O'Neill himself.[450]

O'Neill had spent the funds to uniform his army and the effort put quite a spring in their step. The Irish troops were now trained in part by the English themselves. Calivers, training and fine uniforms, and the inspired leadership of O'Neill, had made true soldiers of the boys of Ulster. The Irish still attacked from the bogs and the woods, made their characteristic sudden thrusts and then disappeared, but they did it much more effectively than in years gone by. The favorite tactics of the Irish proved too much for the English at Clontibret. The Irish burst out of the Ulster woods thick with all varieties of willow, holly and ash and dense brush that seemed impenetrable. They attacked with shot, muskets, calivers, and pikes wielded by bonnaghts and Scots mercenaries. Then they disappeared just as quickly into the bogs and woods where the English dared not give chase.

O'Neill rode to a vantage point across a small stream to observe a stormy clash of pikemen and kerne. As he did, several of the English cavalry drew near on the other side, and one of them recognized O'Neill. They spurred their horses across the stream and attacked O'Neill and the few who were with him. Knocked from his horse, O'Neill suddenly tasted the grit of war, locked in a death struggle on the ground, knowing that whoever was first able to reach his knife would be the only one to rise from the dirt. As they wrestled, his attacker's grip suddenly failed; O'Neill's aide had dealt the Englishman a powerful blow on his arm, and O'Neill's dagger finished him. Shaken, O'Neill remounted and resumed command. He might also have finished Bagenal at Clontibret had he not run out of powder, but he failed to pursue and finish off Bagenal's retreating foot and horse. Once back in Newry after the rout at Clontibret, the stunned English at first would not leave the fort and risk their force by trying to march south to Dundalk or Drogheda. Elizabeth was shocked at the defeat, and enraged to learn of O'Neill's open disloyalty; she proclaimed him a traitor after Clontibret, and she bellowed her outrage at his ungrateful treachery to anyone in earshot.

The Capture of Sligo Castle

In the West, another blow landed on the English. In June 1595, Red Hugh O'Donnell was handed Sligo Castle. It was only days after Clontibret that an aide of Sir George Bingham, Ulick Burke, who had grown to despise Bingham, murdered him. Ulick Burke had suffered insults and indignities from George Bingham; finally he cracked and stabbed Bingham — and he cut off his head. Though the Burkes were loyal, this Ulick Burke was an O'Donnell ally and he sent messengers to Ballyshannon where O'Donnell's men were camped. Burke's message was that he could deliver up the town of Sligo to O'Donnell. Sligo Castle was called by Richard Bingham "the very key of the province and passage from Tyrconnell." [451] O'Donnell went straight to Sligo and captured and destroyed the Castle, throwing open the door from Ulster to Connaught for the northern chieftains. After Sligo Castle was destroyed, O'Donnell and Maguire were able to reap some benefit from the pent up clan discontent in Sligo and Mayo even though the Burkes of Galway and Mayo and the O'Briens of Clare remained loyal. O'Donnell and Maguire found a number of the Irish lords in Connaught quite ready to throw off the Composition of Connaught; but convincing any of the Connaught lords to join fully in a rebellion that would engulf all of Ireland was quite another matter.

Richard Bingham immediately took his forces into the field against O'Donnell, but he had to engage in the equivalent of coyne and livery as he strained to feed and house troops on the march. The local populations were inflamed by the resumption of these hated burdens, imposed by the very man who had portrayed their abolition as one of the great attractions of the Composition of Connaught. Unable to resist the temptations of graft, Bingham also orchestrated new fraudulent confiscations by Crown officials of Connaught lands using typical legal pretense.

O'Neill tried his best to enlist Ulick Burke of Clanrickard to join. O'Donnell meanwhile continued the occasional raids into Connaught even on Clanrickard septs.[452] The game they played did not develop into open warfare between Clanrickard and O'Donnell, but neither did it goad Clanrickard into an alliance with O'Neill. Instead Clanrickard remained loyal and was later appointed the Queen's Commander in Chief for all of Connaught. His son, Richard, Baron of Dunkellin, was even more English, after his return from fosterage and education in England.

O'Neill and the Religion Card

O'Neill found that to maximize support for the rebellion he must emphasize its religious aspect. The schism of Henry VIII sixty years earlier had created an historic gulf in Ireland between the Protestant New English and the Catholic native Irish and Anglo Irish. Though O'Neill's personal practice of religion was spotty,[453] his platform as a leader in the Gaelic world highlighted claims that the Catholic religion was a right of Irishmen and the central tradition of his race. The nine demands O'Neill made for Home Rule were heavy in religious-based freedoms. He called for freedom to preach and practice Catholicism, restoration of Catholic abbeys and churches and erection of a Catholic university. Other of his demands were aimed at the political rights of Irishmen: the Council and all high officials must be Irishmen, anti-Irish statutes must be repealed, conscription by England of Irish soldiers must be forbidden, all hereditary lands must be restored to the Desmond Geraldines, and to the O'Donnells and O'Neills, freedom of commerce and trade must be allowed between Irish and English, and the Irish must have the right to build ships including men-of-war.

Religious content was made a central feature of the list of freedoms, liberties and preferences O'Neill demanded. This was also necessary to attract support from Spain and other Catholic powers and to attract support from the Old English. It did bring promises of aid from Spain, but few promises of active military support from the Anglo Irish of the south.

The Old English of Munster

O'Neill had to make heavy demands to enlist clan leaders and Old English in Munster. Though some of the lords of the south of Ireland showed a willingness to support action by the Irish chieftains of the north, the most powerful flatly refused. Just as earlier Earls of Kildare and Desmond had failed to win over the predecessors of the chieftains of Ulster in their rebellions, O'Neill now failed to win the support of Kildare and others in his. The Thomond earldom by this era of the 4th Earl was staunchly loyal and the earl himself had become quite English. Clanrickard too was anglicized and neither earl would be of any assistance to O'Neill in the Tyrone War.

Many of the Anglo-Irish in the south and the west were distrustful that O'Neill's rebellion was the rebirth of FitzMaurice's rebellion against heresy. Many Anglo-Irish were capable of responding to a truly Catholic demand, but despite O'Neill's claim that this was a holy war, the Anglo-Irish of the south distrusted his rebellion and his purposes, seeing them as nothing but efforts to grab power for himself. One way or another, the Old English of Munster stayed neutral or loyal for the entire Nine Years War.

O'Neill Enlists Southern Chieftains

Munster chieftains had been crushed by the brutal southern campaigns over several years by Lord Deputy Arthur Grey de Wilton and others, rampages of death and famine called "devastatingly violent" by historians.[454] They refused to jump up for the chance to be devastated again so soon after that. O'Neill, however, saw that a narrow Ulster revolt might founder if not supported by Connaught, the Midlands and the south. He realized that the east and southeast were dominated by Pale and Ormond loyalists, but the large Irish population of the Desmond lands at least was home to chieftains of the Gaelic mold who could still turn out a strong contingent of fighting Irish oglach. They, however, would need to be convinced, and would have to accept that fighting the English had become essential for their own survival and that O'Neill could lead them to victory.

In this endeavor O'Neill would recount for them what he knew from his own days spent as a member of the English establishment, and likely he embellished that, but it was convincing to the Munstermen. He could assure them that the torture and extermination at Smerwick was exactly what the English had in mind for the Irish. He could argue that England would no longer tolerate or spare the peaceful Irish in Ulster, Munster or anywhere, but that the English were now about to confiscate their lands and kill them if they resisted. To convince them victory was possible, he was now able to recount several victories. Once they gave O'Neill their attention, some of the Munster chieftains agreed that this was the opportune moment in Ireland's history.

O'Neill's arguments succeeded in convincing the MacCarthy Mor, Florence MacCarthy,[455] leader of the great southwestern clan. He also convinced Donal O'Sullivan Beare, ruler of much of the Beare southwestern peninsula, including areas around Kinsale.[456] He also convinced the so-called "straw earl," the Sugane Earl of Desmond.[457]

O'Neill returned to Ulster to plan the final campaign, emboldened and confident that he had just enough support in the south, and that he had now brought the fighters of Ireland together as no one had before. Now he was determined to make those Irish forces overwhelming. He would add the final piece. He would bring to Ireland the long-promised Catholic fighters from Spain.

Another Promise of a Spanish Fleet

Though sensing the demoralization of the English, O'Neill knew that his heralded victory was in actuality a limited one. More English forces would surely come, and there would be no end to them so long as the Irish rebel force was limited to the northern clans. If, however, Spanish forces arrived to help him, the unimaginable victory could be at hand. Having finally backed the English into near exhaustion in 1595, with Elizabeth's arc losing altitude, she might, in those straits, be willing to strike an accord that could buy Ireland years of freedom and a chance of self-government.

Though Spain was as natural an ally as the Irish chieftains could have designed, Philip II was heavily pre-occupied with England, with revolts in the Netherlands and other parts of its empire. Regardless, Spain was still profoundly in sympathy with the Catholics of Ireland. The late 15th century final defeat of the Muslims at Granada had left Spain an overwhelmingly Catholic country, Catholic not only in its royalty and aristocracy, but the soldiers who would fight the battles were staunch Catholics. Spain was also an implacable enemy of Tudor England. The Tudors annually launched raids on Spanish coastal cities to keep Spain subdued, and every Spanish naval leader vexed by these raids had grown anxious to secure the southern Irish coast for Spain. The more ambitious Spanish wish was to liberate Ireland from the English and use it as a stage from which to invade England. Moreover, Spain detested the injustices done to fellow Catholics in Ireland. Spain, however, was preoccupied.

Pleas to Spain

For many years troubles bankrupted Spain and made it an unpredictable player in the growing struggle between Ireland and England. Unfortunately, Spain often was as inscrutable to the Irish as it was to the English. Spain had been the strongest country in the world prior to the 1588 defeat of the Spanish Armada by the English fleet. Despite Spain's financial stress, Philip II felt an obligation to fight against heresy and he sympathized with the Catholics in Ireland. As recently as 1592 Philip had sent his solemn assurance

SPAIN'S PREOCCUPATIONS–

THE SPANISH NETHERLANDS AND HISPANIOLA

By the mid-sixteenth century, Spain's empire was far-flung, insecure and riddled with revolts, impairing in many ways its ability to rush to the assistance of Irish rebels. The Spanish empire stretched from the Netherlands to the Americas to the Philippines and it was challenged everywhere.

The Netherlands was a continuing source of intense rebellion against Spain in the 16th century. The Netherlands started out as a part of the East Frankish Kingdom and ultimately came under the control of the Dukes of Burgundy. It moved peacefully under the control of Spain when Duke Charles of Burgundy became King Charles V of Spain in 1516 and Holy Roman Emperor in 1519. His son, the fervently Catholic Philip II, inherited the low countries in 1555. With Philip II came Catholic domination, increased oppression and unfair taxation, and life rapidly deteriorated for the Protestants in the Netherlands. Dutch Protestant noblemen, led by William the Silent (William I, Prince of Orange), finally invaded from Saxony and French Huguenots invaded from the south to begin in earnest their long revolt against Philip in 1568.

Spain's soldiers devastated the Netherlands in the summer of 1576 as they sacked Antwerp and achieved the Pacification of Ghent, reuniting the Netherlands with Spain. In 1579, the area that is now Belgium was on its way to return to Spanish rule. However, while the Northern Provinces of Holland and Zeeland where Protestantism was strong, formed the Netherlands by the Union of Utrecht and continued the revolt against Spain, finally declaring an independent Dutch Republic on July 26, 1581. However, the leader of the continuing revolt of the republicans, William the Silent, was assassinated at Delft inside the Prinsenhof in 1584,

(continued)

(Spain's Preoccupations, continued)

and the insurrection began to founder. Next came Spain's Siege of Antwerp, and it became clear that England would have to provide military aid to the Dutch rebels. In 1585, Elizabeth sent 7,000 troops led by Robert Dudley as lord regent to stop the momentum of Spanish forces led by the Duke of Alba. The revolt continued to strain the finances and occupy the best military forces of Spain. This had a major impact on Spain and Ireland for Spain was essentially bankrupt and could not pay its soldiers fighting in the Netherlands let alone send adequate troops to help the Irish chieftains. The additional threat of control of the Netherlands by France was of great concern to Elizabeth.

In addition, raids on the Spanish Main along the coast of South America and in Hispaniola in the Caribbean by the legendary English seadogs were making inroads on the treasures that Spain's adventurers had regularly brought back to Spain. A bankrupt Spain desperately needed this plunder in order to stay solvent. Native rebellions in the Caribbean and in the Philippines further sapped Spain's military resources and finances. These events and the added heavy distraction of the Spanish Inquisition made an otherwise willing Spain financially unable to respond to Irish pleas for military aid.

back to Ireland with Archbishop Edmund MacGauran[458] that if an Irish rebellion could be launched, Spain would send help.

As Spain's distractions kept it from helping Ireland, in June 1596 new discussions between O'Neill and the English seemed about to end the rebellion. Agreement on essential terms seemed to be reached between O'Neill and Sir Geoffrey Fenton, Secretary of State, and Sir John Norrys. It was O'Neill who had initiated them and made a surprisingly modest proposal, seeking a truce and a pardon. O'Neill and O'Donnell said they were willing to accept the shireing of Ulster. O'Neill said he no longer demanded to be the lord of Ulster. Norrys and Fenton were commissioned to negotiate with O'Neill and try to achieve a truce. O'Neill was willing to accept the authority of the Crown, to drop all demands, acknowledge he had committed offenses, and pay reparations, all in exchange for Elizabeth's withdrawal of forces at the various forts in Ulster and her agreement that the shireing of O'Neill's lands would be done without separating Armagh and Tyrone. O'Neill was willing personally to guarantee the peace if he was permitted to retain substantial control over his own lands. But this round of negotiations with Norrys and Fenton may merely have been a ploy to buy more time. Theories abound that O'Neill made such simple demands only to allow Spain time to deliver on its promises and gain time for O'Neill to arm and train his own forces. Those theories may, however, be the product of O'Neill's explanations to his fellow chieftains to justify to them his shifts of positions.

When a pair of enthusiastic Spanish emissaries came to O'Neill with promises of help in 1596, however, their promises were enough to bolster the resolve of O'Neill, O'Donnell and Maguire.[459] O'Neill rejoiced at the Spanish commitment and terminated the agreement he had reached with Norrys and Fenton. The chieftains promised the Spanish emissaries that the Crown of Ireland would be given to Archduke Albert, Governor of the Netherlands, the husband of Isabella, daughter of Philip II. The emissaries gave the chieftains their promise that a Spanish Armada would land at Limerick very soon.[460]

The resolve of the Spanish to invade Ireland, high as it was in the Spring of 1596 was redoubled when the English, led by Drake and Essex, successfully attacked Cadiz in July 1596. The attack on Cadiz gave the Spanish a sense of urgency and a desire for revenge. Philip II was rattled by a new feeling of vulnerability; he now feared conquest by England unless he could launch a successful attack against the English first.[461]

In October, 1596 the day finally arrived when Spain was able to launch an army to invade Ireland. A small armada of Spanish ships set sail for Ireland and England. History, however, was written by a series of violent storms which suddenly appeared and dispersed the Spanish fleet. The tempest swamped a third of the ships and sent the rest scurrying back to Spain. The chieftains were crestfallen. Now they had no choice but to continue the revolt without Spain to help them. But with surprising vigor they resumed combat, winning several victories in 1597.

England was also financially threatened and it too suffered frustrations. The lack of success in putting down the long revolt in Ulster angered the aging Elizabethan Court. Thomas, Lord Burgh, was named Deputy in 1597. He led a renewed effort with reinforced troops to march north to tackle O'Neill. When Burgh encountered O'Neill's troops, he too saw first-hand that this was a different kind of Irish fighting force. Burgh had made plans to join together with Sir Conyers Clifford who was marching north from Sligo, but Clifford was driven back by O'Donnell as he tried to cross into Tyrconnell. Just as Burgh was improving discipline in the English troops, reforming the petty profiteering in the army, and ending the corruption of a host of war profiteers in Dublin, he suddenly died in October 1597, either poisoned by one of his several enemies or a victim of typhus.[462] Burgh was replaced briefly by Richard Bingham, now age 70, but Bingham too died soon after his appointment. It had begun to appear that death and old age were crippling the Tudor effort in Ireland more than O'Neill and O'Donnell. Black Tom Butler, Lord General, was also 70, so Thomas Norris was named Lord Justice. Elizabeth herself was aging, and the anxiety of old age only increased her chronic worry about the financial drain another Irish war would cause.

In December 1597 Black Tom Butler marched his depleted troops to a meeting with O'Neill near Dundalk. O'Neill as usual welcomed the delay of negotiations, and indeed the time he gained was now essential for arming while he waited for Spain, hoping that the Spanish kettle would boil. He and Black Tom called to each other across a brook, the nearly deaf Butler straining to hear O'Neill as he firmly refused to give his sons as hostages. O'Neill recounted for Butler as he had done for others old grievances, even harking back many years to condemn Sir Henry Sidney's long ago decision to support O'Neill's clan enemy, Turlough O'Neill, against him. Yet O'Neill agreed with Butler to hold to a truce into June 1598. During the truce O'Neill diligently prepared for war.

The Yellow Ford

The great victory the Irish had long dreamed of finally arrived just after the truce ended. It was exquisitely satisfying since O'Neill won it against Henry Bagenal, his brother-in law, the rival he most detested. It occurred at the Yellow Ford on August 15, 1598.

The chieftains had destroyed a British fort on the Blackwater and established an earthworks there. Many officers and officials in Dublin had wanted to abandon the outmoded fort, but the English attacked the Irish earthworks and reestablished another rudimentary English fort, an earthworks with a parapet manned by a garrison of 150. O'Neill decided to drive the English out of their billets at the Blackwater fort and then drive them out of Armagh Cathedral. Ormond was tending to disturbances in Kilkenny, so it fell to Henry of the Battleaxes, as Mabel Bagenal's older brother was known, to assume command of an impressive English force of over 4,000. The ensuing battle was not, however, to be a poignant clash of relatives.

On Bagenal's march to the Blackwater fort, as he neared the Yellow Ford, his six marching regiments, each 500 strong, slowed and became separated from each other by over 100 yards. In the march to the Yellow Ford the English had hauled their large saker gun, a useless burden in Ulster terrain where such cannons were almost never used. It became mired in the mud and badly slowed Bagenal's progress.

O'Neill's forces met Bagenal's supply train at the yellowish colored stretch of the River Callan where the road to Armagh crossed the shallows. The Yellow Ford acquired that name due to the peculiar color of a span of the shallows of the Callan cause by the yellow water seeping toward it from bogs nearby. The English were still accustomed to centuries of Irish battle tactics and were reasonably prepared, but O'Neill was as much a student of the English as they were of the Irish. At the Yellow Ford, he employed maneuvers never before confronted by English fighting Irish. Heavy use of muskets, riflemen hiding in trenches shielded by hedgerows, pikemen attacking in waves, an abundance of cannon, all combined to destroy large parts of the 6 English regiments and rout the horsemen.[463] Late in the battle Bagenal paused, lifted his cap, and was dead in an instant, shot in the face.[464]

The English lost 800 men, including 25 officers, plus 400 more wounded, and 300 who defected, and the fort fell. Thomas Wingfield who had also fought at Clontibret, led a difficult English retreat from the Yellow Ford, a withdrawal complicated by efforts to retrieve the reluctant saker cannon. Elizabeth was outraged that, after the killing of Bagenal at the Yellow Ford, the Lord Justices sent a pathetic sounding request to O'Neill asking him to allow the remaining troops safe passage out of Ulster since, after all, he had succeeded in killing his great adversary, Bagenal.

This victory was far more than symbolic; it gained the chieftains the upper hand in European diplomacy. A third of the English army were casualties, and the victory at Yellow Ford became famous throughout Europe. The exhilaration enabled O'Neill's Old English allies, the Sugane Earl of Desmond, James FitzThomas FitzGerald, and others to rouse a large area of Munster in a rising. O'Neill was suddenly being seen by a wider circle than ever before as their leader. The Yellow Ford, however, was apparently as surprising to the Irish and O'Neill as it was shocking to the English. After the Yellow Ford, O'Neill decided not to move on to take Dublin where the poorly defended seat of English power in Ireland was at its most vulnerable after the defeat of Bagenal. But O'Neill was concerned that he lacked the siege weapons needed to take walled cities like Dublin. Nor did he have a Navy to attack from the sea. For this, he must continue to place his hopes on Spain.

Two years after the 1596 Spanish fleet was scattered by storms, as if the long revolt in the Netherlands was not demanding enough, Philip II was still distracted by wars in other countries and by revolts in Spanish territories in Hispaniola and elsewhere.[465] As a result, the armed forces of Spain were spread very thin everywhere. They were also poorly managed and Spain's royal finances were severely depleted. Worse still, in 1598, just as the time approached when the chieftains of Ireland needed Spain the most, Philip II, their expected savior, died.

At the time of Philip II's death, the Ulster insurrection had become Tyrone's war. It had not been his at the start, but by convergence of events and by consensus of the other chieftains, of Spain, of Rome, and even of Elizabeth, the northern chieftains' rebellion had for good or ill become O'Neill's rebellion. It was also now the

TWILIGHT OF THE TUDOR COURT

When the shock of the Yellow Ford defeat reached her, Elizabeth had few trusted counselors. left She had all along been losing the mentors and confidantes and favorites of her youth. Robert Dudley had died in 1588, Christopher Hatton in 1591, and Walsingham in 1590.

She had also lost some of her finest sea captains. Martin Frobisher died in 1594, and Drake and Hawkins were left to launch a raid into the Caribbean in August 1595. Hawkins, however, died at sea near Puerto Rico. Drake died of dysentery at Porto Bello and was buried at sea, and it fell to Sir Thomas Baskerville to bring the fleet home. Elizabeth was having to become more self-reliant, to place her trust in younger captains, and young Essex was one of the most prominent and favored of these.

The Tudor Court's only display of contrarian attitude was Essex' personal treatment of Elizabeth. While others fawned, flattered and flirted, Essex exhibited a shocking familiarity. He believed he had detected insecurity at the root of Elizabeth's indecisiveness, and he mistook it for weakness. Essex confided to others that in confrontations with men whom she favored, Elizabeth would always give way, and to Essex himself most of all. His overbearing egoistic style with her before long produced an abundance of anecdotal evidence to lend support to his thesis. Had he not wildly overplayed his hand, history might have proclaimed him the most astute observer of the Queen. But he pushed not only for favors for himself, and then misunderstood their bestowal as confirmation that he had free reign. He pushed for favors also for his friends, and compiled an unnecessary dossier of enemies from among those left out. Most fatal among his mistakes was alienating the Cecils, then failing to see past their unfailingly courtly manners to the hostility beneath, and underestimating the danger they presented.

(continued)

(Twilight of the Tudor Court, continued)

Essex, in April 1596, sailed for Spain with the best fleet yet, and he temporarily redeemed himself by helping Drake sack Cadiz. He concluded, however, that he could do no more than burn and plunder Cadiz. Though it was a stunning victory, it gained little or nothing for England but it did cause Essex' spotty reputation to soar temporarily. Even Essex' participation in the triumphal attack on Cadiz provided him far less stature than he thought. Disagreements erupted among Essex, Raleigh and Lord Howard of Effingham. Their competition for credit for what was achieved at Cadiz and their flight from blame for the failure to cripple the Spanish fleet as Elizabeth had expected, left Essex with a somewhat checkered stature in Elizabeth's eyes. Another Essex expedition in 1597 set out to attack Spanish ships in the Azores where, after some modest raiding and the capture of a few small islands, the fleet returned with very little to show for their effort, dashing Essex' reputation yet again.

Catholic rebellion against the heretic queen. How it became a religious crusade can be seen by the correspondence with Spain. What had begun as little more than defensive resistance to the first major physical encroachment in west Tyrone, Tyrconnell and Fermanagh, became a rising, a call to arms of the Catholic crusaders of Ireland and Spain.

What Made the Irish Finally Join in Grand Rebellion

The Tudor Irish policy had changed over time, and by the mid-16th century the policy was the extirpation of the native and Anglo Irish and the resettlement of English on their land. The perception of that new Tudor Irish policy by the Irish, and by their chieftains and earls also changed dramatically. Whether or not the Irish perception was an entirely up to date accurate reflection of the actual Tudor plan at each point, it was essentially on point and Ireland was slow, if anything, to appreciate how thoroughly determined the Tudors had finally become to put an end to the Irish. Many Irish did eventually come to the realization that the contention between Tudor England and the Irish had become an existential threat. Many Anglo Irish and native Irish had developed a perception that they were doomed to be impoverished, evicted, hanged, culturally ridiculed, deprived of the leaders they admired and the clergy they leaned on, and punished by a form of colonization difficult to endure. They came to realize they would lose their style of life and worship, and the only language they knew.

Their leaders faced special losses and were confronted with their own unique risks. Such leaders, O'Neill in particular, when they would rally support, would seldom invoke their own risks, but would play on the fears and on the religion of the Irish people. They gained the ability to trumpet their rebellions as a religious crusade. O'Neill, who was not unfairly chastised as having very little interest in religion, was able to fly the banner of God and the Pope when he went to rally support.

Under O'Neill's leadership there was added the exhilaration of victory at The Yellow Ford. When he found he was able to spread word that Spain too could see victory on the horizon for the Irish and that a Spanish army was about to invade and join him, many previously reluctant Irish threw their support to the rebellion.

More clans joined the rebellion, and soon the septs loyal to some of the earls joined. In Connaught, even some of the Burkes joined the rebels. In Munster, a general insurrection required Elizabeth to mass her greatest forces in the south of Ireland, allowing the northern chieftains to continue their attacks.[466] The rebellion spread to the west and to the midlands. O'Neill changed almost imperceptibly with the transformation of the rebellion. He grew to embrace the higher calling and to warm to the historic aura of the struggle while starting to view himself, as many who followed him did, as the new Great Earl, the first in almost a century to renew the promise once thought gone forever with the death of Gerald the Great, 8th Earl of Kildare.

Thomas Norris, Vice President of Munster sent what forces he could spare north under the leadership of his brother Henry Norris and Sir Conyers Clifford to try to cut off O'Donnell in an expected march south, but the English merely suffered another stinging defeat. Clifford, the new governor of Connaught, marched into Tyrconnell and won a victory at Belleek, but then at Ballyshannon he suffered the loss of many of his men. A bloody battle occurred in the Curlew Mountains on August 5, 1599. Richard Burke, Baron of Dunkellin, fighting to help Clifford relieve a castle in Sligo under siege by Red Hugh O'Donnell, led 2,000 men up a mountain pass, but they were attacked by O'Donnell's men and forced to scamper back down. Clifford himself was killed and Richard Burke narrowly escaped.

Preparing for a Winter War

Elizabeth was unusually slow to replace Lord Burgh, and her delay helped O'Neill make progress in rousing support in Munster. O'Neill dispatched an able commander, Richard Tyrrell,[467] into Munster, and Tyrrell went to battle against Ormond near the Butler Castle at Kilkenny. After Yellow Ford, Tyrrell set up camp in Munster in the Aherlow Valley and kept up attacks on castles at Kilkenny and elsewhere. As he marched across Munster, Tyrrell gathered grain and supplies to help if there was to be a winter campaign. The hardship of such campaigns made them a rarity, but Tyrrell could not have known what was in store for the rebels, and how fortunate it would be that the rebels began the practice even in 1598 of preparing for the chance that they would be at war in the dead of an Irish winter.

Tyrrell also mobilized support in Munster. He was joined in October, 1598 by the Sugane Earl of Desmond and his thousands of troops. Soon, Ownie O'More, Florence McCarthy, The O'Sullivan Beare, Lord Maurice Roche, the White Knight, Piers Lacy, the new Seneschal of Imokilly, leaders of cenels of native Irish, began to weigh in with their kerne and galloglass. Black Tom Butler found that he was unable to stop the growth of the rebels or the dismantling of the Munster plantation. Many of the planters fled to walled towns while their homes were burned. The New English settlers left most of Kerry and much of Munster in 1598 and 1599 as their land and cattle were seized by Anglo Irish lords or Tyrrell's men. Many Irish used this opportunity to retaliate against the planters.

The large plantation on the Earl of Desmond's lands that had been awarded to Sir Walter Raleigh simply disappeared as the homes, buildings and fields were burned.

Elizabeth had once proudly proclaimed that the frail woman her subjects beheld had the heart and stomach of a King, but now she longed for the advice of her longtime advisers, especially Lord Burghley, who had steadfastly insisted that Ireland was not susceptible to an affordable military solution, but by then Burghley too had died. Elizabeth's concern over the Irish victories turned to fury. It was directed not only at O'Neill but against those among her command who had failed to subdue him. She felt that Black Tom Butler had let her down, and sent her lifelong friend a strong rebuke for leaving the critical campaign in the north to Bagenal.

Robert Devereaux, 2nd Earl of Essex, saw another opportunity to manipulate Elizabeth's mood to what he was sure would be his great advantage. He lobbied hard for the command in Ireland. Elizabeth, however, was still a shrewd appraiser of those around her, and her experiences with Essex had left her less than confident in Essex' ability to defeat O'Neill. As often, she procrastinated, but Essex persisted in making his case. His boasts became more emphatic, more confident, as he pleaded for the chance, believing it would redeem his tarnished image. Finally, Elizabeth relented, and in March 1599, she dispatched Essex as Lord Lieutenant to Ireland with over 17,000 men.[468] Essex was given the clearest orders from the Queen to go directly after O'Neill. She included an ominous warning reminding Essex that it was he who had long counseled strong military action in Ireland. Almost daring Essex, she sent him with orders that O'Neill was to be killed.

The Tudor Declaration of War

In March 1599 Elizabeth's Proclamation condemned the "bloody and violent outrages" of the Irish and she vowed to "reduce that kingdom to obedience" by sending "an extraordinary and powerful force against them."[469] Thinking she was finally putting an end to The Great O'Neill, Elizabeth had mustered the boldness to spend for her an extravagant sum to end rebellion in Ireland.

At that time O'Neill was in the north, and, by summer 1599, he was in regular communication with Spain. In late June of 1599, emissaries of the new Spanish King Philip III arrived at Killeybegs and met with O'Donnell and O'Neill at Donegal Friary. The emissaries, Hugh Boy MacDavitt, Don Fernando de Barrio Nuevo, and General Marcus di Aramburu, also brought replenishments of weapons, supplies and gun powder.[470]

Essex began his attack in Ireland; however, he did it in Munster rather than Ulster as ordered. As disobedient as this came to be seen at Court, Essex had his reasons. Earlier, Essex had great difficulty with Lord Burghley and the Cecilian Party in the Privy Council. They denied him the carriage horses and ships necessary to establish a base at Lough Foyle. It was the lack of this equipment and inability to set up a base in the north that led Essex to concentrate his efforts on Munster. He believed that it was first essential to reverse the losses being suffered in Munster. By marching into Munster, Essex hoped to discourage a Spanish invasion of Munster. However, he failed to appreciate how his enemies at Court would use the story of this detour against him.

Essex' enemies at Court complained incredulously to Elizabeth that Essex had ignored her clear order to go north and attack O'Neill. It was made to appear to Elizabeth that Essex was merely dallying in the south. His enemies downplayed one very successful Essex attack — his 10-day siege of the seemingly impregnable Cahir Castle of the disloyal sept of the Butlers. The taking of Cahir Castle was trumpeted by Essex, but it was minimized by his enemies as merely a product of inefficient resistance, and Elizabeth was persuaded to view it as a worthless capture.[471] While Essex stayed in the south trying to join with Ormond, he also suffered a crippling defeat and a loss of badly needed men in a battle in the Wicklow Mountains. His men lost faith and began to defect, and soon the expensive force Elizabeth had sent to conquer Ireland was cut in half. In July, Elizabeth sent Essex an ultimatum to strike north.[472] Instead, he camped in Dublin. To protect himself, Essex ordered all his officers and others around him to support his reports to London that his army was no longer in shape to attack O'Neill.[473]

Meeting of Robert Devereaux, 2nd Earl of Essex, and the Earl of Tyrone in County Louth

Essex and O'Neill Meet

Essex was plainly worried. He began to think that his wisest course was to negotiate with O'Neill. Elizabeth renewed her order to Essex to go north and this time he went north, but the 4,000 men he marched with suddenly encountered O'Neill leading an even greater army. Virtually trapped, Essex held a meeting on horseback.

While the two armies camped near each other in September 1599, before preliminary skirmishes had yet given way to battle, O'Neill, still trying to buy time for Spanish help to reach the west coast, sought a meeting with Essex. Tom Lee knew them both and he likely facilitated the unorthodox parley between O'Neill and Essex.[474] Essex was still astride his horse when O'Neill arrived on his horse on the far bank. Each had six retainers, and O'Neill rode into the stream alone and spoke to Essex in private. Essex was 17 years O'Neill's junior and the son of one of the patrons of O'Neill's youth and the stepson of Dudley, another O'Neill supporter. Essex knew

O'Neill and likely had heard many impressive stories about the young Hugh O'Neill from his father and Dudley, spurring Essex to tell O'Neill, that as for the purported religious basis for O'Neill's rebellion: "Thou carest for religion as much as my horse."[475]

Essex returned to his army, broke camp and withdrew south to Dublin. What ensued has been called a truce, but also a grand conspiracy. Some have concluded that Essex and O'Neill conspired in that meeting to cooperate with each other to take the thrones of their respective countries. The willingness of Essex to flirt with such insubordination says a great deal to capture the reality of how far Elizabeth's star had fallen since her glory in 1588.

Essex defended his final failure to attack in a report to London, portraying his delay as an opportunity to regroup over the winter. But he received a scathing written rebuke from Elizabeth, a rejection of the winter truce and a rejection of all excuses for his disobedience of her repeated commands. The suspicious conduct of Essex and O'Neill was leading to increasing rumors and conspiracy theories throughout Ireland and England. Sometime after Ballyclinthe, Essex confided to friends that O'Neill had indeed proposed that Essex rebel against Elizabeth with O'Neill's support. The rumors of a plot between Essex and O'Neill drifted back to Court, and Essex concluded he had better hurry to London to explain himself. Essex rushed to London, then to Surrey, to the hunting grounds of Nonsuch Castle where Elizabeth was residing. He pushed past the royal servants and into the Queen's bedchamber only to find himself distinctly unwelcome, excoriated by an outraged Queen, and under arrest.

In June 1600 Essex was charged with desertion of his post in Ireland, insubordination and conspiracy with O'Neill. He was persuaded to forego a defense and profess remorse, and was then dealt with gently. He was banished from Court, confined to Essex House, removed from one office after another, and he lost his wine custom. His fall led his enemies to conduct intrigue and to forge his name on disloyal writings. For six months he was quarantined in comfortable confinement, but his actions while under quarantine sealed his doom. He continued to appear brave and full of himself, but he had grown unstable and paranoid. He was certain that Walter Raleigh was undermining him and that Elizabeth was simply jealous of him, for he was now sure that he matched her popularity.

Charles Blount, Lord Mountjoy

Frustrated by Essex' failure, Elizabeth's fury was finally consuming her, and her resolve to conquer Ireland reached its zenith.[476] She decided that, after 400 years of England dealing with rebels in Ireland by attainders, executions and martial law, she would, for a second time, send an overwhelming army to conquer Ireland. A fleet carrying another huge Tudor army was sent to Ireland, led by Charles Blount, Lord Mountjoy, the new Deputy replacing Essex.

The appointment of Mountjoy to replace Essex provoked even more recklessness in Essex, whose sister, Penelope Lady Rich, was Mountjoy's mistress. Essex tried to tempt Mountjoy to return to London and instead to lead that same Irish army to save Essex and pave the way for James VI of Scotland to take the Throne. Others around Essex encouraged such disloyalty, and he began to speak far too openly of his distrust of Raleigh and his doubts about the Queen. Essex also continued communications with O'Neill. At the end of the year he sent emissaries to O'Neill signaling his agreement to O'Neill's proposal to back Essex against the Queen.

Finally Essex went entirely over the edge; Essex and his followers finally took action, marching through Ludgate in revolt. He arrested four privy councilors and led two hundred shouting followers up Fleet Street. Despite this bold display, the citizens of London failed to respond, and he fled by small boat back to his home in the Strand where he was captured.

Erratic as he had become, Essex' rebellion was not entirely a product of his quirkiness. Elizabeth's financial stress, penury and her conspiracy-prone Court had by 1600 alienated many aristocrats, and a number of them were behind Essex. Even Mountjoy is believed to have weighed seriously the option of joining Essex against her. But this folly, whatever had led to it, when added to his failure to subdue O'Neill and to the greatly increased alarm over Ireland caused by that failure, was the last straw.

Essex was put on trial before a commission, and prosecuted by Sir Edward Coke, Elizabeth's Attorney General, and he was convicted of conspiring to usurp the Throne. Tom Lee made an ill-fated attempt to rescue Essex, but failed. Elizabeth at first remanded the order to execute Essex, then canceled the remand, acquiesced in the conviction, and her onetime favorite and Lord Lieutenant, now another in a line of wolves who came to grief by the poisoned chalice, was beheaded. O'Neill's old friend, Tom Lee, an Essex intimate, was one of those executed with Essex.

Mountjoy

Mountjoy was unlike Essex; he was a thoughtful, skilled and sometimes inspired tactician, where Essex had been a flashy failure, but Mountjoy would seem an unlikely savior of her policy or the war. He was a hypochondriac, but with good reason; he actually did suffer severe headaches. Mountjoy had been a Catholic in his youth. He also had a long affair with Penelope Rich, the sister of Essex.

In February 1600, Mountjoy arrived with 13,200 men, a smaller but far more effective force than Essex's, because Mountjoy commanded fewer untrained soldiers than Essex. When Mountjoy arrived, he refused to engage in the parlays and truces that had provided O'Neill so much time and preparation. Mountjoy began his battles in Leinster and in the southern parts of Ulster.[477] Sir George Carew had taken charge of the military in Munster and did so very effectively. Carew put the forces of the Sugane Earl on the run. The Earl himself became a fugitive, but was caught and sent to the Tower. To reverse the losses in Munster, Carew set about diluting O'Neill's support, and he achieved considerable success in forcing many of the Munster chieftains and lords to abandon O'Neill. Mountjoy broke with precedent and kept the war going through the winter, taking away the respite O'Neill needed and denying the Irish the chance to tend livestock and plant crops.

The Anger Between Two Clans

Within the rebel clans, ominous divisions were developing. Many were impatient with how the war was dragging on. They hungered for a definitive battle. O'Neill, nevertheless, insisted, that they must continue to hold to the strategy that had served them well – ambushes in the woods and surprise attacks from ideal redoubts. He was firmly opposed to a pitched battle against English cavalry and firearms on open fields. Those battles were the strong suit of the Tudor army, not the Irish.

As the Tyrone Rebellion dragged on, O'Neill was losing influence. Support for O'Neill's rebellion was weakening among lesser captains and younger chieftains. No one wanted to be on the losing side of this war, but pressure from both sides made it necessary to choose a side. Some of the chieftains gave Mountjoy and the Newry garrison quiet assurances of their support if Mountjoy called for it. O'Neill learned such things were happening. He had allies, friends and spies in every clan, and he cautioned several of those leaders against defection, warning that they would not find themselves welcome after the success of the rebellion, to join with the O'Neills and O'Donnells if they had failed to remain loyal to him and come to his aid when he needed them most.

An English Beachhead in the North

Suddenly the English achieved a beachhead in the north. Sir Henry Docwra landed in the north with 4,000 new men in May 1600 and began the fortification of Derry.[478] Red Hugh O'Donnell attacked Docwra and set a siege at Derry, but Red Hugh left Derry at a crucial time; he lead a small force into lower Connaught to raid the earldoms of Thomond and Clanrickard. With their clan leader away, some O'Donnells wavered, and Docwra was able to form an alliance with dissident O'Donnell septs, including the ambitious Niall Garbh O'Donnell, and this helped to secure the fort Docwra established at Derry and to protect this valuable point of access from the sea. Docwra was thus able to create a wedge that split Ulster into two separate, less effective regions. With fresh troops, Docwra, Sir Arthur Chichester and others then set out to make further inroads against O'Neill and O'Donnell.

Docwra provoked a fight over the succession to leadership of the O'Doherty sept. Cahir O'Doherty was passed over in favor of Phelim Og O'Doherty. Docwra spread the rumor that Red Hugh O'Donnell had accepted a bribe to allow Phelim Og to be chosen in preference to Cahir. The O'Dohertys believed it, and they signed on with the English. The O'Donnells then had to fight several battles against the O'Dohertys and their McDaid supporters. Inter clan fights, executions and reprisals in western Ulster soon became the order of the day.

O'Neill suffered losses in the south as well. In early 1600, one brief encounter inflicted a damaging loss on O'Neill's forces. Hugh Maguire accompanied O'Neill in a campaign to the south, and together they scouted out Kinsale. A messenger alerted Sir Warham St. Leger (a nephew of Warham St. Leger who was a friend of Hugh O'Neill), Deputy to the Governor of Munster, and he and his horsemen set out to Cork to intercept Maguire. There Maguire and Warham boldly attacked each other. Maguire stabbed Warham who fell dead on the spot, but was able to fire a single shot as he died. Maguire climbed down from his horse, but suddenly collapsed and died a short distance from the ambush. His death was a severe blow to O'Neill, for Maguire was not only O'Neill's favorite son-in-law, he had been a bulwark of O'Neill's forces.

18

Kinsale—The Chieftains' Darkest Hour

Irish fighters are "great endurers of cold, labor, hunger and all hardness, very active and strong of hand, very swift of foot.... very great scorners of death"[479]
— Edmund Spenser

Momentum had swung to the English by the summer of 1600, and a despondent O'Neill was considering suing for peace. Although the Nine Years War had already provided many exhilarating victories for the Irish, there had been setbacks as well. The Spanish Fleet that had set out for Ireland earlier had been turned back by foul weather. Mountjoy had prevailed in fierce battles at the Gap of the North and built a new fort inside Ulster. The peaks and valleys of emotion of this war took a toll on both sides, but as O'Neill agonized, Philip III of Spain at last sent the promised military force. However, he sent it to the wrong place.

The Landing Site Debate

Prior to launching the new Armada to Ireland, the Spanish themselves debated whether to land at Limerick, Galway, or to sail further north to Sligo or Killybeggs in Donegal. The Spanish feared the northern weather, were very concerned about the North's rockier coastline, and wanted to avoid a long march to the south after landing. Irish coastal waters are dangerous, and many major ports are in river estuaries or deeply penetrating bays: Derry on the Foyle, Belfast on the Lagan, Limerick on the Shannon, Waterford on the Suir, Cork and Cobh on the Lee, and Kinsale on the Bandon. Long

Don Juan Del Aguila

bays at Tralee, Donegal, Galway and Bantry provided equivalent harbor safety.

Those in Spain debating the best landing site were fresh in the knowledge that the 1588 defeat of the Armada had been as much a product of the disease from a three-month ocean voyage as it was of the nimble English fire ships and warships encountered in the Channel. The Armada of 1588 had chosen to sail for England full of soldiers and provisions in summer. On the long voyage food had spoiled, water had become slimy, and disease had taken a heavy toll well before the Armada entered the Channel. Three quarters of the Spanish troops of 1588 ultimately died of wounds or disease. That experience was now the haunting memory which helped the arguments of those favoring a landing at a close southern Irish port.

One Spaniard spoke now with greater credibility than the rest. Hugh O'Neill had sponsored Spanish Archbishop Mateo de Oviedo as the favorite to become Archbishop of Dublin in 1599, for his 20 years of devoted service encouraging Spanish help, and this Spaniard was now one of the key decision makers about to make a crucial decision that set the future course of Irish history. O'Neill had designated Father Edmund MacDonnell, Dean of Armagh, his emissary to Spain, charging him with the role of dealing with Oviedo. Henry O'Neill, the second son of Hugh, had also gone to Spain in the Spring of 1600 both as an emissary to the Spanish and to enroll in school. Oviedo was aware that if Spanish forces landed at Donegal, they would be near O'Neill and O'Donnell, and he appreciated how important it was that Spanish troops landing in the unfamiliar terrain of Ireland receive training from the Irish chieftains. Oviedo also knew that Spanish reinforcements promised by Philip III could easily land at Donegal; that the English had 8,000 foot soldiers and 1,500 cavalry in the South and few in the north; and that if the Spanish landed in the south but failed to break through promptly after landing, provisions would be in short supply because the orders to the Spanish fleet were to depart as soon as Aguila's army landed.

For these reasons the Commander of the Spanish troops, Aguila, strongly favored landing in Donegal Bay. However, Archbishop Oviedo and Captain Don Martin de la Cerda thought they had received contrary recommendations on much earlier visits with O'Neill and O'Donnell. Oviedo was well intentioned, but was using information that was now very badly outdated, but he repeatedly recited with great authority what he had been told earlier by O'Neill and O'Donnell. Earlier, a landing by a large Spanish invasion force at Limerick or Kinsale would have made sense, but now a southern landing by a small army made no sense. The chieftains' earlier preference for a southern landing had been based on the assumption that a powerful army of 7,000 would be sent by the Spanish and that they would immediately be welcomed and bolstered by the galloglass of the native Irish leaders in Cork and Limerick, Florence MacCarthy and James FitzThomas, FitzGerald, the Sugane Earl of Desmond. However, MacCarthy and the Sugane Earl had been captured by the English and were now held in the Tower of London.[480] Even without learning that the Spanish troops would barely be half the number promised, the absence of a native force in Munster made O'Neill conclude that it was essential that the Spaniards land in the north or west to avoid the English troops.[481]

Last Chance

In early August, 1601, O'Donnell had a final chance to update the military intelligence and warn the Spanish that the choice of a southern landing site would be disastrous. Ensign Pedro de Sandoval arrived at Sligo. O'Donnell was quick to advise Sandoval that the support in the south was sharply reduced with the capture of Florence MacCarthy and the loss of the forces of the Sugane Earl of Desmond. O'Donnell warned that there were now strong English reinforcements and fortifications at Waterford and Cork. He urged Sandoval to have the Spanish make for Limerick or any port further north even up to Donegal. Sandoval understood completely and hurried back to Spain; however, the fleet had set sail and it was a small flotilla of only 33 ships carrying only 4,432 troops, crippled by its inadequate manpower and obsolete intelligence.

Archbishop Oviedo had persuaded Don Diego de Brochero y Ania, the naval commander of the expedition before sailing to plan to land in the south of Ireland. Aguila, the army commander, however, continued to argue against Archbishop Oviedo and, by the time they sailed, severe discord had developed between Aguila and Brochero. The fate of Ireland was in the hands of two strong-willed individuals, one of whom wanted to go to the north, the other to the south, neither of whom was willing to reconsider his own views.

Once at sea, however, Oviedo became ill. Aguila, hoping that Oviedo's resolute insistence on a southern port may have weakened, made a final effort to change the landing site. Oviedo was not too sick, however, to refuse. He overruled Aguila once again, and on October 2, 1601, Aguila and his troops were deposited at Kinsale where matters grew worse. They anxiously awaited the rest of the fleet, but eight ships had been lost or driven back to Spain by a storm. By October 9, those ships that did make it to Kinsale had landed their troops and sailed back to Spain; in total, only 3400 men made shore.

With their small force now diminished even further, a wise landing site selection had been especially crucial. The choice they had made was not a mere mistake. It moved the plates of history. O'Neill and O'Donnell were about to learn that they were left with no choice but to drop what they were doing, to leave Ulster, and to execute a forced march to the south lasting more than a month. The main purpose of this destructive detour was to rescue their rescuers.

Badly weakened Munster would now become the site of the historic encounter between the northern clans and the vast Tudor army. By this time there was no longer any serious chance for a widespread Munster rising after the capture of Florence MacCarthy and the Sugane Earl of Desmond.[482] Mountjoy's troops had also succeeded in weakening even the local guerrillas and killing the most effective of the Munster guerillas, Ownie O'More, the midlands legend who, in 1600, had captured Black Tom Butler. O'More's death now allowed Laois to fall to George Carew[483] and Lord Mountjoy. Mountjoy had devastated the crops of Munster before the harvest in 1600 and had stopped the planting of 1601, hoping to cause regional famine in Munster. Carew drove the Irish out of much of Kerry, took their harvest and their herds and conquered or subdued much of western Munster. O'Neill could no longer afford, amid famine and Mountjoy's increasing momentum, to play a waiting game.

Aguila had tried to convince the commanders to put back to sea and land at Killybeggs in the North, but they concluded they had no choice but to stay at Kinsale and prepare for battle. Even then, however, Aguila failed to secure the small castles at Rincorran and Castle Park on the east and west points of the harbor, and English warships and land-based cannon brought about their fall, denying Aguila control of the harbor.

Mountjoy heard the landing site news while meeting with Carew at Kilkenny and the momentary alarm he felt quickly disappeared[484] when he learned where the Spanish had landed.[485]

He wrote London promising Elizabeth that he would soon have the Spanish with "halters about their necks."[486] Carew reported to Mountjoy that he had been saving provisions and munitions for most of the year and could supply the Tudor army for a three-month siege of Kinsale. Mountjoy was jubilant and went immediately to Cork to be closer to the action. He called English troops from as far north as Newry to increase his force at Kinsale to 7,500, and he cautiously left troops in place at Cork and Waterford to guard against a suspected second landing force. Soon Mountjoy's troops were camped on the hills surrounding Kinsale. One was a high meadow, Knockrobin Hill. They seemed to know that O'Neill would have to come out of his lair, to leave the priceless strategic cover of his Ulster woods and come to them.

In Ulster, O'Neill's shock had matured to a healthy anger; he confronted his predicament, hoping for word that Aguila had the sense to put back to sea and make for Sligo or Killybeggs. But, after two weeks, he realized that Aguila would stay at Kinsale and that he and O'Donnell had no choice but to go to Kinsale to relieve Aguila.

O'Neill began the fateful march south after receiving a November 6 appeal that Aguila smuggled out of Kinsale through a Priest. In it Aguila urgently called on the rebels to come and lift the siege. Aguila's message virtually taunted O'Neill and O'Donnell, telling them that they would be disgraced in Spain if they failed to heed this plea after so many years when they had been calling for Spain's help. O'Donnell was persuaded; he pushed hard on O'Neill to start a forced march of over 200 miles from Ulster to the southern coast to relieve Kinsale.[487]

Winter March to Kinsale

O'Donnell preceded O'Neill down the length of Ireland to Kinsale.[488] The delay in deciding had only increased the inclemency of the weather they encountered en route. They brought no wagons, only men and horses, a pure guerrilla force.[489] The British knew O'Donnell was coming and Carew tried to intercept O'Donnell's forces along the River Suir. However, O'Donnell took advantage of the cold, capitalizing on the freezing of the high bogs in the Slieve

Phelim Mountains. Near frozen, the usually impassable bogs had become firm and briefly passable, and the O'Donnell army avoided the lower ground where Carew waited in ambush. O'Donnell marched on and reached Castlehaven by December 12 and there awaited a rendezvous with O'Neill.

On his way down to Kinsale, O'Neill took the time to thrust into Leinster and to pillage no less than 22 villages, taking cattle at will and burning the fields of New English settlers. This uncharacteristic noisy approach may have been O'Neill's effort to try to lure Dublin officials to summon Mountjoy back to protect the Pale and away from Kinsale.

O'Neill marched his men through frozen ground and forded rivers by building temporary wooden bridges, and traversed on foot most of the length of Ireland. He picked up reinforcements in Leinster; the greatest additions were troops led by Captain Richard Tyrell. O'Neill and his forces joined O'Donnell on December 15, having crossed many swollen rivers; but as difficult as all this had been, they both arrived leading formidable forces to join with the Spaniards against the English.

The English were suffering as well; they had begun to lose men. By the time of O'Neill's arrival, the 6000 English at Camphill outside Kinsale were losing 40 men a day from disease. In the days before battle commenced, the weary O'Neill and O'Donnell felt that the Spaniards had proved to Mountjoy that they would be able to endure his siege. They hoped that the English would end the siege themselves, and the centuries old domination by England would be ended forever. However, Mountjoy instead raised the stakes — reinforcements arrived.

At Camp Eiranagh deep in the woods of Coolcarron, near the open field bivouac of Mountjoy's cavalry and infantry, the Irish clans weighed their options. They, too, were exposed to the winter storms that raged around Kinsale. If they held off attacking, the exposed Mountjoy troops might suffer far more from the winter than the Spanish troops interdicted in the town of Kinsale. However, Aguila's men had been suffering winter hardships for many weeks. They were inadequately clothed, and every attempt they had made to sally out from the fortifications around Kinsale to capture cattle for food or horses for cavalry had failed.

As the fate of Ireland hung in the balance, Hugh O'Donnell lost his patience. He began to rage at the reluctant O'Neill, urging attack.[490] O'Neill and O'Donnell were both aware that their successes had been guerrilla style skirmishes and sudden attacks from the woods by pikemen, musketeers and horsemen, avoiding frontal encounters, attacking on the flanks against isolated troops of English on the march. But O'Donnell insisted they attack. O'Neill fought back; he argued that they must continue their blockade of Mountjoy's main camp and use skirmish tactics against approaching reinforcements.

The Irish had succeeded in amassing troops that now outnumbered the English. The Irish were fresher, had enough cover, rations, ammunition and relative comfort to starve or wear out the English trapped at Kinsale. The Irish could accelerate the deterioration of Mountjoy's increasingly infirm troops by pestering them with the dart and disappear attacks that had destroyed English troops in Ulster. Precipitating a battle on open terrain would be foolish. Months of winter remained, and the exposed English were suffering from the siege far more than the besieged Spaniards.

O'Neill's strategy was the soundest and the safest. The Irish army might well prevail if O'Neill was allowed to decide strategy and tactics, and O'Donnell surely must have seen that, but, he was determined to attack, and nothing, it seemed, could sway him. Exactly how perilous the English condition was did not become known until much later, but in fact many English and their horses had already died. Whether O'Neill now lacked the stature needed to govern the war council due to his years vacillating between Irish rebel and loyal Tudor, or whether the ancient hostilities of Clan O'Donnell and Clan O'Neill that had resurfaced were too bitter, it was the young and far less experienced O'Donnell who, through force of will, dictated the attack. At long last, at Ireland's most crucial moment, ancient blood feuds had resurfaced. The *Cenel Conail* and *Cenel Eoghain* clashed once again.[491] The O'Donnell would not yield to The O'Neill.[492]

O'Donnell could explain how in theory an attack might work, but the actual attack would require flawless performance by the attacking armies, precise communication and disciplined timing. The fragmented Irish armies were hostile to each other, amateurs in such an attack and inept at communication.

The Spanish had a voice in the decision as well. Aguila sent a strong plea to the Irish to attack, and O'Donnell built on that.[493] O'Donnell saw himself as the man who had finally brought a serious Spanish army to the aid of Ireland and he felt that the Irish had no choice but to show the Spaniards that they were brave enough to attack to end their suffering. To him, it was a matter of honor; he felt it was shameful to listen to the pleas of the Spanish without rallying to help them. Thus, in the council of war, O'Donnell took an extreme position — that honor required the Irish to attack as urged by the Spanish even if it meant defeat. O'Neill's strategy was rejected.

O'Donnell adopted a posture that seems to have reflected the tone that The Anointed One was about to rid Ireland of the English. His O'Donnell clansmen began lashing out at the O'Neill kerne, bringing to a fresh boil the ancestral grudges they had been suppressing throughout the Nine Years War. The O'Donnell and O'Neill clans spewed Gaelic venom not at Mountjoy or the Tudors, but at each other. That night it all erupted and destroyed the cohesion needed for a battle just hours away. O'Neill and O'Donnell never recovered their focus. The debate ended with a fiat, not a consensus.[494] What had to be a fully embraced plan of battle was by morning just a recognition by O'Neill that O'Donnell was going to attack and that O'Neill had no choice but to do so as well.[495]

Plan of Attack

On December 23rd the decision was made to attack. The Spanish were, at a signal, supposed to come out and attack the Earl of Thomond's Second Camp and O'Neill and O'Donnell together with Tyrell would attack the northern camp. But somehow the English learned that the Irish Army intended an imminent attack, and Mountjoy was poised and ready when the attack came. The crucial warning of the attack was said to have been provided to the English by Brian MacHugh Oge MacMahon, a commander in the Irish army.[496] The English had at least intercepted letters between the Irish and the Spanish and learned enough to infer that an attack would come before dawn. With O'Neill as its leader, Ireland's fate was decided that day — Christmas Eve, 1601.[497] Hugh O'Neill, once the Earl of Tyrone, the Chief of the Name and the head of the great

O'Neill clan of Ulster, exhorted his Irish troops and marched out just before dawn to attack Lord Mountjoy's army at the climactic moment of what had become to that time Ireland's greatest rebellion. The scene that morning, reminiscent of Henry V at Agincourt, became the prelude to 400 years of discord.

The Final Battle

The Battle of Kinsale was fought on December 24, 1601 (under the old calendar).[498] To the Spanish and to some Irish Catholics it was January 3, 1602 under the Gregorian calendar adopted by Spain in 1582. Some 6,000 Irish foot soldiers and 800 cavalry had moved to the outskirts of Kinsale during the last days before the battle. The Irish army was about to abandon its crippling blockade to give the English the extraordinary gift of fighting the battle English style, a battle array in which the English cavalry were nearly invincible and the Irish were notoriously ineffective.

Half an hour before dawn on December 24, 1601, beneath a sky filled with lightning and thunder, the Irish army marching to their first battlefield encounter at Kinsale were in the classic formation of vanguard (Tyrell), main battle (O'Neill), and rearguard (O'Donnell). Another destructive argument began over how the attack should occur and who should lead it. Neither O'Neill nor O'Donnell would yield. The clans marched out of the Irish camp in the dark, before dawn, elbow to elbow, into the breach in unfamiliar formation.[499] Of all battles in which good communication was essential to coordinate the O'Neill, O'Donnell and Spanish forces, miscommunication became the order of the day. O'Donnell and his troops became confused and lost in the dark. The resulting delay threw off the timing and thoroughly confused the Spaniards. They expected the Irish to reach a secure point near Kinsale, then Aguila could burst out to join the fight near where Carew's force guarded the town.

By dawn O'Neill's main force had arrived within sight of the English camps, but O'Donnell's troops failed to reach their position on time. O'Neill stopped to wait for O'Donnell, and by doing so lost the initiative. O'Neill surveyed the battlefield from a ridge near Millwater Ford; he saw that the English regiments and cavalry before him stood on secure ground, but he was alarmed that Aguila and the Spaniards had not come out from Kinsale. He decided to withdraw his troops and cavalry in a tactical retreat, but to do that his men had to cross the Ballinamona bog where they became mired and vulnerable. On the English side, the Marshall, Richard Wingfield, could see that the ground the Irish were crossing was boggy, that only a narrow passage provided a route to solid ground, and that no woods were available to the Irish for cover. He urged attack. Mountjoy hesitated, but finally gave the signal to advance.

The English cavalry attack was led by Sir Henry Danvers and Richard Burke, 4th Earl of Clanrickard; it came at the moment when the woods were unreachable by the Irish in the time needed to escape charging cavalry. O'Neill's main battle group was to have been deployed in the center but at the moment of attack it was his vanguard that was in the center. O'Neill's force revealed what, in essence, it was, a brave army facing its first major fight on an open battlefield.

When the English cavalry attacked, O'Neill's troops formed the tercio, the Spanish style of a phalanx-like cluster with shot posted at all its corners. The English had by 1601 adopted the use of smaller, more controllable tercios, repeatedly tightening the core when men in the tercio fell. The Irish troops, despite all the training they had received producing their three great successes in Ulster, looked as though they had no experience on a field of battle. They were undisciplined in holding the tight tercio formation. When attacked, they opened ranks. Then a store of gunpowder in the Irish supply train exploded and caused momentary panic. The light horse O'Neill had used as his cavalry were routed, and in their effort to retreat, they disrupted their own infantry. The English cavalry was left free to rip into the ranks of retreating Irish foot soldiers, caught for one of the few times in the 9 years of the war out in the open. Richard Burke was one of the very few English casualties, and even he was only slightly wounded. Burke personally killed some 20 Irish kerne, and that day he became "Richard of Kinsale."[500]

So confusing was the melee that it is unclear whether O'Donnell and his forces participated at all in doing battle at Kinsale. It is clear that Aguila and the Spaniards did not. Tyrell failed to take the position from which he was to signal Aguila to bring the Spanish troops out of Kinsale to join the assault, and a confused Aguila stayed put. Thus, the uneven battle was made hopeless by the failure of two major components to participate as planned.

The Irish army suffered an exceptionally steep casualty toll, so steep that the Millwater became known as the Ford of the Slaughter. Many of the retreating Irish were driven into the Blackwater and drowned. Many died in the field, slowed in their retreat by the bog. Many had to discard their weapons to flee, only to become easy prey to capture. Those taken prisoner were hanged. O'Neill's forces lost between 500 and 1,000 dead compared to the English 12, and the English captured 2,000 arms of the Irish as well as their baggage and cows.

Well after the battle was already lost, Aguila heard Lord Mountjoy fire a volley in victory, but mistook it for the signal to attack. He and the Spaniards charged forth from Kinsale to help, but saw quickly what had actually occurred, and scurried lamely back into Kinsale. A battle that could have been won had already been lost, ultimately, due to the well-intentioned help received from a friendly nation.

In the end, the greatest cause of the defeat was that it all occurred at Kinsale rather than in the thick woods of Ulster. It was the choice of the landing site that brought the Irish down. The Irish army lay broken at day's end. The force that could well have relieved Kinsale and, with time, worn the English army out or driven it away, had been fatally crippled. What troops remained alive that night were no longer any match for Mountjoy.

Many things had to go wrong to end the Irish campaign against Tudor England, and they all had. One was the return of ancestral hatreds that had inflamed competing High Kings in 12th century Ireland and now had done the same to 16th century chieftains, once again shackling the Irish for centuries to come.

19

Recessional

[T]hey have left me nothing but ashes and carcasses to reign over[501]
— Elizabeth I

Mountjoy reset the siege of the Spanish in Kinsale and he extravagantly hanged hundreds of Irish prisoners where the Spanish could watch. Aguila was given time to reflect that he and his men would be tortured and slaughtered in the gruesome fashion of Smerwick.[502] Before long, however, he was told that Mountjoy was willing to negotiate. When the negotiators met, confronted by the English, Aguila bitterly denounced the Irish. He claimed that the Spaniards were blameless, that they were able, if necessary, to hold out, comfortable inside the town, compared with Mountjoy's men who were increasingly miserable. Aguila informed Mountjoy that he was willing to leave because the failures by O'Neill and O'Donnell had relieved him of his mission and he was free to return to Spain and to relinquish the three harbors (Kinsale, Castlehaven and Baltimore).

Mountjoy's forces were still in dire straits. They were low on provisions and several of their big guns were now inoperable, and he concluded that England would be better off if the Spanish simply left, and on January 12, 1602, Aguila surrendered to Mountjoy and he and his men were provided ships and allowed to set sail for Spain.

After the Battle of Kinsale, O'Neill, remained firm and tried to continue the war.[503] The Irish regrouped at Inishannon near Bandon, and O'Neill succeeded in escaping back to Ulster using guile to avoid intercept, and spreading false reports that the English had been defeated at Kinsale. But after Kinsale, famine and lawlessness swept Ireland. Many of O'Neill's followers and subjects in Ulster had endured enough. Yet despite limited support, O'Neill was able to muster enough men to spend over a year trying to re-ignite the war.

O'Donnell and his supporters were opposed to any continuation of the war without substantial Spanish help, and King Philip III had at first ordered that plans be made to send additional Spanish forces from Spain and Dunkirk. O'Donnell decided to go to Spain in an effort to convince Philip to send more troops. He turned over command of his army to his brother Rory (*Ruadri*) and sailed from Castlehaven to Spain two days after the battle. Captain Richard Tyrell joined Don Pedro de Zubiaur on a ship for Spain to help in the plan to convince Philip to send help.

In Ulster the O'Donnells were in disarray due to the defection of Neill Garbh O'Donnell and claims of competing chieftains for clan leadership. Neill Garbh O'Donnell had defected to Sir Henry Docwra in October. Several other competing leaders also defected to Docwra, making Docwra's landing at Derry one of the major ingredients of England's continuing success against the Ulster chieftains.

Dunboy Castle

Donal O'Sullivan Beare learned that the Spanish were going to surrender Dunboy Castle, his home. He was joined by Cornelius O'Driscoll and his clan and by the MacCarthys, and they and a thousand Irish went to Dunboy, wrestled it from Spanish control, and led the defense of the Castle. However, months later, Sir George Carew ultimately took Dunboy Castle on June 27 and 28, 1602. The O'Driscoll castles at Castlehaven and Baltimore surrendered also. Many of the O'Sullivans and a number of the O'Driscolls were executed, but Donal O'Sullivan Beare eluded capture and marched the remainder of his force to Leitrim.

O'Donnell in Spain

Spain's confidence, still low as a result of the Armada's failure a decade earlier, was now much lower after the defeat at Kinsale. O'Donnell would find that this second failure broke Philip's will to take precious troops and commit them to Ireland. The Duke of Lerma, who exercised substantial influence over the weak and malleable 23-year-old Philip III, was firmly opposed to renewed aid. O'Donnell based his argument for a new, larger Spanish invasion on the need to rescue Don Juan Del Aguila and his troops from slaughter. At the time O'Donnell left Ireland, Aguila was still trapped in Kinsale. But when Aguila negotiated a surrender and won permission to leave, his success ended the chance for O'Donnell to win the support of Philip III against the contrary advice of the Duke of Lerma. The final blow was the self-serving claims of the returning Spaniards that the defeat at Kinsale was the fault of the Irish.

The Spaniards took these claims seriously and convened a lengthy council of inquiry to determine the causes of the failure. Ultimately this Spanish council absolved Aguila and blamed the Irish. Irish history usually blames the Spanish, but the abundance of miscommunications that led to this defeat defy the naming of a single scapegoat. One person among those most instrumental in bringing about defeat may not have been a military commander at all but Spanish Archbishop Oviedo whose well intentioned insistence led the Spanish fleet to land at Kinsale.

Red Hugh O'Donnell became more and more frustrated in his efforts to convince the Spaniards to wrap up their lengthy inquiry into the failure of the invasion and focus on military and financial support for the Irish chieftains. But on September 10, 1602, O'Donnell died at the Castle of Simancas.

O'Donnell had gone to Simancas on August 10, 1602 to petition Philip III. But by September 10, he was dead after a curious 17-day illness. At the time, O'Donnell's suspicious death was accepted as a death from natural causes, and it was not until years later that evidence appeared suggesting he was murdered on Sir George Carew's orders. Carew's adjutant, James Blake, claimed personal credit for Red Hugh's death, but such a claim is not entirely surprising whether or not the credit was actually his. Carew's correspondence takes credit for sending assassins to Spain to kill O'Donnell. Carew wrote on June 8, 1602 that he had a conversation with Blake in which Blake promised that he would go to Spain to kill O'Donnell. Blake often used the name Diego Blocadell to conceal his identify. O'Donnell had been alerted that Diego Blocadell had landed at Lisbon. Blake was indeed in Spain; he and his servant, Robert Kirwan, were arrested in Spain and interrogated in November 1602 in Valladolid but without resolution. Whatever the cause of his suspicious death, Red Hugh O'Donnell was buried less than a year after Kinsale far from Tyrconnell in a Franciscan church in Valladolid, Spain.

The Running Beast in Ulster

After Kinsale, Mountjoy's troops continued to fight the chieftains. He resumed destroying crops to cause a famine, secured Munster, then headed north. Sir Arthur Chichester advocated the "extermination" of the rebel clans after Kinsale.[504] Mountjoy destroyed the O'Neill's crowning stone at Tullaghoge to strike a note of symbolism of his own. For his success at Kinsale, Mountjoy was named Earl of Devonshire and appointed Lord Lieutenant of Ireland.

O'Neill made it back to Ulster, but Mountjoy's troops had all the momentum and they kept O'Neill on the run. O'Neill at times was reduced to hiding and making nightly moves to elude capture. He and his wife, Catherine Magennis, moved through the Ulster woods, like the Earl and Countess of Desmond 17 years earlier. O'Neill's final forest redoubts were in Antrim at Kylultagh, seat of the Magennis sept,[505] O'Neill's wife's family, and in the dense forest of Portglenone near Glenconkeyne. Often desperate for food, they were unable to stay put long enough to grow and harvest crops. O'Neill was branded "The Running Beast."[506] O'Neill's appetite for the life of guerrilla warfare soon enough disappeared. Once the regrouping of the Irish army failed to roll back the momentum to his favor, he sunk to despair. He could see that his life and that of his children was very much like the endgame of the Rebel Earl of Desmond.

Finding and killing O'Neill, however, was proving next to impossible. After a year as a renegade and guerrilla, as desolation spread throughout Ulster, O'Neill put out feelers for a truce. He offered to lay down his arms and renew his youthful pledge of loyalty to Queen Elizabeth, but Mountjoy refused. O'Neill did not know that Elizabeth had become very ill and was approaching death, and that it was expediency that was about to bring an end to the war. Reports of Elizabeth's lengthy death struggle were raising Mountjoy's anxiety, but Sir Arthur Chichester, the governor of Carrickfergus, was prolonging the end because he was dead set against a pardon; he wanted O'Neill executed as an arch traitor. Finally, by March 1603, several forces came together to end the Nine Years War — the financial drain caused by O'Neill's ability to continue guerrilla warfare, the impending death of Elizabeth, and Mountjoy's in-

Sir Arthur Chichester, Lord Deputy of Ireland

tense anxiety – he needed to get to London to position himself with a coming new king. At long last, near death, Elizabeth authorized Mountjoy to offer O'Neill a pardon.

Submission at Mellifont

The war had taken a great toll on Ireland and on the English treasury. It had become so expensive that in mid-1601 the Irish currency had been debased to keep down the escalating costs of the war, and inflation became virtually uncontrolled. Finally, Mountjoy sent the word that he accepted O'Neill's second offer to submit.

Sir Edward Moore had died in 1602, but Elizabeth and Mountjoy knew that his son Garrett, Viscount Moore of Drogheda, a friend of O'Neill, was the best potential intermediary who might succeed in coaxing O'Neill in from where he and his men were hiding. Moore was also loyal to the Tudors, respected by all, trustworthy and reliable. Elizabeth and her confidantes decided to enlist him to intercede, to convey to O'Neill Elizabeth's and Mountjoy's agreement to favorable terms to end his guerrilla war and to give O'Neill their assurance that this was not a trap.

O'Neill surrendered at Mellifont on March 30, 1603. Thus ended the campaign that could have brought self governance or a Spanish King to Ireland. The Tudor conquest was achieved and the ancient Irish world seemed set to disappear into history. On the day O'Neill arrived to surrender, Mountjoy chose not to reveal to O'Neill that Elizabeth was dead, and that when O'Neill knelt to surrender, it was James I who was now his King.

Succession

In Europe there were over a dozen potential successors (better termed demanding claimants)[507] who could muster support for their lineage-based pretensions to the English Throne. In 1603 the strongest lineage claim was that of King James VI of Scotland, son of Mary Queen of Scots, and thus a direct descendant of Henry VII.[508] James let Tudor courtiers know he was preparing to invade, if passed over, to conquer his way to the Throne he thought rightfully his.

As death reached out to Elizabeth, she shook her weary head and refused to name her successor for fear she would instantly lose the love and loyalty of her people.[509] Hours before she died, she finally signaled it should be King James VI of Scotland, the man she had orphaned. The smooth transition to the coronation of James was negotiated and scripted very effectively by Robert Cecil. Though James' mother, Mary Queen of Scots, had been Catholic, the only Scot allowed to attend Catholic Mass, James VI, like most of Scotland, had been raised Protestant. James never knew his mother.[510] They had not seen each other since he was a baby. Essentially, she had occupied the uncomfortable position of a competitor of his for the Crown of England.[511]

Elizabeth had never met James or his mother, yet she chose him to come from turbulent Scotland to rule England. Hostility to the Scots in Ulster was one of the more impenetrable mysteries surrounding the contradictory enigma that was Elizabeth I. She who had ordered the Scots extirped and driven from Ulster, applauded the massacre of several hundred defenseless Scots on Rathlin Island and over a thousand Scots at Ardnaree in Connaught, had feared the potential challenge of Mary Queen of Scots, but then ordered her execution, now turned over the Crown of England to James Stuart, giving her kingdom to Mary's Scottish son. Whether this was whimsy in her dotage, an archaic devotion to tradition and bloodline, pragmatism, or a gesture of remorse for approving the execution of Mary, it worked. James arrived to an enthusiastic London public,[512] the Stuart era began, and an historic union was achieved — England and Scotland were ruled by a single monarch.[513]

20

The War's Aftermath

[T]he alienation of Our people's minds from Us[514]
— Elizabeth I describing her impact on her Irish subjects.

Before the rebellion, O'Neill had been the ruler of a large portion of Ulster. He was still an earl and he seemed to be at least the landlord of that same large portion of Ulster. Rory O'Donnell (*Rudhraighe O'Domhnaill*), the younger brother of Red Hugh, as the reward for his submission, was made the 1st Earl of Tyrconnell, submitting in London in 1603 and pledging obedience to James I. O'Neill even went hunting with King James during his visit to London.[515] Mountjoy was a pleasant surprise to the earls. He was a tolerant victor in the aftermath of the Tyrone War. A universal pardon of all rebels was granted, sparing O'Neill from "the jaws of death" as Mountjoy groused.[516] The Act of Oblivion pardoned all offenders for offenses committed prior to the accession of King James. In the few months he remained in Ireland, Mountjoy allowed the defeated chieftains to retain their lands and begin attempts to perfect their land titles under English law.

It was not long, however, before O'Neill saw his estates diminishing as more and more lands were settled by a growing tide of planters from England. Despite the confirmation of the grant of lands to the earls, in little more than a year's time the surrogates of James I had proceeded toward doing piecemeal what they had found too expensive to do on a grand scale – taking much of the land and all of the power of the Irish earls with the same shameless legal proceedings as their predecessors had used in other provinces.

O'Neill clung to the hope that Catholic nations would join forces and come to the rescue of Ireland. He began secret efforts to reignite Spanish interest by cautious contacts with influential Spanish military leaders. Spain's records show that as early as 1604 O'Neill and others were back to seeking Spanish help for a new rebellion. O'Neill's 18-year old son Henry helped this effort by going to the Continent as a Colonel in the Irish Regiment of the Spanish army in Flanders.

Hardly had these efforts started when a stunning diplomatic event dashed the earls' hopes for help from Spain. In August 1604 those eternally warring kingdoms, Spain and England, made peace with each other. They announced the Treaty of London. For the bankrupt Spanish, this provided a sigh of relief. Both countries terminated alliances with the rebels in each other's countries. All subsequent pleas by the Irish merely fell on deaf ears at the Spanish Court.

In London, James I proved to be one more disappointment to the earls as he issued starkly anti-Catholic edicts. On July 4, 1605, he ended freedom of conscience for Catholics. Catholic priests were expelled from Ireland and Catholics were ordered to attend Protestant churches and were subjected to recusancy fines or imprisonment if they refused.

The glimmer of hope the Irish had seen amid the stench of conquest, the early conciliatory policies of Mountjoy, were gone; he left as Viceroy in the Summer of 1603. O'Neill misread this changing political landscape, even hoping that he would be named to succeed Mountjoy. But when in February 1605 a successor was named, not only was it not O'Neill, it was the bane of his existence. Sir Arthur Chichester was appointed Deputy and he would stay in that post for the next ten years.

Chichester and the Land Cases

This Deputy was the harbinger of an ominous new order. A British Navy officer who had fought the Armada in 1588, Chichester had also helped Essex sack Cadiz in 1596, and had then served as Governor of Carrickfergus. He saw to it that piecemeal confiscations of Irish lands began promptly. Chichester was determinedly hostile to Catholics.[517] After the war, Crown officials began sending letters on behalf of the new King ordering Irish leaders to attend Anglican services and sending them to prison if they refused. This Mandates policy became a Chichester staple, and it was overt religious persecution.[518] O'Neill's brother-in-law, Sir Patrick Barnewell, was sent to the Tower for a lengthy prison term for his refusal to attend. From the first months of his appointment as Deputy in 1605, and throughout 1607, lordships and parcels were snatched from O'Neill by one means after another in rapid succession. Much of O'Neill's property was taken through legal actions raising challenges to the letters patent he had been granted. The letters patent were customarily imprecise and, when O'Neill's title to a parcel of land was challenged, the documents were seldom tight enough to secure O'Neill's title. The vast lands of the abbeys and church properties within O'Neill's earldom were repeatedly taken by such claims and then were sold at a great profit to wealthy English planters. The Protestant clergy delighted in the willingness of public functionaries and tribunals to reject O'Neill's and O'Donnell's land titles, and the clergy joined aggressively in spreading the word that these loopholes could be a vast windfall for their colleagues throughout Ulster. The new Bishop of Derry, George Montgomery, laid claim to O'Neill's lands around Lough Foyle. Other clergymen made claim to any O'Neill lands that were not specifically included by name in O'Neill's patents, and they rarely were.

Chichester was determined to establish an English-dominated Ulster, to make it the very model of an English Presidency, and himself as the very model of a governor. Chichester bore great animosity not only to O'Neill, but to the Scots as well. The Scots had killed his brother John in a skirmish at Carrickfergus during the war, then decapitated him and kicked his head around as a football.[519] Years later Randal MacDonnell discussed decapitating John Chichester. Viewing a wall plaque of him with a head on it, Randal, with heavy accent, said: "How the de'il came he to get his heid again? – for I was sure I had ance taen it frae him."[520]

Chichester enlisted for his plantation plans Sir John Davies, an English lawyer whose career had rebounded magically after his 1597 disbarment for clubbing a fellow law student. Within six years after that episode, by November 1603, Davies had worked his way to an appointment as Solicitor General for Ireland, and by May 1606, he was Attorney General. Davies specialized in aggressively extending the reach of English law, and he considered himself the legal official who would bring civilization to the barbaric Irish of Ulster.

Davies especially was determined to do in O'Neill. He was offended at how generously the defeated O'Neill had been treated. Together with Chichester, Davies set out to reverse Mountjoy's gracious gestures and he launched a legal campaign against O'Neill, questioning more and more of his land titles at every turn. Then, Davies decided to eliminate O'Neill entirely. He began to conduct surveillance on O'Neill and to compile a file to support a charge of treason. After two years, Chichester and Davies felt they had a case against O'Neill.

Whatever may have been the purpose of the King himself concerning O'Neill, despite King James' occasional announcements that O'Neill should be dealt with honorably and that agreements with him should be honored, he did nothing to stop Chichester and Davies. They worked together, a cunning, manipulative pair who were unwilling to pay O'Neill's property rights anything more than lip service, and, whenever the opportunity presented itself, to confiscate O'Neill's lands. Rory O'Donnell's lands were less in demand, but Chichester and Davies opposed his titles as well, and O'Donnell too lost considerable tracts to his sub chief, Cahir O'Doherty, and to other favorites of the Deputy.

Chichester, together with Hugh Montgomery and James Hamilton, used the lands they took to establish settlements, bringing large numbers of loyal Scots to the O'Neill lands and north Down and Antrim. The Clandeboy lands in East Ulster, which were not within the control of Hugh O'Neill, were simultaneously becoming densely settled with Scots. A commission was convened with great fanfare to plan the complete reconstruction of Ulster. The pace of new arrivals of planters accelerated, and it seemed that the Plantation of Ulster was unstoppable.

The Land Dispute that Foretold the End

One O'Neill land dispute became central to his survival. It was over the vast Coleraine land claimed by Donal O'Cahan, an O'Neill enemy. After Kinsale, Donal O'Cahan, O'Neill's son-in-law and sub chief, became an ally of Chichester in return for Chichester's promise to support his land claims. But, like the fate of the other great defector, Niall Garbh O'Donnell, the promises made to O'Cahan were ultimately scaled back substantially by Chichester. Neither received what he thought was his due, provoking O'Cahan to appeal the decision and to prolong the legal case. Attorney General Davies[521] took the position that all of O'Cahan's country was now held directly by the King and that O'Neill's rights in Coleraine were gone. All the while, Chichester and Davies continued to add to their dossier against O'Neill.

The dispute between O'Neill, O'Cahan and Davies grew from being merely a notorious land dispute to a highly visible case, and eventually King James I announced he would hear the case himself. James wrote Chichester and ordered the case to come before him in the September 1607 Michaelmas Term. O'Neill would have two months to contemplate the import of this strange order to present himself in London. He began to receive warnings from friends in positions close to the King. Henry Howard, Earl of Northampton, a Catholic member of the Privy Council, and Sir Patrick Murray, one of O'Neill's friends at the Court of King James, both warned O'Neill that charges were being prepared against him. Chichester and Davies spread stories that O'Neill was committing abuses and behaving contrary to the obedience required to secure continued enjoyment of his rights. O'Neill was alarmed, so much so that he wrote the King denying any improper conduct. James, however, was easily manipulated by O'Neill's opponents who learned to play on James' neurotic fear of assassination. They succeeded in poisoning the King against O'Neill.

O'Neill knew that Chichester was attempting to convince James that O'Neill, O'Donnell and Maguire were disloyal. Chichester was using mere rumor and speculation and treating it as damning evidence of offenses that would justify James' proclaiming O'Neill and O'Donnell as traitors plotting a new rebellion.

By 1607 O'Neill had seen enough instances of concocted conspiracy charges serving as the guise for land confiscation. He finally came to the realization that the actions undermining him must have had King James' approval. Despite the thin gruel of evidence underlying Davies' accusations, there remains some basis to believe that at least O'Neill and his closest followers were indeed discussing a renewal of the Ulster rebellion.[522] Their level of actual planning[523] is not known, but the rumors of it became extremely graphic. O'Neill and his son Henry, and Rory O'Donnell were also rumored to be implicated in a conspiracy to assassinate Chichester. When this rumor appeared, O'Neill and O'Donnell saw all too clearly what was in store for them and, perhaps, for their families as well, and they began to weigh the need to take flight.

Chichester suddenly called for an increase of surveillance when one of his spies reported to him that O'Neill and his son, together with some of the other chieftains, were about to flee to the Netherlands and that Ulster would then be invaded from Austria. Whatever plan O'Neill's adversaries had for him if he did go to London for the O'Cahan case, there were abundant signs that O'Neill was headed for imprisonment and perhaps execution. He concluded that he and O'Donnell were either to be put to death or lodged in the Tower for life. The Spanish Ambassador to London later wrote that the strong desire among O'Neill's opponents at Court was to poison him.

The slow rumble of approaching tragedy quickened when Cuchonnacht Maguire, the chieftain of Fermanagh, was arrested and questioned pointedly about O'Neill. Though Maguire provided no assistance to support any charges against O'Neill, and was released, the unsettling arrest convinced Maguire to escape from Ireland to Flanders in May 1607.

As the summer of 1607 was ending, an opportunity came, presenting O'Neill with the terrible choice of sacrificing the remnants of his Irish dynasty to save his life and family. A sea captain, John Bath, an old ally of O'Neill, appeared as if from nowhere; he confided to O'Neill that O'Neill's son Henry had sent Bath with a ship now anchored in Lough Swilly, waiting to carry O'Neill away. Aboard it was the fugitive Cuchonnacht Maguire whose risky return to help O'Neill and O'Donnell escape underscored the desperation.

Chichester was surely about to make the arrest. O'Neill met with Chichester at Slane ostensibly to discuss his trip to London for the O'Cahan case. Nothing seemed out of the ordinary to Chichester at the time, but to O'Neill the meeting apparently confirmed his suspicions. Leaving Chichester at Slane, O'Neill spent a night at Mellifont with his old friend, Garret Moore. O'Neill's 8-year old son John, was, living with Garrett Moore's family in fosterage, but on Sunday, September 9, O'Neill took John away with him. As he was about to leave, O'Neill seemed to lose his composure as he bade Moore goodbye. Moore felt compelled to report the visit to Chichester. Too late, Chichester dispatched an agent to try to shadow O'Neill.

Reluctant to the last, O'Neill had by then concluded that, for his family, he had to flee,[524] that the gathering forces were about to close in on them. His lifetime of well-honed intuition, sharpened by 9 long years of war, was not wasted. Somehow he knew he was escaping just in the nick of time.

Their voyage is called "The Flight of the Earls." On Friday, September 14, 1607, Hugh O'Neill, Rory O'Donnell and Cuchonnacht Maguire and many in their families sailed away, creating the historic scene in which the Irish world was given over to England. When the ship sailed, the earls and their contingent turned parting glances to their abandoned horses on the shore.[525]

Conn O'Neill was five years old, at fosterage, and in the hurry to depart, he could not be found, and the ship had to weigh anchor without him. Chichester later succeeded in finding the youngster and held him for years at Charlemont Fort. Cormac O'Neill remained behind when his brother left, while two of Cormac's children, Brian and Art Og, accompanied O'Neill on the ship. Cormac was imprisoned at Dublin Castle and then at the Tower of London where he remained until his death.

The Stuarts braced for the worst; they feared that the Earls' disappearance was a prelude to a Spanish invasion. When calm was restored, it became clear that the "Flight of the Earls" was the end, the finish of Gaelic and Anglo Norman rule of Ireland. England had at last conquered Ireland. The last of the Tudors who had accomplished the conquest was the childless Virgin Queen Elizabeth. Thus, when it came to pass, no Tudor was there to see it.

Chichester wrote with relief and satisfaction that O'Neill had fled, musing that things were easier with O'Neill a fugitive rather than a prisoner. The earls sought help in various places, but eventually went to Rome in May 1608; there they hoped to muster French, Italian, Papal, and Spanish support.

The Ulster Plantation

The secret departure of the earls was treated by King James as confirmation of treason and the estates of the earls were declared forfeited to the Crown. Some large estates were granted to the many other Maguires who remained in Fermanagh and to other Irish elsewhere. The forfeited area consisted of the six counties of Armagh, Cavan, Coleraine (now Londonderry), Donegal, Fermanagh and Tyrone. Great plots were handed out to planters on the condition that the holders plant their estates with English and loyal Scots settlers. This turned the growing infusion of colonists into a surge that became the Plantation of Ulster.

Long before 1607 many settlements and small plantations of English settlers had occurred. Elizabeth's plan of large scale settlements, by which she believed she could replace the hostile native population of Ireland with a grateful loyal population, finally seemed to be taking hold just as she had hoped, because James I

The Departure of O'Neill out of Ireland

followed her lead. These early 17th century Plantation settlers were in the main disenfranchised sons of English families who lacked the wealth or family tenure to acquire land of their own in England. When they received the lands confiscated from the Irish chieftains of Ulster, all involved in the process behaved as if they were oblivious to the deep-seated feeling of outrage these confiscations ignited in the Irish.

The Davies committee formulated the plan for the Plantation of Ulster, and in 1610, London approved the committee's report and its scheme of plantation. Scots, English and Welsh "Undertakers" were awarded 1,000 to 2,000 acre tracts; they brought English and Scots tenants with them to work the land. Others, called "Servitors," obtained smaller tracts upon payment of a socage and they were allowed to use local Irish as workers.

Even some Irish, called "deserving Irish," were awarded lands in areas called precincts. In an effort to keep peace, the severity of the commissioners' treatment of the leading families was offset by a show of generosity to other Irish families – even to some relatives of O'Neill and Maguire. Conor Roe Maguire in east Fermanagh was exempted from plantation and Turlough McHenry O'Neill of the Fenes was shown favoritism. The plantations formed under James I were pointedly independent, loyal to the Crown, and highly resistant to any assimilation with the displaced natives. This suited King James and the Davies Committee. Their goal was never to unify or assimilate, but to overwhelm the Irish population in the settled areas and keep the English and Scots entirely separate from the Irish.

For the native Irish in Ulster, these changes came as a life-altering shock. Everything around them shouted the message that they were now a conquered race. This large scale program of plantation of Scots and English was making Ulster a province with two distinct populations, native Irish Catholics and imported English and Scottish Protestants who dispossessed the Catholics from the land of the Earls of Tyrone and Tyrconnell. The Catholic natives spoke Irish. The new Protestant English spoke English. As the Protestant Ascendancy formed, each day reemphasized that life for the Irish would never again be the life they had led under their chieftains and earls.

The large and small revolts of the *Taoisigh* and earls had failed

THE CAHIR O'DOHERTY INSURRECTION

The Ulster Plantation grew to become more widespread than first attempted in part as a result of Sir Cahir O'Doherty's clash with Sir George Paulet, Governor of Derry. O'Doherty was the foreman of a jury that convicted O'Neill of treason in absentia after the Flight of the Earls. Paulet tried to arrest O'Doherty but it was Lord Deputy Chichester who finally succeeded in imprisoning O'Doherty temporarily in Dublin Castle, but upon his release, O'Doherty attacked Culmore Fort and burned Derry. During that attack O'Doherty killed Governor Paulet. O'Doherty was eventually found and killed at the Rock of Doon at Kilmacrenean in July 1608, but his revolt gave renewed emphasis to the Plantation of Ulster.

The insurrection also brought an end to O'Neill's subchief, Donal O'Cahan, who was suspected of participation in the Cahir O'Doherty plot and was thrown into the Tower of London where he languished until his death.

to stop the capture of Ireland or to deter retribution. In purely military terms they had merely left grisly mementos, the "ashes" and "carcasses" Elizabeth had bemoaned. Shane O'Neill's skull, the head of the Rebel Earl of Desmond, the remains of Silken Thomas FitzGerald and of FitzMaurice — all these had long ago been lost along with thousands of their fallen followers. O'Donnell was dead in Spain and Maguire dead in Cork. But in the centuries to come it would become clear to the Crown that these rebel leaders had themselves been planters of a tradition of resistance. Many who stayed or were left behind to face plantation kept alive resistance against the dismantling of Irish life and tradition. Many of them continued to nurture the hope that someday they would see a new rebellion, another Spanish invasion and the triumphal return of the wiliest Earl, The Great O'Neill, who had disappeared with head intact.

The plantation scheme failed. Although many planters and servitors were willing after Kinsale to take the risk to venture ashore in

Ireland and settle on the free landholdings offered to them, far more had seen the fate of earlier planters. The life of a planter would entail being seen as the usurpers of the property and lands of natives who lived and seethed all around them. To many English, conquest was just not the way to do this. The hostile Irish were abundant and would always be in close proximity to the planters. These planters would bear the opprobrium of being the evictors, and they could see that. The result was that too few came to make it succeed. As Professor Ciarin Brady stated: "Neither the requisite state power nor the necessary number of adventurers was ever available. Even the most heroic of the schemes, the Ulster plantation of 1603, failed, as we know too well, even to establish a bare numerical majority of immigrants over most of the area of the province."[526]

Indeed the hostility of the dispossessed native Irish of early 17th century Ulster grew to become a vestigial bitterness passed down from generation to generation.[527] The Stuart land confiscations "caused great bitterness and long term alienation from royal government of the Gaelic and Old English communities."[528] Even today, Ulster republicans can recite the names of the native families from whom a modern loyalist-owned estate was taken and whether it was taken after Arthur Chichester in 1609 or after Oliver Cromwell in 1651.

For all these reasons, conquest, plantation, and the confiscation of the land of native Irish was no success. It failed to achieve the elimination of the Irish by death or by flight or by assimilation. Instead, the alienation of the Irish people was burned into their ancestral fabric.

The O'Neill never returned. His years on the Continent were spent seeking allies for an invasion and seeking word of his son, Conn, reliving as a father the pain he had experienced as a child after the loss of his own father. His years in Rome were spent in comfort, living along the banks of the Tiber in the handsome Salviati Palace, one of several expatriates there, honored guests of the Pope. But for this former titan it was a decade of frustration. As the shadows descended,[529] it may have become clear to O'Neill that he was to be the last of the great chieftains. Perhaps his final dreams foresaw that others would one day complete what he and O'Donnell and Maguire had started. The deliverance of Ireland, however, would not come to pass while he could see it, and in 1616 Hugh O'Neill died, not in Dungannon, but in Rome.

Something had survived, however, through the bold, resolute, doomed rebellions and the symbol of O'Neill's own survival. To succeeding generations, the Irish fox had endured the full onslaught of the Tudor wolves and they had failed to hoist his head on a pike. The shear grit of outlasting all that Tudor England could unleash kept alive the fire of hope. To the next four centuries of Irishmen and Irishwomen, The O'Neill continued to live in popular imagination. O'Neill always beckoned; he became the "last unconquered Gael" of poetry in the minds of succeeding generations, a ghost who demanded resumption of the struggle after Tudor England's military victory failed to rid Ireland of the Irish. Hugh O'Neill's survival was a symbol of the survival of Irish who, over the next three centuries, would at times be rebels, more often protestors, and at times parliamentary obstructionists. Their dogged resistance to colonial rule of Ireland would continue and preserve the Irish culture and heritage into the modern era and set the stage for a Republic.[530]

Epilogue

O'Brien to James Connolly — "Is there no chance of success?"
Connolly — "None whatever."[531]
— James Connolly, 1916

The chieftains' resolve to fight had been based in large measure on their fear that England was intending to take all of Ireland for itself and to impoverish, enslave, execute or banish the native Irish and the Anglo Irish. Over the next several centuries the Irish were hit with everything they had feared, and their lamentable condition was exacerbated by one of mankind's worst famines. The troubles would include penal laws, atrocities on all sides, yet another Cromwell, demeaning segregation, banishment of Irish to the barren west, terrorism, triumphalism, and virulent societal dysfunction.

The response of the conquered Irish did not help. In 1641 the Catholic population of Ulster began a rampage attacking and killing Protestants, first in Portadown;[532] then throughout Ireland. Whether planned or spontaneous, thousands were killed,[533] and Protestants in turn killed numerous Catholics. The next 10 years were consumed by the Wars of the Three Kingdoms and the conquest of Ireland by Oliver Cromwell.

The Prohibition of Education

Education of the conquered Irish was seen as a danger to the English garrison. From pagan times Ireland had an oral tradition of schooling called Bardic Schools. The Gaelic scholars — bards, files, brehons and seanachies — taught students the Irish language, literature, history and law. When English domination became firm after the Flight of the Earls, Stuart England acted to prevent the majority Catholic population from conducting schools and educating new generations. This policy had previously been implemented in ad hoc fashion under the Tudors, but it was codified and strongly enforced under the Stuarts. After the overthrow of the Stuart King Charles I by Oliver Cromwell, strict enforcement of the laws against Irish education finally wiped out the remaining schools of the native Irish. Historian W. E. H. Lecky summed up the several laws forbidding educating Irish Catholics as "universal, unqualified, and unlimited proscription."[534] Anyone conducting or housing a school was punishable. Thus, the native Irish had to resort to secret schools, and instruction usually had to be held outdoors. The teachers huddled the students behind large hedges and wooded clusters and posted a lookout for informants who were well rewarded.

Schools were closed during the Wars of the Three Kingdoms from 1641 and the 1650 Cromwell Interregnum. Native Irish learning had sunk to its lowest ebb by the early 18th century.[535] It was not until 1782 that legislation was finally passed to repeal the prohibitions on education of Catholics. That, however, was coupled with restrictions designed to assure that no Protestants would be influenced by the teaching methods of Catholics. The new laws also prohibited establishing a Catholic college or endowed school in Ireland.

The Cromwellian Land Confiscation and Banishments

After Cromwell and his Bible-waving Roundheads defeated King Charles I in England, they stormed into Ireland and managed to attract historic opprobrium. In 1649 Cromwell attacked the royalist garrison at Drogheda. His powerful cannons breached the town walls and he and his men rampaged and killed the royal garrison, every priest, non-combatants, elderly, women and children — 2,000 all told. Hated by the Irish for the massacre at Drogheda, Cromwell marched south and did the same to Wexford, massacring another 2,000 there.[536]

Under Cromwell, the Act of Settlement of 1652 confiscated the land owned by Catholics, and the Irish who owned desirable homes or land were evicted and banished to the barren west,[537] all the way to Connaught and the Atlantic shore.[538] Irish workers could remain in the other provinces, but they found they were now working for Cromwell's soldiers who had been awarded the homes and lands of the banished Irish landowners.[539] Ireland's lands soon had fallen wholesale into the hands of English landlords. Many of those sold the land they were awarded to other absentee English who paid Irish workers to farm the land.[540] To a real extent, Ireland had become a vast English-owned farm whose crops were heavily exported to England.

One result of this land confiscation by the English was that large numbers of Irish were left to live on tiny plots — small farms owned by absentee English landlords. They were forced to raise crops but had to sell them to the landlord for export; otherwise they could not pay the rent for the land and would be evicted, and when evicted, the homes and sheds they had built went to the landlord. Squeezed in this way for centuries, the small farmers were able to keep for their own family's nourishment primarily one crop — potatoes. A large percentage of the Irish grew dependent for life on this fragile food, a plant that grew from tubers in the ground where they were highly vulnerable to fungus.

The Penal Laws Disenfranchising Catholics and Presbyterians

By the end of the 17th century and the conclusion of the Williamite War[541] between Protestant King William of Orange and Catholic King James II, The Penal Laws were enacted in full force, and their effect was to ostracize and to repress the Catholics, Presbyterians and others seen as recusants and dissenters.[542] Catholics were forbidden every fundamental right of citizens and deprived of the right to enter professions, hold office, buy land or own a horse worth more than £5.[543] Most of these laws stayed in force until the Catholic Emancipation movement led by Daniel O'Connell in the 19th century produced their successive repeal starting in 1829.

Protestant Emigration to America

The vast majority of the Scots settlers in the plantation of Ulster were Presbyterians and this placed them outside the established

Church of Ireland.[544] Once Queen Anne's Test Act of 1703[545] and the Penal Laws were in full force, some 200,000 of the Scots Irish emigrated to America between 1707 and 1775,[546] bringing with them a hardy industriousness, a fighting spirit and the origins of country music in all its variations from Bluegrass to country western. They settled heavily in Pennsylvania and Virginia, but this period of emigration stalled during the American Revolution.

Ulster Scots Presbyterians were central to the formation of the Society of United Irishmen in the late 18th century and in beginning the great rising of the United Irishmen in 1798.[547] Conditions for the Protestant Dissenters in Ireland had grown so intolerable that they aligned with Catholics to fight against England in a violent, but unsuccessful rebellion. After the conclusion of the American Revolution, which had inspired the United Irishmen, emigration of Irish Protestant dissenters resumed.

The Great Famine

The Great Famine descended on Ireland in 1845 when potato crops were destroyed by a fungus several years running. Virtually the entire potato crop failed again in 1846 and partial failures in other years through 1850 led to the deaths of a million Irish small farmers from cholera, typhus and starvation. The horror led in turn to a desperate flight abroad by another million Irish trying to escape this ghastly fate. *An Gorta Mór*, or The Great Hunger, as it is known, devastated those Irish small farmers who had become dependent on potatoes as their staple. That dependence was due to the Cromwellian land confiscations and banishment of the displaced Irish landowners, and the necessity of exporting the grain, vegetables and meat they raised to England. The death toll, even for a famine, was out of control because of backward policies and crippled relief efforts. Most policy decisions were those of Prime Ministers Robert Peel and John Russell and Chancellor of the Exchequer, Charles Wood, and Home Secretary Sir Charles Grey, but they were rigidly administered by Sir Charles Trevelyan, a reviled British Treasury official. The Great Famine scarred the Irish mind like nothing before. Emigration continued for decades even after the Famine ended due to the fear that the horror was going to recur and claim them all. America, Canada and many other lands became awash with Irish.

The cycle of death produced by the Famine was attributable to a perfect storm of poverty conditions. British policy had made an impoverished population dependent on a precariously vulnerable food source, on outdated farming, on the lenity of land agents who ran evictions for callous absentee landlords, and on cruel and backward policies. This kept Britain's Irish population close to a slave population.[548]

Britain's Corn Laws and Navigation Laws, in effect during the administration of Prime Minister Robert Peel, kept the price of food high and prevented access to inexpensive food to relieve the famine. When the Corn Laws were finally repealed, the Peel government fell in June 1846. Britain still refused to bar the export of food as had been done to ease earlier famines, and the starving Irish were forced to watch armed guards escort the food they grew to the ports to be sold to profit the landlords.[549] Britain ultimately imported maize from America. If the government had distributed the grain, it would have fed many thousands of those who starved, but the famine administrators refused to make the grain imported into Ireland readily available to the starving Irish who could not afford to pay for it. Instead, they insisted that the victims go to work on public works projects, earn pay and then buy the imported food. A Soup Kitchen Act provided a thin gruel for a time, but the government kitchens were closed too quickly.

Many of those who could begin work on the public works projects were weakened by The Famine, and when forced to labor in hard, cold, rainy and windy conditions, many died trying to earn enough to afford the inflated prices demanded by Trevelyan for the imported food. Trevelyan charged 5% above market price for the food he imported; he rejected recommendations of his staff that he make the price substantially lower. He warned that if the Irish found out that they could get food free, the whole country of Ireland would demand welfare.[550] The grain was kept locked in silos and sold only to those who could pay. When desperate victims broke in and stole grain, they were jailed and many were transported to Australia.

A progressive attempt at relief through the Poor Law scheme

and public workhouses crumbled mid-famine under the government's insensitivity and the pinch of Britain's own failing economy. That was followed by more of the same. The roles played by Prime Minister Russell and Trevelyan stand out in Irish memory for their insensitivity, ineptitude or worse in refusing to adopt effective emergency measures to stop the escalation of deaths from famine and The Famine illnesses. Nothing significant changed even after The Famine. When the five years of horror eased somewhat, the Irish remained dependent on the fragile potato; blights recurred several years later and famine conditions erupted again.

By contrast, Quakers from England readily came to the aid of the Irish, particularly William Forster and James Hack Tuke. They and many individual British rallied to help The Famine victims. Quakers established their own soup kitchens in many areas, saving untold lives; and they shared in the suffering from the highly contagious diseases of The Famine.

Different dates are often given for the end of The Great Famine of 1845, but a date cannot be fixed.[551] "The famine was never 'over' in the sense that an epidemic occurs and is over."[552] The British administration declared it over in 1847 when the crop largely survived, but 1847 was a year of typhus and cholera deaths on a grand scale. After a total crop failure in 1848, they declared it over again in 1849 even while bodies lay dead in the roads.

Those who came to believe that some form of intentional genocide was afoot were well off the mark, yet the incompetence of the British response to the cataclysm was a turning point of major proportions, an historical last straw fueling new movements and filling even the most politically disengaged Irish with despair. They concluded they could never enjoy a lasting membership in the United Kingdom. The Great Famine also cemented in many Irish "detestation and distrust of everything and everyone English" and it convinced many that "total separation from England" was the only solution.[553]

The Flight From the Fear

The emigration of Catholic Irish prior to 1845 was small compared to the wave caused by The Great Famine. The Famine started a flight that drove almost a quarter of the population of 1845 out of Ireland, an estimated 2,000,000 people[554] over the next ten years.[555] Fear of famine rose again in the 1870s as famine conditions seemed to approach, and emigration spiked again.

Many Famine emigrants were already very sick; many died in "coffin ships' during the difficult voyage as the unseaworthy ships used by opportunists to make money from those desperate to flee sunk. Many who survived the crossing were perilously ill and held in quarantine. Gross Isle, Quebec in the St. Lawrence River was less restrictive in quarantine than U.S. ports and some of the most wretched victims landed there, often just left on the shore to die.[556]

An astute historian of the Irish emigration to America concluded that the single location that would be least tolerant of Irish immigrants in the era of The Famine was Boston, Massachusetts, a Protestant enclave virulently hostile to everything Irish and Catholic.[557] And that is where they went in record numbers. Many other east coast cities were not far behind Boston in open hostility.

The arrival of so heavy a wave of a single race in 19th century America had a profound impact on the cultures and institutions of the major cities during a period of significant industrial and political developments. The hand-to-mouth existence of the original penniless famine immigrants improved to entry level day labor, then more desirable factory and transport work, municipal jobs, fire and police work. When enough voters or constituents turned out to be Irish, their political demands began to gain attention, even in Boston. Irish candidates and committeemen came to power, and the Curleys, Fitzgeralds and Kennedys gained political power in Boston, and other Irish families became dynasties in other meccas of The Famine diaspora.[558]

When Irish immigrants went to a heavily Catholic city, they found it easier to gain acceptance and begin to assimilate.[559] As Irish immigration spread into the American Midwest, for example, the former French territory west of the Mississippi and the heavily French Catholic city of St. Louis, Catholic Irish immigrants were merely suspect newcomers. While subjected to some discrimination, they were not as vilified or ostracized as in Protestant Eastern cities. Before long, St. Louis had so many Irish that historians have referred to it as "the chief Irish Settlement in the United States."[560]

Home Rule

The trauma of The Great Famine filled many Irish both in Ireland and America with a new resolve. Ireland turned with determination to political movements. A Home Government Association, formed in 1870 under Protestant lawyer Isaac Butt, began to agitate for the enactment of limited Home Rule. A land reform movement dominated late 19th century politics when Protestant gentry and Catholics joined to support Charles Stewart Parnell, leader of the Irish National Party in Parliament. The Irish also became more willing to tolerate and then to embrace and support rebel groups.

When Britain's Liberal Party leader, William Ewart Gladstone, threw his support in favor of Home Rule for Ireland, the momentum seemed unstoppable. The House of Lords was the obstacle, but in the early 20th century its power was curtailed and its ability to block Home Rule legislation was near an end. Then World War I erupted, and Irish freedom was postponed, seemingly until the War's end, but Irish Republicans refused to wait any longer.

Three centuries after O'Neill died, on Easter Monday, April 24, 1916, the iconic doomed insurrection began with the reading of a Proclamation at the General Post Office in Dublin. The Proclamation harked back to these events three centuries earlier and to their successors: "[s]ix times during the past three hundred years," it said, there have been Irish rebellions. The Proclamation declared "the right of the people of Ireland to the ownership of Ireland" and condemned the "long usurpation of that right by a foreign people and government...." The Rising was incited in a 20th century crucible of the native Irish culture which the 16th century rebellions had helped to preserve. The Irish lifestyle and tradition was again in danger of extinction, until The Great War, labor strife and nativist inspiration by the Gaelic League through its devotion to the Irish language, literature, games and traditions, suddenly gave rise to rebellion in the midst of a World War.

To the rebels of the 20th century who rose against British rule, the 16th century failure of the chieftains in the face of an overwhelming foe provided a precedent. Poetic flourish often connects epic events, and among those who rebelled in 1916 were several poets. The dreamers and visionaries among them were more willing than some of the other constituencies involved to brush aside the staggering odds they faced. Patrick Pearse wrote before the Rising of 1916 that there were ghosts in Ireland's history who demanded very big things, and that the Irish people must do what those ghosts demand.[561] This became a part of "Pearse's cultural nationalism" which traces back not only to O'Neill[562] but also to Thomas Davis, Theobald Wolfe Tone and other champions of Irish freedom.[563] That it may be a hopeless challenge was no more to stop them than it had their 16th century ancestors. To them, the ghosts, including the ghost of that "last unconquered Gael" demanded action now.[564]

Despite its apparent failure and the execution of its central participants, just 5 years later, on Tuesday December 6, 1921 Great Britain and Irish plenipotentiaries signed Articles of Agreement, the Anglo Irish Treaty, granting the Irish the *Saorstát* Éireann, the Irish Free State. Ireland was partitioned and 6 counties of the north remained a part of the United Kingdom, but 26 counties obtained, after 700 years, their freedom from Great Britain. And, in 1949, Éire, the Republic of Ireland, was declared. As historian Edmund Curtis has articulated, "Nations are made in many ways" and one of them is by "the heroic example of great men even when they seem to fail."[565] Ireland was made. The Irish had not fallen to a world with only the conqueror's culture — both "traditional cultures" endured.

Since then, much discussion of modern day Ireland has been in sectarian terms,[566] but some of the greatest breakthroughs have come from the efforts of anti-sectarians, from those who focused the cry for reform on human rights rather than religion or culture.[567] The more recent events, the 1998 Good Friday Agreement, and the Northern Ireland Act of 1998, commit Great Britain and Ireland and all the signatories to acknowledge that in 1998 the majority of the people of Northern Ireland wished to remain a part of the United Kingdom but that a substantial section of the people wished to bring about a united Ireland.[568] The Good Friday Accords thus provided that Northern Ireland would remain British until a majority of its own people decided otherwise. The signatories all agreed that they would be bound by the obligation to implement that choice, should it occur.

In the years since, attitudes have fluctuated one way or the other at different times influenced by political, economic and religious events. Birth rates and other demographics have tended at times to raise prospects for a united Ireland. Economic developments have also raised such prospects, as when the Celtic Tiger was vibrant, but those prospects were lowered when bank failures in the Republic of Ireland brought severe austerity measures. As church attendance fell and clerical influence waned, there was less urgency among some citizens of the Republic for unification coupled with less fear of it by some Ulster Protestants.

Peace in Ulster meanwhile has enriched the lives of everyone in Ulster beyond measure. Continued peace could itself have the greatest impact on future governance.

It has often seemed counterintuitive that the failed rebellion that ended at Kinsale and Lough Swilly with the narrow escape of O'Neill in 1607 could provide such inspiration or serve as a source of resolve, renewal or eventual triumph, however, that "escape" became "The Flight of The Earls," a title glowing with reverence and spiritual imagery, and the symbol of the resiliency and resourcefulness that made the Irish unconquerable. Much like others who rallied over defeats at Masada, Dunkirk, The Alamo, or Pearl Harbor, The Flight of The Earls instead became the stuff of legend and lived on in the Irish imagination. No one knows the precise role that these events, or the revered tone that became attached to them, played during the ensuing 300 years of failed uprisings, but the celebrations and reenactments in Ireland in 2007 of The Flight of The Earls demonstrated that these epic events have remained well remembered since 1607.

The Irish people and their traditions and their freedom to be Irish, which those "Grand Disturbers" fought to preserve from extinction, had survived. That "last unconquered Gael" did survive and the nation certainly did not lose its soul. Irish music and dance continue to entertain the entire world. Irish poets, playwrights and novelists contribute their unique voices and special fame to the culture of the world. Over those three hundred years, Ireland became a parent nation to North America, Australia and New Zealand. *Ceilis, seisiuns*, step dancing, set dancing, and all forms of life's activities once outlawed by the Statutes of Kilkenny are practiced and celebrated around the world. What the 16th century Irish fought to save from extinction proved to be ineradicable.[569]

There are many societal shipwrecks in the modern world for which no solution is in sight, but the possibility of resolving the so-called Irish Question, the centuries-long societal trauma once again appears within reach. Despite the persistence of just grievances on all sides, and a need for reforms in the north, the progress made in recent years has proved to be real. Instead of perpetuating grief, fear and a devotion to the cult of the terrible past, many Irish have embraced an agenda of tolerance and have targeted social progress rather than old enemies, and devoted their energies to securing human rights rather than the pursuit of revenge which brought their ancestors years, then decades, then centuries of tragedy.

KEY LIEUTENANTS AND DEPUTIES

Gerald FitzGerald (Kildare)	Deputy	1478 – 1492, 1496 – 1513
Archbishop Walter FitzSimons	Deputy	1492
James Butler (Ormond)	Governor	1492 – 1493
Robert Preston (Viscount Gormanstown)	Deputy	1493 – 1494
Edward Poynings	Deputy	1494 – 1495
Thomas Howard (Surrey)	Lieutenant	1520 – 1522
William Skeffington	Deputy	1529-1532; 1534-1536
Leonard Lord Grey	Justiciar/Deputy	1536 – 1540
Anthony St. Leger	Justiciar/Deputy	1546 – 1548; 1550-51; 1553-1556
Edward Bellingham	Deputy	1548 – 1549
James Croft	Deputy	1551-1552
Thomas Radcliffe (Sussex)	Deputy	1556 – 1558
Henry Sidney	Justiciar	1558 – 1560

KEY LIEUTENANTS AND DEPUTIES
(continued)

Thomas Radcliffe (Sussex)	Lieutenant	1560 – 1564
Henry Sidney	Justiciar/Deputy	1564 – 1571
William FitzWilliam	Justiciar/Deputy	1571 – 1575
Henry Sidney	Deputy	1575 - 1578
Arthur Lord Grey de Wilton	Deputy	1580 – 1584
John Perrot	Deputy	1584 – 1588
William FitzWilliam	Deputy	1588 – 1594
William Russell	Deputy	1594 – 1597
Thomas Lord Burgh	Deputy	1597 – 1597
Robert Devereaux (Essex)	Lieutenant	1599 – 1599
Charles Blount Lord Mountjoy (Devonshire)	Deputy Lieutenant	1600 – 1603 1603 – 1604
Arthur Chichester	Deputy	1605 – 1615

Notes

1. Woodham-Smith, Cecil, *The Great Hunger: Ireland, 1845-1849*, New York: Old Town Books, 1962, 210. The Irish immigrants' view of Americans as "kindred" is from 1859, from contemporary, Thomas Colley Grattan, a Dubliner who lived for a time in Boston as the consul.

2. Michael Hughes, *Ireland Divided: The Roots of The Modern Irish Problem* (New York: St. Martin's Press, 1994), 9.

3. Elizabeth paraphrased Bato: "I find that I sent wolves not shepherds to govern Ireland, for they have left me nothing but ashes and carcasses to reign over." See Frederick Chamberlain, *The Sayings of Queen Elizabeth* (London: John Lane, The Bodley Head, 1923), 308.

4. Elizabethan goals evolved. "By the mid-sixteenth century the Tudor ideal had settled down to the extirpation of the native and so-called Old English population, and the resettlement of the cleared countryside and towns by British immigrants." See Oliver MacDonagh, "Ambiguity in Nationalism: The Case of Ireland," in *Interpreting Irish History: The Debate on Historical Revisionism*, edited by Ciaran Brady (Sallins, County Kildare: Irish Academic Press, 1994), 105. Her goal became the expulsion of the Irish to America or the West Indies or their destruction. Liam De Paor, *The Peoples of Ireland, From Pre-History to Modern Times* (South Bend, Indiana: University of Notre Dame Press, 1986), 140. Froude describes the evolution of British policy and tactics eventually to a plan for the expulsion or destruction of the Irish race. See James Anthony Froude, *The English in Ireland in the Eighteenth Century*, Vol. 1 (London: Longmans, Green, and Company, 1895), 13-14.

5. Elizabeth was a ruler often racked with indecision and contradiction. As for Ireland, she went from teaching the Irish to behave like English, to "transplanting the Irish to some distant colonies, in the Americas or the West Indies, and wholly replacing them with civil and amenable folk." De Paor, *Peoples of Ireland*, 140.

6.   O'Neill wrote to Lord Barry that "the sword of extirpation hangeth over" their Irish subjects, both northern and southern. See Sean O'Faolain, *The Great O'Neill: A Biography of Hugh O'Neill Earl of Tyrone, 1550–1616* (Chester Springs, PA: Dufour Editions, 1997), 206. The term "extirped" was one Elizabeth seemed prone to use. G. A. Hayes-McCoy, "Tudor Conquest and Counter Reformation, 1571-1603." In *A New History of Ireland*, Vol. 3, edited by T. W. Moody, F. X. Martin and F. J. Byrne (Oxford: The Clarendon Press, 1976), 85.

7.   An exceptional map for this era shows the perimeters of all of the many (90 or so) lordships of Ireland. See D. B. Quinn and K. W. Nicholls. *A New History of Ireland*, edited by T. W. Moody, F. X. Martin and F. J. Byrne, Vol. 3, *Ireland in 1534* (Oxford: Clarendon Press, 1976), 3, Map 1 Lordships, c. 1534 [See Illustrations].

8.   Byrne, Charles Artaud. *Ranelagh: The Irish Warlord.* (Tate Publishing, 2008), 20. *Hibernia hibernescit* ("Ireland makes all things Irish") was a mantra of the day and this was troubling to Lionel Duke of Clarence, the proponent of the Statutes of Kilkenny. *Hibernia ipsis hiberniores* ("More Irish than the Irish themselves") was a description depicting "how degenerate" the Norman descendants had become by 1366. The Statutes of Kilkenny were the codification of several earlier laws passed in 1297. Ellis, *Eyewitness*, 23. One historian concluded that "The Statutes of Kilkenny bear comparison with anything attempted under the apartheid laws of twentieth-century South Africa." Marcus Tanner, *Ireland's Holy Wars* (New Haven: Yale University Press, 2001), 40.

9.   It was the purpose of English law to lay "that grievous punishment upon traitors, to forfeit all their lands to the Prince,…" See Barnabe Rich, "A New Description of Ireland, Together With The Manners, Customs, and Dispositions of The People (1610)," in *Elizabethan Ireland, a Selection of Writings by Elizabethan Writers on Ireland*, edited by James P. Myers, Jr. (Hamden, Connecticut: Archon Books, 1983), 75.

10.   A simple timeline of all the rebellions would require distinguishing between a widespread rebellion, a limited uprising and a regional or local outburst. With that in mind, the rebellions most discussed here proceeded in this sequence:
      • Kildares'Lambert Simnel invasion)Battle of Stoke) 1487.
      • Silken Thomas FitzGerald 1534.
      • Shane O'Neill 1562-67.
      • FitzMaurice (first) 1569-73.
      • Clanrickard Burkes 1572 and 1576.
      • Baltinglass 1575-1580.
      • FitzMaurice (second) 1579.

- San Giuseppi landed early November 1579.
- Gerald FitzGerald of Desmond (was proclaimed a traitor and became the Rebel Earl) November 1579. Was killed November 1583.
- Clanrickard Burkes 1579.
- MacWilliam (Mayo) Burkes 1586.
- The Nine Years War/Tyrone Rebellion. (Maguire attacked Sligo May 1593. Ford of the Biscuits August 1593. Maguire retook Enniskillen Castle May 1595. Clontibret 1595. The Yellow Ford 1598. Kinsale December 1601. Submission at Mellifont March 1603).

11. The Munster Rebellion, for example, is described as "scattered and uncoordinated." De Paor, *Peoples of Ireland*, 131.

12. "There was indeed as yet no Irish nation...." Edmund Curtis, *A History of Ireland* (London: Methuen, 1950), 196. The concept of Irishness has been called vague and shifting. Hughes, *Ireland Divided*, 1. Early Modern Ireland was "considerably more than a geographical expression and much less than a political entity." Quinn and Nicholls, *New History*, 1.

13. Crown officials came to realize Ireland's potential for creating wealth. See Edmund Curtis, *A History of Ireland* (London: Methuen, 1950), 159.

14. Froude describes the viciousness of English soldiers posted to Ireland in Froude, *English in Ireland*, 54-55.

15. Elizabeth was exasperated with Sidney and replaced him in 1571 with Sir William FitzWilliam who was also heavily in debt. Colm Lennon, *Sixteenth-Century Ireland: The Incomplete Conquest* (Dublin: Gill & Macmillan, 1994), 186. Even as Sir William FitzWilliam foundered as Deputy, Henry Sidney asked again to be allowed to return as Deputy. Lennon, *Sixteenth-Century Ireland*, 186. He returned in 1576. Ibid.

16. Sir Henry Sidney, for example, owned lovely estates, including Penshurst Place in Kent, but the costs drained him financially. His 1582 memoir complains of "my decayed estate" and discusses his hope to sell some of what is left "to ransom me out of the servitude I live in for my debts." PRO, State Papers, Domestic, SP 12, Vol. 159; Ciaran Brady, ed., *A Viceroy's Vindication? Sir Henry Sidney's Memoir of Service in Ireland, 1556-78* (Cork: Cork University Press, 2002), 43. The competition for position among the courtiers gave rise to jealousy and backbiting. R.W. Church, *Spenser* (New York: Macmillan & Co., 1906), 62. In their competition many of them became devoted enemies and undermined each other at Court. Brady, *Viceroy's Vin-*

dication?, 119, note 38; Ellis, *Eyewitness*, 290. Some accused their predecessors of corruption. See Roger Turvey, *The Treason and Trial of Sir John Perrot* (Cardiff: University of Wales Press, 2005), 25, 28, 41.

17.   The power of English government over Ireland had declined from 1300 to 1460. Ellis, *Ireland*, 18. Less than half of Ireland was under any English control by 1460. Ibid. English control was feeble by the reign of Henry VI. Ibid., 19.

18.   Lord Mountjoy said in 1600 that he sought to make Ireland a "rased table." De Paor, *Peoples of Ireland*, 137. Lord Chichester advocated extermination of the clans in 1602. See McCavitt 44, 47; Cyril Falls, *The Birth of Ulster* (1963; Reprint London: Methuen, 1983), 67.

19.   Lenihan, Padraig. *Consolidating Conquest: Ireland 1603-1727*. (London: Routledge, 2014), 252.

20.   "If England was to become a great power...." Froude, *English*, 12.

21.   Ulster became the last bastion of opposition. Walter J.P. Curley, *Vanishing Kingdoms: The Irish Chiefs and their Families* (Dublin: Lilliput Press, 2004), 44.

22.   Sixteenth century Ulster, protected by "natural defenses of drumlin hills and winding streams, lakes and bogs, was impossible to subdue by the campaigns [the Deputy] could afford to mount." De Paor, *Peoples of Ireland*, 129.

23.   O'Neill had become "a threat to England itself. ..." O'Faolain, *Great O'Neill*, 205.

24.   The rebellions, starting with FitzMaurice in 1579, "were numerous, often interrelated, and they plunged the island into a state of anarchy for over thirty years." Myers, *Elizabethan Ireland*, 6. Desmond's and O'Neill's "almost succeeded." Id. O'Neill and O'Donnell "carried the rebellion throughout the island." They "out-maneuvered and out-fought the English...destroying the career of viceroy after viceroy." Ibid., 8.

25.   The English depended on light cavalry in Ireland, but "the heavily wooded, marshy or mountainous country of the Irishry was much less suitable for English troops." Ellis, *Ireland*, 29.

26.   Chieftains were sometimes "briefly united by self-interest." Ellis, *Ireland*, 29.

27.   Ulster was the last province to succumb. Curtis, *History*, 106.

28.   The Irish kerne fought wearing just linen tunics, carrying swords, light axes and spears. Ibid., 49. Churls typically did not themselves bear arms. Ellis, *Ireland*, 44.

29.   "Men now commonly spoke of O'Neill as Prince of Ireland or King of Ireland." Elsewhere in Europe "his messengers were treated as ambassadors." O'Faolain, *Great O'Neill*, 205. The news of O'Neill's

victory at the Yellow Ford "had an astonishing effect on the country." Within months O'Neill "was virtual master of Ireland and could see the outline of a rapidly forming Confederate Army." Ibid., 203.

30.   Polydore Vergil, *Anglica Historica*, 79. Rich said, "Nature, that hath framed them comely personages, of good proportion, very well-limbed." Id. 130. But he also said "they are very cruel, bloody-minded, apt and ready to commit any kind of mischief." Barnabe Rich, "A New Description of Ireland, Together With The Manners, Customs, and Dispositions of The People (1610)," in *Elizabethan Ireland, a Selection of Writings by Elizabethan Writers on Ireland*, edited by James P. Myers, Jr. (Hamden, Connecticut: Archon Books, 1983), 130. Unlike the bread-eating peasants of other lands, however, before the banishment under Oliver Cromwell, the Irish ate an essentially well balanced diet of high protein foods; greens, milk and raw meat. David Beers Quinn, *The Elizabethans and the Irish* (Washington, D.C.: The Folger Shakespeare Library and Cornell University Press, 1966), 66.

31.   Both Romans and the barbarians missed Ireland. Richard Roche, *The Norman Invasion of Ireland* (Dublin: Anvil Books, 1995), 42-43.

32.   The initial landing of the English was not terribly alarming to the O'Conor, King of Connaught and High King, and seemed "not so very far different from the ordinary feuds and provincial wars." James Wills, editor, *Lives of Illustrious and Distinguished Irishmen: From the Earliest Times to the Present Period, Arranged in Chronological Order, and Embodying a History of Ireland in the Lives of Irishmen* (Dublin: MacGregor, Polson & Co., 1890), volume I, part II, 263, 299. At first the Irish "set no store by them" [the Normans] but soon thought otherwise. Curtis, *History*, 50-51. Thinking their towns were about to be attacked by disorganized footmen, the Irish of Wexford and Waterford were surprised to see skilled Norman knights and archers, horsemen, helmets and shields. Roche, *Norman Invasion*, 126-133.

33.   The Vikings in Ireland had settled coastal towns, several of which have names derived from language of the Norse or Ostmen – Wexford, Waterford. James Lydon, *The Making of Ireland From Ancient Times to the Present* (New York: Routledge, 1998), 20-36. Around Dublin, the area was called Dublin – shire by the Norse; the area north of the Liffey was called Fine Gall, land of the Norsemen. Curtis, *History*, 34.

34.   Ireland culturally "became an area of largely disconnected lordships" after the Norman invasion. Brian O'Cuiv, editor, *Seven Centuries of Irish Learning, 1000-1700* (Dublin: Published for Radio Eireann by the Stationary Office, 1961), 75.

35. The geographical landscape that resulted from the incomplete mix of Normans and native Irish resulted in what historians have called "little islands of Englishness." David Dickson, *Old World Colony, Cork and South Munster 1630-1830* (Cork: Cork University Press, 2005), 7, annotating Ciaran Brady's unpublished 1980 doctoral dissertation, "The Government of Ireland c. 1540-1583," 363, 368, 422-5.

36. Tribal Barbarism was a widespread characterization of the Irish by the English in 1500. G.R. Elton, *England Under the Tudors* (London and New York: Methuen, 1955), 30.

37. There was no central dispositive town or leader for Normans to target whose capture would provide them control of the island, not even their main goal, Dublin. The conquest of Dublin gave the Normans only Dublin. Thus, though in military terms the Native Irish were seriously outmatched, Norman conquest was grueling and piecemeal and gained control only of the ground on which the Norman force stood at the end of a battle. Roche, *Norman Invasion*, 44. This is what prevented a Norman hegemony of the kind the Normans achieved in Great Britain a century earlier. Ibid., 71.

38. Ulster was simply outside of the control of Dublin. G. A. Hayes-McCoy, "Conciliation, Coercion and the Protestant Reformation, 1547-71," in *A New History of Ireland*, edited by. T. W. Moody, F. X. Martin and F. J. Byrne, Vol. 3, *Early Modern Ireland (1534-1691)* (Oxford: Clarendon Press, 1976), 80. The English lordship claimed power over the entire island, but the English did not attempt to exercise power outside The Pale and a handful of walled towns. Ellis, *Eyewitness*, 24.

39. The 1175 Treaty of Windsor signed by Henry II and High King Rory O'Connor divided Ireland into Norman and Gaelic societies. It confirmed O'Connor as High King ruling the native Irish, but subject to the lordship of Henry II. Anthony M. McCormack, *The Earldom of Desmond, 1463-1583: The Decline and Crisis of a Feudal Lordship* (Dublin: Four Courts Press, 2005), 27.

40. The abduction of Dervorgilla, wife of the violent Tiernan O'Rourke, King of Breifne, was committed by Dermot MacMurrough, King of Leinster. Roche, *Norman Invasion*, 48, 53-64.

41. The cooperative relationship between the Pope and the English king was due in part to a unique papal credential held only by Pope Adrian IV – he was an Englishman, Nicholas Breakspear, and the only English Pope. A.H. Tarleton, *Life of Nicholas Breakspear* (London: A. L. Humphreys, 1896), 1.

42. Henry II, concerned that Strongbow and the Normans were about to establish in Ireland a competing Norman kingdom of their own,

came to Ireland in 1171 in full force leading 400 ships filled with fighting Normans. Roche, *Norman Invasion*, 14, 185. He upbraided some of the Norman leaders and even jailed a few, but soon granted them lordships and accepted their fealty. It remains surprising to this day, however, that so many native Irish kings peacefully submitted to Henry II and accepted him as their overlord and protector, but they did. Roche, *Norman Invasion*, 187.

43. The first Norman to land is believed to be Richard FitzGodebert de la Roche; he came in 1167 with King Dermot MacMurrough and a small group of Normans. Others came in 1169, 1170 and 1171. Roche, *Norman Invasion*, 101.

44. Strongbow landed at Passage in August of 1170. Roche, *Norman Invasion*, 163.

45. ("Diarmaid na nGall"). Curtis, *History*, 51.

46. Early Norman Ireland was almost entirely forest. Even the area now seen as a central plain was swamp and bog, impassable, impenetrable. Invaders simply could not get around to conquer and hold fast a sizable conquered territory. Roche, *Norman Invasion*, 36.

47. Most Irish lived not in towns or even villages, but in "small irregular units or in individual farmsteads." The few buildings in any area in Ireland were small, wattle structures. Quinn, *Elizabethans*, 15.

48. Ireland was cattle country. The wealth was cattle and the spoils of war were cattle. Falls 32. Cattle were used much like currency was used later. It was expected that payment of any obligation would be in the form of cattle. Roche, *Norman Invasion*, 41.

49. Native Irish society was not refined, but it was a stratified aristocracy with kings, nobles, freemen, churls and slaves. Roche, *Norman Invasion*, 37. The "Five Bloods." See Curtis, *History*, 76, 115.

50. Cattle raids and small battles were a constant source of hostility between clans. They were often conducted for prestige and "as a sport." Quinn, *Elizabethans*, 15. "Cattle raiding was a universal sport; it was a means by which the young man made a test of his manhood." Ibid., 46.

51. The route to the southwest – the king's highway down the valley of the River Barrow – was besieged by mountain clan raiders and was practically impassable as a result. Ellis, *Ireland*, 20.

52. The Irish were seen by contemporaries as "extremely superstitious." Quinn, *Elizabethans*, 167, 168. Sir John Harington described the Irish people: "strong and able bodies, proud hearts, pestilent wits, liberal of life, subject to incontinency, amorous … lovers of music and hospitality … implacable in their hatred, light of belief, covetous of glory … extremely superstitious…." Ibid., 167-168.

53.   Gerald of Wales, amid his predominantly harsh critique of Irish people, did comment that the native Irish have "strength with beautiful upright bodies and handsome and well-complexioned faces." Gerald of Wales, *The History and Topography of Ireland*, translated by John J. O'Meara (London: Penguin UK, 1982), 100.

54.   The Celtic festivals were *Imbolg* on February 1, *Beltaine* marked by bonfires on May 1, *Lughnasa* on August 1 and *Samhain* on November 1. Wren Day in Dingle was on December 26. All have their start in Celtic and Pagan rituals. Carmel McCaffrey and Leo Eaton, *In Search of Ancient Ireland*. (Lanham, Maryland: New Amsterdam Books, 2002), 82-86.

55.   The central courts were held also at Carlow, but moved back to Dublin by 1394. Ellis, *Ireland*, 21.

56.   Justiciars were called Lord Justice. Peter Berresford Ellis, *Eyewitness to Irish History* (New York: Wiley, 2004), 162. Several English officials posted in Ireland who led the government during the 16th century did so as a Lord Justice or Justiciar, not as Deputy. Some of them were Francis Bryan (1549-1550); William Brabazon (1550); Thomas Cusack and Gerald Aylmer (1552-1553); Adam Loftus, Archbishop of Dublin and Robert Gardiner (1597-1599).

57.   These areas were referred to as a "land of war." Curtis, *History*, 93. The chieftains in these areas would pick off isolated settlements and the fearful occupants would simply abandon their homes and land and leave for The Pale. Ellis, *Ireland*, 32-36. These areas were outside the "land of peace." Curtis, *History*, 93.

58.   By the 16th century, the Norman families with Norman names who had originally spoken French were Irish speakers. Curtis, *History*, 106. They intermarried with the fertile Irish. Many of "these feudal families soon lost their French character and adopted Gaelic law and surnames; …." Curtis, *History*, 107, 116.

59.   One chronicler of Ireland described two native populations found in Ireland, one "gentle and cultured," the other, "wild men of the woods" who were "savage, rude and uncouth." Polydore Vergil, *The Anglica Historica*, 79.

60.   Ambushes in which clans exploited the local terrain posed a great threat to the English. Ellis, *Ireland*, 29.

61.   Jack Cade's rebellion in Kent in 1450 spurred English nobles to call upon Richard Duke of York to return from Dublin to London and serve as "protector" of the realm. ("from Ireland thus comes York to claim his right and pluck the crown from feeble Henry's head.") William Shakespeare, Second Part of Henry the Sixth (New York: Washington Square Press [1966], act 5, sc. 1, lines 1-4). Thomas Her-

ron and Brendan Kane, *Nobility and Newcomers in Renaissance Ireland* (Washington, DC: Folger Shakespeare Library, 2013), 3.

62.   "The Wars of the Roses distracted the attention of the English kings from Ireland and resulted in great lessening of their power over Ireland for close on a century. .... [T]he Norman lords in Ireland were left to manage their own affairs with little control or interference on the part of England. O'Cuiv, *Seven Centuries*, 77.

63.   There were few battles in the Wars of the Roses after Wakefield, mainly St. Albans, Towton, Bosworth and Stoke. Ellis, *Ireland*, 2, 3, 64.

64.   The very first FitzGerald in Ireland was the invader Maurice FitzGerald from Pembroke in Wales. McCormack, *Earldom*, 20, 26.

65.   The 1st Earl of Desmond was Maurice FitzThomas FitzGerald, created Earl in 1329. He greatly increased the Desmond earldom's power and lands. He took and secured considerable land in Munster and he also married well. He married Katherine, the daughter of Richard deBurgh, the Red Earl, and that brought him and the earldom much more land. McCormack, *Earldom*, 31, 32.

66.   The Fitzgeralds also claimed ancestry from the Geraldini of Florence. Herron and Kane, *Nobility*, 24.

67.   The Statutes of Kilkenny almost casually labelled the natives the "Irish enemies." Curtis, *History*, 112. They forbade seanachies, minstrels, poets, Brehon law, intermarriage, and sales to the Irish; they required that speech must be English. Ibid., 113.

68.   The Statutes of Kilkenny have been referred to as the "Outlawry of the Irish race" due to the disabilities they imposed on the Irish. Curtis, *History*, 115-16.

69.   Under the Statutes of Kilkenny, the Irish were excluded from cathedrals, abbeys and benefices. Curtis, *History*, 113. One penalty for violations of the Statutes, approved by the archbishops and bishops of Ireland, was excommunication. Curtis, *History*, 116.

70.   The penalties of English criminal law were too harsh for the native Irish culture. Ellis, *Ireland*, 48.

71.   The Irish recoiled against the "dreadful penalties of the Common Law." Curtis, *History*, 115.

72.   The English expelled the Native Irish from the walled city of Dublin in 1454, sending them to live well outside the walls in an area called Irishtown, now a Dublin neighborhood. John McCormack, *A Story of Dublin* (Denver: Mentor Books, 2000), 44, 287.

73.   Irish natives were isolated in the area beyond the border of the English Pale. They were used as peasant laborers but possessed no rights at all under the common law. Susan Brigden, *New Worlds,*

Lost Worlds, The Rule of the Tudors 1485-1603 (New York: Penguin Books, 2001), 20.

74.   The Statutes of Kilkenny played a role in the land fraud cases of the 16th and 17th centuries. They were cited as a basis for the claim that any chieftain "and his people were mere encroachers and intruders upon some Englishman's land or an inheritance of the Crown." Curtis, *History*, 15.

75.   The Battle of Pilltown near Carrick on Suir was fought in the heart of Butler territory. The Butlers of Poletown, a junior branch in the midlands, and the Berminghams of Meath rose up in 1463 to support an invasion led by Sir John Butler, claiming to be Earl of Ormond. However, the Eighth Earl of Desmond, Thomas FitzGerald, raised an army and defeated John Butler at Pilltown. When Butler withdrew, the Meath rising began to subside. Ellis, *Eyewitness*, 64.

76.   Even Henry Sidney saw that Tiptoft was a tyrant. Brady, *Viceroy's Vindication?*, 61. Tiptoft is also referred to as Tibetot. Curtis, *History*, 144.

77.   John Tiptoft, Earl of Worcester, was called "the butcher." Ellis, *Ireland*, 66, 67.

78.   For the four years from Henry VIII's 1509 coronation to the 1513 death of Kildare the two colossal figures appraised each other. Henry VIII took note of the Council's "affection" for and "dread" of The 9th Earl of Kildare. Ellis, *Eyewitness*, 163; State Papers, Henry VIII, Vol. II, 179.

79.   Despite the many historical references to the Dublin Council, its authority and functional role is not clear. There were seven or more ministers, and the Council conducted many functions of state, but what limits existed on advising the Deputy or taking military or judicial action are unclear. Ellis, *Eyewitness*, 165. When the Lord Lieutenant or his Deputy presided, the Council would be called a parliament. A. J. Otway-Ruthven, *A History of Medieval Ireland*, 3rd ed. (New York: Barnes & Noble Books, 1980), 317. Puritanism in the reign of Elizabeth was led by John Field, Thomas Cartwright, Walter Travers and Thomas Wilcox. Elton, *England Under*, 311.

80.   The early earls of Kildare ruled the Pale as a palatinate. Although English administrators were ambitious to take control, they would arrive in Dublin and find "Dublin's bureaucracy totally infiltrated by men loyal to Kildare and the interests of other Anglo-Norman magnates." James Charles Roy, *The Fields of Athenry: A Journey Through Ireland* (Boulder, CO: Westview, 2003), 104.

81.   To block Grey's authority, Kildare raised hyper-technical issues relating to which seal had been used for Grey's commission. Baron

Portlester used this irregularity to deny Grey access to the Irish great seal. He also broke down a bridge Grey needed to use to reach the castle and the courts. The sheriffs joined the obstruction as well. Some of them declined to come to Grey's parliament. Ellis, *Eyewitness*, 77.

82. *Micel O'Cleirigh* was a lay brother who joined an Irish Franciscan house in Louvain, and dedicated himself to collecting historical materials about Ireland. In 1636 *O'Cleirigh*, along with *Cucoigriche O'Cleirigh, Feargeasa O'Maolchoncaire* and *Cucoigriche O'Duibhghennain* completed the Annals of the Four Masters. Richter, *Medieval Ireland*, 187.

83. Some English saw the Irish as unusually jovial: "the Irishman was born easily and lay on his deathbed listening to the jokes and laughter of his friends" (according to contemporary English observers). Quinn, *Elizabethans*, 82.

84. Kildare had a rough and bawdy style. In London he would talk to Henry VII, take him by the hand, tell him impertinent humorous stories about the Bishop of Meath and spout "Be Jaysus." There was no sign of disapproval. Indeed, Kildare made the King laugh. Ann Wroe, *The Perfect Prince* (New York: Random House, 2003), 98. See also Elton, *England Under*, 31, and Mary Cullen, *Ma Nuad, Maynooth: a Short Historical Guide* (Maynooth: The Maynooth Bookshop, 1995), 27.

85. Kildare was often at serious odds with the unpopular Archbishop of Cashel and he finally burned the Cashel cathedral. Henry VII summoned him to London to answer the charge and Kildare admitted it but playfully jousted: "Never by St. Bride would I have done it but I thought the Archbishop was inside." Cullen, *Ma Nuad*, 27. The King shared the laugh and he restored Kildare as Deputy.

86. Kildare's sister Eleanor married Con Mor O'Neill, son of Henry O'Neill of Dungannon. She was the mother of Con Bacach O'Neill, the grandfather of the Great O'Neill, Hugh O'Neill, Second Earl of Tyrone. Curtis, *History*, 147.

87. The Kildares as Deputies had nominal authority over all of Ireland, but in actuality their authority extended only to the Pale (Dublin north to Dundalk and 40 miles inland), and to the towns-Waterford, Cork, Limerick and Galway, and to the fortress at Carrickfergus in the northeast. Moody xxxix.

88. Young Irish fighters were called oglach. Falls, *Elizabeth's Irish Wars*, 76.

89. Coyne and livery was often just a protection racket. Hiram Morgan, "The End of Gaelic Ulster: A Thematic Interpretation of Events Between 1534 and 1610," *Irish Historical Studies* 8, no. 32 (May 1988), 9.

90. Sir John Davies described coyne and livery as "extortion" and a "crying sin," and he said the consequence of it could be that "when the husbandman had labored all the year, the soldier in one night did consume the fruits of all his labor...." Davies, *Discovery*, 159.

91. The first pretender, Lambert Simnel, a pawn of certain nobles, was thought to have been in reality the child of an artisan from Oxford. Herron and Kane, *Nobility*, 3.

92. A third prince housed in the Tower was yet another Edward, the Earl of Warwick, son of George Duke of Clarence. His claim to the throne was confused due to an earlier family attainder. He was executed in 1499 allegedly for aiding Perkin Warbeck's plot to escape from the Tower.

93. Lambert Simnel pretended to be Edward, Earl of Warwick, one of the 3 princes in the Tower. It is presumed that Richard, Duke of York had already been murdered, but the Earl of Warwick was still alive. He was executed in 1499. Wroe, *Perfect*, 79.

94. The Great Earl of Kildare gave support to Lambert Simnel, the imposter/pretender to the Throne of England. Curtis, *History*, 149. See also Wroe, *Perfect*, 80, 96-97. Elton, *England Under*, 31.

95. The force that invaded England in 1487 in support of the effort to install Lambert Simnel on the throne was led by Thomas FitzGerald, the Earl of Lincoln, who was the brother of Kildare. The substantial force suffered 4,000 fatalities, including the Earl of Lincoln. Simnel himself was captured. Curtis, *History*, 149.

96. Perkin Warbeck was the second imposter/pretender to the throne. Curtis, *History*, 149, 153. See also Wroe, *Perfect*, 226, 491, 502-03.

97. In June 1492 Henry VII replaced Kildare as Deputy but reinstated him. Elton, *England Under*, 31.

98. Poynings law was intended to prevent future Irish Parliaments from endorsing pretenders to the Throne. Myers, *Elizabethan Ireland*, 4.

99. Perkin Warbeck was imprisoned, but when he tried to escape he was executed. He was spared traditional torture; his execution in November 1499 was commuted to simple beheading. Wroe, *Perfect*, 491.

100. The lists of books from the library of Maynooth Castle still exist. Cullen, *Ma Nuad*, 28.

101. The Kildare war cry was "*Crom Abu.*" Cullen, *Ma Nuad*, 24. The O'Brien war cry was "*Lamhlaidir Abu.*" Ibid.

102. The Battle of Knockdoe has been described as "one vast melee of pushing, shoving, hacking, stabbing men." Roy, *Fields*, 107.

103. The Kildare defeat in 1510 near Limerick. Mary Ann Lyons, *Gearoid Og Fitzgerald* (Dundalk: Dundalgan Press Limited, 1998), 28.

104. Kildare was "a virtual king in Ireland and among the most anglicized of the Irish rulers." He encouraged study and supported the Irish culture, but was not himself a scholar. He assembled a great library at Maynooth. Wroe, *Perfect*, 97. The Kildare library contained books in many languages. The Kildares were patrons of poetry and prose in English, Irish and Latin. Herron and Kane, *Nobility*, 19, 23.

105. The Great Earl of Kildare's stature throughout Ireland lasted for forty years. Along with his talents, however, his anger made him at times entirely lose control. Curtis, *History*, 156.

106. Despite early Kildare unruliness and the Lambert Simnel affair, The Great Earl, his father and his son, would never take "that final, ruinous step and yield to the seductive works of the bard...[and] never reached for the crown of Ireland...which on various occasions they certainly could have taken." Roy, *Fields*, 104.

107. The Earl of Kildare summoned a parliament but defied Henry VIII's legislative wishes "with impunity." Lydon, *Making*, 113.

108. For the four years from Henry VIII's 1509 coronation to the 1513 death of Kildare the two colossal figures appraised each other. Henry VIII took note of the Council's "affection" for and "dread" of The 9th Earl of Kildare. Ellis, *Eyewitness*, 163; State Papers, Henry VIII, Vol. II, 179.

109. Wills, *Lives of Illustrious,* Vol. I, Part II, 448-449.

110. Richard II led an English army of 8,000 into Ireland in 1394 and another in 1399. He was the only English King to visit Ireland between 1210 and 1689. Ellis, *Eyewitness*, 24, and Curtis, *History*, 123-130.

111. Henry VIII was less interested in the details of Irish government than his father had been. Even in ruling England, he did so through a single chief minister, first Lord Chancellor Cardinal Thomas Wolsey, then Thomas Cromwell. Ellis, *Ireland*, 114)

112. The English lost their largely military occupation of Normandy to a resurgent French monarchy in the 15th century, holding on only to Calais. Ellis, *Ireland*, 29.

113. Henry VIII knew that Ireland "was not under his effective control." Quinn and Nicholls, *New History*, 1. He had his Irish title changed to King in 1541. Moody et. al., *The Course of Irish History,* 176.

114. Cardinal Wolsey's vanity and accumulation of ostentatious wealth. Elton, *England Under*, 75, 84, 86-87, 92.

115. Garrett Og had been close to Prince Arthur, first husband of Catherine of Aragon. Lydon, *Making,* 117. Youth and education of Garret Og. Lyons, *Gearoid*, 20.

116. The Ormond intra family contest for the earldom. Lyons, *Gearoid,* 31-32.

117. Henry VIII was extremely jealous of the new French King Francis I, who replaced Henry in the esteem of other men. Elton, *England Under*, 89.

118. Piers Roe Butler's appointment as Deputy in 1522. Lyons, *Gearoid*, 36.

119. Con Mor O'Neill's attendance at the 1524 installation of Garret Og as Deputy. Lyons, *Gearoid*, 39.

120. Feuding and political competition between Garret Og and Piers Roe Butler. Lyons, *Gearoid*, 46-48.

121. Finally, the Treaty of Cambrai in 1529 gave Charles V a definitive victory over the Pope that ended Wolsey's chance to squeeze from the Pope a divorce from Charles V's aunt, Catherine of Aragon. Wolsey's fate rested on the kindness of Henry VIII. Elton, *England Under*, 96. Wolsey was not helped by Anne Boleyn's hostility to him. Elton, *England Under*, 120.

122. The rise and fall of Wolsey and Cromwell occurred in the years of the rise and fall of the House of Kildare. Elton, *England Under*, 128-29. Cromwell and the fall of the House of Kildare; playing on Henry's special anxieties. Laurence McCorristine, *The Revolt of Silken Thomas: a Challenge to Henry VIII* (Dublin: Wolfhound Press, 1987), 47, 49. Others in the Dublin Council joined in. McCorristine 42. They urged the appointment of an English Lord Deputy to replace Garret Og. Id. 51. Henry called Garret Og to London in August 1533. He had been called to London once before, in 1519 and removed as Lord Deputy. Ibid., 54.

123. Cromwell undertook to make Henry VIII "the richest sovereign that ever reigned in England." As a result his power with Henry exceeded Wolsey's. It is said Cromwell "had more credit with his master than ever the cardinal had." "Now there is not a person who does anything except Cromwell." Message of Eustace Chapuys, 1535 to Imperial Chancellor Granvelle. C.H. Williams, editor. *English Historical Documents, 1485-1558*. London: Eyre and Spottiswoode, 1967), 412.

124. Archbishop Alen was removed as Chancellor and as a member of the secret council. Lyons, *Gearoid*, 46.

125. Henry VIII and Wolsey were already seeking agreement with the Vatican for control of the Church in Ireland and England. Lennon, *Sixteenth-Century Ireland*, 135. In 1529, Wolsey sent the "secret council" of John Alen, John Rawson and Patrick Bermingham to bring about the same ecclesiastical changes he had made in the north of England. McCormack, *Earldom*, 68; Lennon, *Sixteenth-Century Ireland*, 102, 103.

126. The "crucial" role leading to the Kildare rebellion played by Thomas Cromwell. McCorristine, *Revolt*, 55. Cromwell was planning a full reformation of the governance of Ireland, the type embodied in his 1534, The Ordinances for the Government of Ireland. Ibid., 55. The Ordinances contained little substance of note ("a high sounding pamphlet" containing "a ragbag of instructions") but the significance of Cromwell's issuance of the Ordinances was his tactic to command wide observance of rules promulgated by the royal Court. Ellis, *Eyewitness*, 135. Historians differ over whether Cromwell's plan was aimed only at reigning in the House of Kildare. Ibid., 56.

127. It is said Thomas was "more alive to flattery" than to "fear or reason", Wills, *Lives*, Vol. 4, Part II, 442. Thomas' actions are described as impetuous and the result of his own folly. Wills, *Lives*, Vol. I, Part II, 451. References appear of Thomas' "personal beauty and magnificent appearance" and the "richness of his attire ... embroidered with silk." Ibid. 442.

128. Descriptions of Silken Thomas come largely from Richard Stanihurst. McCorristine, *Revolt*, 16. Silken Thomas' rudeness in keeping the Council waiting, his acerbic remarks, love of flattery are described by James Wills. Wills, *Lives*, Vol. I, Part II, 440-443.

129. Thomas would keep the Council waiting for hours, then greet them rudely. Wills, *Lives*, Vol. I, Part II, 441. Thomas' statement that he was now the King's foe. Ibid.

130. The plot was allegedly intended to goad Silken Thomas to some foolish act. Garret Og and Thomas both believed that Thomas Cromwell intended to get them both to come to London and have them both executed. This, more than impetuosity, undoubtedly motivated Thomas' dramatic, public declaration of rebellion. Curtis, *History*, 162. Silken Thomas was, however, deceived by the report of his father's death. Elton, *England Under*, 180. The report that Garret Og had been "cut short." Fitzgerald (The Geraldine's) 204. Some historians doubt the story of the plot and the fake letter; they assert it was a scenario written up later by Richard Stanihurst to justify Thomas' rebellion and to argue in favor of the restoration of the 11th Earl of Kildare. Ellis, *Eyewitness*, 136.

131. St. Mary's Abbey was a Cistercian abbey where the Council was meeting. McCormack, *Earldom*, 80.

132. The influence of the harpist cannot be so easily dismissed; the influence of bards and poets on the Irish was excessive. It is said that they less feared the Lord Deputy than "the least song or ballad these rascals might make against them." Quinn, *Elizabethans*, 42.

133. In a "gesture of profound medieval drama," Thomas threw down his sword to begin the rebellion." McCorristine, *Revolt*, 65.
134. The killing of Archbishop Alen at Artane on July 28, 1534. Wills, *Lives*, 444.
135. Both the cause of Garret Og's death and the date are uncertain. It is reported that he died on September 2, 1534; if so, he was dead before Silken Thomas was excommunicated. McCorristine, *Revolt*, 82, and 161n75. Whatever, the cause of his death, Richard Stanihurst's theory that Garret Og died of grief is merely undocumented theory. Ibid.
136. Skeffington's and Boys' rejection of the plea of Christopher Paris (Parese) after he helped them with the fall of Maynooth Castle. Wills, *Lives*, Vol. I, Part II, 448-49.
137. Lord Leonard Grey was a military man who served as Deputy and was a favorite of Thomas Cromwell, but in 1541 when Cromwell fell from power, Leonard Grey was charged with treason and executed. Ellis 149. Henry VIII's reasons for executing Lord Leonard Grey are still unclear. Roy, Fields, 119.
138. The violence was such that the Irish were "utterly devoured by it." Edwards, et al, *Age of Atrocity*, 69.
139. Lord Leonard Grey executed the women and children of Carrigogunnell Castle in Limerick in 1536, a total of 46 victims. Edwards, et al, *Age of Atrocity*, 59. At Bellahoe in 1539 Grey himself recounted killing many herdsmen, peasants and common people. Edwards, et al, *Age of Atrocity*, 60. In 1540, Grey beheaded the members of the Franciscan community in Monaghan, including the Prior. Edwards, et al, *Age of Atrocity*, 60.
140. The "utter extinction" of the culture of Gaelic aristocracy "was the declared colonial policy of England from 1541 forward." Ellis, *Erin's*, xii.
141. "*Cujus regio, ejus religio,*" Ford 55.
142. The Reformation of religion instituted under Henry VIII took many steps and its form changed and evolved. Henry declared himself head of the church in England and broke with the Pope in 1534 by The Act of Supremacy, but the central religious disputes raging in Europe since Martin Luther and others challenged Catholic beliefs and practices were mostly yet to be resolved. Henry's wars had cost the monarchy its fortune, but he began to replenish it through the taking of the lands of the monasteries and abbeys in England and Ireland in 1536 and 1539. Russell, Conrad. "The Reformation and the Creation of the Church of England, 1500-1640," in *The Oxford Illustrated History of Tudor and Stuart Britain*, edited by John Morrill

(Oxford: Oxford University Press, 2000), 275, 277. On the subject of doctrine, Henry had initially rejected Luther's doctrinal changes. Id. 271. Debate continued in England as elsewhere over salvation by Faith alone or by good works or by observance of rituals and ceremonies, and over the mass, confession, celibacy, icons and other features of religion. When Henry first legally curtailed diversity by the 1539 Act of Six Articles, it was continental Protestant edicts that were curtailed. Catholic practices and beliefs, such as transubstantiation and the mass and clerical celibacy, were endorsed. Russell, "Reformation," 277.

143. The sincerity in religion of the Wild Irish was dismissed by the English who insisted the Irish were only nominal Christians whose Christian identification was stressed only when it was important to try to attract support from the papacy, Spain and France. Elton, *England Under*, 386-87.

144. Cork and other walled cities often evidenced a split between their New English and Old English occupants. In Cork City the Old English moved toward rejecting the Protestant reforms; their opposition to the reforms was spurred by the influence of foreign-trained priests. Dickson, *Old World*, 7.

145. The Lordship of Ireland dating back to Henry II thereby became the Kingdom of Ireland under King Henry VIII. Richter, *Medieval Ireland*, 132-134; Elton, *England Under*, 180.

146. Henry VIII's policy of surrender and regrant ignored "fundamental facts of their tribal and nomadic culture: that the clan, not individuals, possessed ultimate ownership of the land...." Myers, *Elizabethan Ireland*, 6. Under clan law and custom the chieftain's surrender did not bind his successor. Ibid.

147. Sir Anthony St. Leger, a member of a prominent Kent family, arrived as Deputy in 1540. He was experienced in Irish affairs; he had served there before. Unlike many Deputies, he was not a military man. Ellis, *Eyewitness*, 149. Anthony St. Leger served as Lord Deputy from 1540 to 1548, crucial years for the administration of surrender and regrant. He was a wise and decent administrator and was able to win over many Irish to accept this procedure peacefully. Curtis, *History*, 168. Anthony St. Leger became concerned that so many Irish had been speaking of the Pope as King of Ireland that he prevailed on the Council to propose to Henry VIII that Henry declare himself King of Ireland, and Henry did so. Curtis, *History*, 168. Henry VIII sent St. Leger as Deputy to campaign to achieve surrender and regrant in south Leinster and he succeeded in bringing peace with the O'Mores, MacMurroughs and O'Connors and se-

curing their acceptance of the King. He had similar success in west
Munster with the Desmonds and in Connaught with the Burkes of
Clanrickard. Ellis, *Eyewitness*, 150. St. Leger and his chief administrator, Thomas Cusack, were even successful in resolving old disputes and achieving conciliation among rival Irish chieftains. Ellis,
Eyewitness, 150-51. The two made "remarkable progress towards a
settlement of the Irish question." Ibid., 154. They even took the time
to address the internal politics within lordships. Ibid., 155. Under St.
Leger, native Irish lords attended Parliaments held in Dublin and in
Drogheda. Ibid., 154. Yet even under St. Leger there was graft, corruption and embezzlement in the King's Dublin administration. It
tainted St. Leger and Lord Justice Brabazon. Ibid., 158-59.

148.   The Old English and the New English sharply conflicted. The Old
English benefitted from St. Leger's program, but the New English
needed to take over substantial Irish lands to entrench themselves
in what they hoped was going to become a new entirely English
world free of the "native customs" of the Irish. Ellis, *Eyewitness*, 157.

149.   St. Leger, as others, had disputes with the earl of Ormond; both of
them were summoned to London to appear at court to resolve one
dispute. Ellis, *Eyewitness*, 157. St. Leger lost the King's ear when
Henry VIII became totally preoccupied with war against France.
Ibid., 153. Henry VIII recalled St. Leger in 1546, then Henry died in
January 1547. Ibid., 156-57. This ended a promising peace initiative
with the Irish lords and gentry. Ibid., 157.

150.   Another official derogatory phrase used was "mere Irishman." Curtis, *History*, 93.

151.   "Irish Enemies" and "Wild Irish" were official terms. The native
Irish were treated as "aliens and foreigners." Ellis, *Eyewitness*, 23.
"[A]n Irishman found inside the border [of the Pale] was liable to
arrest as a spy." Froude, *English*, 29. "Intermarriage with the Irish,
or fostering with the Irish, was made treason." Froude, *English*, 27.
Richard II came to Ireland with an army in 1394 to retake much of
Kildare and Carlow from the chieftain Art MacMurrough. Curtis,
History, 124-126. While there, he formally divided the population
into "the wild Irish, our enemies; English rebels; and obedient English." Ibid., 125. Many chieftains submitted to Richard II (Ibid., 126).
MacMurrough was thereby weakened, and he was induced to agree
at Tullow to abandon the lands in Leinster but he was permitted to
conquer and hold under the King any lands he took from the Irish
enemies (Ibid., 128).

152.   Normans, too, are chronicled as possessing a savage "untamable
temper." Roy, *Fields*, 38.

153. The title of the modern position of *Taoiseach*, leader, came from the *Aire Tuisi*, noble of leadership. Eugene O'Curry, *On The Manners and Customs of the Ancient Irish*, vol 1, edited by W. K. Sullivan (London: William and Norgate, 1873), 27; Richter, *Medieval Ireland*, 203, 205.

154. A family group was a *deirbhfhine*. Quinn, *Elizabethans*, 16.

155. Barnabe Rich described Irish weather: "I say, we do not find Ireland to be cold in the winter, nor so hot in the summer, as it is in England....yet the country is very cold, with a kind of rawish moisture..." Rich, "New Description," 129.

156. Gerald of Wales admired the "quick and lively" music of the Irish. He wrote that it was "sweet and pleasant." Gerald of Wales, 103. He marveled at "the great speed of the fingers" of Irish musicians playing the harp and the tympanum. *Id.* 104. The native Irish had, however, formed "social and cultural institutions [and] created a substantial racial and cultural unity." Ellis, *Ireland*, 46.

157. A somewhat independent evaluation of 16th century Irish people is contained in a contemporary description of Ireland during the Tyrone Rebellion. It was published a few years later by one of the soldiers who served under Richard Burke in the cavalry at Kinsale. That author, Thomas Gainsford, wrote a book, "The True Exemplary, and Remarkable History of the Earle of Tyrone" in 1619. He described how fertile Munster was. He also described how devilishly quick the Irish were in creating obstacles in the woods and attacking in bogs, then quickly fleeing. He wrote of the sweet rivers full of fish. He described mountainous Ulster with very few towns, neither as cold or as hot as England, continual showers and mists, little frost, short snowfall, abundant wolves, and people who were "beyond measure proud". Quinn, *Elizabethans*, 165-66.

158. Although Catholic, "[Edmund] Campion writes more as an Englishman." Myers, *Elizabethan Ireland*, 22. Even Edmund Campion, amid his recounting of base Irish habits, described the Irish people he encountered favorably at times: "They are sharp-witted, lovers of learning, capable of any study whereunto they bend themselves, constant in travail, adventurous, intractable, kind-hearted, secret in displeasure." Campion, "History," 24-25. Publications like those by Stanihurst and Campion were censored by the government. The "cruel nature of guerilla warfare, made the Crown extremely sensitive to publicity. Most of the manuscripts apparently failed to obtain the official authorization required for publication until the events of which they spoke were well in the past." Myers, *Elizabethan Ireland*, 11.

159. The "Five Bloods." See Curtis, *History*, 76, 115.

160. Thomas Radcliffe, Earl of Sussex (earlier Lord Fitzwalter), replaced Anthony St. Leger as Deputy in 1556. Sussex served under Queen Mary and thus was commissioned to restore and promote "the true catholic faith and religion." Though Mary burned many Protestants in England, even under Sussex and martial law, there were no such burnings in Ireland. Hayes-McCoy, "Conciliation," 76. Sussex was Deputy until the summer of 1560 and then was named Lieutenant. Ibid., 79. Sussex in his official memoranda about his time in office urged that reform in Ireland should focus on undermining the powerful factions in Ireland, most of all the Geraldines in Kildare and in Desmond. Brian S. J. McCuarta, *Reshaping Ireland, 1550-1700: Colonization and Its Consequences: Essays Presented to Nicholas Canny.* Dublin: Four Courts Press, 2011), 31. See also Ciaran Brady, *From Policy to Power: The Evaluation of Tudor Reform Strategies In Sixteenth-Century Ireland.*

161. The putative heir of the House of Kildare had been whisked off to Florence for his safety. Once the Catholic Queen Mary ascended the Throne, the House of Kildare was restored and this Wizard Earl returned to Ireland. Curtis, *History*, 168.

162. The alliance established by the Great Earl of Kildare remained even after the 1537 execution of Silken Thomas. They formed what has been called The Geraldine League consisting of the O'Donnells, the Earl of Desmond, MacCarthy Mor, O'Connor Offaly and the northern chieftain Conn O'Neill. Their hope was to restore Geraldine power, to do this through the remaining heir, Gerald FitzGerald, who was Silken Thomas' half-brother. They also planned to revolt and overthrow the Deputy Lord Leonard Grey and Crown Conn O'Neill at Tara as King of Ireland. Their one chief assault, however, was stopped in 1539 when Grey defeated Conn O'Neill's clan at Bellahoe. Curtis, *History*, 168.

163. The O'Connors and O'Mores in Laois were evicted during the reign of Queen Mary, and Laois became Queen's County. These colonizations were "improvisations," not the substantial organized plantations later begun under Queen Elizabeth. Michael McConville, *Ascendancy to Oblivion: the Story of the Anglo Irish* (London: Quartet Books, 1986), 21.

164. The native Irish were not considered natural subjects of the king and were denied the rights and protection of the law. Ellis, *Ireland*, 122.

165. Elizabeth executed many English Catholics; 130 priests and 60 lay Catholics were executed in her reign with abundant torture. Among them was the Jesuit, Edmund Campion, who was hanged, drawn

and quartered at Tyburn in 1581. McFarnon 1. Catholics and priests were executed for showing one way or another that they sided with the Pope. Elton, *England Under*, 307-08.

166. Francis Bacon wrote that Elizabeth "allowed herself to be wooed and courted and even to have love made to her." John Guy, *The Tudor Monarchy* (London: Hodder Education Publishers, 1997), 234.

167. Elizabeth very nearly died in 1562. Hayes-McCoy, "Conciliation," 80.

168. The state papers contain a contemporaneous observation reporting that: "The Queen is much aged and spent, and is very melancholy. Her intimates say that this is caused by the death of the earl of Leicester; but it is very evident that it is rather the fear she underwent and the burden she has upon her." COSPEA. 1587-1603. Entry 470. Nov. 5, 1588. 481.

169. Philip II of Spain had ambitions to rule England. Moody Hayes-McCoy, "Conciliation," 80.

170. Chambers, *Eleanor*, 58.

171. Gerald is designated as the 15th Earl of Desmond in McCormack's work on the Desmond Earldom. McCormack, passim.

172. Butler was Elizabeth's childhood playmate. Berleth, 36.

173. Elizabeth called Tom Butler her "Black Husband". Anne Chambers, *Eleanor, Countess of Desmond: A Captivating Tale of the Forgotten Heroine of the Tudor Wars in Ireland* (Dublin: Wolfhound Press, 2000), 35.

174. The Desmond earls could call upon many fighting men, including anyone occupying the vast Desmond lands, as many as fifty lordships. Chambers, *Eleanor*, 40.

175. Askeaton Castle on the River Deel in western Limerick offered lavish hospitality, fine meals and strong drink served and eaten on couches. Berleth, 26. The garden at Askeaton Castle was the scene of long dances and fiddle music. Ibid., 83. At Irish castles bards would sing and guests would drink "the dainty drink of nobles" (ale and mead) and whiskey (*uisge beatha* or *aqua vita*), and play cards and backgammon. Chambers, *Eleanor*, 27. The Castle at Askeaton was old, but renovated and reinforced. It was not a place of grandeur but bore touches of the FitzGerald's pride in their Italian blood, their Gherardini (Gheraldini) Florentine ancestry. Ibid., 75.

176. The Rebel Earl had a complex and disputed inheritance to the earldom. For that reason, and perhaps others, he is referred to variously as either the 14th, 15th or even the 16th Earl of Desmond. Lennon, *Sixteenth-Century Ireland*, 378. See also Hayes-McCoy, "Conciliation," 86. Gerald FitzGerald is referred to as the 16th Earl of Desmond. Wills, *Lives*, Vol. II 11.

177. Early in his life Gerald had been loyal. Indeed, when Lord Deputy Thomas Radcliffe, Earl of Sussex, assembled supporting forces from loyal lords to march to Ulster in 1561 to challenge Shane O'Neill and stop Shane's attacks on The Pale and Connaught, Gerald, Earl of Desmond, joined forces with him and marched with him to Ulster on behalf of the Crown. Lennon, *Sixteenth-Century Ireland,* 271, 272.
178. Gerald was a strong man despite his infirmities, and he was attractive to women. Berleth, 80.
179. Gerald FitzGerald, the 14th Earl of Desmond, was called the "madbrained earl." Berleth, 68, 124.
180. Staple towns where the staples – wine, wool, skins, and salt—could be sold to foreign merchants were Dublin, Limerick, Waterford, Cork and Drogheda. Lennon, *Sixteenth-Century Ireland,* 30, 39. Surrounded by the sea, Ireland "was also a seafaring society, with a coastal fishing and seafood exporting tradition which was a significant part of its economy. Its agriculture was based on oats rather than wheat, and it used part of its grain for winter cattle feed." Quinn, *Elizabethans,* 14.
181. Joan fervently loved both Gerald, her husband, and Black Tom, her son. Chambers, *Eleanor,* 43.
182. Early in her reign Elizabeth turned a blind eye to certain illegalities of her Irish earls. Brigden, *New Worlds,* 228.
183. Elizabeth was warned that "Irish lords will have all that their swords can keep." Brigden, *New Worlds,* 345. The Bohermor confrontation was in early summer 1562. Berleth, 82. Shane O'Neill had appeared before Elizabeth earlier that year. Berleth, 82; Ellis, *Eyewitness,* 277.
184. Gerald, the Earl of Desmond, went before the Privy Council in London just months after Shane O'Neill had made his submission at the Tudor Court. Berleth, 82; Ellis, *Eyewitness,* 277.
185. Elizabeth "spat" with anger at Gerald. Chambers, *Eleanor,* 43.
186. The death and burial of Joan FitzGerald, Countess of Desmond. Berleth, 82.
187. Shane O'Neill wanted to be King of Ulster. Hayes-McCoy, "Conciliation," 76.
188. The English believed that Ulster consisted of tribes still living in the savagery of the Bronze Age. Elton, *England Under,* 386. In a letter to Queen Elizabeth, Captain Nicholas Dawtrey wrote describing the Irish: "an ape will be an ape, though he were clad in cloth of gold." Quinn, *Elizabethans,* 36. He told her of their "tyrannous customs" and said that their ancestral personality was that "they will have all that their sword can command. ..." Dawtrey was one of the models for Falstaff. Ibid., 37.

189. Con Bacach O'Neill's mother was Eleanor FitzGerald, the daughter of the 7th Earl of Kildare and sister of The Great Earl of Kildare. Berleth. Geneologies. The Earls of Tyrone, III.

190. The French Ambassador reported back excitedly that he had witnessed the surrender of the greatest Barbarian, Con Bacach O'Neill, to Henry VIII. Ellis, *Eyewitness*, 153.

191. Some historians report that it was Con Bacach's continuing romance with Alison O'Kelly, not respect for Mathew, that led to his naming of Mathew as his heir. McConville, *Ascendency*, 55.

192. Shane was called *Séan an Diomáis* and *Sean Donnghaileach*. Brady, *Shane O'Neill*, 23.

193. The tales of Shane, whiskey and women, being buried to his neck in hot or cold moist sand have become legendary. Berleth, 248. It is also reported that Shane would have himself buried up to the neck in earth to treat fever. Wills, *Lives*, Vol. II, 4. The works of Edmund Curtis treat Shane O'Neill as no more a drunk than most others, particularly when comparing Shane's drinking to that of Turlough O'Neill. Curtis also reports that Shane was a skilled politician, quite handsome, and entertaining company even to the highest members of Elizabeth's Court. Curtis notes that Shane's uncivilized native appearance at the Tudor Court was a subject of laughter and ridicule mainly by Shane's avowed enemies at Court, but that others expressed a more flattering opinion of Shane. Curtis, *History*, 185.

194. Much of the harsh biography of Shane O'Neill is attributed to Richard Stanihurst; an Oxford educated Dublin Englishman who wrote history firmly from the English bias. His view is attacked more as unproven rather than contradicted by other direct evidence or credible first-hand accounts. Edmund Campion, a friend and tutor of Stanihurst, is also a contributor to the wild tales of Shane O'Neill and some others as well. Brady, *Shane O'Neill*, 4, 6. A good deal of the drama surrounding Shane O'Neill is attributable entirely to the writings of Stanihurst and Campion. Stanihurst, *Holinshed's Irish Chronicle*, 15-18, 39-52. Richard Stanihurst and Edmund Campion lived in the Pale with the Stanihurst family, and later in the household of the 11th Earl of Kildare. They were at least contemporaries to the events they described. Vincent Carey *Surviving the Tudors: The Wizard Earl of Kildare and English Rule in Ireland, 1537–1586* (Dublin: Four Courts Press, 2002), 46-47, 190-91. The background of Stanihurst and his New English viewpoint is recounted in Wills, Vol. II, 295, et. seq.

195. Shane O'Neill is said to have been a combination of great talents and great flaws. He is described as cunning, with native intelligence,

subtlety, politeness and wit. He is also said to have been brutal and cruel. Wills, *Lives*, Vol. II, 4. These mixed elements in him were "in no way inconsistent with the simplicity of a barbaric chief." Ibid.

196. Internal dissension in native Irish families was common. Ellis, *Ireland*, 41.

197. Con Bacach O'Neill died in Meath in 1558 at the home of the Bishop of Meath a year after Shane killed Mathew. Brady, *Shane O'Neill*, 35.

198. Shane O'Neill appears to have been the first chieftain willing to arm virtually any peasants. Lennon, *Sixteenth-Century Ireland*, 273. Shane especially alarmed the English by his unprecedented conscription. He was seen by English intelligence operatives "as the first Irishman to make use of the ordinary people." De Paor, *Peoples of Ireland*, 135.

199. Calvagh O'Donnell's wife, Catherine MacLean, a Scot, was also the step mother of the powerful Scot, the Earl of Argyll. Burghley was seeking help from the Earl against Shane; he wanted the Earl to deploy the Scots MacDonnells against Shane. The Earl in turn requested that Burghley use the negotiations with Shane to demand that Shane release the Earl's stepmother. Brady, *Shane O'Neill*, 46-47.

200. The Scots 5th Earl of Argyll, Archibald Campbell, was an important figure in the equation of Ulster as well as the sagas swirling around Mary Queen of Scots. He was the leader of the Clan Campbell, rivals of the MacDonnells, and Argyll was seeking ways political and otherwise to gain dominance over lands in Antrim for control of which the MacDonnells and O'Neills had long been competing. Jane Dunn, *Elizabeth & Mary: Cousins, Rivals, Queens* (New York: Alfred A. Knopf, 2004), 305.

201. Shane O'Neill sought to conspire with Scotland through the powerful Earl of Argyll and with the Wizard Earl of Kildare who had lived in France. Hayes-McCoy, "Conciliation," 80. The Wizard Earl of Kildare was Shane's cousin. Ibid., 81.

202. Elizabeth, Sussex and Sidney reacted against Shane when he attacked the O'Donnells because the O'Donnells had pledged loyalty and were honoring their pledge. Falls 91. His attacks on the Scots were much more acceptable to, and often encourage by, the Tudors who wanted the Scots out of Ulster. Falls 90.

203. Edmund Campion's description of Shane's visit to the Tudor Court became legend and served as grand entertainment. Campion, History Ireland, ed. Ware, 189-190. Shane appeared at the Tudor Court with "a gorgeous train of his followers, arrayed in the rude magnificence of ancient Ulster." They were wearing "long curled locks" and "hairy cloaks" said to be wolfskins. Wills, *Lives*, Vol. II, 5. Shane was depicted as letting forth a deafening howl at Court and carry-

ing a battle ax, speaking only in Irish, accompanied by two columns of warriors. Falls 89. So strange and peculiar was Shane O'Neill's behavior at Court that some described his contingent "as if they had come from China or America." Carey, *Surviving*, 118; quoting Ellis, *Eyewitness*, 277. It was said that he shocked and intimidated many at Court. They addressed him with excessive politeness as "O'Neill the Great." In private, they referred to him as the "Grand Disturber." Berleth, 24-25. Shane did, however, prostrate himself and acknowledge his rebellious conduct. Lennon, *Sixteenth-Century Ireland*, 272.

204. It is even reported that Elizabeth found Shane O'Neill physically attractive. Curtis, *History*, 185.

205. Shane O'Neill procured his recognition as *Taoiseach* of Tyrone. Lennon, *Sixteenth-Century Ireland*, 272. At the end of his stay in London, Shane was confirmed as the Captain of Tyrone, O'Cahan's Country (Derry) and part of Antrim. Hayes-McCoy, "Conciliation," 83. Elizabeth had decided that she would approve Shane O'Neill's request to be named Earl of Tyrone, but protocol required the Deputy's approval, and Sussex was adamantly opposed to it, and so Shane O'Neill did not become an earl. Lennon, *Sixteenth-Century Ireland*, 270, 272.

206. "Before departing, Shane secured an indenture which recognized him as *Taoiseach* of Tyrone with a reservation concerning the rights of Hugh [O'Neill], but his overlordship claims over most of Ulster were tacitly rejected...." Lennon, *Sixteenth-Century Ireland*, 272.

207. Earl of Ulster was long considered one of the greatest earldoms of Christendom. Ellis, *Eyewitness*, 153. Shane O'Neill is quoted: ("I am O'Neill King of Ulster") dismissing the notion of becoming an earl. Dolby, 184. See also O'Faolain, *Great O'Neill*, 45. ("I care not to be an earl. ... My ancestors were Kings of Ulster. ..."). Shane's quotes about an earldom and his ancestors who had been kings of Ulster. Wills, *Lives*, Vol. II, 8.

208. In 1205 King John had conferred the Earldom of Ulster on Hugh de Lacy the younger. Curtis, *History*, 68.

209. As negotiations and inquiries went on with Shane O'Neill and The Tudor Court, Elizabeth suddenly decided she should hear first-hand from Shane's rival for O'Neill leadership, Brian O'Neill, son of Matthew. Shane was alarmed at this hostile and surprising turn in the negotiations. Moreover, Brian had just been found and killed by Turlough O'Neill in April 1562 to the satisfaction of Shane and to the great benefit of both of them. Shane at least saw that Elizabeth's request was a negative sign suggesting his failure in the negotiations. Brady, *Shane O'Neill*, 40.

210. Turlough O'Neill carries the most direct culpability as the chieftain who procured the murder of Brian O'Neill (Mathew's son and Hugh's brother). Shane O'Neill was the principal beneficiary of the murder, but it occurred during Shane's long absence from Ireland to attend the Elizabethan Court, and Turlough was undoubtedly motivated by his own ambitions as well. Lennon, *Sixteenth-Century Ireland*, 272. Shane, when he appeared before Elizabeth, claimed he was innocent of the murder of Brian; he accused Turlough O'Neill. Brady, *Shane O'Neill*, 41.

211. Some reports say that Shane O'Neill actually fled Whitehall when he saw his political opponents at Court were carrying the day, but he signed the terms Elizabeth had approved and he did receive her approval to leave. Brady, *Shane O'Neill*, 40-41. Shane O'Neill's departure from the Tudor Court was in any case not an actual escape. Carey, *Surviving*, 122.

212. The Dublin Council did not accept Shane as The O'Neill until they signed the 1563 treaty. Carey, *Surviving*, 122. Shane argued that Ulster was better run than Dublin. He said it was "a very evil sign that men shall forsake the Pale and come and dwell among wild savage people." Hayes-McCoy, "Conciliation," 84.

213. Sussex and Shane hated each other, and Shane delighted in embarrassing Sussex. Sussex's rearguard were repeatedly ambushed by Shane, and fled in disarray. Hayes-McCoy, "Conciliation," 80-81.

214. Sussex bungled his attempt to have Shane O'Neill assassinated. Brady, *Shane O'Neill*, 37.

215. Shane continued to oppress Maguire, MacMahon and O'Reilly and to worry the Armagh garrison. Another attempt was made to poison him, but it failed as well. Finally, Sir Thomas Cusack brokered the 1563 peace with Shane, and Shane was finally acknowledged as The O'Neill. Hayes-McCoy, "Conciliation," 85.

216. In the Treaty of Drumcree Shane was promised that the earldom of Tyrone would be conferred on him by statute. Brady, *Shane O'Neill*, 51-52.

217. Froude, too, states that England had everything to lose by treating Ireland as a conquered province, and by seizing lands and governing by force. Froude, *English*, 12.

218. Cusack's advice was emphatic that it was essential for England's own benefit that a peaceful settlement be reached by diplomacy and that Ireland should not be reduced to submission by force. Brady, *Shane O'Neill*, 51.

219. Sussex was crushed by Elizabeth's agreement to withdraw the Armagh garrison and he resigned in 1564. Lennon, *Sixteenth-Century*

Ireland, 274. Sussex was succeeded as Deputy by Sidney in 1565. Sir Henry Sidney was a major figure who had not only an active mind, but a forceful personality. Hayes-McCoy, "Conciliation," 85.

220. Gerald FitzGerald, the 14th Earl of Desmond, offered his support to Sidney against Shane O'Neill. Chambers, *Eleanor,* 53.

221. Many of the 4,500 O'Donnells killed by Shane O'Neill were common people, not warriors. Darren McGettigan, *Red Hugh O'Donnell and the Nine Years War* (Dublin: Four Courts Press, 2005), 33.

222. Sussex and Sidney were bitter enemies. They constantly defamed each other. The successor (in the case of this pair that was Sidney) was naturally better able to second-guess the abundant mistakes of his predecessor. Cook, *Pirate Queen,* 60. The problem of fighting Shane was ever-present because outposts had to be resupplied, and getting to them meant fighting a path through Shane's men over and over. Hayes-McCoy, "Conciliation," 81.

223. Shane O'Neill is described by contemporary David Wolf, S. J., as "a cruel, and impious heretical tyrant...." He imprisoned the Bishop of Dromore, burned the Church of Armagh, "took away the wife of one of his kinsmen, and had three sons by her...." In addition, he hanged a priest. COSPRome, Vol. I, 482.

224. Sussex as Lord Deputy was followed by Sidney. These early deputies lobbied hard for the position, perceiving it as a path to great wealth, stature and advancement at Court. Judith Cook, *The Pirate Queen: the Life of Grace O'Malley, 1530-1603* (Cork, Ireland: Mercier Press, 2004), 59-60. Sir Henry Sidney was no exception. He was nearly broke and was not ordered to Ireland; he offered to serve as Lord Deputy. Lennon, *Sixteenth-Century Ireland,* 186.

225. Randolph conducted an amphibious operation landing a 1,000 man army at Derry. Hayes-McCoy, "Conciliation," 86.

226. By 1566, the hunt was on for Shane O'Neill in Ulster. The O'Donnells and the Scots MacDonnells were in sufficient pursuit that Shane O'Neill was on the run, and Sidney felt that his principal focus and use of troops could be in Munster where the Earl of Desmond continued to test Black Tom Butler and threaten skirmishes with the Ormond earldom. Lennon, *Sixteenth-Century Ireland,* 275. Sir Warham St. Leger, son of Sir Anthony, served as President of Munster under Sidney in 1566. Warham and Earl Gerald got along well. Warham was not as intrusive in the earldom as others had been. Ellis, *Eyewitness,* 289.

227. Shane reached out to France. He wrote the French court asking for an army to help him expel the English. Shane burnt Armagh Cathedral. Elizabeth finally asked wearily how Shane, that "cankered

dangerous rebel" might be "utterly extirped." Hayes-McCoy, "Conciliation," 85.

228. Shane had a violent history with the MacDonnells, so his effort to become their ally is inexplicable. Shane had soundly defeated the MacDonnells in 1565 at the Battle of Glenshesk, and had taken James and Sorley Boy MacDonnell prisoner. Ellis, *Eyewitness*, 286. Lennon, *Sixteenth-Century Ireland*, 273.

229. The preamble to The Bill of Attainder of Shane O'Neill contains a description of his murder during a feast marked by heavy drinking. See 11 Eliz. I, c. 9, Stat. Ire. i, 322-328. Some contend, however, that there was no drunken feasting at Cushendun. Brady, *Shane O'Neill*, 65. Some claim that the tale about the killing of Shane O'Neill in a heated drunken brawl may have been a story designed to portray the Scots as wild, better justifying expulsion of the Scots from Ulster. Lennon, *Sixteenth-Century Ireland*, 276.

230. The murder of Shane O'Neill at Cushendun in June 1567 at the hands of Alexander Oge MacDonnell had earlier been urged by Captain William Piers, Constable of Carrickfergus. Afterwards, Sir Henry Sidney claimed some credit for achieving this victory over O'Neill, and reminded the Tudor Court that Shane had long eluded Lord Sussex. Lennon, *Sixteenth-Century Ireland*, 276.

231. It is said that Shane O'Neill's life was a fight to prevent "the very extirpation of his people...." Brian Mallon, *Shane O'Neill: The Grand Disturber of Elizabethan Ireland* (New York: Red Branch Press, 2015), 767. It is said in his defense: "He was fighting bitterly a people who were intent on expelling the Irish from their lands and colonizing it with their own settlers." Mallon, *Shane O'Neill*, 2.

232. Captain Piers years later acknowledged that he had pocketed the bounty placed on Shane O'Neill, admitting that he was paid 1,000 marks for delivering Shane O'Neill's head. Nicholas Canny, *Making Ireland British 1580-1650* (Oxford: Oxford University Press, 2001), 87.

233. Shane's death was a very important event in Ulster and London, but of little direct moment in the south. Hayes-McCoy, "Conciliation," 86.

234. Henry Sidney refused to allow Turlough O'Neill to exercise lordship over Maguire. Brady, *Viceroy's Vindication?*, 123 n81. Turlough O'Neill was married to a Scot, Agnes Campbell. Agnes was a good counsellor to Turlough and a "grave, wise and well-spoken lady, both in Scots, English and French". Brady, *Viceroy's Vindication?*, 76. Agnes Campbell supplied Scottish forces to help Turlough O'Neill. Brady, *Viceroy's Vindication?*, 118, note 30.

235. Quinn, *Elizabethans*, 157, 158.

236. Rory MacSheehy led the Rebel Earl's galloglass. McCormack, *The Earldom of Desmond*, 164. The galloglass were not merely added fighters; they were a professional class of soldier, the trained, experienced backbone of the soldiers serving every significant Irish political unit. Quinn, *Elizabethans*, 15.

237. Fynes Moryson, who served in Ireland as secretary to Lord Mountjoy, writing of the Tyrone Rebellion said the Irish "use no saddles: and so "they may easily be cast off from their horses, yet being very nimble do as easily mount them again,...." Fynes Moryson, "An Itinerary (1617-c.1626)," in *Elizabethan Ireland, a Selection of Writings by Elizabethan Writers on Ireland*, edited by James P. Myers, Jr. (Hamden, Connecticut: Archon Books, 1983), 212.

238. Gerald lost 280 men at Affane. Wills, *Lives*, Vol. II, 12.

239. Sidney received a letter from Elizabeth instructing him to conduct an inquiry into the Butler and Desmond disputes, but telling him in no uncertain terms to favor Butler in making his judgments. Sidney resisted to an extent, but ultimately did as the Queen instructed. Wills, *Lives*, Vol. II, 12-13, 127.

240. Sidney considered Ormond hypocritical; his territories were a "sink of criminality and baseness." Brady, *Viceroy's Vindication?*, 24. "The system was begun on a large scale in Leinster in the reign of Mary, when the immense territories belonging to the O'Mores, the O'Connors and the O'Dempseys were confiscated, planted with English colonies, and converted into two English counties.... The confiscation being carried out without any regard for the rights of the humbler members of the tribes, gave rise, as might have been expected, to a long and bloody guerilla warfare...." W.E.H. Lecky, *A History of Ireland in the Eighteenth Century*, Vol. 1. (New York: Longmans, Green and Co., 1892), 18.

241. Sidney confronted Gerald at Youghal. Chambers, *Eleanor*, 57.

242. In 1565, MacCarthy Mor was created Earl of Clancare by Elizabeth to free him from the rule of the Earl of Desmond. Chambers, *Eleanor*, 52.

243. In 1567, Sidney arrested Gerald on charges of treason and jailed him in the Tower and then elsewhere in London. Gerald's cell was a drab state prisoner cell, but larger than a jail cell and equipped with a fireplace. His followers, the hundreds accompanying him to London, had daily access to him and brought him abundant food. Chambers, *Eleanor*, 60, 75. Gerald's two brothers, John and James, were also arrested and brought to London. Berleth, 38.

244. Sidney thought that the goal of Elizabeth's Irish policy in her early years was a limited conquest consisting of overthrowing Shane

O'Neill in Ulster followed by limited strategic colonizations in Ulster and Laois-Offaly, forming a model community which could provide an example of civility to Anglicize the unruly Native Irish. Ibid., 287. But sending the seneschals out, giving them their own forts and garrisons, and permitting them to execute masterless men, led to horrible killings and the killings were flaunted. Ibid., 287. Soon, Sidney's rosy view disappeared. He found "he had been fobbed off with half-promises." He had not the budget or the troops to achieve the peaceful panacea. Instead, the brutality of the seneschals became the face of Tudor England to the horrified Irish victims, and the response of the native Irish was not civility but violent self-defense. Ellis, *Eyewitness*, 287, 295-299.

245. An English captain in charge of a band of soldiers was appointed as seneschal for a district corresponding to a lordship. Lennon, *Sixteenth-Century Ireland,* 166. They were to verify which inhabitants were under which landowners and which were "masterless" men. Their assignment included "extirpating those who were 'masterless'." Ibid., 166. From 1565 on, Sidney gave the seneschals judicial powers. Ibid., 196. The seneschals competed with all the others against the native Irish for land titles. Ibid., 197.

246. These appointed seneschals should not be confused with the Anglo Irish lord called by the hereditary title, the Seneschal of Imokilly, leader of a small lordship in the far south with a castle at Ballymartyr. At the time of the Munster rebellion the Seneschal of Imokilly was the Rebel Earl's uncle and ally, John FitzEdmund FitzGerald. In 1573, however, he submitted to Perrot. He died in 1589 and his cousin of the same name from Cloyne succeeded him. Berleth, 69.

247. Even lowly offices—Edmund Spenser's post as Clerk of Decrees and Recognizances in the Irish Chancery Court where he merely certified state documents—was a "lucrative" job. Church, *Spenser*, 74-75.

248. The "expulsion or destruction" of the incurable Irish race. Froude, *English*, 13- 14.

249. MacDonagh, "Ambiguity," 105. ("...extirpation of the native and so-called Old English population").

250. De Paor, *Peoples of Ireland,* 140.

251. The Irish were being killed like "foxes or jackals." Froude, *English*, 54-55. "Elizabeth's soldiers ... were little better than banditti ..." Ibid., 54-55.

252. "The progress of a Deputy, or the President of a province, through the country is always accompanied with its tale of hangings. There is sometimes a touch of the grotesque." Church, *Spenser*, 65.

253. Elizabeth needed money. The English soldiers sent to Ireland went

as long as two years without pay. Cook, *Pirate Queen*, 60; COSPI, 15 July 1573 and 13 March 1595. She expected Anglicization to be accomplished at no expense. Cook, *Pirate Queen*, 60.

254. Lecky, *A History of Ireland in the Eighteenth Century*, 18.

255. The murder of the O'Mores at a "peaceful conference" is called a "treacherous murder." Lecky, *Eighteenth Century*, 18. Violence escalated fiercely in 16th century Ireland. The killings at Maynooth in 1535, Belfast in 1574, Rathlin Island in 1595, Mullaghmast in 1577, Smerwick in 1580, Ardnaree in 1586, and Dunboy in 1602 are among the most notable. Edwards, Lenihan and Tait (Edwards, *Age of Atrocity*, 34). Skeffington's troops also massacred over 100 victims at Naas in 1535. Edwards, Lenihan and Tait (Edwards 55) Smerwick became a legendary story.

256. Lord Grey de Wilton's "administration...was...a rule of extermination." Church, *Spenser*, 66.

257. Grey wrote that he executed nearly 1,500 "chief men and gentlemen." Church, *Spenser*, 67. "If taking of cows, and killing of kerne and churles had been worth advertising, I would have had everyday to have troubled your Highness." Lord Grey de Wilton to Elizabeth I. Church, *Spenser*, 65.

258. Some English reformers wanted to expel all Irish clergy, but one cleric sent to Ireland directed it be done gradually: "For it is necessary that we eradicate them little by little and by stages." Tanner, *Holy War*, 37.

259. By 1568 the many retainers were gone, and Gerald's situation and his quarters in the Tower had deteriorated. He pleaded with Eleanor to come to London and bring money. Chambers, *Eleanor*, 70.

260. Eleanor undoubtedly hoped to come to London to comfort Gerald and to live outside the Tower, but after a short time, she joined him living in his Tower cell. Anne Chambers, *Granuaile: Grace O'Malley, Ireland's Pirate Queen* (Dublin: Wolfhound Press, 2003), 72.

261. Gerald was allowed to live under restriction in Sir Warham St. Leger's house in the Bankside area just east of London Bridge, a neighborhood of brothels, breweries, bear pits and the jail (Clink Prison). Berleth, 39-40.

262. Martin Frobisher contrived an historic "sting." He set up Desmond, then informed on Desmond's escape attempt. By this maneuver he had begun the steps that started the Munster Plantation. He had put the English in position to threaten Desmond with execution for treason, and then to mercifully pardon Desmond if he "voluntarily" forfeited his vast landholdings, and he did. That began the Munster Plantation. McConville, *Ascendency*, 24.

263. Frobisher sought out the Earl of Desmond and introduced the idea of escape. Chambers, *Eleanor*, 82. Gerald signed away his palatine rights to avoid execution. Ibid., 84.

264. For the English leaders prone to "jealousies and backbitings and mischief-making, [and] their own bitter antipathies... there was only one point of agreement, and that was their deep scorn and loathing of the Irish." Church, *Spenser*, 62.

265. Dudley was Henry Sidney's brother in law. Brady, *Shane O'Neill*, 58.

266. Perrot's son wrote of the job of Lord Deputy: "What a slippery seat they sitte that govern that kingdom. ..." Roger Turvey, *The Treason and Trial of Sir John Perrot* (Cardiff: University of Wales Press, 2005), 42.

267. Crown officials came to realize that Ireland's potential for creating wealth made it a delicious prize. Curtis, *History*, 159. Irish lands were communal tribal property under Brehon law. Control passed not from common law descent or title but by election of the tribal leader who controlled the clan area. McConville, *Ascendency*, 20.

268. Surrender and regrant injected a legal paradox into land ownership, one which would give New English "a legalistic validity to much stylishly justified theft." McConville, *Ascendency*, 20. It was done by repossessing land as a "penalty for 'misbehavior' of an Irish Chieftain" to give it to loyal English planters. Ibid. Often they simply resold it to another absentee English investor. Ibid., 47.

269. "There was prolonged legal examination of old titles, some going back for centuries, some of straightforward authenticity, some the ambivalent products of past Geraldine intimidation or fraud." McConville, *Ascendency*, 44.

270. The legal gambits used to take the property and to title it in the hands of the English were shameless. "A sanctimonious and rather unreal preoccupation with legal niceties contributed a last element to the piece." McConville, *Ascendency*, 25. They needed an Englishman "who could put up an adequately plausible claim to a land title in Munster....One presented himself almost immediately. Sir Peter Carew....had more rough edges than most....He was physically tough, as ruthless as any Gaelic or Norman Irish Chief,... and he had a good lawyer." Ibid., 25.

271. The lawyer, John Hooker, was adept at using "the ingenious illegible deeds" that Hooker argued gave Carew "hereditary right to the ownership of large expanses of the forfeited Geraldine lands." McConville, *Ascendency*, 25. Hooker presented this foggy evidence to the Queen and she approved Carew as the owner of vast Irish lands. Ibid., 26. Other courtiers used Carew's tactics. Sir Richard Grenville,

Sir Walter Raleigh, Sir Humphrey Gilbert, Sir Warham St. Leger and others. Ibid., 26-27.

272. "The lands that had been Geraldine for four hundred years were once again forfeit." McConville, *Ascendency*, 44.

273. The Old English leaders in Ireland perennially complained to the royal Court that they should be appointed to the posts of deputies, sheriffs and to other official positions because the New English who sought those positions were motivated exclusively by the desire to enrich themselves at the expense of native Irish. Canny, *Early Modern Ireland*, 100.

274. Sir Peter Carew took Idrone from the Kavanaughs, Edmund Butler and others based on contrived evidence and a strained theory in support of a claimed inheritance from an invading Norman. He and his politically connected lawyer, John Hooker, shopped for a favorable forum to rule on the claim and exploited the appearance of inconsistencies between English property rights, boundary descriptions, and the very different concepts and customs of the Irish Brehon law of property relationships. Curtis, *History*, 190-191. Carew then convinced a court to evict the Kavanaghs from their estates in Idrone. Ibid., 190.

275. Carew presented his hereditary claim to the Dublin Parliament. McConville, *Ascendency*, 26. It declared that Peter Carew and his family were the rightful heirs to the Barony of Idrone, not the Kavanaghs who had farmed it "immemorially." Ibid. Grenville, St. Leger and others followed suit in Cork and around the River Blackwater and "the cycle followed by all these communities was identical: eviction of the Irish, distribution of land, construction of the first buildings, clearance and cultivation." Ibid., 27.

276. This was "armed confiscation of the source of the [Irish] race's wealth." McConville, *Ascendency*, 27.

277. In response, "a murderous opposition accumulated among the dispossessed Irish," and they began to ambush and attack Carew. The Roches, Barrys and Muskerry McCarthy's began such attacks before the Carew program had the chance to fall upon them. McConville, *Ascendency*, 29. A "formidable soldier "emerged as their leader – James FitzMaurice. Ibid., 30.

278. "What caused destabilization in Leinster was Sidney's allowing of the claims of Sir Peter Carew from Devon to the Barony of Idrone in Carlow ... and the manor of Maston in Meath, ..." Lennon, *Sixteenth-Century Ireland*, 185. "Carew's research and legal proceedings were aided by the Lord Deputy ...." Lennon, *Sixteenth-Century Ireland*, 185. These were done using the Dublin parliament. Ibid.

279. Edward Butler's men raided cattle on Carew's new land, and Carew invaded Kilkenny itself and "destroyed, looted, burnt and raped" in the process. McConville, *Ascendency*, 28. Carew and his men overran Kilkenny Castle in the process with "extensive massacre;" the rape victims included Sir Edward Butler's wife and they captured Sir Edward. Ibid., 29. Carew went on to take Sir Edmund Butler's Clogrennane Castle and slaughtered the garrison and their men, women and children. Ibid.

280. Under the Tudors it was very easy for the Irish to have their land confiscated by escheatment to the Crown; they only had to behave in a way that Crown officials found disloyal or unruly. Roy, *Fields*, 119.

281. Irish lands were owned, in the English sense, not by individuals but by a clan. Ellis, *Ireland*, 40.

282. FitzMaurice lost his Kerrycurrihy manor to a contrived claim by Sir Warham St. Leger. Lennon, *Sixteenth-Century Ireland*, 216.

283. The lands confiscated from their Irish owners and tenants were vast. Curtis, *History*, 176. Curtis observed that the Irish were slow to realize what was in store: "[H]ad the Irish realized it the terrible weapon of confiscation threatened them all." Curtis 176. The legal pretext was often a sham. Id. "[I]n Ireland it became common for a century and a half to declare vast countries forfeited and all the local landowners attainted." Curtis, *History*, 176-77. English were installed in their place. Ibid. In Laois and Offaly only one third of the Irish kept their land. Ibid., 177.

284. The Lord Deputy was charged with confiscating Irish lands and awarding them to reliable Englishmen. Lennon, *Sixteenth-Century Ireland*, 185.

285. Even after FitzWilliam became Deputy "the reverberation of the Carew land claims in Idrone continued to be felt." Lennon, *Sixteenth-Century Ireland*, 186.

286. It was reported to Sir Henry Norris on July 22, 1569 that Fitz Maurice, working with Turlough O'Neill, had "demanded of the King of Spain to send an army into Ireland to resist the Queen's power, and has offered to give into the Spaniards' hands all his castles and towns upon condition that, winning others, they shall restore him his own again." COSPFS 1569-71 entry 341 98, 99.

287. FitzMaurice was described as so devout a Catholic he was of a mind to enter a religious order. COSPEARome Vol. I, 481. (An account by David Wolf, S. J.).

288. The Earl of Desmond designated FitzMaurice to lead the Desmonds in his absence, but FitzMaurice had to campaign to obtain support from the lords of the earldom. McCormack, *Earldom*, 109-10.

289. One of FitzMaurice's ancestors, an earlier James FitzMaurice, had aspired to succeed his grandfather, Thomas, the 12th Earl of Desmond, at Thomas' death, but legitimacy issues about Thomas swung the earldom to the ancestors of Gerald (The Rebel Earl). McCormack, *Earldom*, 68-71.

290. Eleanor of Desmond saw the FitzMaurice rebellion as a coup against Gerald, not a religious crusade. Chambers, *Granuaile*, 70-71.

291. The White Knight, Thomas FitzGibbon, who ruled Clangibbon on the west of the Decies, died in 1570; he was attainted and his lands confiscated in 1571 and 1572. Brady (*Viceroy's Vindication*) note 58, 121. The White Knight ruled lands around Kilmallock in County Limerick. McCormack, *Earldom*, 32.

292. The native Irish and Anglo Irish responded with violence and murder of their own, including murder of noncombatants. Edwards 70.

293. The English under Sidney and Perrot conscripted loyal Anglo Irish and brutally responded to the Irish assaults. The "butchery of prisoners" was commonplace. McConville, *Ascendency*, 30. The Deputy and President "used large trees as mass gallows." Ibid. The non-cooperating civilians became the victims of "slaughter by both sides." Ibid., 31. Malby too committed "the murder and torture of as many non-combatants as he could find." Ibid., 38. He devastated a large part of Munster. Ibid.

294. When the Irish won a victory at Springfield, they too massacred their prisoners. When the English scored a technical win at Monasternenagh, they in turn massacred the Irish prisoners. McConville, *Ascendency*, 38.

295. The lordships of the Seneschal of Imokilly, the White Knight, the Knight of Glin, and the Knight of Kerry were small. They were called "the lesser landlord class". While they were allies of the Rebel Earl when he instructed them to be, absent a compelling provocation affecting them, many were reluctant rebels who were more abused by the Earls of Desmond, particularly Gerald, than bonded by gratitude or loyalty. Lennon, *Sixteenth-Century Ireland*, 220. The Seneschal of Imokilly, John FitzEdmond, was a more staunch rebel follower of the Earl of Desmond than some of the others. McCormack, *Earldom*, 164.

296. Sidney was replaced by FitzWilliam in 1571, and then Sidney returned to replace FitzWilliam in 1575. Lennon, *Sixteenth-Century Ireland*, 186. As Deputy, FitzWilliam allowed great autonomy to the provincial presidents, Perrot, Bingham and Fitton and even to the First Earl of Essex while Essex was briefly governor of Ulster. Ibid.

297. FitzMaurice had the support of Catholic clergy; five were Bishops,

including Bishop Tanner of Cork and Bishop O'Herlihy of Ross. Dickson, *Old World*, 6.

298. Sir Humphrey Gilbert was appointed colonel and governor of Munster in 1569. Gilbert "deemed it his task to extirpate the rebels" and he reported that he "put man woman and childe to the sword." His statements and actions "served to convince FitzMaurice and his remaining supporters that...the English had been intent on their destruction." McCormack, *Earldom*, 118-19.

299. Perrot continued the reign of terror begun by his predecessor, Sir Humphrey Gilbert, sending 800 rebels to the gallows. Turvey, *Treason*, 10. He served from February 1571 to July 1573. Ibid., 10.

300. Perrot was "a man in stature very tall and bigg, exceeding the ordinary stature of men by much. ..." Perrot's bastard son James described him thus: "[w]hen he was angry, he had a terrible visage or look; and when he was pleased, or willing to show kindness, he then had as amiable a countenance as any man. ...: Quoted in R. K. Turvey (ed.), *A Critical Edition of Sir James Perrot's 'The Life, Deedes and Death of Sir John Perrot, Knight'"* (London, 2002).

301. Though little is known of Perrot's early life, Turvey states definitively that Perrot's mother was never a mistress of Henry VIII, and thus concludes that Perrot was not the King's bastard son. Turvey, *Treason*, 4-5.

302. "The unremitting attempts made by the English in the sixteenth century to exterminate the Irish aristocracy were carried out with a ferocity and perfidy seldom equalled even in that violent age." Curley, *Vanishing*, 44.

303. Perrot was not the first choice to succeed Gilbert as President of Munster. What attracted Elizabeth's interest in Perrot was that he had "a rugged individualism and uncompromising approach to resolving problems." Turvey, *Treason*, 9-10.

304. Lordship over a part of Gaelic Ireland was not an ownership of a defined territory precisely in the English way, or with property rights of the kinds defined in the common law of England; it was a "complex of rights, tributes and authority." It was exercised by a leader who was chosen because of his power and might, or who had fought his way to the leadership of the clan or the lordship. Ellis, *Ireland*, 41-43.

305. After almost seven years, Gerald was allowed to return to Ireland, as far as Dublin, but then escaped loose restraint in Dublin and made it back to Askeaton in 1573. Back at Askeaton, Gerald was thinking of and preaching rebellion. Lennon, *Sixteenth-Century Ireland*, 214, 218-19.

306. Gerald escaped Dublin and walked for several days to reach Kerry, where he was welcomed. O'Donovan, *The Four Masters*, Vol. V, 1665.

307. Gerald's correspondence with the Crown after his pardon was voluminous and he purported to be helpful and informative about the state of affairs in Ireland; but he was not in any respect grateful and humble. The information he sent to London was full of lies. Berleth, 68.

308. Sir Henry Sidney was heavily in debt. Brady, *A Viceroy's Vindication?*, 43.

309. Sidney planned in 1575 to exact taxes and to make Ireland self-sustaining within three years. Lennon, *Sixteenth-Century Ireland*, 187.

310. The Deputies were critical of each other as well. Relations between Sir Henry Sidney and Sir William FitzWilliam were never good; Sidney tried to undermine FitzWilliam as Deputy, and FitzWilliam's response was venal. Brady, *Viceroy's Vindication?*, 119 note 38. FitzWilliam was a special enemy of Perrot. Sidney even challenged Sussex to a duel. Ellis, *Eyewitness*, 290.

311. Sidney's heavy handed taxation of the old English of Dublin to pay for his campaigns against the Irish in the midlands caused intense discontent. Herron and Kane, *Nobility*, 15.

312. To Elizabeth, Ireland was a world of "ravening beasts" as she wrote to Henry Sidney. Brigden, *New Worlds*, 227.

313. Gerald failed to cooperate with Davells and was evasive. McConville, *Ascendency*, 36.

314. It was asserted that Lord Justice Drury had intended to pay Sir John FitzGerald of Desmond a royal pension for loyalty prior to the murder of Henry Davells. Berleth, 99.

315. The English and the Irish respected Davells. He had helped and befriended Sir John Fitzgerald, yet John and his brother James murdered Davells and Arthur Carter. McConville, *Ascendency*, 36.

316. John FitzGerald in effect succeeded FitzMaurice as rebel leader. McCormack, *Earldom*, 21, 146. In September 1579 Sir John FitzGerald led the rebels to victory at the Battle of Springfield. McCormack, *Earldom*, 146.

317. The reasons given for the FitzMaurice and Desmond rebellions vary. Some say the goal of FitzMaurice was to oppose the Reformation. Others say his goal was to free his cousin, Earl Gerald. Some blame Gerald's rebellion on Gerald's own deficiencies and excesses and on the momentum created by the FitzMaurice rebellion. McCormack, *Earldom*, 21.

318. In November 1579 Sir William Pelham, as Lord Justice proclaimed Gerald a traitor. De Paor, *Peoples of Ireland*, 132; McCormack, *Earl-*

dom, 146. Elizabeth demanded to know "Why was Desmond proclaimed a traitor before he was in hand." Berleth, 125-26.

319. The Desmond battle cry was *"Shanid Abu."* The Ormond battle cry was *"Butler Abu."* The Catholic cause or Papal-banner battle cry was *"Papa Abu."* Berleth, 125.

320. Townspeople in Munster, unlike the rural native Irish, remained heavily loyal to the English. McCormack 153. Attacks on towns like Youghal likely began with the rebels' need to stock up on victuals. McCormack, *Earldom*, 153. Desmond's forces killed 140 townsmen at Youghal. Ibid. They also attacked Tracton in County Cork, a Cistercian abbey on which the Earl of Desmond held a lease. Ibid., 80. The earl's men pillaged and raped in their attack against the English who occupied the town of Youghal. Lennon, *Sixteenth-Century Ireland*, 227.

321. Descriptions of Irish kerne, cavalry and even horseboys by such observers as Edmund Spenser and Richard Stanihurst are replete with scathing assertions, yet also with abundant admiration for their fighting skills, calling them "great endurers of cold, labor, hunger and all hardness, very active and strong of hand, very swift of foot … very great scorners of death." Quinn, *Elizabethans*, 41. Spenser also said the Irish soldier was willing to engage in "beastly behavior" and to be "cruel and bloody" and "delighting in deadly execution." Spenser's harshest accusation was that the Irish soldiers were "common ravishers of women and murderers of children." Ibid.

322. The case against Chief Justice Nugent has been called an "utter travesty of justice." Ellis, *Eyewitness*, 316.

323. English officials in Dublin always feared that one Earl of Ormond or another might be named Viceroy; they wanted that post and the power and prosperity it carried for themselves. Brady, *Viceroy's Vindication?*, 24.

324. Elizabeth wrote to Lord Grey de Wilton expressing her "joy" over his killings at Smerwick: "The mighty hand of the Almighty's power hath showed manifestly the force of his strength in the weakness of the feeblest sex and mind this year, to make men ashamed ever after to disdain us. In which action I joy that you have been chosen the instrument of his glory, which I mean to give no cause to fore think." Berleth, 175.

325. In Irish legend *Graia Fides* (Grey's faith or Grey's promise) mirrored the perfidy of the Pardon of Maynooth of 1534. McCormack, *Earldom*, 153.

326. The British response to the Rebel Earl of Desmond's rebellion has been described as a "devastatingly violent suppression. …" Dickson, *Old World*, 5.

327. Lord Grey deWilton intentionally induced the famine so grimly depicted in the writings of Spenser. De Paor, *Peoples of Ireland*, 132.

328. "Lord Grey had been ruthlessly severe, and yet not successful." This was so, "In spite of the thousands slain, and a province made a desert." Church, *Spenser*, 70.

329. Church, *Spenser*, 65.

330. Grey's report listed in matter of fact terms: "1,485 chief men and gentlemen slain, not accounting those of meaner sort, nor yet executions by law, and killing of churles, which were innumerable." Church, *Spenser*, 67. Ormond boasted killing over 3,000. Ibid. 66. Warham St. Leger reported 30,000 famine deaths and he added that "Munster is nearly unpeopled" by the killings by both sides. Ibid.

331. To some contemporaries, Arthur Lord Grey de Wilton merited praise as Deputy succeeding Sidney; it was said that he ran a godly and just administration. Herron and Kane, *Nobility*, 16. Edmund Spenser saw Lord Grey as the image of "perfect and masculine justice." He said Grey had a "heroic spirit." Church, *Spenser*, 74. His role in deciding the torture and slaughter of the invasion force at Smerwick, however, stands out as an unforgettable event in history. His brutality at Smerwick is not vulnerable to claims that it is exaggerated. Spenser recounts the slaughter of the 600 at Smerwick based upon the first person account given to him by Lord Grey; it includes the torture by breaking arms and legs. Ibid., 59-60. Grey's report and Spenser's report recount Grey himself ordering the breaking of arms and legs. Ibid., 60. When Lord Grey left Ireland in 1582, he left behind him "unappeasable animosities" and "an ill satisfied mistress." Ibid., 73.

332. "Out of every corner of the woods and Glynes they came creeping forth upon their hands, for their legs could not bear them; they looked like anatomies of death, they spake like ghosts crying out of their graves; they did eat the dead carrions ...." Church, *Spenser*, 68 (quoting Spenser). Edmund Spenser came over to Ireland with Lord Grey de Wilton to serve as his secretary. Church, *Spenser*, 57. Spenser was rewarded with an estate in Cork. Ellis, *Eyewitness*, 69.

333. Black Tom Butler was sent to offer difficult terms to Desmond – surrender his castles, his brothers and Nicholas Sander or be charged with treason. He refused the offer of exile in London, and he was charged with treason. McConville, *Ascendency*, 39.

334. Lord Grey de Wilton was recalled in August 1582. Ellis, *Eyewitness*, 317, 369.

335. Desmond's plight was desperate by the summer of 1583 when his band was reduced to 20 men. McCormack, *Earldom*, 148. Gorehe

MacSweeney, the last of the captains of Desmond's galloglass was killed. Ibid.

336. A posse went after Desmond and undoubtedly knew who it was who was hiding in the cabin. McCormack, *Earldom*, 148. The Earl of Desmond was killed on November 11, 1583. Ellis, *Eyewitness*, 318. O'Moriarty is reported to have rebuffed the Earl's pleas for mercy saying "Thou hast killed thyself long ago." A. L. Rowse, *The Expansion of Elizabethan England*, 2nd ed. New York: Palgrave Macmillan, 1955, 107.

337. The confiscation of The Earl of Desmond's vast lands by the legal process of attainder took 3 years. McConville, *Ascendency*, 45. It gave the Crown "the largest expanse of land in Ireland held by one man,…" Ibid. It was allocated to English for their services to the Crown and to English developers. Ibid., 44. The biggest shares of the Desmond lands were doled out to the British military commanders – Sir William Herbert, Sir Edward Denny, Sir Warham St. Leger and even Edmund Spenser. Ibid., 46.

338. Lecky wrote of the policy that drove the plantation of Munster: "It was intended to sweep those who had survived the war completely from the whole of this enormous territory [Munster], or at least to permit them to remain only in the condition of day-labourers or ploughmen, with the alternative of flying to the mountains or the forests to die by starvation, or to live as savages or as robbers." Lecky, *Eighteenth Century*, 18.

339. The Irish had endured excessive violence but from the mid Tudor period they were "utterly devoured by it…." Edwards 69.

340. There arose considerable alarm in England about the extent of Catholic plots which may still be undiscovered. McCavitt 59, 171.

341. Archbishop Dermot O'Hurley of Dublin was hanged in 1584. Lennon, *Sixteenth-Century Ireland*, 319-20.

342. Queen Elizabeth's was "a solution that was shrouded in enormous slaughter, suffering and devastation." McConville, *Ascendency*, 22.

343. After Perrot served as President of Munster, he also served at sea, patrolling for pirates, one of whom wound up saving his life. Turvey, *Treason*, 12.

344. Sidney failed in his attempt to secure a third term as Deputy. Perrot, however, had been sending frequent reports and analyses to the Queen with recommendations on how to better govern Ireland. These ideas convinced her to send him as Lord Deputy of Ireland in 1584. There he served until 1588. Turvey 20, 41. Sidney himself had rated Sir John Perrott "the most complete and best humored man to deal with that nation, that I know living." Brady, *Viceroy's Vindica-*

tion?, 73. Perrot had been warned by Sir Henry Jones, his step brother, not to go to Ireland, but he went anyway. Turvey, *Treason*, 20, 34.

345. As Deputy, Perrot was left to govern Ireland in his own way, to implement the legislative goals he had urged Elizabeth to enact in the Dublin Parliament, and to flesh out the details for making Ireland fiscally sound by extending the policies and methods of the Composition of Connaught to all of Ireland. Ellis, *Eyewitness*, 320. Any more complete Anglicization would require the cooperation and assistance of the most powerful chieftains. Ibid., 288.

346. Ulick Burke's sobriquet, "the Beheader," likely came from the attitude displayed by the dozen galloglass he kept close at hand who "think no man dead until his head be off." Roy, *Fields*, 106; Quinn, *Elizabethans*, 168.

347. Connaught was ruled by a junior branch of the Burkes. Curtis, *History*, 105. The two families became known as the Upper MacWilliam (Clanrickard) and Lower MacWilliam (Mayo). Ibid., 106.

348. In the 14th century, William Burke left two sons named Ulick and Edmund (Albanach). Ulick took Galway and founded the Clanrickard Burkes and Edmund took the Mayo lands. Curtis, *History*, 105.

349. Elsewhere, another Edmund Burke founded the lordship of Castleconnell in Limerick; that family was called Clanwilliam. Curtis, *History*, 105; Canny, *Making Ireland*, 528.

350. The rest of the west was ruled by others: The O'Connor Sligo ruled the county and town of Sligo. The O'Briens ruled Thomond (Clare). Leitrim was ruled by the O'Rourkes as *uirrithe* or sub chiefs under the O'Donnells. Curtis, *History*, 106.

351. Richard Burke, Second Earl of Clanrickard, was called The Sassanach. Sassanach, based on old Irish, means variously Englishman, Saxon or lowlander. Wills, *Lives*, Vol. I, Part II, 489. The Sassanach's sexual activities were so unrestrained they were likened to reproductive practices of the poultry yard. Roy, *Fields*, 125.

352. Ulick Burke, the 3rd Earl of Clanrickard, in the "tradition of Gaelic chieftains from ages long past,...lied, cheated, and dissembled whenever circumstances demanded,..." Roy, *Fields*, 152.

353. The MacWilliam submitted to Henry Sidney in 1575. Chambers, *Granuaile*, 70.

354. The "Iron Burke," Richard Fitzdavid MacWilliam an iarain Burke. Chambers, *Granuaile*, 63-64.

355. Malby helped settle the "Iron Burke's" 1580 fight to succeed The MacWilliam. Chambers, *Granuaile*, 88.

356. Richard Burke joined the Rebel Earl of Desmond for a time, but Richard submitted in 1580. Chambers, *Granuaile*, 77-79.

357. Grace was a man's woman; she had charisma and did not practice the modesty of some women of the day. Chambers, *Granuaile*, 52-53, 68. She gambled, used snuff and had a number of sexual exploits. Chambers, *Granuaile*, 53; Cook, *Pirate Queen*, 153.

358. The tales of Grace and her many lovers. Cook, *Pirate Queen*, 47-48, 65.

359. Grace O'Malley's first husband, Donal-an-Chogaidh O'Flaherty was killed in an attack by the Joyces around 1560. Chambers, *Granuaile*, 47-50. As a woman, Grace was ineligible under Brehon law to be elected Chief of the Name O'Flaherty, but she was a skilled commander, and many O'Flaherty's and other clan members followed her when she moved back to Clare Island. Chambers, Granuaile, 50.

360. Grace's lover, Hugh De Lacy, a shipwrecked sailor, was murdered by the MacMahons. Cook, *Pirate Queen*, 47-48; Chambers, *Granuaile*, 55-56. Grace caught the MacMahon murderers. Ibid., 69-70.

361. Grace may have had 20 vessels under her command. Cook, *Pirate Queen*, 152.

362. Sidney brought his son Philip Sidney with him to Mayo and Philip and Grace became friends. Chambers, *Granuaile*, 72. Grace submitted to Sidney and pledged ships and men. Ibid., 73, 73, 74. Despite that, Grace led a pirate raid in March 1578 in Desmond land. Ibid. 74.

363. Sir Richard Bingham's methods of enforcing order and establishing the Composition were rough and gruesome. He came into Connaught, including the domain of the MacWilliam Burkes, and took cattle and stripped the land bare. He also subdued septs and required their leaders to end allegiance to native overlords as a means of ending the power of local chieftains. Some killings in this process were unusually arbitrary. One was the murder of Owen O'Flaherty, Grace's eldest son by Captain John Bingham, Richard's brother. Chambers, *Granuaile*, 96. Bingham gave only a vague reason in a report attempting to provide some basis for executing Grace's son Owen. Chambers, *Granuaile*, 96.

364. Richard Bingham took Grace's younger son Tibbot as a hostage and sent him to serve Bingham's brother. Chambers, *Granuaile*, 94-95.

365. Chambers, *Granuaile*, 96.

366. Grace was on the brink of being hanged after Bingham had her arrested for, among other suspicions, trying to draw the Scots in to help the Irish. Many Burke hostages were being held at the time by Bingham and they were virtually all executed. Grace, however, was released because of the arrival of a royal warrant ordering her release signed by Walsingham, or because her feared son in law,

known as the Devil's Hook, pledged peace and loyalty. Chambers, *Granuaile*, 97- 98.

367.   The Mayo Burkes had colorful nicknames. Grace was called "Grace of the Gamesters." Cook, *Pirate Queen*, 171. The "Devil's Hook" was Grace's son-in-law, Richard Burke. Cook, *Pirate Queen*, 114. Another leader was known as "The Blind Abbott." Id.; O'Faolain, *Great O'Neill*, 183.

368.   In 1586 the Mayo Burkes enlisted the support of 2,000 Scots for their Connaught campaigns. The Scots arrived at Ardnaree, but Bingham's men captured them, then proceeded to hack to death "every man woman and child of them-just over 1,000." Rowse 115; Lennon, *Sixteenth-Century Ireland*, 257. One English captain complained of fatigue from hacking and stabbing so many. Rowse 115.

369.   Perrot's quarrels spread to Richard Bingham, Norris and Geoffrey Fenton. Perrot accused Bingham of corruption and cruelty, but Sir Henry Wallop rose to Bingham's defense. Such an array of enemies, when added to Loftus and Henry Bagenal, found Perrot surrounded. Turvey, *Treason*, 25, 28, 41.

370.   In May, 1587, Grace went to Dublin to plead before Lord Deputy Sir John Perrot. Perrot pardoned Grace. Cook, *Pirate Queen*, 108; Chambers, *Granuaile*, 100.

371.   Richard Bingham was charged with corruption but was tried and acquitted in 1590. Chambers, *Granuaile*, 109.

372.   Elizabeth and Grace probably met at Nonsuch or Richmond, perhaps twice. Cook, *Pirate Queen*, 150, 154.

373.   Bingham accused Grace in 1593 of being a nurse to all rebellions. Chambers, Granuaile, 83.

374.   One stubborn tale is that Elizabeth gave Grace a present of a lovely handkerchief to use for her snuff habit. Later, Grace tossed it away. Even later, she was heard growling a curse about the useless gift. Cook, *Pirate Queen*, 153.

375.   Grace's son, Tibbot ("Tibbot of the Ships") and her half brother, Donal, were held by Bingham in 1593. They were ordered released by Elizabeth. Cook, *Pirate Queen*, 55, 156, 158.

376.   The Queen granted Grace an income from clan lands and that concession appalled Bingham. Chambers, *Granuaile*, 137; Cook, *Pirate Queen*, 155.

377.   It has been said of Grace's end, as far as history goes, "she simply disappears without a trace." Cook, *Pirate Queen*, 170. The belief is that she died in 1603 and may be buried in the Cistercian Abbey on Clare Island. Ibid; Chambers, *Granuaile*, 153. If so, she and Elizabeth ended their careers simultaneously.

378. But problems – notably harvest failures in Ireland and England – cut the troops in Ireland in half. War in the Netherlands became very real and raised an expensive existential threat. These problems made it essential that Perrot succeed, that his legislative agenda pass, that he make political friends, and that he govern Ireland at no expense to the financially pinched, genetically frugal Queen. But Perrot had no luck on any front. Ellis, *Eyewitness*, 319-322.

379. When Perrot came home to London, it was initially more in triumph than disgrace. He received a seat on the Queen's Privy Council. It was later that the reports of his many enemies led Elizabeth to send him to the Tower. Turvey, *Treason*, 20, 34, 41.

380. Later deputies learned that the lofty sounding post was actually a "poisoned chalice." Cook, *Pirate Queen*, 60.

381. Perrot's failures were capped by the failed parliament. Chancellor/Archbishop Adam Loftus deliberately frustrated Perrot's 1585 Parliament in Dublin. Success of the Parliament meant a great deal to Perrot and he was mortified by its failure. Turvey, *Treason*, 36-37, 39. Most of what Perrot presented for enactment in the 1585 Dublin Parliament failed. He suffered excruciating highly public failure inflicted with glee by his Old English enemies. His composition bill failed. So bitter was the parliamentary defeat that no parliament was held in Dublin thereafter for over a quarter of a century. Ellis, *Eyewitness*, 321.

382. Under Perrot tensions grew high over efforts to establish a university in Dublin. This effort pitted Perrot against Loftus over Perrot's proposal to establish the school on the grounds of St. Patrick's Cathedral and to dissolve the Cathedral and use the assets to support the university. Ultimately, Loftus prevailed. Dublin found a spot and donated it, and in 1591 Trinity was founded, based on the model of Trinity College, Cambridge. Lennon, *Sixteenth-Century Ireland*, 322.

383. Perrot and Archbishop Loftus of Dublin kept at each other's throats. Perrot wrote to Sir Francis Walsingham of Loftus: "The ungodly gain that this archbishop doth suck out of that church to pamper himself, his children and friends, as well in that realm as in this, is so sweet as he cannot endure any man to look towards it." Turvey, *Treason*, 27. He said Loftus "hath so well feathered his nest as he hath purchased, in this realm and in that, above iiic li a year." Ibid., 28.

384. Lord Burghley and Christopher Hatton played large roles in the fall of Perrot. Burghley kept in contact with FitzWilliam and framed the accusation-laced questions of witnesses at Perrot's trial. Turvey,

Treason, 81. Burghley and FitzWilliam were linked by marriages of relatives. Thus, Burghley helped bring down Perrot less out of animosity to Perrot than to elevate his kinsman. Ibid., 82. Essex, Robert Devereaux, remained a friend of Perrot. Perrot was Essex' sister's father-in-law. Ibid., 86.

385.   Dennis O'Roughan, from Ireland, a priest, but a devout criminal, was in jail in Dublin facing possible execution when Archbishop Adam Loftus, Perrot's bitter enemy, availed himself of O'Roughan's willingness to make false accusations against Perrot to save himself. Loftus feared Perrot, who had risen to the Privy Council. FitzWilliam, too, now feared attack from Perrot. They forged a letter from Perrot to the King of Spain and brought a copy to use against Perrot, claiming O'Roughan was reported to be compiling a book against Perrot, but was not finished because one of the constable's men had bit off a piece of O'Roughan's nose. O'Roughan had a history of trafficking in forged documents. In fact, he had earlier worked for Perrot, and Perrot had once pardoned O'Roughan and enlisted him as a spy. O'Roughan blackmailed priests whom he was investigating at Perrot's instance. Turvey, *Treason*, 88-90.

386.   Richard Bingham was removed in 1596 and summoned to Dublin, but when he left Dublin for London without permission, he was jailed at Fleet prison for extortion. Cook, *Pirate Queen*, 167.

387.   Wills, *Lives*, Vol. II, Part II, 5.

388.   Ulster was the province that was the most Irish, the most rebellious and the least pacified of the four provinces. Hughes, *Ireland Divided*, 7.

389.   Ulster was the most difficult of the Irish provinces from the English perspective. The English thought Ulster was still in the Bronze Age. Elton, *England Under*, 386. "By 1590, English rule had been gradually extended until only Ulster lay outside the system of shire government." Ellis, "Tudor Borderlands," 72.

390.   The Scots had a legitimate claim to land in Ulster. Marjerie Bissett was an heiress of the O'Neill clan, the lords of Antrim and Tyrone. Her mother was Sabia O'Neill, daughter of the King of Ulster and wife of John Bissett, lord of the Glens. Marjerie inherited the Glens of Antrim. She became a central figure of the Scots MacDonnell clan, marrying John Mor MacDonnell in 1399, thereby giving the Clan Donald of Scotland a claim to the Glens. Marjerie's heirs include many MacDonnells of Antrim and also many MacDonalds of Dunnyveg. Her children were Donald Balloch MacDonnell and Ranald Bane MacDonnell. John Leonard Roberts, *Feuds, Forays and Rebellions: History of the Highland Clans, 1475-1625* (Edinburgh: Edin-

burgh University Press, 1999), 16; Curley, *Vanishing*, 1; George Hill, *An Historical Account of the MacDonnells of Antrim* (Belfast: Archer & Sons, 1873), 16.

391. Essex dined as a guest of Sir Brian O'Neill, then had his men surround the house, arrest O'Neill and his wife, send them to Dublin for execution, and massacred the O'Neill guests and retainers. Lecky, *Eighteenth Century*, 5.

392. Mary Stuart was vivacious, had a tall, graceful, strong body, a beautiful complexion unstained by the pox marks Elizabeth wore. Dunn, *Elizabeth*, 10. Mary longed to meet Elizabeth and wrote her sycophantic letters pledging loyalty, but the planned meeting was cancelled. Dunn 332. Mary Queen of Scots was Elizabeth's most likely successor. Hayes-McCoy, "Conciliation," 80.

393. James I was an unattractive youth and from an early age was timid, subject to anxiety attacks, and he stuttered. Dunn, *Elizabeth*, 304.

394. The Casket Letters are believed by many to have been forgeries. Elton, *England Under*, 293. Mary Queen of Scots' connection to the "Casket" letters provided the evidence that she had been involved in plotting against her husband, Lord Darnley, and that she was Bothwell's lover. Elton, *England Under*, 293-94.

395. Bothwell and Mary were tried for the murder of Darnley but were acquitted due to insufficient evidence. Dunn, *Elizabeth*, 297.

396. Mary's life was surrounded by plots: the Ridolphi conspiracy. Dunn, *Elizabeth*, 345; the plot to kill her husband, Lord Darnley; and the Anthony Babbington plot to kill Elizabeth. Dunn, *Elizabeth*, 328, 385-88; Peter and Fiona Somerset Fry, *The History of Scotland* (New York: Barnes and Noble, 1982), 150-152.

397. Mary Queen of Scots marriage in 1568 to her 3rd husband, James Hepburn, the 4th Earl of Bothwell, in a Protestant ceremony cost her the loss of the support of the Catholic countries, Spain and France. Elton, *England Under*, 292; Dunn, *Elizabeth*, 185.

398. Even the language of Elizabeth's letter to James VI professing her innocence in the execution of Mary Queen of Scots was so stilted and exceedingly literal that it was apparent that she had participated in the decision. It has been called a "breathtakingly hypocritical" statement. Dunn, *Elizabeth*, 411. Almost equally disingenuous was James's reply announcing that he chose to accept her profession of innocence. Ibid.; Somerset Fry, *Scotland*, 154.

399. Pope Pius V had issued the earlier Papal Bull *Regnans in Excelsis* in 1570 excommunicating Queen Elizabeth. Elton, *England Under*, 303.

400. The Vatican edicts not only excommunicated Elizabeth, they encouraged her overthrow and death (as well as the death of the Prince of

Orange, William the Silent). These condemnations were reissued by the Pope at the time of the Spanish Armada. Dunn, *Elizabeth*, 375-76, 416.

401. Ireland "threatened to become a vantage-ground to the foreign enemy." Church, *Spenser*, 54.

402. The Battle of Gravelines on July 28, 1588 is memorable for the fire ships used by the English to scatter the Spanish Armada. Elton, *England Under*, 374.

403. In 1588 Richard Bingham's cousin, George, executed over 700 survivors of the Spanish Armada. Lennon, *Sixteenth-Century Ireland*, 257.

404. The Queen wrote Walsingham that "she was moved to incline to an offer of marriage with the Duke of Alencon, but found the matter somewhat strange...considering the youngness of the years of the Duke of Alencon;..." COSPFSE Entry 502. Elizabeth wrote this just days before the beginning of the St. Bartholomew's Day massacre which lasted several weeks during which some 5,000 to 30,000 Huguenots and others were killed by French Catholic mob violence. The State Papers attribute some level of guilt for the St. Bartholomew's Day killings to the House of Guise. COSPFS, 1572-74. Entry No. 583 Sept. 1571 183.

405. "Thou carest for religion as much as my horse." Rowse 427.

406. Tyrone's country was west of Lough Neagh. There, at the top of a steep hill, stood the well guarded Dungannon Castle of Hugh O'Neill. Rowse 422.

407. Hugh O'Neill was accused of having hanged Hugh Gaveloch O'Neill with his bare hands from a thorn tree. He denied that, but admitted he ordered his hanging for murder and treason and said that two McMurrehys hanged him. O'Faolain, *Great O'Neill*, 110-11.

408. Sidney found Hugh O'Neill tending horses in Dungannon. McConville, *Ascendency*, 55.

409. Henry Sidney was very close to the Tudors and a childhood friend of King Edward VI who, it is said, died in Sidney's arms. O'Faolain, *Great O'Neill*, 39.

410. Sidney was described as a humane man. McConville, *Ascendency*, 55.

411. Sidney found Hugh O'Neill as a horseboy. The horseboys were viewed by Edmund Spenser as "rake-helly horseboys, growing in knavery and villainy." Quinn, *Elizabethans*, 41. He was taken either to the Pale or to England in 1559 and he was still there in 1562 when Shane visited the royal Court. Hayes-McCoy, "Conciliation," 82. Paor and O'Faolain both conclude that Hugh O'Neill was taken to London and brought up at Court. De Paor, *Peoples of Ireland*, 133;

O'Faolain, *Great O'Neill*, 38-39. However, some historians conclude that he did not live in England. Hugh did apparently live for some time under the guardianship of the New English family of Giles Hovenden in the Pale. However, Sir Henry Sidney's own Memoir recites that O'Neill lived with Sidney. (Hugh O'Neill "whom I had bred in my house from a little boy....") Brady, *Viceroy's Vindication?*, 54; Micheline Kearny Walsh, *An Exile of Ireland: Hugh O'Neill, Prince of Ulster* (Dublin: Four Courts Press, 1996), 19-20. Some say that the time Hugh O'Neill spent in England as a boy began in 1562. O'Faolain, *Great O'Neill*, 282, note 3. He was under the overall tutelage of Sir Henry Sidney from age 9 to 16. He is said to have lived for some period with the Sidney family at Penshurst in Kent. There, Hugh served as a page to Mary Sidney and was a friend of Philip Sidney. Berleth, 247, 248. A number of historians have provided convincing detail that indicate that young Hugh O'Neill lived at Penshurst Place in Kent with the Sidney family for several years. Elton describes O'Neill being taken to England to be educated at Court. Elton, *England Under*, 388. Robert Kee observed that O'Neill had been "brought up for eight years in England as a boy and man—a young protege of leading Englishmen with access to Elizabeth's court" and that Elizabeth "had helped him since childhood in his disputes with other branches of the O'Neills...." Kee, *Ireland*, 35. Berleth recounts that Sidney virtually adopted O'Neill, and states that O'Neill spent several years living at Penshurst Place and that he grew up beside Philip Sidney. Berleth, 246, 247. Professor Hiram Morgan cautions that the references to O'Neill being bred in Sir Henry Sidney's house and other contemporaneous references to O'Neill living as a youth in London and being raised among the English do not prove that he was raised or educated in England, but suggest that he was raised in the Pale by the Hovenden family. Morgan, "End," 92-93. Professor Morgan, however, notes that had Hugh been raised at Penshurst, he likely would have been Protestant. He notes that the Hovendens were a Protestant, New English family also, but less so. Morgan, "End," 214-15. Sir Henry Sidney in his later years also lent occasional political support to Hugh O'Neill. Morgan, "End," 97.

412. Edmund Curtis states that Hugh O'Neill "was rescued by the government and brought over to London, where he was taken in the Earl of Leicester's household." Curtis, *History*, 185.

413. At Penshurst, O'Neill met poets and scholars, Walsingham and Leicester, Ormond and Perrot. McConville, *Ascendency*, 55-56.

414. O'Neill's foster brothers from the Hovenden family of Laois, Henry,

Richard, Piers and Walter Hovenden, all served O'Neill in his loyal years. Morgan, "End," 97.

415. Eventually, no Irishman knew as many English as O'Neill. Berleth, 249. His other English and New English friends included Sir Warham St. Leger, Sir Christopher Hatton, and even the Spymaster, Sir Francis Walsingham. Ibid.

416. O'Neill as Baron of Dungannon had been a member of the 1585 Dublin Parliament which approved the Plantation of Munster. De Paor, *Peoples of Ireland*, 133. Mr. Justice Robert Gardiner was a good friend of O'Neill and an outspoken Englishman in Dublin who warned the Council and the Tudor Court that corruption of officials in Dublin was costing England by alienating potentially loyal Irish. Canny, *Making Ireland*, 91. Edward Moore was recognized among his fellow English as an ally of Hugh O'Neill. Ibid., 90.

417. By 1590 only Ulster lay outside the system of Shire government. Ellis, "Tudor Borderlands," 72. The English thought Ulster was still in the Bronze Age. Elton, *England Under*, 386.

418. Sidney and other Deputies had long attempted without success to free the uirrithe clans who were beholden and loyal to O'Neill from the control of the O'Neill clan. Lennon, *Sixteenth-Century Ireland*, 269.

419. Ulster was "as inaccessible to strangers as the Kingdom of China," according to Sir Arthur Chichester. Rowse 97. Three routes led through the drumlins into Ulster: Dublin to Newry and Armagh; Ballyshannon and the ford across the River Erne; and by sea to Lough Foyle to Derry. Rowse 422.

420. Hugh O'Neill's desire to gain power is ranked by some as his main motivation. Morgan, "End," 214.

421. Nicholas Bagenal was granted a lease of Newry Abbey. Canny, *Making Ireland*, 79-80.

422. The Bagenals were from Staffordshire. They were initially sponsored by the aggressive Lord Deputy Sir Edward Bellingham. G. A. Hayes-McCoy "Tudor Conquest and Counter Reformation, 1571-1603," in *A New History of Ireland*. Vol. 3, edited by T. W. Moody, F. X. Martin and F. J. Byrne (Oxford: The Clarendon Press, 1976), 70.

423. Nicholas Bagenal based at Newry and Andrew Brereton based at Lecale, northeast of Newry, commanded the forces the English relied upon to control the Wild Irish in Ulster and to assure that the Irish did not venture south into the Pale marches or into the maghery to launch raids. Lennon, *Sixteenth-Century Ireland*, 166.

424. Nicholas Bagenal's own ambitions in Ulster may have motivated him to turn into an enemy of Hugh O'Neill. Hugh in turn saw the

Bagenals, first Nicholas, then his son Henry, as among the main obstacles to his own domination of Ulster. Canny, *Making Ireland*, 81.

425. Another O'Neill opponent was Sir Roger Wilbraham, the Irish solicitor general, who favored other O'Neills and the Bagenals in the 1592 disputes over O'Neill's lordship. Morgan, "End," 77.

426. Hugh O'Neill is described as "dashing and courtly." McConville, *Ascendency*, 57.

427. Mabel Bagenal and Hugh O'Neill were very attracted to each other. Berleth, 249-250. Hugh O'Neill is described as handsome. Cook, *Pirate Queen*, 144.

428. Elizabeth was unconvinced that the marriage of Hugh and Mabel would accelerate the Anglicization of Ulster, so she withheld consent for a time. She did eventually relent and approve the marriage, but Hugh and Mabel had gone ahead and married without Elizabeth's knowledge. Berleth, 250. Canny 81. The Bagenals did not take the news of the marriage well. Berleth, 250.

429. Life at O'Neill's castle, with its majestic corner turrets was described by a visiting English lord, Sir John Harington, with enthusiasm. He praised O'Neill's outdoor dining at a "fern table and fern forms, spread under the stately canopy of heaven." Quinn, *Elizabethans*, 101. Hugh went to London and bought elegant fineries for Mabel and fine furniture, tapestries and art for Dungannon. Berleth, 251. Records reflect that feasting at Castles like Askeaton and Dungannon included many meats, light Spanish wine, ale and whiskey. Fynes Moryson describes Irish whiskey (*uisce beathadh*) as "the best in the world in that kind." The whiskey of that era is described by Luke Gernon as "a very wholesome drink and natural to digest the crudities of Irish feeding." He counselled: "you may drink a naggin without offense" (a fourth of a pint). Quinn, *Elizabethans*, 67.

430. O'Neill hired English craftsmen to renovate Dungannon and stocked it with continental furnishings. McConville, *Ascendency*, 22. After remodeling, Dungannon almost approached the elegance of Penshurst Place. McConville, *Ascendency*, 57.

431. O'Neill admitted in a letter to impregnating the two women, but took umbrage at Mabel complaining about it to the Council. O'Faolain, *Great O'Neill*, 221.

432. Red Hugh O'Donnell fulfilled an O'Donnell clan superstitious prophecy, and that stood him in good stead in drawing even greater than usual reverence. McGettigan, *Red Hugh*, 37-40. Red Hugh O'Donnell was viewed as The Anointed One. Morgan, "End," 204.

433. The "Spoilers of the Pale" were the chieftains Rory Oge O'More of Leix, Feagh MacHugh O'Byrne of Wicklow, and Brian O'Connor

of Offaly who raided homes in the Pale. Rowse 129, 131. The raiders were also less glamorously referred to as bandits and outlaws. Carey, *Surviving*, 168.

434. The escape of Red Hugh O'Donnell required that he make it safely back to Ulster. During his flight north, Red Hugh was helped by stopping at the estate of Garrett Moore, a friend and supporter of Hugh O'Neill. Morgan, "End," 132. O'Neill had a strong friendship with Sir Edward Moore of Louth and his son Garrett. Ibid., 97.

435. Red Hugh O'Donnell went to spend several days with O'Neill immediately after his escape from Dublin Castle. Walsh, *Exile*, 21.

436. Many believed that Hugh O'Neill engineered the escape of Red Hugh O'Donnell from Dublin Castle. O'Faolain, *Great O'Neill*, 123.

437. Hugh was obsessed with killing Shane O'Neill's children. McConville, *Ascendency*, 56.

438. The chieftains felt the threat of Tudor England as the English increased their pressure. English garrisons and forts in the approaches to Ulster and within Ulster at the Yellow Ford, Armagh and elsewhere were tightening the knot. De Paor, *Peoples of Ireland,* 133.

439. O'Neill "saw the end of ancestral sovereignty of the O'Neills approaching." De Paor, *Peoples of Ireland*, 135.

440. Conor Roe Maguire was the loyal "Queen's Maguire". O'Faolain, *Great O'Neill*, 137.

441. O'Neill is described as "dissembling and meditative" and also as "a consummate liar" in pretending to be loyal during the run up to his rebellion. Morgan, "End," 217.

442. Rowse, 426.

443. Tom Lee was a friend of O'Neill but an enemy of Ormond. Rowse 133. Lee and O'Neill slept together in Irish style a number of times. Rowse 132, 135. Tom Lee led the band that killed Feagh MacHugh O'Byrne. Lee sent O'Byrne's head to Queen Elizabeth. Rowse 130, 131.

444. Warham St. Leger, Justice Robert Gardiner and Adam Loftus were authorized by the Dublin Council as commissioners to negotiate with O'Neill. All three were known to be friends of O'Neill but loyal to the Crown. Morgan, "End," 160.

445. O'Neill claimed that Justice Robert Gardiner was his best friend, but Gardiner scolded and rebuked him for rebelling, and O'Neill again wept. O'Faolain, *Great O'Neill*, 141. Hugh O'Neill was "always liable to a flood of tears." Ibid., 111.

446. Prior to the military reforms introduced by Hugh O'Neill, the Irish kerne were distinctly inferior to British forces due to their lack of training, simple fighting skills, absence of discipline and commu-

nication, and their inferior weapons, ammunition and equipment. Elton, *England Under*, 387. The strong suit and special expertise of Irish kerne was "hit and run tactics." Quinn, *Elizabethans*, 41. They were trained "to skirmish upon bogs and difficult passes or passages of woods, and not to stand or fight in a firm body upon the plains, they think it no shame to fly or run off from fighting, as their advantage." In battle, the Irish had one equipment advantage; they used the bagpipe instead of a trumpet. Quinn, *Elizabethans*, 41-42.

447. Turlough O'Neill, ill and under pressure, resigned as the O'Neill in favor of Hugh in May, 1593. Lennon, *Sixteenth-Century Ireland*, 293. O'Neill appears not to have performed the Irish coronation at Tullaghoge until Turlough died in 1595. De Paor, *Peoples of Ireland*, 134.

448. The Irish were very deficient in weapons compared to the English. In 1534 Connor O'Brien of Thomond was among the first Irish leaders to report that his men were equipped with arquebuses as well as bows, arrows and swords. Ian Heath, *The Irish Wars, 1485-1603* (London: Asprey Publishing. 1993), 12. But there are few recorded mentions of Irish use of arquebuses before an event in 1558. Ibid., 13. Black Hugh O'Donnell used some guns as early as 1516. By 1600 it is reported that, even when the Irish captured ordnance, they often failed to use it. Ibid., 18.

449. The English out-shone the Irish in technique, equipment, horse and artillery. The Spanish could help the Irish make up for their lack of any sea power. The Ulster terrain, however, almost always benefitted the Irish. Rowse 416.

450. The reports describing the order and discipline of O'Neill's troops at Clontibret "shocked the Dublin government." Morgan, "End," 179.

451. Richard Bingham called Sligo Castle the key to Connaught. Morgan, "End," 189.

452. O'Donnell repeatedly raided Mayo and stole cattle and plundered the Mayo Burkes. He had earlier taken Sligo Castle, then Sir Conyers Clifford took it back. Cook, *Pirate Queen*, 168.

453. O'Neill's life had not been the life of a fervent Catholic. Canny, "Early Modern, 113.

454. A "devastatingly violent suppression". "Dickson, *Old World*, 5.

455. In 1599, O'Neill marched south and secured support from the Sugane Earl, James FitzThomas FitzGerald, and from Florence MacCarthy. Rowse 427. Wills, *Lives*, Vol. II, 117.

456. Donal O'Sullivan Beare was the chieftain in Kerry's deep southwest controlling Dunboy Castle and Berehaven. McCormack, *Earldom*, 65; John J. Silke, *Kinsale: The Spanish Intervention in Ireland at the End of the Elizabethan Wars* (Dublin: Four Courts Press, 2000), 132, 163.

457. The Munster leaders who promised the greatest help to O'Neill were the Sugane Earl of Desmond and Florence MacCarthy. Rowse 427. But, alliances in Munster were insecure and changing. In 1596, the White Knight, Edmund FitzGibbon was seen as sufficiently loyal that he was appointed Sheriff of Cork. Thereafter, however, he was suspected of supporting O'Neill's rebellion, but that could not be proved. Prior to the Battle of Kinsale, the White Knight submitted to the Crown. The White Knight was Clangibbon, the Black Knight was the Knight of Glin, and the Green Knight was the Knight of Kerry, all hereditary titles conferred by the Earl of Desmond long after the Norman invasion. McCormack, Earldom, 35, 51.

458. Archbishop MacGauran of Armagh had travelled to Spain where he personally secured the assurance that Spain would assist an Irish rebellion. Walsh, *Exile*, 20.

459. The Spanish and Irish collaborators regaled each other with history, suggesting that the Milesians from whom the Irish race proceeded were Spaniards from the Bay of Biscay near Santander on the Sea of Cantabria. Morgan, "End," 208-09.

460. When O'Neill and O'Donnell advised the Spanish that they would become loyal to King Philip, Spain saw the chance to rule a new kingdom, and Philip believed that Ireland was willing to remain under a foreign king. Brigden, *New Worlds*, 333-34.

461. The English fleet's attack on Cadiz, Spain in 1596, led by a competitive group—Lord Howard of Effingham as Lord Admiral, Essex as Lord General of the Army, Francis Vere as Marshal of the Army, and Walter Raleigh as captain of the War Spite—achieved a stirring victory, but the attack provoked Spain, setting the stage for Spain's willingness in 1600 to send military help to the northern Irish chieftains. Brigden, *New Worlds*, 338-39. Spain was financially stressed and was also preoccupied with the Turkish Empire. Though Spain won the historic sea battle at Lepanto in 1571, Philip's fleet had still not fully recovered from the heavy losses suffered in its effort to attack Tripoli in 1560. Silke, *Kinsale*, 16. However, in retaliation for Essex' and the others' attack on Cadiz, Philip II in 1596 approved a plan of Don Diego de Brochero to send forces to help O'Neill. Ibid., 30-31.

462. There was suspicion that Lord Burgh, an effective and principled man, was poisoned by his English colleagues because he was obstructing their lucrative corrupt practices. Berleth, 260.

463. Hugh O'Neill engaged in violence and killing and has been called "a past master of it." Morgan, "End," 95. He especially killed collaborators. Ibid., 107.

464. When O'Neill saw Henry Bagenal leading the English force at the Yellow Ford, O'Neill "directed his entire fury" at Bagenal in the first charge, and Bagenal "fell by the hand of his enemy." Wills, *Lives*, Vol. II, 116. Bagenal was killed at the August 1598 Battle of the Yellow Ford. Elton, *England Under*, 392. Afterward, the Lords Justices sent a plea to O'Neill to let the English force hiding in Armagh go. Rowse 423.

465. Spain maintained control of much of the Caribbean and of Mexico, Chile and Peru, but maintaining that control placed heavy demands on the fleet. Elton, *England Under*, 339.

466. In October 1598 when many of the Munster men broke into rebellion, they committed the all too typical outrages of pillage and plunder against the New English in Munster. Ellis, *Eyewitness*, 74, quoting Fynes Moryson.

467. Richard Tyrrell was a seasoned leader from an early Norman family. He had proved exceptionally capable by leading a small force to victory over the English at the Battle of Tyrellspass in 1597.

468. Essex felt he was successful in intimidating Elizabeth because "she doth not contradict confidently." He also had a need to be an alpha male, and he especially indulged his compulsion to dominate any woman. Brigden, *New Worlds*, 336. Essex claimed Mountjoy was too bookish for this task. Rowse 424. He argued against Elizabeth's desire to send Mountjoy to Ireland, and Essex instead led the command himself. Rowse 424.

469. Elizabeth's proclamation of war against Ireland promised and threatened "to reduce that kingdom to obedience by using an extraordinary power and force against them...." Berleth, 287.

470. On June 29, 1599 three Spanish ships carrying 1,000 arquebuses and other arms for O'Neill and O'Donnell, commanded by General Marcos de Aramburu, landed at Killybegs in the northwest. O'Donnell and O'Neill met with them. Silke, *Kinsale*, 60. The Spanish sergeant – major, Don Fernando de Barrio Nuevo, gave the chieftains Philip III's assurance that he was going to send them troops to support the rebellion. Silke, *Kinsale*, 59-60.

471. The Essex victory at Cahir was ridiculed by Elizabeth; she referred to his captives as mere "beggarly rogues." Brigden, *New Worlds*, 346. Elizabeth also called the captives the "base rogues" of Cahir. O'Faolain, *Great O'Neill*, 215.

472. Elizabeth's letters castigated Essex for vacillating in Ireland. Wills, *Lives*, Vol. II, 124-127; Rowse, 424-426; Berleth, 286-289. She scolded Essex for his ineffectiveness and unresponsiveness in his Ireland campaign. She pointed out her view of the ease of the task of catch-

ing and defeating O'Neill ("taking of an Irish hold from a rabble of rogues.") Rowse, 425. She scolded Essex ("How often have you told us that others that preceded you had no judgment to end the war...."). Rowse 425. Elizabeth urged him again to attack O'Neill, questioning his resolve and ultimately chastising him and expressing suspicion about his private meeting with O'Neill out of the earshot of his officers. Brigden 346-347; 394-398. Rowse 425, 426. Elizabeth, finally, was on to Essex' duplicity ("you and the traitor [O'Neill] spoke half an hour together without anybody's hearing.") Rowse 426.

473. Elizabeth's letters confronted Essex, saying that she has seen a document in which he forbade his men to criticize his conduct in Ireland. Wills, *Lives*, Vol. II, 127.

474. Essex "had known O'Neill personally in England." Froude, *English*, 67.

475. At the meeting with Essex at Ballyclinthe O'Neill rode into the stream until the water was up to his knees. Wills, *Lives*, Vol. II, 123. Essex derided O'Neill's assertion that religion motivated him in his rebellion ("thou carest for religion as much as my horse.") Rowse, 427. Berleth, 288. Essex admitted to those close to him that O'Neill had urged Essex to rebel and O'Neill offered to join him. Brigden, *New Worlds*, 347.

476. Elizabeth recorded her recognition of "the alienation of Our people's minds from Us." Brigden, *New Worlds*, 354. The alienation of the Irish and their developing hatred for the English was also vividly described by Spenser in a report to Elizabeth during the Munster rebellion. Berleth 282, 283. Some Deputies blamed their predecessor or successors for instilling such hatred. The lasting effect of actions of some of the worst Deputies was acknowledged by later Deputies. The "alienation of the Queen's subjects ... had resulted from the forceful and sometimes rash actions" of prior deputies, according to a speech by Sir John Perrot. Canny, *Making Ireland British*, 104.

477. Mountjoy went directly to challenge O'Neill, both to fulfill Elizabeth's wishes and to contrast his campaign with the failed campaign of Essex. He marched north in September 1600 with a force intending to dislodge O'Neill from the Moyry Pass at the Gap of the North, then to establish a fort in O'Neill's territory. In foul weather during September and October Mountjoy and O'Neill fought head to head with substantial casualties. Ultimately O'Neill withdrew to Armagh. Mountjoy established Mountnorris Fort between Newry and Armagh. The battle, however, gave Mountjoy a taste of the improved Irish fighting forces under O'Neill. Falls 265, 266.

478. The ford across the river at Ballyshannon at the western end of lower Lough Erne was an entry to Ulster; but another was from the North Sea into Lough Foyle and then along the River Foyle to Derry. Rowse 422. O'Neill's greatest concern after Mountjoy and Carew were named to replace Essex when he fell from power was that the new English administration would land a major force to his rear at Derry through Lough Foyle. The Docwra landing there raised his anxiety. Silke, *Kinsale*, 74.

479. Quinn, *Elizabethans*, 41.

480. Florence MacCarthy and the Sugane Earl of Desmond had both been captured and sent to the Tower. O'Faolain, *Great O'Neill*, 231-32, 245. Silke, *Kinsale*, 119-20; Lennon, *Sixteenth-Century Ireland*, 301.

481. O'Neill and O'Donnell agreed they should warn the Spanish that they should not land south of Limerick because of the loss of support there and the heavy presence of the Queen's Army in the south. Silke, *Kinsale*, 86, 102-03.

482. The Sugane Earl of Desmond, James FitzGerald, remained a prisoner in the Tower of London until his death in 1607. McCormack, *Earldom*, 197; Curtis, *History*, 215.

483. Sir George Carew, Lord President of Munster, accompanied Mountjoy at Kinsale. Carew was very capable and he had the strong support of Lord Burghley. Rowse, 427.

484. A Report of the Council of State to King Philip III at the end of December 1601 described the English elation over the landing site: "The enemy was very confident in Ireland, since he learnt the small number of the Spaniards; and was approaching the Spanish force and intercepting the Catholics." COSPEA Vol. IV 1587-1603. Entry 713 696. Eight of the Spanish ships had gone "astray" and many of General Zubiar's men were sick. Id 695. The Report recommended sending troops from Dunkirk to Ireland after the battle. Id. 695.

485. The coded message referring to the "Low Countries" did not fool Mountjoy when he intercepted it. He knew it meant Ireland. O'Faolain, *Great O'Neill* 243.

486. When the news of the landing came, Mountjoy was at Kilkenny and he wrote Burghley promising to affix "halters about their necks." Rowse, 431.

487. Even before arriving at Kinsale, Red Hugh O'Donnell, was said to have come to think less of O'Neill and "to think himself as good a man: which was not the case." Rowse, 427.

488. O'Donnell went to Kinsale before O'Neill. O'Donovan, *The Four Masters*, Vol. VI, 2275.

489. O'Neill and O'Donnell in 1599 had an estimated 20,000 fighting

men in total, but it is estimated that less than half of them were adequately armed. Silke, *Kinsale*, 55.

490. The debate at Kinsale occurred on the night of December 23, 1601 (on the old calendar) and the battle on December 24. Falls. 304. The debate rehashed all the reasons for O'Neill's opposition to launching an attack. Falls 302.

491. Jealousy as well as old enmities arose between O'Neill's men of Tyrone and O'Donnell's men of Tyrconnell. Wrangling erupted between O'Neill and O'Donnell even over the question of who should lead the attack. Falls 305. Earlier in the rebellion in a more collegial setting, O'Neill and O'Donnell had entered a written agreement that they and their clans would work as equals. McGettigan, *Red Hugh*, 66-67.

492. The chieftains and their clans "had a tradition of mutual family and territorial enmity." De Paor, *Peoples of Ireland*, 135.

493. Father Mateo de Oviedo, who was trapped in the town of Kinsale, recorded that Don Juan Del Aguila sent a message to O'Neill and O'Donnell through Lieutenant Bustamente urging that the Irish attack the enemy, and assuring them that the Spaniards would charge out of the town and attack at the same time. Silke, *Kinsale*, 105.

494. Some have claimed that O'Neill was persuaded: "Yet O'Neill was persuaded to gamble on a joint operation...." Lennon, *Sixteenth-Century Ireland*, 302.

495. Historians have debated the relative contributions of O'Neill and O'Donnell. McGettigan makes a case for O'Donnell's virtues (McGettigan, *Red Hugh*, 66-67) and Morgan for O'Neill's (Morgan, "End," 191, 196, 200). MeGettigan observed that O'Neill was the "more elder, more cautious and more subtle" of the two and O'Donnell the "more forceful." McGettigan, *Red Hugh*, 67.

496. There are credible sources for the story that a bribe of a bottle of whiskey given to a chief in the O'Neill clan was what provided Sir George Carew a crucial tip-off about the imminent attack by the Irish against the English at Kinsale. Elton, *England Under*, 388n1. The Irish plan to attack before dawn was said to be betrayed by Brian MacHugh Oge MacMahon, a member of the O'Neill forces. His message was delivered to Captain William Taaffe for transmission to Sir George Carew. Falls 303.

497. Kinsale, in the history of Ireland, is the decisive battle. G. A. Hayes-McCoy *Scots Mercenary Forces in Ireland, 1565-1603* (London: Edmund Burke Publisher, 1996), 334.

498. The Julian calendar was 10 days behind the new Gregorian calendar, and the old style calendar was used in England and Ireland.

Just before dawn on December 24, 1601 (under the old calendar – January 3, 1602 under the new Gregorian calendar) an English sentry reported sighting the Irish troops approaching. Falls. 304.

499.   There was a final standoff, a disagreement over who should lead the attack at Kinsale. Then, O'Donnell lost his way in the dark. Falls 305. O'Donnell insisted on marching his troops side by side with O'Neill's rather than behind them. Silke, *Kinsale*, 142. How they lost contact with each other despite this is a mystery. The march to the battlefield started late and O'Donnell lost his way, took the wrong route and did not arrive at the battle until daylight. He saw the English cavalry rout the Irish cavalry and foot soldiers, then he turned and withdrew his men. Falls 305. O'Donnell and his men simply left the battle field without fighting when he saw the charge of Clanrickard's cavalry overwhelm the Irish cavalry. Rowse, 435.

500.   The English cavalry attack was commanded by Richard Wingfield and executed by Richard of Clanrickard's and Henry Danvers' horse. Some 1,200 Irish bodies were dead on the field. Clanrickard killed 20 men with his own hand. Falls 306- 307.

501.   Elizabeth said of her Irish courtiers, "I find that I sent wolves not shepherds to govern Ireland, for they have left me nothing but ashes and carcasses to reign over." Chamberlain, *Sayings*, 308; See also Dennis Taafe, *An Impartial History of Ireland*, 434 (Dublin: J. Christie, 1809); Thomas Leland, *The History of Ireland*, 287 (London: Printed for J. Nourse, 1774).

502.   After the Battle of Kinsale, on January 30, 1602, Philip III wrote Don Juan Del Aguila: "I learn of the rout of the earls O'Neill and O'Donnell, and I recognize that our only hope now rests upon your bravery and prudence which I prize highly. I trust....you will be able to keep the army together until help can reach you in the form of ships, arms and munitions, which are now being prepared here, and will be despatched promptly." COSPEA Vol. IV. 1587-1603. Entry 715. Jan. 30, 1602, 703. The Report recommended that "reinforcements should if possible be sent to Don Juan Del Aguila and the Irish Catholics." COSPEA Vol. IV. Entry 71 697.

503.   O'Neill was determined to continue the war after the defeat at Kinsale, but others went their own separate ways, some back to their homes to attend to great discord and to repel challenges to their authority. Falls 324, 326. Richard Tyrrell submitted to George Carew. Silke, *Kinsale*, 163.

504.   Chichester's strategy was "extermination" of the rebel clans near war's end. Falls, *Ulster*, 67; McCavitt 47, 44. "The fight of the Northern chiefs was an apparent failure. Nations, however, are made in

many ways, and among these is the heroic example of great men even when they seem to fail. Few of the great names of Irish history come better out of the tangled treachery, cruelty, self-seeking, and indifference of their times than the wise and long-lived Hugh O'Neill and Red Hugh O'Donnell, that fiery spirit soon quenched." Curtis, *History*, 220.

505. Magennis was the captain of Kylultagh. Brady, *Viceroy's Vindication?*, 61.

506. O'Neill was referred to in this period as "The Running Beast." Mc-Cavitt 47.

507. James VI had let the Tudor courtiers know he was gathering troops to fight, if necessary, to establish his rightful claim to the throne. But the dying Elizabeth feared the loss of the loyalty of her people once a successor was identified. "Even until her last hours she would never name her successor...." Brigden, *New Worlds*, 356. Of the 12 or so potential successors, one was the Infanta Isabella of Spain, wife of the Archduke Albert, Governor of Flanders. James VI of Scotland was the most direct claimant as the only direct descendant of Henry VII. Finally, on Wednesday, March 23, 1603 on her deathbed, Elizabeth signaled her approval of James VI as her successor. Ibid.

508. The line of descent of Henry VIII ended with Elizabeth. James VI (James Stuart) of Scotland, as a direct descendant of Henry VII, had the superior claim to succeed Elizabeth, but there were a dozen, including the Infanta Isabella of Spain, holding some claim to the Throne. Elizabeth had the ability to name her heir but did not do so definitively until her last days. Brigden, *New Worlds*, 356.

509. There are many references to O'Neill crying ("he hath divers times bemoaned himself with tears in his eyes.") Rowse, 132. Most peculiar is that O'Neill wept again when he learned of Elizabeth's death though he had been at war with her for years. J.C. Beckett, *The Making of Modern Ireland, 1603-1923* (1966; Reprint, Mackays of Chatham PLC, 1981), 24, 293. "The Great O'Neill openly wept at the news... [he said] out of genuine love for his royal antagonist...." Myers, *Elizabethan Ireland*, 2.

510. James never knew his mother. They had not seen each other since he was a baby. She was Catholic. He was Protestant. Essentially, she occupied the uncomfortable position of a competitor of his for the Crown of England. Somerset Fry, *Scotland*, 153.

511. The Stuart line's claim to the Throne was viewed by the English as a strong one, and it was greatly strengthened when Mary Queen of Scots delivered a baby boy. Dunn, *Elizabeth*, 275. Many believed that he had a superior claim to his mother's. Elizabeth, however,

declined to clarify her succession until her deathbed. Bridgen, *New Worlds*, 356.

512.   Prior to ascending the Throne, James I had never been to England. Dunn, *Elizabeth*, 304. After his ascension, he chose to rule his two kingdoms from London; he returned to Scotland only once in the 22 years of his reign. Somerset Fry, *Scotland*, 162-63.

513.   There was some effort in some areas of Ireland to resist the new King. Cork and Wexford, for example, were on the whole loyal to the crown from 1598-1601 until James became King. Cork publicly announced through aldermen and clergy that it would not recognize James; Wexford began a brief rebellion. This was all quickly ended after it had lasted just a few weeks with few hangings and many pardons by Mountjoy. Dickson, *Old World*, 7.

514.   Elizabeth expressed anguish over the Irish rebellion, saying it has become such that "the Crown of England cannot endure, without the extreme diminution of the greatness and felicity thereof, and alienation of Our people's minds from Us...." Rowse, 437; Moryson, "Itinerary," 172.

515.   O'Neill went hunting with King James. McCavitt 54.

516.   The Act of Oblivion pardoned all offenders for offenses committed prior to the accession of King James. The pardon spared O'Neill from "the jaws of death." McCavitt 50.

517.   "[T]he eventual pattern of military conquest left a bitter legacy of racial and religious animosity." Ellis, "Tudor Borderlands," 72. It was infused in addition with "cultural imperialism." Ibid., 73.

518.   After the war, Crown officials began sending letters under the Mandates policy ordering Irish leaders to attend Anglican services or go to prison. McCavitt 58.

519.   Sir Arthur Chichester hated the MacDonnells even more than he hated O'Neill for a very personal reason. James MacSorley MacDonnell led the Scots to victory against the English at the 1597 Battle of Carrickfergus. The commander at Carrickfergus was John Chichester, Arthur's brother. John's forces encountered the Scots four miles from Carrickfergus and he decided to attack them. Canny 188. John Chichester was killed by the Scots, beheaded. The Scots proceeded to kick John's head around, using it for a football. After Kinsale, Arthur arranged to have James MacSorley MacDonnell poisoned at Dunluce Castle in 1601. Falls 208.

520.   The decapitation of John Chichester after being killed by a headshot has also been attributed to Sir Randal MacDonnell. Canny 188; Falls 208. Some reports are that James MacSorley MacDonnell simply passed away, with no mention of being poisoned. Falls. 277. Years

later Randal MacDonnell discussed decapitating John Chichester. Viewing a statue of John Chichester with a head on it, Randal said with heavy accent: "How the de'il came he to get his heid again?-for I was sure I had ance taen it frae him." A.P.B. Chichester, *History of the Family of Chichester* (London: Printed by author, 1871), 53; McCavit 136.

521. Sir John Davies, Attorney General of Ireland under the reign of King James I, called Ireland "the land of Ire." Myers, *Elizabethan Ireland*, ix.

522. Spain's records confirm that by 1604 O'Neill was again seeking Spanish help. McCavitt 61.

523. Brigid FitzGerald, a descendant of an Earl of Kildare, was married to Rory O'Donnell, Earl of Tyrconnell (one of the earls in the "Flight" in 1607). A year prior to the flight of the Earls, Hugh O'Neill and Rory O'Donnell came to Maynooth and attempted to enlist Lord Delvin of the FitzGeralds to take part in a new insurrection. Cullen, *Ma Nuad*, 32.

524. Enroute to Lough Swilly and the flight, a tired and exasperated O'Neill ranted at his wife when she slipped from her horse from fatigue. Walsh, *Exile*, 71.

525. The Flight of The Earls is generally referred to as the end of the old order, the end of life under the Gaelic system, laws and traditions that were thousands of years old. Beckett, *Modern Ireland*, 44. The Earls brought more than eighty individuals with them. The full total is believed to be ninety nine passengers. McCavitt 98 Just as O'Neill in the haste to depart, left his son Conn, O'Donnell also had to leave without his pregnant seventeen year old daughter who was in Fosterage with her Grandmother, the dowager Countess of Kildare at Maynooth. Hill, *Historical Account*, 213. By the Earls' own recounting of the Flight, as stated in Conde de Fuentes April 13, 1608 letter to King Philip III, the departing earls lamented "leaving their horses on the shore with no one to hold their bridles." Walsh, *Exile*, 136.

526. The plantations failed. MacDonough, "Ambiguity," 105-06.

527. One writer describing the failure of the Ulster plantation attributes it to "lax enforcement" and "corruption" by the Crown, "absenteeism," "inaccurate land surveys," "large numbers of still unmoved Irish," and of "segregation and expropriation." Myers, *Elizabethan Ireland*, 10. Whereas the Munster Irish "were killed or driven from their land during Desmond's Rebellion, the Ulster colonists, actually imported in large numbers and segregated from the Irish, multiplied and so entrenched their position by means of persecution and a pliable legal system that the plantation and its aftermath became a

watershed for problems, largely insoluble, that continue to this day to plague Ulster." Ibid., 10.

528. At the end of the Tudor conquest "many natives were totally alienated from government." The manner of the conquest and the Stuart land confiscations "caused great bitterness and long-term alienation from royal government of the Gaelic and Old English communities." Ellis, *Eyewitness*, 352. The Old English (*Sean Ghaill*), the descendants of the Normans who came to Ireland in the 12ᵗʰ Century, were predominantly Catholic; the New English (*Nua Ghaill*), who came later as planters, English soldiers who stayed, or as adventurers, were virtually all Protestant after Henry VIII's Reformation. Moody, *A New History*, xlii.

529. After the flight, once in Rome O'Neill became "a heavy drinker and a pensioner of the Pope." Roy, *Fields*, 152. Hugh O'Neill is described as "a lonely, grand, tragic figure." Rowse, 416. He is also described, at his end, as "a miserable old exile living on Italian charity." Falls 90.

530. Although the developments triggered by the Grand Disturbers took three centuries to produce their eventual effects, "these developments also promoted conditions conducive to the gradual emergence, mainly after 1603, of a new Irish nation with a nationalist ideology based on faith and fatherland." Ellis, *Eyewitness*, 356. Indeed, The Prime Minister is the *Taoiseach*, the National anthem is in the Irish language, and the Irish culture infuses modern life. "Some historians have seen the beginning of nationalism in this period." But it was not modern, nor was it animated by "romantic ideology." De Paor, *Peoples of Ireland*, 137. This era did, however, throw the spotlight of Irish history on being and remaining Irish in all its human and ancestral facets. The different customs and habits of English and Irish persisted right through the Middle Ages. The "traditional cultures" endured – both of them. De Paor, *Peoples of Ireland*, 137. The Irish language, speech, culture, music, poetry and epic tales proved captivating to the Old English. Curtis, *History*, 114.

531. That the Easter Rising was seen by its leaders as doomed prior to its start is dramatized in a nearly carefree-sounding response by one of its leaders, James Connolly. As he headed out of Liberty Hall in Dublin that morning, one of Connolly's men, Bill O'Brien, heard Connolly remark that very few had turned out to commence the fight against the British army; Connolly said: "We are going out to be slaughtered." When O'Brien asked, "Is there no chance of success?" Connolly responded "None whatever." James Hyland, *James Connolly* (Dundalk: Published for the Historical Association of Ire-

land by Dundalgan Press, 1997), 52; DeRossa 251. Many historians and commentators concluded in retrospect that the Rising in 1916 was doomed, and some say the leaders knew that, but willingly embraced death. Edwards 277; DeRossa 247, 248 (of 1,000 men on one of the rolls, only 130 showed up). Id. 249. An estimated 2,500 participated in the Rising. Pearse had said: "I shall die very cheerfully." Edwards 317. There is also evidence, however, that some of the leaders harbored a hope of victory though they considered it unlikely in view of the confusion, the cancellation of a general call and the diminished likelihood of a strong turnout. Edwards 276.

532. In 1641 the Catholic population of Ulster began a rampage attacking and killing Protestants in Portadown. There were claims that a wholesale massacre of Protestants was planned, but in what has been termed a "dispassionate analysis," historian W. E. H. Lecky wrote: "There was no such plan and no such massacre, but in the first months of the rising the insurgents committed many murders, often savagely." Corish, "The Rising," 291.

533. Thousands of Protestants were slaughtered by Catholics during 1641 and 1642, and Protestants retaliated killing numerous Catholics in return. In the next few years several armies formed in or came to Ireland to wage The Wars of the Three Kingdoms—a Scots Covenanteer Army, a Catholic Confederacy Army, a royalist force, and eventually Oliver Cromwell's Parliamentarian Army. Patrick Corish, "The Rising of 1641 and the Confederacy, 1641-45," in *Elizabethan Ireland, A Selection of Writings by Elizabethan Writers on Ireland*, edited by James P. Myers, Jr. (Hamden, Connecticut: Archon Books, 1983); Kee, *Ireland*, 42-43.

534. Prohibition of Catholic education. P.J. Dowling, *The Hedge Schools of Ireland* (Cork, Ireland: Mercier Press, 1968), 22. The secrecy requiring the use of hedges to hide classes. Ibid., 35. The low ebb of Irish schools after Cromwell. Ibid., 10-11. The prohibition of Catholic colleges or endowed schools. Ibid., 23-24.

535. It became the practice of Native Irish people to assemble around a home fire where each would recite poems, history and the stories of their heroes in a style of exceptional beauty and feeling. Dowling, *Hedge*, 11.

536. Cromwell's massacres at Drogheda and Wexford. Kee, *Ireland*, 46-48.

537. By 1652 it was estimated that one third of the total Irish population had perished by war and attendant diseases. Ellis, *Erin's*, 65. After that "The English Administrations began to enact policies that were designed to eradicate the Irish people by ordering them first into a

'reservation', that is, the territory west of the River Shannon, in the province of Connacht and County Clare....Any Irish person found on the east bank of the River Shannon after May 1, 1654, could be, and was, executed on the spot....Many were." Ellis, *Erin's*, 65.

538.   By the Act of Settlement enacted in 1652 at the end of the Cromwell campaign in Ireland all land in Ireland owned by Catholics was confiscated, and the land in Ulster was planted by English rather than by Scots who had opposed Cromwell's Parliamentarian forces. One estimate is that 80% of the land in Munster and Leinster changed hands in a "gigantic act of robbery." Hughes, *Ireland Divided*, 8.

539.   After Cromwell ordered the banishment of the Irish to the west, it was firmly enforced and administered by investigative inquisitions which conducted surveys to determine who was politically acceptable to own the properties. Roy, *Fields*, 181. The native Irish after Cromwell possessed but did not always own roughly one third of the land—"certainly the poorest lands, primarily in far reaches to the west." Roy, *Fields*, 166.

540.   Some 100,000 Irish were seized from their villages between 1654 and 1660 and banished to Barbados and other colonies as "indentured laborers." Ellis (*Erin's Blood Royal*) 65.

541.   Later, the Williamite War against Jacobites in England and Ireland from 1689-1691 resulted in a Protestant victory and the Treaty of Limerick, and secured the "Glorious Revolution" and the reign of William and Mary. Kee, *Ireland*, 49-51.

542.   Religious toleration was a key promise of the Treaty of Limerick ending the Williamite War, but there was none for Catholics or Presbyterians. When The Penal Laws were passed, Presbyterians and Catholics were the focus. Intermarriage between people of different religions was forbidden. Couples married by a Presbyterian minister would be hauled into an Anglican church service to be denounced for fornication. As for restoration of land, only 14% of Irish land was held by native Irish by the start of the 18th century. Ellis, *Erin's*, 122.

543.   Catholics were not allowed to own horses or property worth more than a few pounds sterling. They could not practice professions or hold office even in municipal government. Ellis, *Erin's*, 67.

544.   Ulster Scots were a distinct ethnic and religious group with their own traditions, their predominately Presbyterian religion and a Scots Irish dialect. Many of the Scots in Ulster came from the Scottish Borders and lowlands. The Scots Presbyterians suffered under some Penal Laws along with Catholics. Only members of the established Anglican Church of Ireland entirely escaped the sanctions of the laws. Hughes, *Ireland Divided*, 9.

545. A famine in Scotland late in the 17th century led to widespread flight of Scots to Ireland and they became a dominant presence again in Ulster. But in 1703 Queen Anne's Test Act denied Scots Presbyterians and Catholics a variety of rights, and by 1707 heavy emigration of Ulster Scots began, largely to America. The enactment of the Act of Union creating the historic union of England and Scotland did little to stem emigration by dissenters. Kee, *Ireland*, 65-66.

546. Ulster Scots who did not join the Church of Ireland were treated as dissenters and were required to tithe to the Church of Ireland, and they began to emigrate to America from 1707 until the American Revolution interrupted them. Kee, *Ireland*, 243. They represented several religious groups, but were mainly Presbyterians. Peter Gray, *The Irish Famine* (New York: Harry N. Abrams, Inc., 1995), 98.

547. England was alarmed by one of the most significant threats to its rule of Ireland and its own security during the French Revolution. In 1796 a substantial French fleet carrying an invasion force arrived in Bantry Bay in the southwest. It was preparing to go ashore at a point where no British defenses would impede their landing or advancement, but a troublesome storm turned into a gale and became so intense it prevented a landing. The storm forced the French to flee Bantry Bay for the open sea and they returned to France. The inspiration of the French Revolution, however, took hold among the disaffected Presbyterians of Belfast. They formed the Society of United Irishmen, aligning with groups called Volunteers and with Catholic groups in Ireland to launch a challenge to British rule. What ensued was the United Irishmen's uprising, a fierce rebellion following the organizational model of the French Directory. The rebellion was put down by Britain's Lord Charles Cornwallis and others in the most brutal fashion. The British and the United Irishmen fought many fierce battles, but the failure of the rebellion was assured by British success in using torture, mainly public flogging, to learn the names of rebel leaders and members. After the rebellion was ended, Britain abolished the Irish Parliament and, by the 1800 Act of Union, swept Ireland into the United Kingdom on January 1, 1801. Kee, *Ireland*, 65, 66.

548. The Irish people were dependent for survival on not being evicted from the tiny plots on which they grew potatoes . They sustained themselves by eating the "lumpers," coarse potatoes. They were forced by circumstances to sell to their absentee British landlords any food they grew to pay the rent or else face prompt eviction and a very great risk of a resulting slow death. In some areas – Cork, Donegal, Mayo and Clare- they produced little but potatoes. When the potato crop failed, there was an immediate existential crisis for

these native small farmers. Woodham-Smith, *Great Hunger*, 76, 84; Edwards, *Atlas*, 179. Even when starving, the Irish had to sell any food they could raise to avoid eviction. Woodham-Smith, *Great Hunger*, 75-76.

549. The Great Famine. Kee, *Ireland*, 77-101; Woodham-Smith, *Great Hunger*, 74-84. The requirement to export crops and food even in the depths of the famine. Gray, *Famine*, 46.

550. Sir Robert Peel's government fell in June 1846 over repeal of the protectionist Corn Laws. He was succeeded by Prime Minister John Russell, who with his Chancellor of the Exchequer, Sir Charles Wood, were laissez faire economists devoted to insistence that problems of the famine must be allowed to run their natural course without government aid. Woodham-Smith, *Great Hunger*, 87. Trevelyan, for example, refused to lower the price of food. Kee, *Ireland*, 94. Russell, Wood and Trevelyan declined to replenish the grain and meal in the silos after those able to work on new public works projects bought the grain. The most destitute were too sick to work and could not earn money to buy grain. Woodham-Smith, *Great Hunger*, 74-84.

551. There was no photographic record of The Great Famine. Sexton and Kinealy 39.

552. Woodham-Smith, *Great Hunger*, 406. The Great Famine was not over in the ordinary sense. Crop failure recurred and people continued to die after 1849. Ibid., 407-08.

553. The bitterness left by British famine policy lead to a widespread distrust that fueled the ensuing movements for total separation from Britain. Woodham-Smith, *Great Hunger*, 406.

554. Famine emigrants were as many as 2,000,000 in the years after the start of the Famine. Kee, *Ireland*, 119. Another estimate is 1,800,000 during the ten years from 1845-1855. Gray, *Famine*, 97.

555. The impact The Great Famine and the flight from the Famine had on the population could only be estimated because baseline census figures were uncertain and no reliable record was kept of the deaths. In 1841 the population was recorded as 8,175,124 and in 1851 as 6, 552,385, with an adjusted calculation concluding that some 2 1/2 million people were lost by death and flight during and soon after the Famine. Woodham-Smith, *Great Hunger*, 411-12.

556. The condition of famine immigrants was seldom good, but Gross Isle, Quebec was notoriously overrun with desperately ill Irish. Kee, *Ireland*, 97, 98.

557. "If there had existed in the nineteenth century a computer able to digest all the appropriate data, it would have reported one city in the entire world where an Irish Catholic, under any circumstance,

should never, ever set foot. That city was Boston, Massachusetts. It was an American city with an intensely homogeneous Anglo-Saxon character, an inbred hostility toward people who were Irish, a fierce and violent revulsion against all things Roman Catholic....Yankee Boston was unique in the depth and intensity of its convictions." Thomas H. O'Connor, *The Boston Irish, A Political History* (Boston: Back Bay Books and Northeastern University Press, 1995), xvi.

558. Ireland had an outsized parental impact on the US due to the formation of clusters of Irish yielding high birth rates in cities just when they were in need of workers, just as the political backbone of US cities was forming, exporting Irish style Catholic traditions to the US resulting in a large and influential Catholic population with strong Irish tradition. The Irish caste was reinforced and increased in the next generations by Irish clerical hierarchical control of parishioners and schooling in the U.S. The Irish, such as the O'Dwyers of NYC, the Daleys of Chicago, the Fitzgeralds, Curleys and Kennedys of Boston, were often the founders of modern political organizations. O'Connor, *Boston*, 137-140.

559. The Irish model of Catholicism kept parishioners very close to their clergy. Priests were from poor families; they remained poor as priests and depended on their parishioners for food and support. They were a nationalist clergy. Auricular confessions were a strong tradition, and morality focused heavily on sexual abstinence. Regular attendance at Sunday Mass made the parish the social, cultural, civic and political center of life in early America for most Catholics. O'Connor, *Boston*, 137-140.

560. Soon St. Louis had so many Irish that historians have referred to it as "the chief Irish Settlement in the United States." March 529. Faherty 12. Irish politicians in St. Louis named Igoe, Sullivan, Cochran and Hannegan came to dominate political office there. William Barnaby Faherty, S. J., *The St. Louis Irish: An Unmatched Celtic Community* (St. Louis: Missouri Historical Society Press, 2001), 167.

561. Patrick Pearse wrote "There is only one way to appease a ghost. You must do the thing it asks you. The ghosts of a nation sometimes ask very big things; and they must be appeased, whatever the cost!" *Ghosts* (Dublin: Irish National Committee, 1915); Edwards, *Patrick Pearse*, 254.

562. "O'Neill ... was in a sense the father to Irish nationhood, the last defender of the Gael." Berleth, 246.

563. Theobald Wolfe Tone and Thomas Davis are sources for the spirit that has been referred to as "Pearse's cultural nationalism...." Edwards, *Patrick Pearse*, 255.

564. "The Irish nation could survive as long as the repositors of the Gaelic tradition remained. Had 'the last unconquered Gael' died, the nation would have died with him, for the nation would have lost its soul." Edwards, *Patrick Pearse*, 256.
565. Curtis, *History*, 220.
566. The distinction between loyalist and unionist is that unionist is used to denote any who have a determined desire to remain part of Great Britain. Hume, *New Ireland*, 43-44. Loyalist is used to refer to the groups who long had paramilitaries. Ibid., 94. The distinction between republican and nationalist is that nationalists seek to work for their goals through traditional constitutional methods; republicans for theirs through force, and they long had paramilitaries. Ibid., 35.
567. Human rights, not religion, became the distinguishing issue separating some of the Irish from the political/religious cacophony of the ensuing centuries. Many became not only non sectarian, but anti sectarian. John Hume, *A New Ireland* (New York: Roberts Rinehart, 1996), 35.
568. The events of the 16th and early 17th century are identified as the roots of today's partition separating The Republic of Ireland from Northern Ireland. Hughes, *Ireland Divided*, 6-7. The partition itself was part of the Anglo Irish Treaty of 1921. The boundary was fixed by a Boundary Commission. That, in turn, is said to be one of the root causes of the Troubles that traumatized Ireland from the early 1970s to 1998. Ibid., xiii.
569. The Irish have shown "a survival against incredible odds – endurance against confiscations, the destruction of books and records, genocidal warfare, artificial famines and an enforced dispersal of the princes and their people throughout the world in a manner as incredibly poignant as the Jewish diaspora." Ellis, *Erin's*, xiv.

Select Bibliography

Bagenal, Philip. *Vicissitudes of an Anglo-Irish Family*. London: C. Ingleby, 1925.

Bartlett, Thomas and Keith Jeffery, eds. *A Military History of Ireland*. Cambridge: Cambridge University Press, 1996.

Beckett, J.C. *The Making of Modern Ireland, 1603-1923*. 1966; Reprint, Mackays of Chatham PLC, 1981.

Berleth, Richard. *The Twilight Lords. Elizabeth I and the Plunder of Ireland*. New York: Roberts Rinehart. 2002.

Bowker, John. *The Concise Oxford Dictionary of World Religions*. Oxford: Oxford University Press, 1997. www.encyclopedia.com.

Brady, Ciaran. *Shane O'Neill*. Dundalk: Published for the Historical Association of Ireland by Dundalgan Press, 1996.

Brady, Ciaran, ed. *A Viceroy's Vindication? Sir Henry Sidney's Memoir of Service in Ireland, 1556-78*. Cork: Cork University Press, 2002.

Brigden, Susan. *New Worlds, Lost Worlds, The Rule of the Tudors 1485-1603*. New York: Penguin Books, 2001.

Byrne, Charles Artaud, *Ranelagh: The Irish Warlord*. Mustang, OK: Tate Publishing, 2008.

Byrne, F. J. *Irish Kings and High Kings*. Dublin: Four Courts Press, 1973.

Camden, William. *The History of the Most Renowned and Victorious Princess Elizabeth, Late Queen of England*. 1688; Reprint, RareBooksClub. com, 2012.

Campion, Edmund (Saint). "A History of Ireland (1571)." In *Elizabethan Ireland, a Selection of Writings by Elizabethan Writers on Ireland*, edited by James P. Myers, Jr., Hamden, Connecticut: Archon Books, 1983.

Canavan, Tony. *Frontier Town: An Illustrated History of Newry*. Belfast: Blackstaff Press, 2009.

Canny, Nicholas. *Making Ireland British 1580-1650*. Oxford: Oxford University Press, 2001.

Canny, Nicholas. "Early Modern Ireland c. 1500-1700." In *The Oxford History of Ireland*, edited by R. F. Foster, 88-133. Oxford: Oxford University Press, 1989.

Carey, Vincent. *Surviving the Tudors: The Wizard Earl of Kildare and English Rule in Ireland, 1537–1586*. Dublin: Four Courts Press, 2002.

Chamberlain, Frederick. *The Sayings of Queen Elizabeth*. London: John Lane, The Bodley Head, 1923.

Chambers, Anne. *Eleanor, Countess of Desmond: A Captivating Tale of the Forgotten Heroine of the Tudor Wars in Ireland*. Dublin: Wolfhound Press, 2000.

Chambers, Anne. *Granuaile: Grace O'Malley, Ireland's Pirate Queen*. Dublin: Wolfhound Press, 2003.

Chichester, A. P. B. *History of the Family of Chichester*. London: Printed by author, 1871.

Church, R. W. *Spenser*. New York: Macmillan & Co., 1906.

Cook, Judith. *The Pirate Queen: the Life of Grace O'Malley, 1530-1603*. Cork, Ireland: Mercier Press, 2004.

Corish, Patrick. "The Rising of 1641 and the Confederacy, 1641-45." In *Elizabethan Ireland, A Selection of Writings by Elizabethan Writers on Ireland*, edited by James P. Myers, Jr., Hamden, Connecticut: Archon Books, 1983.

Cruickshank, C. G. *Elizabeth's Army*. Oxford: Clarendon Press, 1966.

Cullen, Mary. Ma Nuad, *Maynooth: A Short Historical Guide*. Maynooth: The Maynooth Bookshop, 1995.

Curley, Walter J. P. *Vanishing Kingdoms: The Irish Chiefs and their Families*. Dublin: Lilliput Press, 2004.

Curtis, Edmund. *A History of Ireland*. London: Methuen, 1950.

D'Alton, Rev. E. A. *History of Ireland: From the Earliest Times to the Present Day*. Vol. 2 and 3. London: The Gresham Publishing Co., 1913.

Davies, John. *A History of Wales*. London: Allen Lane, 1993.

Davies, John. *A Discovery of the True Causes Why Ireland Was Never Entirely Subdued* Washington, DC: Catholic University of America Press, 1988.

De Paor, Liam. *The Peoples of Ireland, From Pre-History to Modern Times*. South Bend, Indiana: University of Notre Dame Press, 1986.

Dickson, David. *Old World Colony, Cork and South Munster 1630-1830*. Cork: Cork University Press, 2005.

Dolby, William, and a Committee of Admirers of Irish History. In O'Halloran, Sylvester, editors. *A General History of Ireland*. New York: Virtue and Yorston, c1840.

Dowling, P. J. *The Hedge Schools of Ireland*. Cork, Ireland: Mercier Press, 1968.

Dunn, Jane. *Elizabeth & Mary: Cousins, Rivals, Queens*. New York: Alfred A. Knopf, 2004.

Edwards, David. *The Ormond Lordship in County Kilkenny, 1515-1642: The Rise and Fall of Butler Feudal Power*. Dublin: Four Courts Press, 2003.

Edwards, David, Padraigh Lenihan, and Clodagh Tait. *Age of Atrocity; Violence and Political Conflict in Early Modern Ireland*. Dublin: Four Courts Press, 2007.

Edwards, Ruth Dudley. *An Atlas of Irish History*, 2nd ed. London: Methuen, 1986.

Edwards, Ruth Dudley. *Patrick Pearse: The Triumph of Failure*. London: Faber and Faber, 1977.

Ellis, Peter Berresford. *Eyewitness to Irish History*. New York: Wiley, 2004.

Ellis, Peter Berresford. *Erin's Blood Royal, The Gaelic Noble Dynasties of Ireland*. New York, Palgrave, 2002.

Ellis, Steven G. *Ireland in the Age of the Tudors 1447-1603*. London and New York: Longman, 1998.

Ellis, Steven G. "The Tudor Borderlands." In *The Oxford Illustrated History of Tudor and Stuart Britain*, edited by John Morrill. Oxford: Oxford University Press, 2000.

Elton, G. R. *England Under the Tudors*. London and New York: Methuen, 1955.

Faherty, William Barnaby, S. J. *The St. Louis Irish: An Unmatched Celtic Community*. St. Louis: Missouri Historical Society Press, 2001.

Falls, Cyril. *The Birth of Ulster*. 1963; Reprint London: Methuen, 1983.

Falls, Cyril. *Elizabeth's Irish Wars*. Syracuse, New York: Syracuse University Press, 1950.

Fenlon, Jane. *Clanricard's Castle: Portumna House, County Galway*. Dublin: Four Courts Press. 2012.

FitzGerald, Brian. *The Geraldines; An Experiment in Irish Government, 1169-1601*. Devin-Adair, 1952.

FitzPatrick, Elizabeth. *Royal Inauguration in Gaelic Ireland, c. 1100-1600: A Cultural Landscape Study*. Suffolk, UK: Boydell Press, 2004.

Ford, Alan. *The Protestant Reformation in Ireland*. Dublin: Four Courts Press, 1997.

Foster, John T. *Saint Mary's Press Glossary of Theological Terms*. Winona, MN: Saint Mary's Press, 2006.

Foster, Roy F. *Modern Ireland, 1600–1972*. London: Penguin Books, 1988.

Froude, James Anthony. *The English in Ireland in the Eighteenth Century*. Vol. 1. London: Longmans, Green, and Company, 1895.

Gainsford, Thomas. *The Glory of England*. London: Printed by Edward Griffin, 1618.

Gerald of Wales. *The History and Topography of Ireland.* Translated by John J. O'Meara. London: Penguin UK, 1982.

Gray, Peter. *The Irish Famine.* New York: Harry N. Abrams, Inc., 1995.

Guy, John. *The Tudor Monarchy.* London: Hodder Education Publishers, 1997.

Hadfield, Andrew and John McVeagh. *Strangers to That Land: British Perceptions of Ireland From the Renaissance to the Famine.* Buckinghamshire: Colin Smythe Ltd., 1994.

Hayes-McCoy, G. A. "Conciliation, Coercion and the Protestant Reformation, 1547-71" In *A New History of Ireland. Edited by T. W. Moody, F. X. Martin and F. J. Byrne.* Vol. 3, Early Modern Ireland (1534-1691). Oxford: Clarendon Press, 1976.

Hayes-McCoy, G. A. "The Battle of Kinsale, 1601." *Irish Historical Studies* 38 (1949): 307-456.

Hayes-McCoy, G. A. *Scots Mercenary Forces in Ireland, 1565-1603.* London: Edmund Burke Publisher, 1996.

Hayes-McCoy, G. A. "Strategy and Tactics in Irish Warfare, 1593-1601." *Irish Historical Studies* 2, no. 7 (1941): 255-79.

Hayes-McCoy, G. A., "Tudor Conquest and Counter Reformation, 1571-1603." In *A New History of Ireland.* Vol. 3, edited by T. W. Moody, F. X. Martin and F. J. Byrne. Oxford: The Clarendon Press, 1976.

Heath, Ian. *The Irish Wars, 1485-1603.* London: Asprey Publishing. 1993.

Herity, Michael and George Eogan. *Ireland in Prehistory.* London: Routledge, 1977.

Herron, Thomas and Brendan Kane. *Nobility and Newcomers in Renaissance Ireland.* Washington, DC: Folger Shakespeare Library, 2013.

Hill, George. *An Historical Account of the MacDonnells of Antrim.* Belfast: Archer & Sons, 1873.

Hughes, Michael. *Ireland Divided: The Roots of The Modern Irish Problem.* New York: St. Martin's Press, 1994.

Hume, John. *A New Ireland.* New York: Roberts Rinehart, 1996.

Hyland, James. *James Connolly.* Dundalk: Published for the Historical Association of Ireland by Dundalgan Press, 1997.

Johnson, Paul. *Ireland, A Concise History from the Twelfth Century to the Present Day.* Chicago: Academy Chicago Publishers, 1984.

Jones, Frederick M. *Mountjoy, 1563-1606: The Last Elizabethan Deputy.* Dublin: Clonmore & Reynolds, 1958.

Kee, Robert. *Ireland: A History.* New York: Little Brown, 1982.

Kinsella, Thomas, translator. *The Tain.* New York: Oxford University Press, 1969.

Lecky, W. E. H. *A History of Ireland in the Eighteenth Century.* Vol. 1. New York: Longmans, Green and Co., 1892.

Leland, Thomas. *The History of Ireland*. London: Printed for J. Nourse, 1774.

Lenihan, Padraig. *Consolidating Conquest: Ireland 1603-1727*. London: Routledge, 2014.

Lennon, Colm. *Sixteenth-Century Ireland: The Incomplete Conquest*. Dublin: Gill & Macmillan, 1994.

Lennon, Colm. *An Irish Prisoner of Conscience of the Tudor Era: Archbishop Richard Creagh of Armagh, 1523-86*. Dublin: Four Courts Press, 2000.

Lennon, Colm. *Richard Stanihurst the Dubliner, 1547-1618*. Dublin: Irish Academic Press, 1981.

Lydon, James. *The Making of Ireland from Ancient Times to the Present*. New York: Routledge, 1998.

Lyons, Mary Ann. *Gearoid Og Fitzgerald*. Dundalk: Dundalgan Press Limited, 1998.

Mac Airt, Sean, editor and translator. *The Annals of Inisfallen*. Dublin: The Dublin Institute for Advanced Studies, 1951.

MacDonagh, Oliver. "Ambiguity in Nationalism: The Case of Ireland." In *Interpreting Irish History: The Debate on Historical Revisionism*, edited by Ciaran Brady, Sallins, County Kildare: Irish Academic Press, 1994.

MacNiocaill, G., editor. *The Red Book of the Earls of Kildare*. Dublin: Irish MSS Commission, 1964.

Maginn, Christopher. *Civilizing Gaelic Leinster: the Extension of Tudor Rule in the O'Byrne and O'Toole Lordships*. Dublin: Four Courts Press, 2005.

Mallon, Brian. *Shane O'Neill: The Grand Disturber of Elizabethan Ireland*. New York: Red Branch Press, 2015.

March, David, *The History of Missouri*. Vol. 1. New York: Lewis Historical Publishing Company, 1967.

McCarthy, Justin, editor. *Irish Literature*. Vols. 1, 3, and 8. Philadelphia: John D. Morris & Company, 1904.

McCaffrey, Carmel, and Leo Eaton. *In Search of Ancient Ireland*. Lanham, Maryland: New Amsterdam Books, 2002.

McCann, Colum. *TransAtlantic*. New York: Random House, 2013.

McCavitt, John. *The Flight of the Earls*. Dublin, Gill & Macmillan, 2005.

McConville, Michael. *Ascendancy to Oblivion: the Story of the Anglo Irish*. London: Quartet Books, 1986.

McCormack, Anthony M. *The Earldom of Desmond, 1463-1583: The Decline and Crisis of a Feudal Lordship*. Dublin: Four Courts Press, 2005.

McCormack, John. *A Story of Dublin*. Denver: Mentor Books, 2000.

McCorristine, Laurence. *The Revolt of Silken Thomas: a Challenge to Henry VIII*. Dublin: Wolfhound Press, 1987.

McCuarta, Brian, S. J., editor. Reshaping Ireland, 1550-1700: Colonization and Its Consequences: Essays Presented to Nicholas Canny. Dublin: Four Courts Press, 2011.

McFarnon, Emma. "Elizabeth I's War on Terror: How the Virgin Queen Persecuted England's Catholics." *BBC History Magazine* 15, no. 5 (May 2014).

McGettigan, Darren. *Red Hugh O'Donnell and the Nine Years War*. Dublin: Four Courts Press, 2005.

Mitchell, George J. *The Negotiator: A Memoir*. New York: Simon and Schuster, 2015.

Moody, Martin, and F. J. Byrne. *A New History of Ireland*. Vol 3. Oxford: Clarendon Press, 1976.

Moody, T. W., and F. X. Martin, editors. *The Course of Irish History*. Lanham, MD: Roberts Rinehart Publishers, 1994.

Mooney, Canice. *A Noble Shipload*. Irish Sword, ii. 1954-6, 195-204 (in Irish) (translated in Walsh, Kerney. *Destruction by Peace*, document 40a).

Morgan, Hiram. "The End of Gaelic Ulster: A Thematic Interpretation of Events Between 1534 and 1610." *Irish Historical Studies* 8, no. 32 (May 1988): 8-32.

Morrill, John, editor. *The Oxford Illustrated History of Tudor and Stuart Britain*. Oxford: BCA and Oxford University Press, 1996.

Moryson, Fynes, "An Itinerary (1617-c.1626)." *Elizabethan Ireland, a Selection of Writings by Elizabethan Writers on Ireland*, edited by James P. Myers, Jr., Hamden, Connecticut: Archon Books, 1983.

Myers, James P., Jr., editor. *Elizabethan Ireland: A Selection of Writings by Elizabethan Writers on Ireland*. Hamden, Connecticut: Archon Books, 1983.

Ni Cathain, Proinseas, and Michael Richter, editors. *Ireland and Europe in the Early Middle Ages: Texts and Transmissions*. Dublin: Four Courts Press, 2002.

O'Brien, Conor Cruise. *Ancestral Voices: Religion and Nationalism in Ireland*. Chicago: University of Chicago Press, 1995.

O'Brien, Jacqueline and Peter Harbison. *Ancient Ireland: From Prehistory to the Middle Ages*. New York: Oxford University Press, 1996.

O'Connor, Thomas H. *The Boston Irish, A Political History*. Boston: Back Bay Books and Northeastern University Press, 1995.

O'Cuiv, Brian, editor. *Seven Centuries of Irish Learning, 1000-1700*. Dublin: Published for Radio Eireann by the Stationary Office, 1961.

O'Curry, Eugene. *On The Manners and Customs of the Ancient Irish*. Vol 1. Edited by W. K. Sullivan. London: William and Norgate, 1873.

O'Donovan, John, translator. *The Four Masters: The Annals of the Kingdom of Ireland*. Dublin: Hodges & Smith, 1851.

O'Faolain, Sean. *The Great O'Neill: A Biography of Hugh O'Neill Earl of Tyrone, 1550–1616*. Chester Springs, PA: Dufour Editions, 1997.

Otway-Ruthven, A. J. *A History of Medieval Ireland*. 3rd ed. New York: Barnes & Noble Books, 1980.

Painter, Sidney. *William Marshall: Knight-Errant, Baron and Regent of Ireland*. Toronto: University of Toronto Press, 1982.

Palmer, Patricia. *The Severed Head and the Grafted Tongue*. Cambridge, UK: Cambridge University Press, 2014.

Paris and Skeffington quotes. *Notes and Queries*. Third Series – Volume 11. London, 1867, 333.

Pawlisch, Hans. *Sir John Davies and the Conquest of Ireland: A Study in Legal Imperialism*. Cambridge: Cambridge University Press, 1985.

Pearse, Padraic. *Ghosts*. Dublin: Irish National Committee, 1915.

Perraud, Cardinal Adolphe Louis Albert. *Ireland in 1862*. Dublin: J. Duffy, 1863.

Poblacht na h Éireann. *The Easter Proclamation of the Irish Republic*. 1916.

Quinn, D. B., and K. W. Nicholls. *A New History of Ireland*. Edited by T. W. Moody, F. X. Martin and F. J. Byrne. Vol. 3, *Ireland in 1534*.Oxford: Clarendon Press, 1976.

Quinn, David Beers. *The Elizabethans and the Irish*. Washington, D.C.: The Folger Shakespeare Library and Cornell University Press, 1966.

Raftery, Joseph. *Prehistoric Ireland*. London: Batsford, 1951.

Rich, Barnabe. "A New Description of Ireland, Together With The Manners, Customs, and Dispositions of The People (1610)." In *Elizabethan Ireland, a Selection of Writings by Elizabethan Writers on Ireland*, edited by James P. Myers, Jr., Hamden, Connecticut: Archon Books, 1983.

Richter, Michael. *Medieval Ireland: The Enduring Tradition*. New York: St. Martin's, 1995.

Roberts, John Leonard. *Feuds, Forays and Rebellions: History of the Highland Clans, 1475-1625*. Edinburgh: Edinburgh University Press, 1999.

Roche, Richard. *The Norman Invasion of Ireland*. Dublin: Anvil Books, 1995.

Rowse, A. L. *The Expansion of Elizabethan England*, 2nd ed. New York: Palgrave Macmillan, 1955.

Roy, James Charles. *The Fields of Athenry: a Journey Through Ireland*. Boulder: Westview, 2003.

Russell, Conrad. "The Reformation and the Creation of the Church of England, 1500-1640." In *The Oxford Illustrated History of Tudor and Stuart Britain*, edited by John Morrill, Oxford: Oxford University Press, 2000.

Savine, A. *English Monasteries on the Eve of Dissolution*. Oxford: The Clarendon Press, 1909.

Sexton, Sean and Christine Kinealy. *The Irish, a Photohistory 1840-1940*. London: Thames & Hudson, 2002.

Silke, John J. *Kinsale: The Spanish Intervention in Ireland at the End of the Elizabethan Wars*. Dublin: Four Courts Press, 2000.

Simms, Katharine. "The Norman Invasion and the Gaelic Recovery." In *The Oxford History of Ireland*, edited by R. F. Foster. Oxford: Oxford University Press, 1989.

Somerset Fry, Peter and Fiona. *The History of Scotland*. New York: Barnes and Noble, 1982.

Stanihurst, Richard. *Holinshed's Irish Chronicle, 1577*. Dublin: Dolmen Editions, 1979.

Taaffe, Dennis. *An Impartial History of Ireland*. Dublin: J. Christie, 1809.

Tanner, Marcus. *Ireland's Holy Wars*. New Haven: Yale University Press, 2001.

Tarleton, A. H. *Life of Nicholas Breakspear*. London: A. L. Humphreys, 1896.

Turvey, Roger. *The Treason and Trial of Sir John Perrot*. Cardiff: University of Wales Press, 2005.

Vergil, Polydore. *The Anglica Historica of Polydore Vergil 1485-1587*, edited by Denis Hay. London: Royal Historical Society, 1950.

Walsh, Micheline Kerney. *An Exile of Ireland: Hugh O'Neill, Prince of Ulster*. Dublin: Four Courts Press, 1996.

Williams, C.H., editor. *English Historical Documents, 1485-1558*. London: Eyre and Spottiswoode, 1967.

Wills, James, editor. *Lives of Illustrious and Distinguished Irishmen: From the Earliest Times to the Present Period, Arranged in Chronological Order, and Embodying a History of Ireland in the Lives of Irishmen*. Vols. 1 and 2. Dublin: MacGregor, Polson & Co., 1890.

Woodham-Smith, Cecil. *The Great Hunger: Ireland, 1845-1849*. New York: Old Town Books, 1962.

Wright, Thomas. *The History of Ireland from the Earliest Period of the Irish Annals to the Present Time*. Vol. 1. London: The London Printing and Publishing Company, 1854.

Wroe, Ann. *The Perfect Prince*. New York: Random House, 2003.

State Papers

Calendar of State Papers, Letters and Papers, Foreign and Domestic, of the Reign of Henry VIII. Vol. 21, Part I, *1546*.

Council Book of Ireland, 1558-71, MS 24 F 17.

Crosby, Allan James, editor. *Calendar of State Papers, Foreign Series, of the Reign of Elizabeth, 1569-71*. London: State Paper Department of Her Majesty's Public Record Office, 1874.

Crosby, Allan James. *Calendar of State Papers, Foreign Series, of the Reign of Elizabeth, 1572-74.* State Paper Department of Her Majesty's Public Record Office.1876. Kraus Reprint Ltd, 1966.

Cunningham, Bernadette. *Calendar of State Papers, Ireland, Tudor Period.* Revised edition. Vol. 1: 1568-1571. Dublin: Irish Manuscript Commission, 2010.

Gairdner, J., and R. H. Brodie, editors. *Letters and Papers, Foreign and Domestic, of the Reign of Henry VIII.* Vol. 21, Part 1, *1546.* London: His Majesty's Stationery Office, 1908.

Hume, Martin A. S., editor, *Calendar of State Papers. English Affairs.* Vol 1. London: Hodges, Figgis, & Co. 1899.

Letters of Queen Elizabeth on Public Affairs Relating to Ireland, Addressed to the Lord Deputy, Sir Henry Sidney, 7 January, 1565–30 June, 1570. MS 745.

Lomas, Sophie Crawford, editor. *Calendar of State Papers Relating to Ireland.* Vol 1, *August 1584-August 1585.* The Hereford Times Limited, 1916.

Mahaffy, Robert Pentland, editor. *Calendar of State Papers Relating to Ireland, of the Reigns of Henry VIII, Edward VI, Mary, and Elizabeth, 1509-[1603].* Vol. 1, *1601-3,* with addenda *1565-1654.* London: His Majesty's Stationery Office, 1912.

Riggs, J. M., editor. *Calendar of State Papers Present Principally at Rome in the Vatican Archives and Library.* Vol. 1, *Elizabeth 1558-1571.* The Hereford Times Limited, 1916.

Russel, C. W. and John Prendergast, editors. *Calendar of the State Papers relating to Ireland, of the reign of James I, 1603-[1625] preserved in Her Majesty's Public Record Office, and elsewhere.* Vol. 1, *1606-1608.* London: Longman & Co, Truebner & Co, Parker & Co, Macmillan and Co, A&C Black, A. Thom, 1874.

State Papers Published under the Authority of his Majesty's Commission: King Henry the Eighth, 1830-1852. Vol. 1, Part 3, *Correspondence between the Governments of England and Ireland, 1515-1538.* London: His Majesty's Commission for State Papers, 1834.

About the Author

Jack Bray is a lifelong student of Irish and British history, and a senior member of the Bar in Washington DC where he served in government and private practice, ultimately as a senior partner at King & Spalding. While he has published many legal articles in University law reviews and Institutes, this is his first publication of a history. He was educated at Jesuit schools, including Saint Louis University and its Law School, and served for nearly a quarter century on the University's Board of Trustees. His Irish ancestors were from Bruree, County Limerick and Cork. His role in performing and publishing an assessment of the Saville Tribunal's Report on the Bloody Sunday killings during a January 30, 1972 civil rights march in Northern Ireland was favorably mentioned during debates in the British House of Commons. He and his wife, Joan, live in Washington DC and have two children, Kathleen and John.

Index